Handbook of hospitality human resources management

Handbook of hospitality human resources management

Edited by

Dana V. Tesone

Rosen College of Hospitality Management
University of Central Florida
9907 Universal Boulevard
Orlando, FL, USA
Elsevier Limited

AMSTERDAM • BOSTON • HEIDELBERG • LONDON • NEW YORK • OXFORD
PARIS • SAN DEIGO • SAN FRANCISCO • SYDNEY • TOKYO
Butterworth-Heinemann is an imprint of Elsevier

ELSEVIER

Butterworth-Heinemann is an imprint of Elsevier
Linacre House, Jordan Hill, Oxford OX2 8DP, UK
30 Corporate Drive, Suite 400, Burlington, MA 01803, USA
First edition 2008

Notice
No responsibility is assumed by the publisher for any injury and/or damage to persons
or property as a matter of products liability, negligence or otherwise, or from any use
or operation of any methods, products, instructions or ideas contained in the material
herein. Because of rapid advances in the medical sciences, in particular, independent
verification of diagnoses and drug dosages should be made

British Library Cataloguing in Publication Data
A catalogue record for this book is available from the British Library

Library of Congress Cataloging-in-Publication Data
A catalog record for this book is available from the Library of Congress

ISBN: 978-0-08-045081-0

Printed and bound in Hungary
08 09 10 11 10 9 8 7 6 5 4 3 2 1

For information on all Butterworth-Heinemann publications
visit our website at books.elsevier.com

Contents

About the authors

Akin Aksu was born in 1971 in Ankara. He graduated from Akdeniz University School of Tourism & Hotel Management in 1993. He got the Ph.D. degree from Gazi University in 1999 by fulfilling his doctorate thesis entitled "Reengineering in 5 Star Hotels and A Research on Its Applicability". Akin Aksu currently works as an associate professor at Akdeniz University School of Tourism & Hotel Management. Dr. Aksu has published many articles on tourism and he has one book entitled "Modern Management Techniques in Tourism Establishments".

Dr. George Alexakis has had three distinct careers: full-service restaurant and banquet operations management, foodservice and hospitality consulting, and university teaching and administration. He has been a full time business and hospitality management professor for universities in the State of Florida since 1995. He is also a professional speaker and presents training seminars on topics such as communication, customer service, managing conflict, management/leadership, and human resources development for a variety of domestic and international organizations. Before entering the world of education, he worked for Cini-Little International, Inc. as a hospitality/foodservice consultant and marketing manager. His operations experience of more than 15 years includes managing his family's businesses: a formal dinning room and a family-style restaurant just outside of Toronto, Canada. In addition to teaching, Dr. Alexakis holds a Doctor of Education with a concentration in Hospitality Management, a Master of Science in Hospitality Administration, a Bachelor of Commerce in Hospitality and Tourism Management, and a Diploma (Associate's equivalent) in Hotel and Restaurant Management.

Debra Cannon, Ph. D. specializes in hotel management and human resource management in the hospitality industry. Prior to joining Georgia State University, she worked with the Ritz Carlton Hotel Company and Hyatt Hotels. Her research interests have focused on high performance service organizations, organizational culture, organizational commitment, and work teams.Cannon's research has been published in journals including the Journal of Hospitality & Tourism Research, International Journal of Hospitality Management, Hospitality and Tourism Educator, and the International Journal of Contemporary Hospitality Management. She was the founding Executive Editor of Praxis—The Journal of Applied Hospitality Management, a scholarly research journal formerly published by the Cecil B. Day School of Hospitality. She has conducted funded research for hospitality organizations such as the Atlanta Convention and Visitors Bureau and the Georgia Hospitality and Travel Association. She has a doctorate degree in Human resources from Georgia State University.

Frank J. Cavico is a full professor who teaches Business Law and Ethics at the H. Wayne Huizenga School of Business and Entrepreneurship of Nova Southeastern University. In 2000, he was awarded the Excellence in Teaching Award by the Huizenga School. Professor Cavico holds a J.D. degree from St. Mary's University School of Law and a B.A. from Gettysburg College. He also possesses a Master of Laws degree from the University of San Diego School of Law and a Master's degree in Political Science from Drew University. Professor Cavico is licensed to practice law in Florida and Texas. He has worked as a federal government regulatory attorney and as counsel for a labor union, and he has practiced general civil law and immigration law in South Florida.

Catherine Curtis is a third year doctoral student at the University of Central Florida in Orlando where she also earned her Master's of Science Degree and finished a thesis regarding the differences between tipped and non-tipped employees in the casual restaurant industry. Her industry experience includes many hotel settings with the latest being Starwood International. Catherine enjoys teaching, researching, and speaking on a broad array of topics in the hospitality industry. Aside from the hospitality industry, Catherine's background also spans elementary education. Her hobbies are spending time with her new son and singing.

Margaret Deery is Professor in Tourism and Events and a Professorial Research Fellow in the Centre for Tourism and Services Research at Victoria University, Melbourne, Australia. Her background is in Human Resource Management, having published in the areas of employee turnover, internal labor markets, promotional opportunities, and career development. Her Ph.D. dissertation focused on the concept of turnover culture. She has previously held the positions of Director of the Centre for Hospitality and Tourism Research at Victoria University and Professorial Research Fellow with the Australian government funded Sustainable Tourism Co-Operative Research Centre. She has published extensively in hospitality and tourism management areas and attracted numerous competitive research grants.

Robin B. DiPietro, *Ph.D.* is an assistant professor at the University of Nebraska-Lincoln in the Hospitality, Restaurant and Tourism Management program. Prior to her work at the University of Nebraska-Lincoln, Dr. DiPietro worked at the Rosen College of Hospitality Management, at the University of Central Florida. She has 20 years of experience with chain restaurants in the operations, human resources, and training areas. Dr. DiPietro worked with Horizon Foodservice, Inc. dba Burger King in Lincoln, Nebraska as the Director of Training and Director of Operations for over 10 years developing restaurant leaders and managers. She has research interests in multi-unit chain restaurant operations and human resources issues inherent in restaurant operations including motivation, employee retention, and staffing issues of organizations.

R. Thomas George, MBA, Ed.D. is an Associate Professor in the Hospitality Management Program at The Ohio State University. He teaches courses in hotel and restaurant management as well as human resource management and organization behavior. His research has centered on the manager and employee relationship and has appeared in the Journal of Hospitality and Tourism Research, International Journal of Hospitality Management, Journal of Human Resources in Hospitality and Tourism, Journal of Foodservice Business Research, and others.

Dr. Leo Jago is a Professor in Tourism at Victoria University and Director of the Centre for Tourism and Services Research For the last 6 years, he has been seconded to the position of Deputy CEO and Director of Research for Australia's national Cooperative Research Centre for Sustainable Tourism. He is a former national Chair of the Council of Australian Universities in Hospitality and Tourism Education and is a director of a range of public and private sector organizations in tourism. Leo has undertaken a wide range of research projects in tourism including the management of paid and unpaid staff in tourism and recreation organizations. Outside academe, Leo has owned and operated a range of small tourism enterprises in various parts of Australia.

Osman M. Karatepe is an associate professor of marketing at the School of Tourism and Hospitality Management at Eastern Mediterranean University in the Turkish Republic of Northern Cyprus. He received his Ph.D. in business administration from Hacettepe University in 2002, M.S. in production management and marketing from Gazi University in 1997, and B.S. in tourism and hotel management from Bilkent University in 1992 in Turkey. His research interests entail service quality and customer satisfaction, customer complaint management, customer equity, scale development and validation, work-family conflict and facilitation, emotional labor, customer aggression, and burnout and work engagement. Dr. Karatepe has contributed to a number of journals such as the Journal of the Academy of Marketing Science; the Journal of Business Research; the International Journal of Service Industry Management, Managing Service Quality; the Journal of Retailing and Consumer Services; the International Journal of Bank Marketing; the Journal of Travel & Tourism Marketing, The Service Industries Journal, Tourism Management; and the International Journal of Hospitality Management. Currently, he teaches marketing and strategic management courses at the undergraduate and graduate levels at the School of Tourism and Hospitality Management at Eastern Mediterranean University.

Dean A. Koutroumanis is an adjunct professor of business for the John H. Sykes College of Business at the University of Tampa, and an entrepreneur in the restaurant industry. He received his doctorate in business administration, with a concentration in Human Resources from Nova Southeastern University in 2005. Dr. Koutroumanis' research interests have been focused on the development of human capital, commitment, service, and organizational culture in the restaurant industry. He has worked on developing academic models that could prove to have a significant impact on restaurant operations from a human relations perspective and has had his work in this area published in Journal of the American Association of Behavioral and Social Sciences and Business

Research Yearbook. In addition to his academic interests, Dr. Koutroumanis has been involved in the restaurant business since childhood in his family's restaurant in New Haven, CT. He began his professional restaurant career as a manager for a national restaurant chain in the mid-west, where he refined his management skills in restaurant operations. His passion for the business prompted him to start his own restaurant company and has been responsible for the development and growth of multiple restaurant concepts in the Tampa Bay area. Dr. Koutroumanis has also served on the board of directors for several restaurant companies in Tampa.

Bahaudin G. Mujtaba is Chair for Management Department and an Associate Professor in Nova Southeastern University's H. Wayne Huizenga School of Business and Entrepreneurship in Fort Lauderdale, FL. Bahaudin has worked with various firms in the areas of management, cross-cultural communication, customer value/service, and cultural competency. His doctorate degree is in Management, and he has two post-doctorate specialties: one in Human Resource Management and another in International Management. During the past 25 years he has had the pleasure of working in the United States, Brazil, Bahamas, Afghanistan, Pakistan, St. Lucia, Thailand, India, and Jamaica. Bahaudin is author and co-author of 15 books regarding mentoring, diversity, management, leadership, change, and ethics.

Dr. Jalane Meloun is an Assistant Professor and the Academic Coordinator of Human Resources Administration in the School of Adult and Continuing Education at Barry University in South Florida. She has recently passed the national certification exam to become a Senior Professional in Human Resources (SPHR) and, as such, has taken over the position of chapter advisor for the Barry University Society for Human Resource Management (SHRM). Dr. Meloun earned her Ph.D. in Industrial/Organizational Psychology from the University of Akron, which has consistently had its I/O program ranked as one of the top ten such programs in the nation. As for research, Dr. Meloun's interest in human–computer interaction began over a decade ago when she was a computer software instructor and eventually led to her conducting extensive research on computer anxiety. Thus far, she has published two journal articles, a book chapter, given several presentations, and won three awards for her technological anxiety research. In 2005, Dr. Meloun has won the Best Paper Competition for the International Public Management Association Assessment

Council's annual contest. Dr. Meloun's teaching experience is both broad and deep. She began teaching business and secretarial skills in private small business colleges in Ohio. Then she taught for several years at each the University of Akron and Kent State University before relocating to Florida. Besides her academic specialty of Industrial-Organizational Psychology, Dr. Meloun has spent years teaching computer skills to both older adult and visually impaired populations.

Dr. Fevzi Okumus joined the Rosen College of Hospitality Management at UCF in August of 2005. He holds a Bachelors of Science degree in Tourism and Hospitality Management from Cukurova University and a Masters of Science degree in Tourism and Hospitality Management from Erciyes University, Turkey. From Oxford Brookes University, UK, he received his second Masters degree in International Hotel Management in 1995 and his Ph.D. in Strategic Hotel Management in 2000. He worked in the hotel business and held managerial positions before starting his academic career. Before coming to UCF, Dr. Okumus was the Department Head for Hospitality Management at Mugla University Turkey. Previously he held positions as Associate Professor at Mugla University, Turkey, Research Fellow at the Hong Kong Polytechnic University, Part-Time Lecturer at Oxford Brookes University and Lecturer at Erciyes University. During his Ph.D. studies he worked as a consultant for InterContinental and Forte Hotel groups on the implementation process of some specific projects in their hotel units. His research areas include strategy implementation, change management, competitive advantage, learning organizations, knowledge management, crisis management, cross-cultural management, destination marketing, and developing countries. He has widely published in leading journals, including Annals of Tourism Research, Service Industries Journal, Tourism Management, Management Decision, International Journal of Hospitality Management, Journal of Hospitality and Tourism Research and International Journal of Contemporary Hospitality Management. He has over 75 academic publications (journal articles, book chapters, and conference presentations). His publications have been cited over 90 times by other academics and industry practitioners in numerous academic and industry publications.

Dr. Michael Ottenbacher is an Associate Professor at San Diego State University, CA, USA. He received his Ph.D. in Marketing from the University of Otago, New Zealand and his Master and Bachelor of Science in Hospitality Management from

Florida International University, USA. In addition to academia, he has extensive business experience. Dr. Ottenbacher worked in senior hospitality positions in the USA, UK, France, and Germany. Professor Ottenbacher has numerous publications in the areas of innovation, new product development, and hospitality management.

Robert C. Preziosi was named "Faculty Member of the Year in 2003". He is a professor of management with the Wayne Huizenga Graduate School of Business and Entrepreneurship at Nova Southeastern University. He is faculty chair of HRM. He was the recipient of the school's first Excellence in Teaching Award. In December 2000 he was named Professor of the Decade. He has been vice president of management development and training for a Fortune 50 company. In 1984, he was given the Outstanding Contribution to HRD Award by the American Society for Training and Development. In 1990, he received the Torch Award, the highest leadership award that the society can give. He was named HRD Professional of the Year for 1991. He has been named to the first edition of *International Who's Who in Quality*. In June 1996, he received his second Torch Award from the society—the first time ASTD has given a second Torch Award to one individual. Bob has worked as a human resource director, line manager, business school dean, and leadership-training administrator. He has published in various national publications, including Training Professor, and Quality Review. He has been a consultant to consultants, educator of educators, and a trainer of trainers. Bob's management education consulting experience includes all levels of management with many organizations including American Express, AT&T, Burger King, FP&L, NCCI, and Pollo Tropical and a large number of hospitals, banks, and government organizations at the local, state, and federal levels. He has trained entire departments of trainers. He has been interviewed for Fortune, Meeting Management, Savings Institutions, Technical and Skills Training, the Miami Herald, and the Sun-Sentinel. Recently, *Training and Development* referred to him as a member of Who's Who in HRD. He as a B.A. degree in social science and an M.Ed. degree in educational psychology. He received his doctoral degree in management. He has a special certification in coaching skills, participative leadership, and consulting skills, and has completed study at Harvard University's Institute for the Management of Lifelong Education. He is listed in *Who's Who in Finance and Industry*, *Who's Who in the World*, and *Who's Who in American Education*. Four times he has been selected for *Who's Who Among America's Teachers. In a recent book, North American Adult Educators, he was named 1 of 50 quintessential adult educators of the 21st century.* Bob has been a national seminar leader for the American Management Association and Dun & Bradstreet. He has presented to regional, national, and international conferences on various aspects of leadership, management, and adult learning. He has recorded a video titled "The High Performing Trainer," and a six-part audio program titled, "Executive Success Strategies," in addition to his six-part audio series on "Maximizing Adult Learning". He is the Editor of the Pfeiffer Annual on HRM and a new Annual on Management Development. He has just completed a book on leadership, *The Leadership Zone.*

Dr. Claire Michele Rice is Assistant Professor of Conflict Analysis & Resolution at the Graduate School of Humanities and Social Sciences, Nova Southeastern University. Dr. Rice is also co-founder of Rice Training Solutions, Inc. along with her husband Dr. Larry A. Rice. Their firm specializes in providing consultation and training in conflict resolution, diversity issues, mediation, and leadership development. The Rices have facilitated over 10,000 hours of training for institutions of higher learning, businesses, private and non-profit organizations. As certified Inclusive Community Building Trainers (ICB Trainer); for the past 10 years, the Rices have served as consultants to businesses, civic organizations, and institutions of primary to higher education in the Caribbean and in the U.S. Michele Rice received a Ph.D. at Florida International University in Comparative Sociology with concentrations in race and ethnicity, sociolinguistics and cultural analysis. Rice's research and community organization activity have focused on the use of the Ellison Executive Mentoring Model to build inclusive communities. Thus, she credits much of her work in inclusive community building to the mentorship of the developer of the model, Dr. Deryl G. Hunt, Sr., CEO of ICB Productions. Some of her consulting career's highlights include her work with Margaret McDonald Policy Management & Administration Center in Nassau, Bahamas and the Grand Bahama Community Builders Organization in Freeport, Bahamas for a number of years in training and program development. She also enjoyed her work with FAVACA, the Florida Agency for Volunteer Action in the Caribbean and the Americas, based in Florida. As part of a team of trainers, she assisted the Women in Democracy organization in Haiti in developing community building programs and in enhancing their conflict resolution skills. Dr. Rice has volunteered her services to various community service organizations and has spent years mentoring middle school, high school, and university students. Her focus in mentoring students has been in assisting them in developing conflict resolution and diversity skills, academic skills, career goals, and professional interpersonal skills. Dr. Rice was award the Dr. Israel Tribble Jr. Award from the Florida Education Fund. She was recently recognized as *Humanitarian of the Year* at Florida Memorial University for her commitment to community service. In July 2006, she was recognized by the Margaret McDonald Policy Management & Administration Centre in their Banquet of Honour Celebrations 2006 with an *Outstanding Service Award* for her work as an international consultant in management training for MMPMAC and various organizations in the Bahamas.

Dr. Larry Rice is a television personality, teacher, and civic leader, Dr. Larry Rice has flourished from his humble beginnings in Union, South Carolina, to be acclaimed as an expert in the hospitality and education field. He currently is Dean of Academic Affairs at Johnson & Wales University, Florida Campus, where he oversees all faculty and operations of the administration of college academia, which includes oversight of the campus' Academic Services, Library, and Student Success departments. Rice has kept himself in the forefront of the business and hospitality industries as Chair of the Board for the Visitors Industry Council of Greater Miami and as a Board member of the Greater Miami Convention and Visitors' Bureau and the Adrienne Arsht Center for the Performing Arts of Miami-Dade County, Inc. A highlight of Rice's career was co-hosting the television show "Leadership in the New Millennium," a half hour show which aired on Cable TAP—Channel 36 in Dade County. The show focused on various leadership tactics and the vision of success in the new millennium. Dr. Rice has been part of several educational and hospitality-related organizations such as the American Association of Higher Education (AAHE), Council on Hotel & Restaurant Institutional Education (CHRIE), Multicultural Food Service & Hospitality Alliance (MFHA), and the National Black MBA Association (NBMBA). Dr. Larry Rice has been featured in Miami Today magazine; The National Black MBA magazine; Hospitality Lodging Magazine, U.S. News & World Report; the Miami Times, The Black EOE Journal; and The Black Ph.D./Ed.D. magazine. He was also featured on the cover of the November 2004 addition of the *South Florida CEO* magazine. Rice's upcoming book, *The Recess Effect*, discusses teambuilding practices from the perspective of the effect of childhood socialization during recess and draws upon parallels between these childhood experiences and adult teambuilding behavior.

Peter Ricci, *Ed.D., CHA* is an associate professor in the Barry Kaye College of Business at Florida Atlantic University (FAU). Dr. Ricci holds over 20 years of hospitality management experience including director of sales and marketing, general manager, and consultant roles for some of the hospitality industry's most noteworthy brands including: Crowne Plaza, Best Western, Holiday Inn, and Radisson. Dr. Ricci's passion for locating the "right employee" for the "right position" at the "right time" has led to his lifelong pursuit of study in the area of job competencies relevant to managerial positions in the global tourism and hospitality industry. Dr. Ricci may be reached at priccil@fau.edu.

Denver Severt has been teaching hospitality tourism management with emphasis on service and accounting at the University of Central Florida for 5 years. Prior to that, Denver taught at Eastern Michigan University for 7 years. His industry experience spans 20 years in country clubs, family dining, and fine dining management. Denver's latest publications regarding service management have been featured in Tourism Management, Journal of Hospitality and Leisure Marketing and the Journal of Hospitality and Tourism Research. Denver enjoys teaching, researching, and speaking on service management across various settings.

Dr. Stephen E. Sussman received his MPA and Ph.D. (Political Science) from Georgia State University. His research and general teaching interests include public administration, public policy, public law, and judicial politics. He is an Assistant Professor of Public Administration at Barry University's School of Adult and Continuing Education. Recent courses taught, include Public Policy, Research Methods, Productivity Improvement, Nonprofit Administration, and Public Budgeting and Finance. Prior to joining the Barry University faculty, Dr. Sussman was the Director of Research at the Economic Council of Palm Beach County. The Economic Council is a not-for-profit organization, involved in the political, economic, and social processes of the region.

Dana V. Tesone, *Ph.D.* is an associate professor with the Rosen College of Hospitality Management at the University of Central Florida where he teaches management and technology courses. His background includes administrative and executive positions with academic institutions and corporate organizations, including VP of Human Resources at a leading resort corporation in Florida. Tesone is currently conducting research in the areas of human resource management and technology. He has more than 90 scholarly publications.

Michael J. Tews is an assistant professor at The Ohio State University in the Department of Consumer Sciences. He earned a Ph.D. from the School of Hotel Administration at Cornell University and a M.S. from the London School of Economics and Political Science. Michael's research focuses on employee selection, training and development, and retention, specifically in the context of service employees. His work has appeared in the Cornell Quarterly, Journal of Hospitality and Tourism Research, Journal of Vocational Behavior, and Organizational Research Methods.

J. Bruce Tracey is an Associate Professor of Management at Cornell University's School of Hotel Administration. His current research focuses on the effectiveness of human capital investments, particularly the relationship between training and development initiatives and firm performance. He has also conducted research on staffing, leadership, employee turnover, and labor and employment law. He has presented his work at numerous regional, national, and international conferences, and his work has appeared in diverse outlets such as the Journal of Applied Psychology, the Cornell Quarterly, and the University of Pennsylvania Journal of Labor and Employment Law. Recent sponsors for Professor Tracey's research and consulting include Hilton Hotels and Resorts, Moevenpick Hotels and Resorts, and Wynn Resorts.

Sean A. Way is an Assistant Professor of Human Resource Management at Cornell University's School of Hotel Administration. He earned a Ph.D. from the school of Management and Labour Relation at Rutgers University. Sean has taught undergraduate and graduate courses in HR management, HR strategy, and training and development in the U.S., Canada, and Hong Kong. His current research focuses on a number of strategic human resource management topics, including the effects of HR systems, flexibility, and marketing orientation on the performance and effectiveness of organization and their employees. He has presented his work at numerous national and international conferences, and his work has been published in diverse outlets such as the journal of Management, Human Resource Management Review, and journal of small business and entrepreneurship. Research and consulting sponsors include Shangri-la Hotels and Resorts, Marriott International, R.P. Scherer Canada.

Dr Nick Wilton is a lecturer in Human Resource Management at Bristol Business School and member of the Centre for Employment Studies Research (CESR) at the University of the West of England, Bristol. His research interests include employment relations and HRM in the hotel sector, careers in the 'knowledge' economy and the relationship between higher education and the labour market. A business administration graduate, his MPhil research examined HR strategy formation in the UK hotel sector and he has a PhD in labour market studies. Dr Wilton is an affiliate member of the Chartered Institute of Personnel and Development (CIPD).

Preface

Successful human resource management practices require integrated strategic thinking. The role of human resource managers is to protect the assets of the organization as well as maximize the development and productivity of human capital. It is widely known that the hospitality industry is labor intensive and requires high levels of interaction between staff and guests. In certain sectors, such as lodging, the guest interacts with staff members on an intimate level over long periods of duration. The purpose of all hospitality operations is to create guest experiences that evolve into magical memories. These memories bring a guest back to a previously visited establishment.

The human resource practitioner is charged with balancing the needs of all stakeholder groups. They are charged with handling the people issues within complex operational settings in certain sectors. This requires a wide array of strategic knowledge, skills, and abilities. Hence, human resource management is a holistic thinking practice.

The book is an edited collection of papers from senior practitioners as well as renowned scholars in the field of human resource management. Certain chapters focus on practitioner perspectives, while most are academically oriented. The book is divided into four sections. The first section presents chapters that discuss issues related to the acquisition of human capital. Next, there is a section dedicated to the retention of quality employees. The third section focuses on issues related to the development of human resources. The final section presents chapters related to critical human resource management issues.

Chapter 1: Tracey: HR in the hospitality industry: strategic frameworks and priorities.

Chapter 2: Meloun: Job analysis: the basis for all things H.R.

Job analyses are truly the basis of all things related to human resources. Relationships between job analyses and eventual applications of the resulting documents are addressed as well as a current review of the hospitality industry. This paper examines the numerous legal and other reasons to conduct job analyses and talks about the advantages and disadvantages of the different means of collecting job analysis data. Steps for actually doing the job analysis are given, as well as valuable resources and a job analysis example.

Chapter 3: Ricci: Getting it right the first time: using job competencies for positive hiring outcomes in the hospitality industry

The goal of this edited textbook is to showcase, demonstrate, and illustrate the human resources (HR) function within the greater context of hospitality and tourism marketing. It is important to note that human resources strengths and capabilities can be a strong factor in the performance of a culture that, in turn, adds greatly to marketing strength and profitability of a hospitality organization. While communication, internal guest focus, leadership, empowerment, and a host of other concepts add to the strength of a culture, hiring right is a "must have" in order for organizations to match internal guest success with their desired external guest satisfaction levels. Those who are adequately matched with competencies, either inherent traits or learned protocols, will help lead our industry venues to be more productive and profitable while leading its employees toward future careers with higher levels of satisfaction.

Chapter 4: Koutromanis: Organizational culture in the casual dining industry: the impact that culture has on service quality and customers' intention to return

The study posits a model to describe the organizational culture process applicable to the development of superior customer service practices of the full service, casual dining, and restaurant industry. The premise of this study is found in the academic disciplines of organizational culture and hospitality, as they relate to service quality and behavioral intentions theories. The chapter will look at the implications organizational culture has on service quality and customers' intentions to return in the casual dining restaurant segment. The implications of the findings of this research will add to the hospitality literature that currently exists and can be used as a blueprint for practitioners to develop and improve their service quality practices.

Chapter 5: Mujtaba and Cavico: Ethical principles and practices in human resources management

Human resource management centers on fairness, justice, and advocacy for a company's most critical resource, its human resources. In other words, human resource management is about ethics ethical principles, and ethical practices. For ethics to be taken seriously by people in modern organizations, it must be related to business and management activities and, most importantly, to a competitive advantage and successful business performance. The purpose of this chapter, therefore, is to discuss ethics, ethical principles, and the requirements of morality in conjunction with claims of business, management, and personal self-interest. Overall, basic ethical practices and discussions regarding ethics, values, law, and why business professionals need to focus on morality, are examined in this chapter.

Chapter 6: Severt and Curtis: Human resource management and a service culture

An internal culture of service is critical to effective service delivery. Human resources can play many roles in developing this internal service culture in a hospitality and leisure organization. First, organizational culture, organizational climate, and service vision must be defined. After definitions, and for the realization of a service culture, the service climate and the service culture must be aligned. Next, the various roles of HR in creating and sustaining a service culture is presented. This includes using multiple methods across major HR functions such as the promotion of company values from recruitment, training, correction, and communication. To an end, steps that HR can take towards the promotion of an internal service culture are presented. After that, specific human resources and culture literature is briefly discussed and future research is suggested.

Chapter 7: George: Employee relations: a problem solving approach

Along with the acquisition of employees, the retention of qualified employees has been a major concern of all businesses. The hospitality industry is in a highly competitive situation in which the presentation of service is often a distinguishing characteristic and a major contributor to the success of the enterprise. It employs individuals who come to the workplace with a variety of degrees of skill, motivation, and differing goals. This scarcity and variation of individuals necessitates the supervisor be flexible in working with those who may be exhibiting performance problems. Performance problems may surface through a variety of means. They may be related to skill deficiencies or to issues causing a distraction in concentration to the task at hand. While the term employee relations may refer to a department, it is also considered to be a process of relating to employees and helping to bring about quality performance. With this in mind, this chapter will present three approaches to working with employees sometimes labeled as "problem" employees.

Chapter 8: Meloun and Sussman: Human resource management role in ethics within the hospitality industry

Ethics is an important part of business and should be a key factor in many business-related decisions. It is of particular interest in the hospitality industry where many employees operate in an unsupervised fashion and handle cash. This paper examines the current state of ethics in this country, how values impact ethics, some ethical systems, the ethical environment, and how human resource departments can increase the overall level of ethics in an organization. These topics are all presented within the context of the hospitality and tourism industries.

Chapter 9: Deery and Jago: Ogranizational communication in the hospitality industry

This chapter examines current practices in communication within organizations generally, and in hospitality establishments specifically. The chapter, first, provides a review of these practices as portrayed in academic literature. Second, the chapter focuses on some of the difficult issues associated with effective communication and finally, a case study of a five star hotel is included to illustrate some of the issues discussed in the literature.

Chapter 10: Aksu: Employee turnover: calculation of turnover rates and costs

In terms of economic perspective service industries play critical role in world economy and as an important component of service industry, tourism industry has direct effect on service industry (Varoglu and Eser, 2006, p. 30). Today like other establishments, touristic establishments are trying to survive under conditions of high-level competition. In order to survive they are trying to realize greater economic aims (such as profitability) and social aims (supporting recruitment and raising employee motivation). In this context, employee turnover can be seen as one of the indicators of the touristic establishment's working conditions.

Chapter 11: Rice and Rice: The role of conflict management in human resource development in human resource management in the hospitality industry

Cliques are quite common in the hospitality field. Many industry professionals can identify with the lines of separation between the "front-of-the-house" and "back-of-the-house." The front-of-the-house is comprised of areas visible to or in direct contact with the guests. Such are the cashier, dining room, front desk, concierge, reception desk, and bars. On the other hand, the back-of-the-house areas are behind the scenes and not as visible to guests. These are areas such as the kitchen, housekeeping, accounting, and engineering departments. In the hospitality industry, while most workplace conflicts are interpersonal (Babin & Boles, 1998), such disputes between employees are often symptoms of much larger problems—inter-departmental conflicts (Bittner, 1995; Cybulski, 1997; Freidman, 2006). On a broader level, workplace conflicts are rooted in departmental disputes and lines of divisions between departments that sprout micro-level conflicts between staff members belonging to different departments.

Chapter 12: Karatepe: Work-family conflict and facilitation: implications for hospitality researchers

Faced with the influx of dual-earner couples, single parents, and single women in the workforce as well as changes in gender-role norms, researchers have devoted much attention to examining the complexities of the interrelationships in the work-family nexus. In this chapter, we focus on a selective review of the relevant literature on the antecedents, outcomes, and moderators of both directions of conflict and facilitation in order to identify gaps in the research in our knowledge and delineate various research issues that have been largely ignored in the hospitality management literature.

Chapter 13: Alexakis: The optimal hospitality leader: creating a thriving, self-motivating leadership-followership organizational network

Technological advances have caused the rapid decline in employment and purchasing power internationally. Global unemployment is now at its highest levels since the Great Depression (Rifkin, 2004). Although the Information Age has decreased the need for organizational workers, the hospitality industry remains labor intensive. The motto that "human resource is our most valuable resource" does not hold up to scrutiny in most organizations. There is typically a mountain of evidence refuting the claim, which can even elicit laughter among many hospitality employees.

Chapter 14: Wilton: The path of least resistance? Choice and constraint in HRM strategy in the UK hotel sector

Guerrier and Deery (1998) suggest two central questions that are recurrent in HRM research in the hotel sector. First, to what extent is the work of hospitality managers influenced by the industry context? Second, to what extent do hospitality managers engage in reaction or reflection? In this chapter, research exploring patterns of HR practice and policy in the UK hotel sector will be used to address these questions. The chapter discusses the factors that appear to be influential in determining HRM strategy across the hotel sector and how different approaches to HRM translate into employee relations' practices in respect of employee involvement and participation, skills utilization and employment flexibility. In particular, it discusses the contextual pressures on HRM in the sector, particularly those relating to labor and product markets, the extent to which HR managers in the sector are able to formulate a range of strategic approaches and how HRM strategy relates to wider competitive strategy.

Chapter 15: Mujtaba: Employee orientation and mentoring programs

Employee orientation and socializations programs are an important element of making sure employees is successful in achieving their goals and the goals of the organization. Human resource managers and staff are responsible for maximizing the productivity of their organization's human resources through effective employee orientation and mentoring programs. Through a comprehensive coverage of socialization and mentoring programs, this chapter provides a reflection of employee orientation and development practices that can be used by human resource staff members and departments. The chapter emphasizes that mentoring is an art as it requires experience, and it is a science since it can be formalized, structured, and taught.

Chapter 16: DiPietro: Human capital development: a return on investment perspective

The chapter presents information concerning the benefits associated with investments in existing human capital within hospitality and tourism enterprises. It begins with an introduction that discusses the research framework. The author then discusses concepts and definitions concerning human resource development, human capital, resource-based view of the organization, training and development, and return on investment. Next, the service-profit chain will be reviewed as one of the strategic framework models that capture the essence of the role of human capital in the hospitality/service industry. Following that, a review of research is presented on the topic of human capital as it relates to the hospitality industry with a return on investment perspective. Finally, applications of the concept of human capital and return on investment (ROI) will be discussed, as well as suggestions concerning directions for future research on the subject of human capital and ROI.

Chapter 17: Cannon: Contributing to employee development through training and development

Training and professional development are vital elements to hospitality organizations. Development of job skills and knowledge necessitate on-going and consistent training processes. In addition, an organizational culture that supports continual quality improvement including exemplary guest service requires a commitment to ongoing effective employee training and development. Horst Schultze, former COO of the Ritz-Carlton Hotel Company and now President of West Paces Hotel Company, developer of some of the world's finest lodging properties, has described the role of training as "creating consensus between the employee and the customer" (Iverson, 2001). Without this consensus built on constant refinement of skills and knowledge, employees (the organization) cannot consistently meet and exceed customer (guest) expectations.

Chapter 18: Preziosi: An HR practitioner's view: four actions that HR executives can take to get their services used

Because of its central positioning within an organization, human resources departments often face the challenge of creating cooperative relationships with other departments, while also attempting to manage the internal foundation in which the organization is built upon. This chapter provides a set of guidelines that human resource practitioners can use to ensure that their services are utilized by their departmental business partners, focusing on the creation of new relationships, the development of reputable services, the recognition of responsiveness, and the realization of organizational success.

Chapter 19: Ottenbacher: Employee management and innovation

Given increasing global competition and even more rapid changes in technology and in consumer needs and expectations, hospitality firms' ability to innovate is regarded more and more as a key factor in ensuring success. Hospitality firms can no longer rely on their existing service portfolio, as customers increasingly demand and expect—and competitors will do their best to provide—new and improved services. To succeed in such a turbulent environment, hospitality businesses must systematically develop innovations and become more customer focused (Cooper & Edgett, 1999). In this context, innovation can be seen as a fundamental marketing activity and an important resource for the survival and growth of service firms. Accordingly, customer focus requires managers to understand customer needs and behavior and to manage service encounters between employees and customers in ways that create satisfaction (Lovelock & Wirtz, 2004).

Chapter 20: Tesone: Development of a sustainable tourism hospitality human resources management module: a template for teaching sustainability across the curriculum

This chapter presents a module to be used to teach sustainable tourism practices as part of a course in hospitality/tourism human resources management. It is designed with the intention to infuse sustainable practices into topics that would be covered in a hospitality/tourism human resources management course at an institution of higher learning. The module was developed in conjunction with the leadership of Business & Entrepreneurial Sustainable Tourism (BEST), who provided the framework, as well as formative and summative reviews throughout the development process. This module serves as a template for others to be developed for teaching sustainable tourism practices across the curriculum in hospitality/tourism programs at institutions of higher learning.

Chapter 21: Okumus: Strategic human resource issues in hospitality and tourism

This chapter discusses strategic human resources management (SHRM) issues in hospitality and tourism (H&T) organizations. A critical review of relevant literature suggests that being able to manage people strategically is the main critical HR issue in H&T organizations. This requires that the HR function becomes a strategic partner and a player in the strategic management process and help organizations create and maintain a competitive advantage through employing numerous exemplary HR practices successfully. In addition, the HR function has to demonstrate that managing HR strategically influences companies' overall performance positively. In many H&T organizations, this may not be an easy task to achieve in a short period of time. One essential factor in this process will always be finding and developing executives as well as HR managers who would view HRM practices more from the strategic management perspective. Certainly this requires fundamentally changing organizational culture and structuring these organizations where the HR function is seen as a strategic partner rather than a cost center. This may mean that a radical shift is needed in the minds of many senior executives as well as HR managers. This chapter provides detailed discussions about these issues and provides recommendations for practice and future research.

Part One

Acquiring human resources

HR in the hospitality industry: strategic frameworks and priorities

J. Bruce Tracey

School of Hotel Administration, Cornell University
530 Statler Hall, Ithaca, NY 14853, USA

Sean A. Way

School of Hotel Administration, Cornell University
541A Statler Hall, Ithaca, NY 14853, USA

Michael J. Tews

College of Education and Human Ecology
The Ohio State University
265-A Campbell Hall, Columbus, OH 43210, USA

Introduction

Creating and sustaining a long-term competitive advantage. These are the buzzwords that are uttered with increasing frequency in the board rooms, executive-planning sessions, and managerial meetings that occur throughout the industry today. Much has been written on the ways in which firms may accomplish their strategic objectives. Many scholars have emphasized the importance of environmental forces that may influence and shape a firm's strategic position, while others have stressed the roles of a firm's internal structures and coordinating mechanisms that may be used to execute the chosen strategies. What is clear is that there must be an alignment between the forces outside the firm—many of which are beyond the firm's control—and the policies, programs, and systems that are used to manage the firm's day-to-day operations[1].

To achieve this alignment, firm leaders make choices about identity, values, and goals as a means for reacting to and anticipating market conditions that affect their firm's competitiveness. These choices can have a significant impact on operational quality, customer satisfaction and loyalty, and profitability. So rather than accept the fates of the environment, it is critically important that executives and managers take considered, purposeful, and sometimes bold actions that not only respond to competitive forces, but anticipate market influences in order to create value, gain the upper-hand in competitive position, and achieve long-term strategic objectives.

One of the key considerations for creating alignment is an understanding of the role that human capital plays in delivering value and sustaining competitiveness. Managing people is arguably one of the most vexing challenges in the hospitality industry. Indeed, human resource concerns top the list of the most critical managerial challenges in our industry. Tight labor markets, increasing and rapidly changing labor legislation, and high turnover are among the numerous problems that pose serious threats to maintaining a strong competitive position. Therefore, rigorous efforts must be taken to make sure that the policies, procedures, and systems for attracting, selecting, developing, and retaining the best employees are consistent with the firm's business strategies and account for the dynamic conditions within the firm's competitive markets—in

---

[1] It is important to note that firms really do not behave—people do. However, for the sake of convenience and convention, we will refer to firm actions in a manner that is similar to those of the people who are associated with it.

other words, support strategic and functional alignment (cf. Wright & Snell, 1998; Way, 2006; Way & Johnson, 2005).

The outline of this chapter is as follows. We will begin by presenting some of the realities (at least a sampling thereof) about HR in the hospitality industry, followed by an overview of the resource-based view (RVB), one of the most predominant frameworks that has been developed for explaining how HR can enhance firm performance and sustainability. We will then extend this framework and present a discussion on flexible HR systems and the associated policies and practices that support such systems which may enhance the capacity of hospitality firms to achieve their strategic objectives and gain sustainable competitive advantage.

Some of the realities

While HR remains one of the top concerns in the industry, this function is often viewed as a transactional-based, administrative part of business and not an integral part of the firm's strategic decision making and planning efforts (Tracey & Nathan, 2002). The result is that the HR function is typically managed through the lens of efficiency and cost-minimization. This narrow view compromises the alignment between the HR function and the firm's overall business strategy and thus, creates significant competitive concerns. In a recent article, Tracey and Nathan (2002) argued that the lack of HR alignment exists on two levels. The first is on a strategic formulation level wherein HR priorities are not fully considered when business leaders formulate their firm's overall business plan. This is not to say that executives and managers place little value on the HR function. Rather (and to reiterate the point made above), the prevailing view is that HR is primarily an enabling function, and as such, does not—and should not—play an instrumental role in developing firm goals. However, failing to consider the role of HR in strategy formulation can have significant negative consequences. By way of example, a few years ago, the owners of an upscale independent hotel decided to get on the spa bandwagon. They earmarked almost US$20 million for a high-end, full-service facility. A significant amount of time and effort were spent on financing (e.g., decisions about the amount of capital that would come from reserves vs. debt) and design (e.g., number and types of treatment rooms), but very little emphasis was placed on HR considerations (e.g., sourcing and hiring a capable spa manager). The HR planning discussions were primarily limited to expenses associated with pre-opening training, as well as payroll and benefits costs. The implications for failing to examine the HR priorities became evident soon after the construction process had commenced. The opening was delayed by several months, in large part because the property was unable to recruit and select individuals for key positions in the new spa. In addition, there were significant operational and service problems during the first several months that the facility was open because the newly hired staff did not possess the knowledge, skills, and attitudes (KSAs) necessary to perform their roles effectively.. For the owners, the result was a much lower rate of return of invested capital. Many of the problems highlighted above could have been avoided if a comprehensive labor market analysis and staffing plan were completed during the planning stages of this effort.

The second level of disconnect resides in strategy execution. As noted above, many firms have adopted a transactional, administrative approach to managing the HR function. The primary focus is on record keeping, payroll and benefits administration, and employee relations. While these tasks are important, this type of work does not add much value to the firm—economic or otherwise (cf. Huselid, Jackson, & Schuler, 1997). Moreover, if HR professionals spend the bulk of their time managing administrative tasks, they are unable to fulfill other role responsibilities and engage more important value-adding activities that can help the firm achieve its strategic objectives. Part of this problem stems from a lack of infrastructure support that can be used to enhance the efficiency and quality of transactional work. Fortunately, many hospitality firms have adopted information systems and decision support tools that can save a significant amount of time and money on the administrative components of the HR function (e.g., maintenance of employee records, performance management support, benefits and payroll administration, etc.).

However, while efforts to incorporate technology for facilitating the administrative back-office work may be helpful, and even necessary, many firms still do not fully utilize the HR function as they should. HR departments routinely fail in helping operations managers execute the basic HR functions—hiring capable and motivated employees, providing relevant and timely training, implementing meaningful performance management programs, and delivering incentive schemes that stimulate extra-role performance. This concern stems in part from a lack of awareness among business leaders and HR professionals regarding the nature and scope of influence that HR can have on a firm's business strategies, as well as a lack of understanding about the specific needs of operational staff. In addition, HR professionals have not been able to provide clear and convincing evidence regarding how they can facilitate the achievement of strategically important goals. Thus, it is imperative that HR professionals gain a greater understanding of the strategic and operational needs of the firm, and use reliable and valid data for supporting strategy formulation and strategy execution.

A guiding framework: the resource-based view

Over the past several years, a number of frameworks and models regarding the roles of HR have been developed. The most predominant explanation is the RVB (Way & Johnson, 2005; Wright, Dunford, & Snell, 2001). This explanation focuses on factors within the firm (vs. factors outside the firm) as sources of competitive advantage and proposes a way by which internal resources may contribute towards developing and maintaining a competitive advantage (Barney, Wright, & Ketchen, 2001). One such internal resource is the firm's HR capital, which refers to the knowledge, skills, attitudes (KSAs), and behavioral repertories held by the firm's employees (cf. Becker & Huselid, 1998; Wright *et al.*, 2001; Wright & McMahan, 1992; Wright & Snell, 1998).

Based on the work by Wernfelt (1984), Rumelt (1984), Dierickx and Cool (1989), and others, Barney (1991, 1995) presented what are considered to be the seminal RBV articles which describe the role of a firm's capital—which includes people—for creating and sustaining competitive advantage. Barney stated that for a firm's resources to hold the potential of a sustained competitive advantage, they must be valuable, rare, inimitable, and "there cannot be strategically equivalent substitutes" (1991, p. 106). Valuable resources are those that exploit opportunities and minimize threats, and can be linked in objective terms to a firm's key performance indices—financial and otherwise. Rare resources are those that are scarce and in high demand. For example, given a normal distribution of ability, individuals with high levels of ability are, by definition, rare and have prompted the "war for talent." Non-substitutable resources are those that cannot be acquired or developed by competitors. For example, technology per se is not a source of competitive advantage, but the ways in which a firm uses technology may be a key driver for sustainability[2]. And finally,

---

[2] There may be exceptions to this claim. For example, firms that develop and hold patents on certain forms of technology may enjoy some degree of sustainable competitiveness. However, given the rather short half-life of technology and information systems, it can be argued that the degree of sustainability achieved by this type of resource will be short-lived.

inimitable resources are those that are difficult to replicate due to unique historical and contextual conditions, such as a firm's culture.

Most of the RBV explanations within the human resources management literature are based on the assumption that a particular business strategy requires a unique set of people requirements, both in terms of employee knowledge, skills, and attitudes (i.e., human capital "stock" or the human capital "pool"), as well as HR policies, practices, and systems. That is, in order to create a source of competitive advantage, a firm's human capital must be characterized by high levels of skill, motivation, and high-performance behavior on the part of employees, and supported by a set of HR policies, practices, and systems that are unique, create value for the firm, causally ambiguous, and thus, inimitable. It is also important to develop an "alignment of interests" among employees. When employees have a high degree of consensus and commitment to the firm's objectives, and as a collective are capable of learning and growing, then the firm may be more agile and adaptable to the changes it faces during its lifecycle (Boxall, 1998). In addition, it is important to emphasize that some employees are more instrumental in creating competitive advantage, and as such, they need to be managed differently (Lepak & Snell, 1999). Therefore, a firm's HR strategy must account for the variance in employee contribution (which of course, changes over time), while providing a means for developing the talents and commitment among all employees. Therefore, a "best practices" HR system is one that has complementary and interdependent components and is able to develop talented, committed employees who are capable of continuous learning and growth. That is, effective HR systems are dynamic and flexible—they not only respond to the external and internal forces of change, but can also help forecast the future competitive conditions and implement plans accordingly.

While the specific propositions that are embedded within the RVB framework have yet to be examined directly (Wright *et al.*, 2001; Wright, Gardner, Moynihan, & Allen, 2005), there is a growing body of evidence that has demonstrated links between numerous HR policies, practices, and programs and measures of firm performance. One of most influential studies was conducted by Huselid (1995), which showed that a set of HR practices termed as "high performance work systems" (e.g., selective staffing procedures, continuous learning and development programs, pay-for-performance compensation systems, etc.) were related to employee turnover, profitability, and market value. Since then, a number of studies have demonstrated a positive association between HR systems ("bundles" as well as individual policies and practices) and measures of firm performance (Appelbaum, Bailey, Berg, & Kalleberg, 2000; Becker & Huselid, 1998; Combs, Liu, Hall, & Ketchen, 2006; Delery & Doty, 1996; Way, 2002; Youndt, Snell, Dean, & Lepak, 1996). While there appears to be a general consensus that HR systems do have a positive impact on measures of performance, there are still some important questions that remain unanswered (Huselid & Becker, 2006; Way & Johnson, 2005). It has been suggested that HR system research has provided little evidence regarding the specific HR practices that may contribute to performance (Becker & Huselid, 1998; Chadwick & Cappelli, 1999; Dyer & Reeves, 1995; Wright & McMahan, 1992). Of greater concern is that there is little explanation regarding how HR systems produce higher levels of firm performance (Becker & Gerhart, 1996; Delery & Shaw, 2001; Way & Johnson, 2005). Indeed, the literature has only vaguely described how HR systems impact firm-level outcomes. To address this need, one of the most important considerations is the nature and type of HR systems that may be most effective in firms that face dynamic, changing environments—specifically, flexible HR systems (cf. Dyer & Shafer, 1999; Way, 2005).

HR flexibility

Flexibility refers to the capacity for change and adaptation over time (Snell, Shadur, & Wright, 2001). Building upon the work on Sanchez and colleagues (Sanchez, 1995, 1997; Sanchez & Heene, 1997), Wright & Snell (1998), and others (e.g., Milliman, Von Glinow, & Nathan, 1991; Snell, Youndt, & Wright, 1996), Way (2005) defined HR flexibility as the capacity to develop (redevelop), configure (reconfigure), and deploy (redeploy) systems of HR practices/policies/structures which acquire, develop, coordinate (re-coordinate), and deploy (redeploy) human resources who possess competencies that enhance the capacity of the firm as a whole to quickly—compared to competitors—meet and/or generate a variety of dynamic market demands. Consistent with previous research, Way's conceptualization of HR flexibility highlights the skills, behavioral scripts, and motivation of the firm's human capital, and its internal pro-cesses and routines, that may enhance the firm's capacity to quickly meet and/or generate a variety of dynamic market demands (Way, 2006). So for firms operating in dynamic environments, HR flexibility is expected to be a source of competitive advantage and have a positive effect on firm performance and effectiveness because they provide firms with access to human capital with two important features—employees who "can do" (i.e., employees who possess the appropriate KSAs and behavioral repertories) and employees who "will do" (i.e., employees who are engaged in and motivated to perform their role responsibilities) a diverse set of alternative work-related activities that are required to operate effectively in dynamic competitive contexts. As such, flexibility enhancing HR systems are expected to increase the organization's ability to adapt to environmental change by increasing the latitude, KSAs, and behavioral repertories of human capital that is available to the organization.

Flexibility enhancing HR systems are comprised of two elements—resource flexibility, and structural coordination flexibility. Resource flexibility is defined as the extent to which a resource can be used—and the time and cost associated with using the resource—for a wide-range of purposes. Coordination flexibility describes the extent to which resources can be assigned, re-assigned, configured, and re-configured in the firm's internal processes and routines. Thus, flexibility enhancing HR systems allow organizations to achieve the purpose of effectively adapting to environmental changes in a proactive and reactive manner, or both (see Brown & Eisenhardt, 1998; Way, 2005). The sections that follow will describe the key aspects of resource and structural coordination flexibility and specify the HR practices, processes, and structures that support these two components of flexible HR systems.

Resource flexibility

The primary components of resource flexibility include cognitive staffing, multi-skill training, job rotation, involvement in decision-making, group-based compensation systems, and employment stability.

Cognitive staffing

The general cognitive ability construct has received robust support in the selection literature as a strong indicator of performance for most jobs (Deadrick, Bennett, & Russell, 1997; Hunter & Hunter, 1984; Schmidt, Hunter, Outerbridge, & Goff, 1988), including those in the hospitality industry (Tracey, Sturman, & Tews, 2007). These results suggest that general cognitive ability is an indicator of the individual's capacity to perform their essential tasks, duties, and responsibilities, but also to learn and adapt to new situations—a key component of HR flexibility (Snow & Snell, 1993; Wright & Snell, 1998). As such, recruiting and selecting employees for their general cognitive ability will enhance resource and HR flexibility and aid the organization in adapting to changes in the environment (i.e., employees will have the cognitive ability to learn and/or create new behaviors required by the organization). Thus, it is expected resource and HR flexibility will be enhanced when cognitive ability is used a criterion for staffing decisions.

Multi-skill training

Training can enhance employee KSAs (Blanchard & Thacker, 1999), behavior repertories (Wright & Snell, 1998), productivity (Lynch & Black, 1995), efficiency (Cooke, 1994), and HR flexibility (van Ham, Paauwe, & Williams, 1986; 1987; Wright & Snell, 1998). However, different types of training influence performance in different ways (Lynch & Black, 1995; Morrow, Jarrett, & Rupinski, 1997) as well as have different impacts on KSAs and behavioral repertoires (Blanchard & Thacker, 1999). Results reported by Sesil (1999) indicate that training may have a greater impact when training focuses on building broad KSAs and behavioral repertories (i.e., multi-skill training) as opposed to those that may be specific to a function or task. Therefore, multi-skill training of employees will create the KSAs and behavioral repertoires that promote learning and/or the creation of new behaviors required by the system, and it is expected that multi-skill training will enhance resource and HR flexibility.

Job rotation

Practices such as job rotation, cross-functional assignments, task forces, and other activities that expose individuals to a broad array of work activities are expected to broaden an individual's skills and behavioral repertoires (Wright & Snell, 1998). It is expected that these experiences will increase the employees' capacity to recognize a greater variety of contingencies that may affect their job performance and thus, enhance behavioral repertoires (Noe, Wilk, Mullen, & Wanek, 1997). Wright and Snell (1998) suggest that employees who possess a variety of behavioral repertoires that are developed through job rotation are more likely to identify and adapt to dynamic situations (i.e., be more flexible). Thus, resource and

HR flexibility will be enhanced when employee KSAs and behavioral repertories are developed through job rotation.

Involvement in decision-making

Processes in which employees have voice/participation mechanisms may lead to increased efficiency (Ichniowski, Shaw, & Prennushi, 1997; Levine & Tyson, 1990). Appelbaum *et al.* (2000) and Rubinstein (2000) suggest that a process in which front-line workers gather, process, and act on information is key to the successful link between HR systems and performance. Furthermore, Wright and Snell (1998) suggest that HR systems in which employees have voice, participate, and are involved in decision making may lead to increased HR flexibility because it builds a broader awareness of the firm's plans and priorities. Thus, resource and HR flexibility may be enhanced through a system that includes a process in which employees participate in regular meetings in which work issues are presented and discussed. In addition, participatory decision making, suggestion programs, and other means for involving employees in key work processes can also enhance employee voice and assist in the development of superior knowledge and motivation that is required to perform desired behavioral repertories.

Group- and performance-based compensation systems

Gomez-Mejia and Balkin (1994) suggest that many traditional pay systems cannot be adapted to changing environments and that compensation should be a flexible system used to align the outcomes desired by employees and the establishment. Using agency theory (Sesil, 1999) and game theory (Weitzman & Kruse, 1990) the economics literature has proposed that profit sharing (Kruse, 1993) and stock options (Blasi, Kruse, Sesil, Kroumova, & Carberry 2000) are two compensation systems that can create alignment between the desired outcomes of the employees and those of the firm. Empirical results have supported the association between performance and stock options (Blasi *et al.*, 2000) and profit sharing (Kruse, 1993). Furthermore, these group-based compensation systems are by design flexible systems in that some component of compensation is based upon environmental and performance factors. Thus, group-based compensation systems are expected to provide the motivation and incentive for individuals to act on their KSAs (that are enhanced through the other components of a flexibility enhancing HR system) and demonstrate the behavioral repertories desired by the system, which should enhance resource and HR flexibility.

Employment stability

In an HR system that is trying to develop HR flexibility, the gains produced by such a system are developed through long-term relationships with core (permanent/long-term) employees (Way, Lepak, Fay, & Thacker, 2004). This long-term employment will allow the organization to develop (via multi-skill training, job rotation, involvement in decision-making and group- and performance-based pay) employee KSAs and behavioral repertoires. Theory suggests that superior performance gains and the extra employee effort required in employee participation/involvement practices (policies, or mechanisms) are unlikely to manifest if the organization is not prepared to provide employment stability (Kochan & Osterman, 1994; Osterman & Kochan, 1990). Empirical evidence demonstrates that job stability may be required for team and/or voice processes to have a positive impact on performance (Batt, 1995). That is, establishments that invest in employees and enhance resource and HR flexibility rely on a stable workforce that is willing (i.e., motivated) and has the capacity (i.e., the KSAs) to demonstrate the behavioral repertoires that are required by the system. Therefore, employment stability is an important facet of resource flexibility and HR flexibility systems.

In terms of performance, there are several important outcomes that may be affected by resource flexibility. Specifically, the resource flexibility element (i.e., cognitive staffing, multi-skill training, job rotation, involvement in decision-making, group-based compensation systems, and employment stability) is expected to enhance the KSAs and behavioral repertories of the establishment's human capital, which will result in greater levels resource and HR flexibility. Firms with greater levels of resource and HR flexibility are expected to gain competitive advantage and superior performance due to the higher levels of quality and efficiency that such resources generate. Thus, the resource flexibility element will be associated with enhanced service quality and labor productivity, as well as lower voluntary turnover.

In addition, firms which have an enhanced resource flexibility element should possess employees with the KSAs and behavioral repertoires that are required to adapt to environmental change in a timely manner. That is, these establishments will have human capital that are able to adapt in a timely manner to an increase in the skills that are required of them to perform their job at an acceptable level versus those establishments that do not have enhanced resource flexibility. Moreover, resource flexibility will be a critical concern to firms which face considerable environmental change and require employee adaptation. Thus, the resource flexibility element and an increase in the required skills of the establishment's front-line employees to perform their job at an acceptable level (i.e., environmental change requiring employee adaptation) will have an interactional association with higher labor productivity and lower turnover. That is, resource flexibility will be even more important when firms operate in dynamic competitive markets.

The coordination flexibility element

As noted earlier, coordination flexibility refers to the HRM mechanisms that provide the establishment with human capital that have the latitude, KSAs, and behavioral repertories to adapt to change in a timely manner. We contend that the key components of coordination flexibility element include contingent workers and self-directed teams.

Contingent workers

Through the use of contingent workers, coordination and HR flexibility is enhanced by the establishment's ability to hire workers with the appropriate skills in a just-in-time fashion (cf. van Ham, Paauwe, & Williams, 1987; Way et al., 2004). Furthermore, when the establishment requires a new set of narrow skills for a specific purpose or specific problem, contingent employees can be utilized (Kochan, Smith, Wells, & Rebitzer, 1994). Thus, contingent workers enhance coordination and HR flexibility by allowing the establishment to select or buy a narrow set of skills (expertise) that does not exist within the establishment to solve specialized problems or perform specific projects (van Ham *et al.*, 1987; Wright & Snell, 1998) in a timely manner.

Self-directed teams

Wright and Snell (1998) suggest that coordination and HR flexibility will be enhanced by HR processes that allow employees to use different behavioral scripts in appropriate situations, rather than following standard operating procedures. Furthermore, the ability to adapt may be enhanced through mechanisms in which employees and teams can make rapid decisions and effective use of resources and share their insights (Dyer & Shafer, 1999). Indeed, self-directed teams may provide a mechanism which allows human capital to use different behavioral scripts, make rapid decisions, make effective use of resources, and share their insights. That is, self-directed teams should provide employees with exposure to a greater number of behavioral scripts, new KSAs, and provide the motivation and latitude (to make decisions), which should enhance the ability of employees and the establishment to adapt to environmental change.

In terms of performance, the components of coordination flexibility element should provide firms with human capital that has the appropriate KSAs and behavioral repertories to adapt in a timely manner to environmental change, which should result in greater coordination and HR flexibility. Firms with greater levels of coordination and HR flexibility have responsive and are expected to achieve superior performance and over time, competitive advantage, due to the responsiveness and engagement of the firm's employees that are associated with the use of contingent workers and self-directed teams. Thus, similar to resource flexibility, the coordination flexibility element will be associated with higher service quality and labor productivity, and lower voluntary turnover.

In addition, organizations that have enhanced coordination flexibility will have in place the mechanisms that provide the firm with human capital that possesses the appropriate KSAs and behavioral repertories, which should aid human capital and the establishment as a whole to adapt to environmental change. That is, these establishments will be able to adapt in a timely manner when environmental change requires employee adaptation versus those establishments that do not have enhanced coordination flexibility. Therefore, it is within establishments in which environmental change requiring employee adaptation has recently occurred that the coordination flexibility element is expected to have its greatest impact on competitive advantage and superior performance. Thus, the coordination flexibility element and an increase in the required skills of the establishment's front-line employees to perform their job at an acceptable level (i.e., environmental change requiring employee adaptation) will have an interactional association with higher labor productivity and lower turnover.

Conclusion

It is clear that human capital is one of the most important resources that firm's can leverage for creating competitive advantage. As such, it is critical that firms adopt HR systems that not only attract, develop, and retain top talent, but also have a degree of flexibility to account for the dynamic qualities of internal and external environments. To date, the focus of most strategic HR scholars has typically been on the relationship between firm performance and various systems of HR practices. While we have learned a great deal about the role and influence of HR, we contend that a critical and overlooked component of previous inquiry is the extent to which HR systems can adapt to environmental change.

Strategic HR (SHRM) research has accumulated a substantial body of empirical evidence that supports the HR–firm performance relationship (Becker & Huselid, 1998; Combs *et al.*, 2006). Scholars who examine this relationship maintain that human resources are the organization's primary resource to be strategically leveraged for competitive advantage, and thus, examine systems of HR practices as the means through which human resources can be deployed to gain competitive advantage and enhance firm performance (Wright, 1998). However, the focus of most empirical SHRM studies has not considered the situational contingencies that may affect the relationship between various systems of HR practices and firm performance. To advance the field, numerous scholars have suggested that future empirical SHRM research must focus on illuminating the "black box" (i.e., explicating the mediating mechanisms) between HR systems and firm performance (Becker & Gerhart, 1996; Huselid & Becker, 2000; Snell *et al.*, 2001; Way & Johnson, 2005; Wright & Boswell, 2002). We contend that consideration of the components of flexible HR systems will provide some of the needed clarity and provide a means for opening this black box and learning more about the ways in which HR can be used to help firms achieve their strategic and operational objectives.

In addition to assessing the direct effects of HR systems on important firm-level outcomes, there is a need for research that allows practitioners and scholars to gain a better understanding of the mediating mechanisms (the process) through which HR systems create value and enhance firm performance. Future research should develop and include valid measures of meditating variables (e.g., workforce competencies, motivation, attitudes, perceptions, etc.) in research that empirically examines the relationship between HR systems and firm performance (Way, 2006). This type of inquiry will help identify the system characteristics that support HR flexibility, and offer prescription to practitioners that will help them create work contexts that address the demands of their competitive environments.

Finally, in order to truly understand the role of HR systems, the performance effects of HR flexibility are probably best assessed using longitudinal research designs. Longitudinal data will provide a greater opportunity to examine how in the long run, and after many changes in environmental demand, HR flexibility is associated with the most important firm-level outcome measure of all—organizational survival. Longitudinal studies will allow researchers to control for fixed characteristics of the firm, and look for changes in performance, systems, strategies, etc. and aid researchers in identifying causality.

HR flexibility is an important construct that may allow practitioners and scholars to gain a better understanding of the process through which HR systems in firms that operate within dynamic environments can create value and enhance firm performance. Business research indicates that for firms operating within dynamic environments, competitive advantage and firm performance are a function of the firm's capability to become responsiveness and innovation (Chakravarthy, 1982; Sanchez, 1997; Schumpeter, 1934; Teece, Pisano, & Shuen, 1997). Congruently, HR scholars have suggested that within dynamic competitive environments, HR flexibility is a critical concern for enhancing firm performance and competitive position (Wright & Snell, 1998). We hope that this review and our contentions encourages research attention on HR flexibility, and that firms take purposeful actions to incorporate the policies and practices associated with resource and coordination flexibility as they attempt to manage the dynamic environments in which they compete.

References

Appelbaum, E., Bailey, T., Berg, P., & Kalleberg, A. (2000). *Manufacturing competitive advantage: The effects of high performance work systems on plant performance and company outcomes*. Ithaca, NY: Cornell University Press.

Barney, J., Wright, M., & Ketchen, D.J., Jr. (2001). The resource-based view of the firm: Ten years after 1991. *Journal of Management*, 21: 625-641.

Barney, J. B. (1991). Firm resources and sustained competitive advantage. *Journal of Management*, 17(1), 99–120.

Barney, J. B. (1995). Looking inside for competitive advantage. *Academy of Management Executive*, 9(4), 49–61.

Batt, R. (1995). Performance and welfare effects on work restructuring: Evidence from telecommunications ser-vice. Ph.D. dissertation, MIT Sloan School of Management, Cambridge, MA.

Becker, B., & Gerhart, B. (1996). The impact of human resource management on organizational performance: Progress and prospects. *Academy of Management Journal*, 39: 779–801.

Becker, B. E., & Huselid, M. (1998). High performance work systems and firm performance: A synthesis of research and managerial implications. In G. R. Ferris (Ed.), *Research in personnel and human resources management* (Vol. 16, pp. 53–101). Stamford: JAI Press Inc.

Becker, B.E., & Huselid, M.A. (2006). Strategic human resources management. Where do we go from here? *Journal of Management*, 32: 898–925.

Blanchard, P. N., & Thacker, J. (1999). *Effective training: Systems, strategies, and practices.* Upper Saddle River, NJ: Prentice Hall.

Blasi, J., Kruse, D., Sesil, J., Kroumova, M., & Carberry, E. (2000). *Stock options, corporate performance, and organizational change.* Oakland, CA: The National Center for Employee Ownership.

Boxall, P. (1998). Achieving competitive advantage through human resource strategy: Towards and theory of industry dynamics. *Human Resource Management Review*, 2(2), 265.

Brown, S., & Eisenhardt, K. (1998). *Competing on the edge: Strategy as structured chaos.* Boston: Harvard Business School Press.

Chadwick, C., & Cappelli, P. (1999). Alternatives to generic strategy typologies in strategic human resource management. In G. R. Ferris (Ed.), and P. M. Wright, L. L. Dyer, J. W. Boudreau & G. T. Milkovich (Vol. Eds.), *Research in personnel and human resources management* (Suppl. 4, pp. 1–30). Stamford: JAI Press Inc.

Chakravarthy, B. (1982). Adaptation: A promising metaphor for strategic management. *Academy of Management Review*, 7, 35–44.

Combs, J., Liu, Y., Hall, A., & Ketchen, D. (2006). How much do high-performance work practices matter? A meta-analysis of their effects on organizational performance. *Personnel Psychology*, 59: 501–528.

Cooke, W. (1994). Employee participation programs, group-based incentives, and company performance: A union-nonunion comparison. *Industrial and Labor Relations Review*, 47(4) 594–609.

Deadrick, D., Bennett, N., & Russell, C. (1997). Using hierarchical linear modeling to examine dynamic performance criteria over time. *Journal of Management*, 23(6) 745–757.

Delery, J., & Doty, H. (1996). Modes of theorizing in strategic human resource management: Tests of universalistic, contingency, and configurational performance predictions. *Academy of Management Journal*, *39*(4) 802–835.

Delery, J.E., & Shaw, J.D. 2001. The strategic management of people in work organizations: Review, synthesis, and extension. In G.R. Ferris (Ed.), *Research in personnel and human resources management*, 20. Stamford, CT: JAI Press.

Dierickx, I., & Cool, K. (1989). Asset stock accumulation and sustainability of competitive advantage. *Management Science*, 35(12): 1504–1511.

Dyer, L., & Reeves, T. (1995). Human resource strategies and firm performance: What do we know and where do we need to go? *The International Journal of Human Resource Management*, *6*(3), 656–670.

Dyer, L., & Shafer, R. A. (1999). A duality-based prospective from strategic human resource management. In G. R. Ferris (Ed.), and P. M. Wright, L. L. Dyer, J. W. Boudreau & G. T. Milkovich (Vol. Eds.), *Research in personnel and human resources management* (Suppl. 4, pp. 145–174). Stamford: JAI Press Inc.

Gomez-Mejia, L., & Balkin, D. (1994). Compensation, organizational strategy, and firm performance. *South-western series in human resource management*. Cincinnati, OH: South-Western Publishing Company.

Hunter, J., & Hunter, R. F. (1984). Validity and utility of alternative predictors of job performance. *Psychological Bulletin*, *96*, 72–98.

Huselid, M. A. (1995). The impact of human resource management practices on turnover, productivity, and corporate financial performance. *Academy of Management Journal, 38*(3), 635–672.

Huselid, M. A., & Becker, B. E. (2000). Comment on "measurement error in research on human resources and firm performance: How much error is there and how does it influence effect size estimates?" by Gerhart, Wright, McMahan, and Snell. *Personnel Psychology*, *53*(4), 835–854.

Huselid, M. A., Jackson, S., & Schuler, R. (1997). Technical and strategic human resource management effectiveness as determinants of firm performance. *Academy of Management Journal*, *40*(1), 171–188.

Icniowski, C., Shaw, K., & Prennushi, G. (1997). The effects of human resources management practices on productivity: A study of steel finishing lines. *American Economic Review*, *87*(3), 291–313.

Kochan, T., & Osterman, P. (1994). *The mutual gains enterprise*. Boston, MA: Harvard Business School Press.

Kochan, T., Smith, M., Wells, J., & Rebitzer, J. (1994). Human resource strategies and contingent workers: The case of safety and health in the petrochemical industry. *Human Resource Management*, *33*, 55–77.

Kruse, D. (1993). *Profit sharing: Does it make a difference?* Kalamazoo, MI: W.E. Upjohn Institute for Employment Research.

Lepak, D. P., & Snell, S. A. (1999). The human resource architecture: Toward a theory of human capital allocation and development. *Academy of Management Review*, *24*, 31–48.

Levine, D., & Tyson, L. (1990). Participation, productivity and the firm's environment. In A. Binder (Ed.), *Paying for productivity* (pp. 183–237). Washington, DC: The Brookings Institution.

Lynch, L., & Black, S. (1995). Beyond the incidence of training: Evidence from a National Employers Survey. *National Bureau of Economic Research Working Paper Series, working paper 5231*.

Mager, R.F., & Pipe, P. (1984). Analyzing performance problem: or, You really oughta wanna (2nd ed.) Belmont, CA: Lake Management and Training.

Milliman, J., Von Glinow, M. A., & Nathan, M. (1991). Organizational life cycles and strategic international human resource management in multinational companies: Implications for congruence theory. *Academy of Management Review*, *16*, 318–339.

Morrow, C., Jarrett, Q., & Rupinski, M. (1997). An investigation of the effect of economic utility of corporate-wide training. *Personnel Psychology*, *50*(1), 91–119.

Noe, R, Wilk, S., Mullen, E., & Wanek, J. (1997). Employee development: Construct validation issues. In J. K. Ford (Ed.), *Improving training effectiveness in work organizations*. Mahweh, NJ: Lawrence Erlbaum Associate.

Osterman, P., & Kochan, T. (1990). Employment security and employment policy: An assessment of the issues. In K. Abraham & R. McKersie (Eds.), *New developments in the labor market: Toward a new institutional paradigm*. Cambridge, MA: MIT.

Rubinstein, S. (2000). The impact of co-management on quality performance: The case of the Saturn corporation. *Industrial and Labor Relations Review*, *53*(2), 197–218.

Rumelt, R. (1984). Toward a strategic theory of the firm. In R. Lamb (Ed.), *Competitive strategic management* (pp. 556–570). Englewood Cliffs, NJ: Prentice-Hall.

Sanchez, R. (1995). Strategic flexibility in product competition. *Strategic Management Journal*, *16*, 135–159.

Sanchez, R. (1997). Preparing for an uncertain future: Managing organizations for strategic flexibility. *International Studies of Management & Organization*, *27*: 71–94.

Sanchez, R., & Heene, A. (1997). Managing for an uncertain future: A systems view of strategic organizational change. *International Studies of Management and Organization*, 27(2): 21–42.

Schmidt, F., Hunter, J., Outerbridge, A., & Goff, S. (1988). Joint relation of experience and ability with job performance: Test of three hypotheses. *Journal of Applied Psychology*, 73(1), 46–57.

Schumpeter, J.A. (1934). The theory of economic development. Cambridge, MA: Harvard University Press.

Sesil, J. (1999). The impact of employee Involvement and group incentives on performance in UK high technology establishments. In R. Oakey, W. During & S.-M. Mukhtar (Eds.), *New technology firms in the 1990s* (pp. 297–308). New York, NY: Elsevier Science Ltd.

Snell, S.A., Shadur, M.A., & Wright, P.M. (2001). Human resources strategy: The era of our ways. In M.A. Hitt, R.E. Freeman, & J.S. Harrison (Eds.), *The Blackwell handbook of strategic management* (pp. 627–649). Malden, MA: Blackwell Publishers Inc.

Snell, S. A., Youndt, M. A., & Wright, P. M. (1996). Establishing a framework for research in strategic human resource management: Merging resource theory and organizational learning. In G. R. Ferris (Ed.), *Research in personnel and human resources management* (Vol. 14, pp. 61–90). Stanford: JAI Press.

Snow, C., & Snell, S. A. (1993). Staffing as strategy. In N. Schmitt, W. Borman, et al. (Eds.), *Personnel selection in organizations*. San Francisco, CA: Jossey-Bass.

Teece, D.J., Pisano, G., & Shuen, A. (1997). Dynamic capabilities and strategic management. *Strategic Management Journal*, 18: 509–533.

Tracey, J. B., Sturman, M. C., & Tews, M. J. (2007). Ability versus personality: Factors that predict employee job performance. *Cornell Quarterly*, 48, 313–322.

Tracey, J. B., & Nathan, A. E. (2002). The strategic and operational roles of HR: A new model emerges. *Cornell Quarterly*, 43, 17–26.

van Ham, J., Paauwe, J., & Williams, R. (1986). Personnel management in a changing environment. *Personnel Review, 15*(3), 3–7.

van Ham, J., Paauwe, J., & Williams, R. (1987). Human resource flexibility: Some necessary conditions for success. *Personnel Review, 16*(2), 27–30.

Way, S. A. (2002). High performance work systems and intermediate indicators of firm performance within the U.S. small business sector. *Journal of Management*, 28, 765–785.

Way, S.A. (2005). *A firm-level analysis of HR flexibility*, Ph.D. dissertation, Rutgers University (School of Management & Labor relations), New Brunswick, NJ, U.S.A.

Way, S. A. (2006). A firm-level analysis of HR flexibility. *Ralph Alexander Best Dissertation Award*. Academy of Management: HR Division.

Way, S. A., & Johnson, D. E. (2005). Theorizing about the impact of strategic human resource management. *Human Resource Management Review*, *15*, 1–19.

Way, S. A., Lepak, D. P., Fay, C. H., & Thacker, J. W. (2004). Contingent labor strategies, HIHRS, and HR outcomes for full time employees: A firm-level analysis. In K. M. Weaver (Ed.), *Proceedings of the Sixty-fifth Annual Meeting of the Academy of Management* (CD), ISSN1543-86432.

Weitzman, M., & Kruse, D. (1990). Profit sharing and productivity. In A. Blinder (Ed.), *Paying for productivity: A look at the evidence* (pp. 95–140). Washington DC: Brookings Institution.

Wernfelt, B. (1984). A resource-based view of the firm. *Strategic Management Journal*, *5*, 171–174.

Wright, P.M. (1998). Introduction: Strategic human resource management research in the 21st century. *Human Resource Management Review*, 8: 187–191.

Wright, P. M., & Boswell, W. R. (2002). Desegregating HR: A review and synthesis of micro and macro human resource management research. *Journal of Management*, *28*, 247–276.

Wright, P. M., Dunford, B. B., & Snell, S. A. (2001). Human resources and the resource-based view of the firm. *Journal of Management*, *27*(6), 701.

Wright, P. M., Gardner, T. M., Moynihan, L., & Allen, M. R. (2005). The relationship between HR practices and firm performance: Examining causal order. *Personnel Psychology*, *58*(2), 409–446.

Wright, P.M., & McMahan, G.C. (1992). Theoretical perspectives for strategic human resource management. *Journal of Management*, 18: 295–320.

Wright, P. M., & Snell, S. A. (1998). Toward a unifying framework for exploring fit and flexibility in strategic human resource management. *Academy of Management Review*, *23*(4), 756–772.

Youndt, M., Snell, S. A., Dean, J. W., & Lepak, D. (1996). Human resource management, manufacturing strategy, and firm performance. *Academy of Management Journal*, *39*(4), 836–866.

CHAPTER 2

Job analysis: the basis for all things H.R.

Jalane M. Meloun

School of Adult and Continuing Education, Barry University 11415 N.E. 2nd Avenue Miami Shores, FL 336161, USA

Introduction

Job analysis is the root of all things H.R. Its implications are broad and deep, spanning workforce planning, recruitment, selection, placement, job classification and evaluation, compensation, performance appraisal, training, employee development, succession planning, workforce analysis, HRIS designs, and organization analysis. In this chapter, the topic of job analysis will be explored, with emphasis on why and how to conduct a job analysis, with implications for the hospitality industry.

Although job analyses are typically done at the person level of analysis (as opposed to the team/departmental or organizational levels), it is useful to have a rudimentary understanding of the current industry situation and trends before beginning the job analysis. For example, if the industry is experiencing rapid international growth, then perhaps more job analyses will have to be preformed as a position such as a front desk clerk in a hotel can have vastly different duties depending on whether the job is in the U.S. or Great Britain.

Current industry review

Lodging

To better understand the implications for the hospitality industry, it is wise to examine the current state of different segments in the industry. According to Datamonitor (2006), the lodging industry, comprised of hotels and motels in the United States, has enjoyed a compound annual growth rate of 6.9% over the recent five year time period of 2002–2006, with an 8.9% growth in 2006 alone. Currently, the U.S. hotel and motel industry is valued at $133.7 billion and accounts for over 27% of the global lodging's value. This becomes dramatic, when coupled with the forecasted 42.9% growth projected from 2006 to 2011. Major players include Cendant Corporation (Avis, Budget, and Ramada), Starwood Hotels & Resorts Worldwide, Inc. (Sheraton, Westin, Four Points, W, Meridien, St. Regis), Marriott International, Inc. (Mariott, Ritz-Carlton, Courtyard, Renaissance, Fairfield Inn) and Hilton Hotels Corporation (Hilton, Doubletree, Embassy Suites, Hampton) (Datamonitor, 2006). Looking more closely, Cendant employs nearly 84,000, Starwood approximately 110,000 (Datamonitor, 2006) and Mariott approximately 151,000 (www.mariott.com). So many workers translate into many positions and, thus, many jobs that need to be analyzed.

Food service

The service of food industry contains the subcategories of profit foodservice, and fast food. Foodservice is defined as "the sale of food and drinks for immediate consumption either on the premises from which they were bought, or in designated eating areas shared with other foodservice operators, or ... freshly prepared food for immediate consumption" (Datamonitor, 2007, p. 7). As compared to the lodging industry, foodservice has a higher value, at $188.1 billion, but only grew by a 3.3% compound annual growth rate from 2002 to 2006 with a 3.9% increase in 2006 and is predicted to grow 18% between 2006 and 2011. When making an international comparison, the United States holds 29.3% of the global industry's value (Datamonitor, 2007). Given the vast number of restaurants across the United States, there are a few key companies that have a strong foothold in their respective segments. Yum! Brands, Inc. does the development, operation, and franchising/licensing of the following: KFC, Pizza Hut, Taco Bell, Long John Silver's and All American Food (A & W). Primarily serving in the United States and Canada, Darden Restaurants, Inc. focuses on casual dining and operates Olive Garden, Red Lobster, Smokey Bones, and Bahama Breeze. As half of a duopoly with Burger King, McDonald's Corporation owns and franchises worldwide, operating 31,667 restaurants in over 119 countries (Datamonitor, 2007). Up and coming foodservice establishments are Starbucks, the unquestionable leader in coffee houses and Subway, known for its healthy fare. Across the segments of foodservice, a universal compensation maxim is that pay to employees is low, and many work for minimum wage. However, the industry as a whole is labor-intensive, so wages still present themselves as a corporate financial burden and a focal point of human resources.

Definitions

A *job analysis* is the actual process of gathering information about jobs. From this information, both a job description and a job specification may result, often combined in one document generally referred to as the job description (see Appendix A). The *job description* highlights the work duties required of the position, often including a description of the working condition, whereas the *job specifications* focus on the requirements demanded by the employee who fills this position. The job specifications typically are written to the minimum qualifications necessary to fulfill the job and may include examples of task duties requiring such skills, abilities, etc. Technically, there are two types of job analyses. The first type is either called *job-based* or *task-oriented*, because the primary concern is the job. The focus of the second, termed *person-based* or *worker-oriented*, places far more emphasis on the qualifications necessarily possessed by the worker in the job. Of the two, the job-based is more common. To better clarify, a job-based analysis for a travel agent might contain the following sentence: *Operates Amadeus travel software to find best transportation and lodging options to suit customer preferences.*

Whereas, a person-based job analysis might list the same major work duty with emphasis on the employee's skill at using the software in this way: *Evaluates customer's transportation and lodging preferences and chooses which options presented in Amadeus travel software will best please the client.*

With either focus, it is important to understand some vocabulary generally associated with the job analysis. Starting at the macro level and working toward the microlevel, let us begin with job family. A *job family* is comprised of two or more jobs that share common duties, but are sufficiently different from each other not to be considered as one job. For example, a hotel might have the job family of clerical workers, including front desk employees, reservationists, rooms manager, night auditor, accounts pay and receivable clerks. Next comes a *job*, which consists of a group of positions that have similar duties. *Positions* are also composed of duties, but only one person holds a position. To clarify, a waiter/waitress is a job, but in a given restaurant, there may be 22 such positions. Only one person occupies each of those 22 positions. As mentioned, jobs and positions are made up of *duties*, which is the highest level of actual work requirements. Duties are comprised of many tasks. Further, *tasks* are constituted by job *elements* that are at the level of actual movements required to complete the task. To demonstrate: someone employed in a small travel agency may be responsible for the work duty of communicating with customers. This breaks down into a number of tasks, including answering the phone. Said particular task may be further dissected into numerous elements, such as reaching out to grasp the headset, lifting the headset to one's head, and placing the headset on one's head with the earpiece on an ear, etc. Typically job analyses focus on both duties and tasks, but rarely get into the finer task elements.

KSAs, *KSAOs*, and *KSAPCs* (a.k.a. competencies) are common acronyms referencing the knowledge, skills, abilities, and other or personal characteristics that a job demands (see Appendix A).

The simplest definitions of each follow: *knowledge* is knowing how to perform the work, but not actually having performed it. *Skills* involve actually being able to perform the work, and *ability* references having the emotional, physical, intellectual, and psychological ability to perform the work, but neither having done the work, nor having been trained to perform the work (Clifford, 1994). *Other* may include years of experience, certain educational requirements or other credentials. Typically, however, other refers to *personal characteristics* such as motivation. Looking at KSAs another way, an individual must first have the capability or ability to gain the knowledge or exhibit the skill. Next comes the know-how and only then may a developed skill follow. Keep in mind that having an ability and knowledge does not guarantee skill as often skills take time to develop and imply a certain acceptable level of proficiency. Think of all the golfers who physically can hit a tiny ball with a club and all the readers of Golf Digest and the like, but those who have mastered true skill number few.

Turning focus to a hospitality example, a hotel front desk employee may have just attended a class on how to use new rooms-tracking software, but because the employee has not actually used the software, this exemplifies knowledge. When the employee puts the knowledge garnered into use, then this becomes a skill. Abilities are a bit different as they are forward focused, emphasizing potential capabilities and not current states of affair. Let us slightly modify the example to a job seeker applying for a front desk position. If the candidate had low computer anxiety, good eyesight, adequate finger/hand/arm coordination, sufficient memory, etc. to handle using the room-tracking program, such would constitute an ability to master the software.

Brief History

The first known standardized job analysis dates back to 1922. Industrial psychologist Morris Viteles used a job analysis as the basis for selecting trolley car employees (Viteles, 1922). Vitales included something called a job psychograph which essentially assigns attribute levels necessitated by the job qualifications. Otherwise, when making a comparison between Viteles's work and any given modern-day job analysis, the job description and the job qualifications are remarkably similar. Such a lack of marked modifications over so many decades suggests that the process is well-established, time-tested, and worth doing.

Why should job analyses be done?

Legal reasons

Probably one of the most compelling reasons to perform job analyses is to avoid being sued. As our society ostensibly tends to become more litigious, it is important to exercise every additional precaution to avoid costly lawsuits. Although correctly performing a job analysis is not free and does cost not only money but employee productivity time, there is an inherent associated opportunity cost as well. However, when weighted against potential lawsuits that can be in the millions, doing a job analysis is often the least costly option.

Specifically, doing a job analysis insulates against lawsuits stemming from the Americans with Disabilities Act (ADA) of 1990 and the Rehabilitation Act that covers federal contractors and grant recipients. The ADA is more far-reaching, imposing compliance by all employers. In essence, it protects disabled individuals (i.e. those who have a physical or mental impairment that substantially limits one or more major life activities such as walking). Employers cannot discriminate against otherwise qualified disabled applicants who can fulfill the "essential functions" of the position. "Essential functions" are those parts of the job that require more time and generally have greater importance, perhaps by having great consequences of errors, while being parts of the position that cannot easily be tasked to someone else. Let us take the example of a "barback," or person whose main job is to ensure the bar is adequately stocked. This individual predominantly carries heavy cases of alcohol from the back of the bar/restaurant to the bartending area and would have the essential function of carrying heavy items. To reassign this part of a barback's job would be to basically remove his/her position, thus it would be deemed an essential function.

To deal with otherwise qualified disabled individuals, employers must make "reasonable accommodations" (e.g. restructuring the job or the workplace) for the nonessential functions, unless making such accommodations would present "undue economic hardship" on the organization. The logical question is: "What constitutes 'undue economic hardship?'" and such a question is not answerable as it is too subjective, forcing the courts to decide on an individual basis.

The question that *may* easily be answered is: "What constitutes an essential function of a job?" This question is one of the main functions in conducting a job analysis. The job description section basically lists out the major work duties, or essential functions, in order of important or frequency and thus gives a preemptory legal rationale as to why someone was or was not hired on the basis of whether that individual could accomplish the essential functions of the position.

Non-legal reasons

The root of all things H.R.

Beyond the avoidance reason to conduct a job analysis, there are many uses for the results of a job analysis and hence the name for this chapter: *Job Analysis: The Basis for All Things H.R.* For example, conducting job analyses let an organization know what jobs comprise the organization and what associated skills are demanded for those jobs. Finding skill deficiencies suggests direction for workforce planning. Once human resource needs are determined, naturally the recruitment of qualified talent and the selection of such individuals ensues. Job analyses color both important organizational processes of recruitment and selection. Recruitment will be based on open jobs and human attributes needed to fulfill those positions. Selection completely depends on the job description and the job qualifications as those determine selection methods (i.e. interviewing, testing, assessment centers). To give a more specific example, consider a job interview for a tour guide. Asking the job applicant if she can stand for prolonged periods of time is a legally defensible question as it is defined in the job description as a major work duty. Boiled down to its barest elements, testing for or selecting on any criteria is permissible, as long as job-relevancy may be demonstrated, and it is not in violation of an employment law. Believe it or not, even asking if a candidate is of a particular religion is legal if, for example, the person was applying to be a priest in a Catholic church.

A good rule of thumb to keep in mind during any selection activities is to remember the term "job-relevant." Whenever an organization uses a means of selection that can directly be traced back to something on the job analysis, be it a duty or KSA, then the selection procedure may better be deemed "content valid." Thus, the job analysis governs the recruitment and selection process, which will be elaborated on in the next chapter.

Job analysis also plays an important role in placement. Sometimes an organization, such as a new hotel may have a need to hire a great number of employees quickly. Perhaps there will be mass hiring and then, on the basis of the job analysis that pinpoints what KSAs are necessary for each position, new employees may be assigned.

Compensation systems are heavily influenced by the results of the job analyses. Specifically, job classification requires using job descriptions resulting from a job analysis to decide which jobs should be slotted into which job grades (range of like jobs). The jobs become relatively easy to group when the job descriptions are side by side. Beyond classification, the job evaluation, or determining pay levels and differentials among jobs within one organization, is also highly dependent upon the job analysis. Although determining pay during the job evaluation process is never easy and different results come about if different methods are utilized, nonetheless using the job analysis outcomes does ease this procedure. As well, it increases the likelihood of jobs that require more critical duties and more extensive or rare KSAs, to be paid more than those positions requiring less or fewer.

Often tied to compensation are performance appraisals, which also are directly linked to job analyses. Organizations are able to target desired employee behavior on the basis of what is rewarded. The performance outcomes are determined to a large degree on the job analysis's resulting job description and how well the job incumbent met those duties. There is likely to be a greater perception of procedural justice (Cropanzano & Folger, 1989) if the employee is rewarded based on how well he or she carried out the major work duties delineated in the job description. This becomes another example of content validity with rewards directly tied to the fundamentals of the job. Put another way, if a job analysis were not done, there would be no systematically written job description and thus no solid basis on what behavior to reward. Given the scenario, it would be easy to imagine employees crying "foul" about who was rewarded and to what extent, even in cases when everyone was given the exact same pay. Thus, again, job analyses are shown to be the root of important fundamental HR functions.

For success in the marketplace, it is critical to keep top-notch talent. One way to better ensure this is to provide frequent and relevant opportunities for employees to keep their skills finely tuned and to increase their knowledge bases. The initial step in planning employee training is to first conduct a job analysis to reveal what KSAs are relevant to current positions. This is naturally followed by a needs analysis that assesses KSA deficits. Also based on the job analysis is the whole concept of employee development, which focuses more on career planning. When employees are looking to make either upward (promotions) or lateral moves within the company, one way for them to better ensure their success is to first examine the job description and job qualification for their target job. If they believe they can handle the major work duties and they think they either have or can acquire the necessary minimal KSAs, then the job becomes a natural fit for them. In the case of KSA deficiencies for a coveted position, the employee finds him/herself directed toward which KSAs need sharpening or acquiring. Likewise, from the employer's perspective, open jobs may be filled with internal candidates by examining the job description and job qualifications, both outgrowths of the job analysis. Many times qualified and interested individuals are already on staff, a situation that cuts down on time mandated when hiring externally. Namely, external candidates inherently cost not only time from the recruitment phase to when the employees are oriented and socialized to the time they reach productivity, but also eliminates the expense of advertising and selection.

In the same vein, succession planning is aided by the job analysis. Analysis of which employees move into which positions after attrition or promotion is succession planning. This is often done with key positions in the upper echelon of management. Without time spent developing succession plans, many organizations would be sunk. Imagine what would happen were a large hotel chain CEO to be killed in a car accident. Unless one of his/her underlings were groomed to fill those shoes, much knowledge, finesse, skills, etc. would go undeveloped and the hotel may stumble a bit in recovery. Planning saves scurrying about to make do and can be more easily done with solidly performed job analyses.

Workforce analysis involves a structural examination of the organization to forecast which jobs need to be filled, who is filling them, etc. One easy way to do this is via technology. In regards to the varied human resources tasks that have been made facile with a computer program, there is a whole HR subfield termed Human Resources Information Systems or, more commonly, HRIS. Such systems retain vast quantities of information about employees or jobs and enable data to be stored, queries to be run, reports to be generated, and regulatory mandated statistics to be compiled for easy reporting. Again, all of these HR functions are facilitated by conducting job analyses.

Job migration

Another reason to conduct job analyses is that jobs tend to migrate over time. Some are done away with while others are added. Jobs also morph to take on the characteristics of the incumbent. For example, let us say a busser (formerly bus boy) at a restaurant is detail-oriented and has the skill for organizing. By virtue of his abilities, his job during slow bussing times is expanded to include inventory control. After he vacates the position, the manager now searches for a busser who can also handle inventory control tasks. Thus the person has changed the job duties.

Sometimes positions become altered because of technological improvements. Years ago cashiers in a souvenir shop, for example, would have to ring up items by tapping the numerical keys on the cash register. Now, they tend to scan bar codes linked to the correct price to trigger whether the good is taxable and concurrently subtract the good from inventory all the while adding one quantity of it to the outgoing inventory order. In some cases, as in fast food restaurants, cashiers simply push a button on the cash register that says "small fry" and the price is rung. Such cash registers also count out and dispense the correct amount of change directly to the customer, thus eliminating the cognitive demand of performing math from the required KSAs for the cashier position. Following that example, fewer KSAs are required. At other times, automation demands more or different KSAs as in the example of small hotel front desk clerk who must feel comfortable using computers and changing toner in the copy machine, fixing the FAX machine, etc.

Regardless of the reason jobs change over time, the important thing to keep in mind is that job analyses should be done regularly to keep job descriptions and job qualifications current. With so much riding on the job analysis outcomes, keeping on top of this HR tool is a wise means of not only staving off lawsuits, but also ensuring that all of the other HR functions that rest on job analyses run more smoothly.

What to include in a job analysis

The Uniform Guidelines on Employee Selection Procedures (Uniform Guidelines) is one piece of literature that strongly influences job analyses, from how they are done to what is included (Equal Employment Opportunity Commission, Civil Service Commission, Department of Labor, Department of Justice, 1978). This document (available free at www.uniform-guidelines.com) was set forth with blessings from the Equal Employment Opportunity Commission, the Civil Service Commission, the Department of Labor, and the Department of Justice to ensure fair selection procedures for both public and private organizations. Although technically only those organizations that have been shown to have used selection procedures that caused adverse impact against a protected group must follow these uniform guidelines, it is wise for any business to adhere to these principles to avoid legal issues. In brief, adverse/disparate impact means a statistically shown difference in selection rates (i.e. who is hired versus who applied for the position) for those in protected groups (i.e. those protected by national laws such as minorities, women, or those over 40) compared to those not in protected groups. This difference favors those not in protected groups. (For more information on adverse impact or protected groups, please refer to the chapter on recruitment and selection.)

As for content, section 15(c)3 of the Uniform Guidelines more specifically suggest that the following be included:

1. a description of the method used to analyze the job;
2. the work behaviors, associated tasks, and, if applicable, the work products;
3. measures of criticality and/or importance of work behaviors and method for determining these measures;
4. the operational definition for each KSA, with focus on observable behaviors and outcomes;
5. the relationship between each KSA to each work behavior, as well as the method used to determine this relationship;
6. a description of the work setting, where the work behaviors will be performed and the KSAs put to use (recommended, but not essential).

How should the job analysis data be collected?

There are a variety of different means for collecting the job analysis data. It is not difficult to see that the best collection means is by way of triangulation. This simply means utilizing more than one means of data collection to better approximate the truth, in this case about the job. Each method of performing a job analysis inherently has advantages and disadvantages. Triangulation allows some of the disadvantages to be offset by using another collection method as well as capitalizing on the advantages of the different methods.

Self-report methods

Perhaps one of the easiest ways of collecting job analysis data is by means of self-report by an *incumbent*—someone who currently holds a position in the job to be analyzed. The person may complete a step-by-step work diary of everything done over a couple of days, including the durations and detailed descriptions of each. This can be time consuming and expensive as employees are losing valuable productivity time by recording every move. A faster, and less expensive option for this is to have incumbents complete a structured questionnaire that directs employees to focus their answers on the major work duties, tasks, etc. of the job. Allowing workers to complete this at home or as their schedule permits is an advantage for the organization. Perhaps the most widely used such structured interview survey is the Position Analysis Questionnaire (PAQ) which is comprised of 194 job elements that are evaluated on an ordinal scale of one to five on each of six scales (i.e. importance to job, extent of use, etc.) (McCormick, Jeanneret, & Mecham, 1972). One of the nice things about the PAQ is that it is easily scored via computer. However, while leaving human job analysts out of the equation at this juncture saves time, it may also have the disadvantage of unintentionally arousing suspicion on the part of the job incumbents. Sometimes the whole process of analyzing jobs, and particularly in cases of less human interaction, leads employees to the conclusion that their positions are in jeopardy. They may worry of potential organizational restructuring or down-/right-sizing.

Another means of self-report involves a job analyst interviewing an incumbent about what he/she does in his/her position. Compared to the PAQ, this method is more time-consuming as it takes not only the employee's time, but also the job analyst's. However, one advantage lies in the ability of the information taker to gain immediate clarification when an ambiguous work duty, task, or KSA is presented. The other plus of utilizing this technique is that some jobs that involve much cognitive work can be analyzed. Often, this takes the form of the "think aloud" technique (Ericsson & Simon, 1993). Employees will verbalize the step-by-step thinking process they use when they are doing a cognitive task. For example, a computer programmer who works for a cruise line may be trying to debug some computer code. The programmer would verbalize his/her thoughts on what to test as a means of troubleshooting the problem. This leaves the job analysts with a much clearer picture of the programmer's mental demands and thus the suggested KSAs more appropriate to such a position.

While there are a great many advantages to the self-reported means of data collection, there is a sizable disadvantage and that is observed when incumbents tend to inflate aspects of their positions. In particular, research shows incumbents tend to add importance to the KSAs required to perform the job, when compared with job analysts and supervisors who also rated the same position (Morgeson, Delaney-Klinger, Ferrara, Mayfield, & Campion, 2004). Fear, baseless or not, could impel workers to engage in a general "rounding up" of how important duties are, the frequency with which certain tasks are done, or even the fabrication of additional duties. As previously mentioned, workers may be fearful that this microscopic examination of what they do on a daily basis may be for the purpose of trimming the organizational fat, i.e. their positions. If they give the impression that a higher level of KSAs are required for anyone to fill the position, for example, it makes finding a replacement all the more difficult and thus secures their positions.

In order to combat the self-reported inflation that often occurs, there are a couple of techniques that get around this problem. One of them is direct observation of the worker in action. This prevents the employee from saying his work is so much more important than it is or that he accomplishes five times as much as he typically does. However, as was seen in the now-famous Hawthorne studies, employees tend to behave differently when they know they are being observed (Mayo, 1933). This may lead to such changed behaviors as fewer breaks and increased productivity.

Non-self-report methods

Another job analysis collection method is to have the job analyst actually perform the work. This only works for jobs that are easily learned and that do not involve hazardous consequences for poor performance (i.e. tour bus driver). While this gives the job analyst an excellent idea of the working conditions and necessary KSAs, there may not be the exposure to infrequent occurrences such as end-of-year inventory duties of kitchen staff.

Utilizing the critical incidents technique (CIT) is yet another data collection technique. It differs from other techniques by focusing on either outstandingly good or bad performance of employees in that particular position. These critical incidents end up forming anchors on rating scales of work behavior for that particular job. Other than taking a great deal of time to compose, the main disadvantage is that the embedded emphasis on extreme work performance, by definition omits typical behavior on the job, which is the whole point of conducting a job analysis.

There are variants of the above, often involving an incumbent's supervisor(s). However, it is important to remember that sometimes supervisors are unaware of what their supervisees do, or, worse yet, they are under severe misimpressions. It is generally considered best that the incumbent is the subject matter expert (SME) for the position. Yet, it is standard procedure in conducting a job analysis to have the final product reviewed by one or two people, often supervisors, to verify accuracy. This can ameliorate the inflated importance problem previously mentioned. It is also wise, wherever possible, to focus on observable behaviors rather than outcomes that are more subjective.

Steps in conducting a job analysis

As the chapter title suggests, job analyses are done for a variety of purposes. As such a multi-functional tool, the purposes of the job analysis might govern the breadth and depth or means of conducting the job analysis. For example, the CIT lends itself to an organization gathering the data to revise its performance appraisal system as it delivers high and low behavioral ratings. So, keep in mind that these steps are generalized and will vary depending upon many factors such as who conducts the analysis, etc. But, in general,

1. determine the purpose of the job analysis;
2. determine which jobs will be analyzed;
3. review existing literature (i.e. job description, job specification);
4. conduct initial tour of worksite;
5. collect data from incumbent (i.e. self-report, interview, observation);
6. verify the collected information* (i.e. with supervisor);
7. consolidate the job information;
8. draft job description and job specification; and
9. verify job description and job specification* (i.e. with supervisor).

For more information on jobs and job analyses

An excellent resource for so many aspects of jobs is called O*NET and found at www.online.onetcenter.org. This website is an occupational network that basically replaces the Dictionary of Occupational Titles (DOT). The Department of Labor manages this online source that includes databases, job families, taxonomies, questionnaires, career exploration tools, etc. Moreover, to be more accessible, many of the features, including databases, are available in Spanish versions. Thus, there are many available resources to aid you in your understanding of the job analysis process.

References

Clifford, J. P. (1994). Job analysis: Why do it, and how should it be done? *Public Personnel Management, 23*(2).

Cropanzano, R., & Folger, R. (1989). Referent cognitions and task decision autonomy: Beyond equity theory. *Journal of Applied Psychology, 74*, 293–299.

---

*Sometimes only one verification step takes place.

Datamonitor. (2006, December). *Hotels & motels in the United States: Industry profile* (Reference Code: 0072-0520).

Datamonitor. (2007, July). *Foodservice in the United States: Industry profile* (Reference Code: 0072-2333).

Equal Employment Opportunity Commission, Civil Service Commission, Department of Labor, Department of Justice. (1978). Adoption by four agencies of uniform guidelines on employee selection procedures. Federal Register, 43, 38290–58315.

Ericsson, K. A., & Simon, H. A. (1993). *Protocol Analysis: Verbal Reports Data*. Cambridge, MA: MIT Press.

Mayo, E. (1933). *The human problems of an industrial civilization*. New York: MacMillan.

McCormick, E. J., Jeanneret, P. R., & Mecham, R. C. (1972). A study of job characteristics and job dimensions as based on the Position Analysis Questionnaire (PAQ). *Journal of Applied Psychology, 56,* 347–368.

Morgeson, F. P., Delaney-Klinger, K., Ferrara, P., Mayfield, M. S., & Campion, M. A. (2004). Self-presentation processes in job analysis: A field experiment investigating inflation in abilities, tasks, and competencies. *Journal of Applied Psychology, 89,* 674–686.

Viteles, M. S. (1922). Job specifications and diagnostic tests of job competency designed for the auditing division of a street railway company. *Psychological Clinic,* 14, 83–105.

Appendix A

Jalane Meloun, Ph.D., SPHR

Director, Affirmative Action
SME: Thomas Kuthy, Incumbent

Summary

The director of affirmative action has two main job duties: (1) to research and handle discrimination charges and (2) to ensure company's adherence to affirmative action and equal employment opportunity rules and regulations.

Duties

Frequency: 75%

I. Researches and addresses discrimination charges against company
   A. Receives notification of a discrimination charge.
   B. Contacts plant or specific location from where charge stemmed.
   C. Requests and collects proper documentation from all company employees involved in the charge.
   D. Reviews documentation.
      1. May need to meet with those involved for clarification on documentation or situation.
   E. Determines appropriate comparatives based on company's current or past employees.
      1. Begins to search for a comparative at the same location as incident causing the charge.
      2. If none occurred at that locale, other company locations are examined for similar situations.
   F. Composes via computer a sufficiently long statement (can be 10–12 single-spaced page with attached supporting documents) addressing charge.
   G. Submits statement to company's attorney and employees involved in charge (excepting the person or persons making the charge) for review and feedback.
   H. Revises statement as needed.
   I. Submits completed statement to proper authorities addressing the charge.
   J. May need to defend company in court.

Frequencies of skills used in specific tasks of Duty I:
5% analysis
10% reading/research
10% oral communication
75% written communication

Frequency: 25%

II. Performs duty of keeping company's selection, promotion, and retention, consistent with affirmative action and EEO plans, laws, and regulations. This serves to waylay potential charges.
   A. Reads current literature to keep abreast of law or regulation updates.
      1. BNA (Bureau of National Affairs)
      2. CCH (Commerce Clearing House)
      3. Labor Relations Week (and other newsletters)
   B. Delivers formal, 4-hour, affirmative action/EEO presentations to supervisors.
      1. Meets with other human resource employees as need arises to give input on affirmative action and EEO concerns.
   C. Implements company policies or programs for compliance with affirmative action plans and EEO guidelines.
   D Advises inquirers about Americans with Disabilities Act (ADA), (1990) reasonable accommodations.
   E. Prepares an annual utilization of workforce review in anticipation of future need by government regulatory bodies or charging parties.
   E. Prepares mandatory government reports via the computer and submits them.
      1. EEO1 report.
      2. VETS100 report.
   F. Handles periodic on-site compliance reviews by the Department of Labor.

Frequencies of skills used in specific tasks of Duty II:
33% reading/research
33% oral communication
33% written communication

Knowledge, Skills, and Abilities

The following were deemed important for this position:
   I. Knowledge of current affirmative action/EEO laws and regulations
      A. Learn by reading:
         1. BNA (Bureau of National Affairs)

2. CCH (Commerce Clearing House)
3. Labor Relations Week (and other newsletters)
B. Learn through on-the-job training
II. Good written and oral communication skills, particularly using effective persuasion
A. Personality disposition and refined through schooling
III. Strong analytical skills
A. Personality disposition and refined through schooling
IV. Ability to organize
A. Personality disposition and refined through schooling
V. Flexibility to multitask and switch focus with little notice
A. Personality trait and refined through job-related experience
VI. Emotional resilience to the many negative aspects of the position
A. Personality trait and refined through on-the-job exposure

Job specifications

Knowledge required by the position

The position requires in-depth knowledge of affirmative action plans and EEO laws and regulations. This knowledge must be continuously updated through reading current literature and manuals. Minimally a Bachelor's degree in human resources or a quantitative field is required.

Previous experience

This position requires either previous experience working with affirmative action and EEO laws and regulations or a several years' experience in the company. Supervisory experience is a plus.

Supervision exercised

The position does not include supervisory duties.

Supervision received

The position is overseen broadly by the head of the human resource department. However, the incumbent is extremely independent in deciding what, when, and how to accomplish tasks. Incumbent essentially does not have supervision.

Guidelines

This position is very much governed by guidelines. The affirmative action plans, EEO law and regulations, and company policies are the reasons this job exists. Although the guidelines are detailed and in written form, much analysis and judgment must be used to apply the conceptual laws on a case-to-case basis.

Complexity

This position requires the incumbent to multitask. The work is varied in so much as there may be no notice before a discrimination charge is filed.

Scope and effect

The nature of this position's duties has a significant impact on the company. If the company does not comply with the governmental regulations, there could be financial repercussions. Further, if the company is found to be at fault for a discrimination case, not only might there be financial penalties, but the company might be forced to rehire or promote the person bringing the charge.

Personal contacts

This position requires contact with internal company legal counsel. It also mandates external contact with Ohio Civil Rights, EEOC, and Department of Labor personnel at a rate of 12–15 contacts per year depending on number of charges against company.

Purpose of contacts

This position requires factual exchanges of information, explanation of research/analysis, and negotiation between opposing parties.

Physical demands

This position occasionally requires incumbent to drive to company plants four or less hours away; therefore the incumbent must be mobile. Otherwise, this position is sedentary.

Work environment

This position usually requires incumbent to be in a minimally hazardous office environment. However, during the occasional on-site plant compliance review, incumbent is expected to accompany inspector on the tour. This requires proper plant dress, including: goggles, hardhat, and steel-toed.

Get it right the first time: using job competencies for positive hiring outcomes in the hospitality industry

Peter Ricci

Florida Atlantic University
Barry Kaye College of Business
Hospitality and Tourism Management
Boca Raton, FL 33431

Introduction

The goal of this edited textbook is to showcase, demonstrate, and illustrate the human resources (HR) function within the greater context of hospitality and tourism marketing. It is important to note that HR strengths and capabilities can be a strong factor in the performance of a culture that, in turn, adds greatly to marketing strength and profitability of a hospitality organization. While communication, internal guest focus, leadership, empowerment, and a host of other concepts add to the strength of a culture, hiring right is a "must have" in order for organizations to match internal guest success with their desired external guest satisfaction levels. Those who are adequately matched with competencies, either inherent traits or learned protocols, will help lead our industry venues to be more productive and profitable while leading its employees toward future careers with higher levels of satisfaction.

It is the goal of this chapter to briefly examine and explore the job competency dimension as it relates to HR practices within the hospitality industry. The author incorporates the concept of job competencies into a possible paradigm which will help lead today's hospitality operations toward a more stable and effective performance level. By using job competencies as effective tools in one's HR cache, it is the hope that employees will offer higher levels of quality of work while experience higher quality levels of work. Strong cultures with happy staff members lead to stronger performance on the balance sheets. Effective HR managers not only have happy employees, they have happy owners and investors. As an HR manager, tactics and procedures surrounding the concept of job competencies need to be a part of your arsenal.

Hospitality management education at the college level: a brief history

Hospitality is defined as "hospitable treatment, reception, or disposition" by *The Merriam-Webster Dictionary* (2003, p. 601). However, hospitality *management* is the comprehensive term for the business management disciplines which include the services to travelers, visitors, and even local residents (Walker, 1999, 2004). It is a focus on hospitality management to which this text is dedicated, and specifically, to HR functions and practices within the hospitality industry. Those employed in HR capacities are dedicated to the hiring, training, development, and growth of hospitality employees within organizations of all types and sizes. The number of positions, titles, and designations within the vast hospitality industry seems limitless. One need only consider the various segments within the overall hospitality industry to understand the challenges facing HR individuals today. A non-inclusive listing of these segments would include such areas as airline, cruise line, destination marketing, theme park, food service, lodging, event planning, and vacation ownership. Each area is a large "industry" within its own right. One shall quite easily realize the need for an ongoing cadre of trained professionals in the hospitality industry.

Indeed, by the year 2005, 7.5 million jobs were directly generated by the travel industry in the United States alone and the payroll for those directly employed in the travel industry was over $170 billion (Travel Industry Association of America, 2006). The high number of employees has led to the need for college-level training of the workforce. Although "the concept of hospitality is as old as civilization itself" (Walker, 1999, p. 4), the offering of a hospitality management degree at the college level is much more recent. The first program was offered by Cornell University in 1922 (Cornell University School of Hotel Administration, 2007). Thereafter, programs appeared at Purdue University in 1926, Michigan State University in 1927, and The Pennsylvania State University in 1937 (Guide to College Programs, 2004).

The increase in worldwide travel from the 1940s to the 21st century and its resultant need for talented employees far outpaced the growth of hospitality education at the managerial level (i.e., baccalaureate degree). The growth of the industry led to an ever-present need for highly educated and well-trained employees in all segments of hospitality management (Guide to College Programs, 2004; Lattin, 1995; Marriott, 2001; Walker, 1999, 2004). As hotelier J. W. Marriott, Jr., remarked in 2001: "Finding and keeping employees has never been easy. But now full employment has converged with a service and information economy making recruitment and retention the most pressing challenge facing American business today" (p. 18).

It took over 50 years for lodging and hospitality management programs at the baccalaureate level to grow to an even moderate number. By the year 1974, only 41 programs offering baccalaureate degrees in hospitality management or hospitality administration existed in the United States (Brady, 1988). The latter part of the 21st century, however, saw a more rapid growth cycle in the number of these degree-granting programs. By 1986 there were 128 baccalaureate-level programs available to future hospitality managers (Tanke, 1986). By 2004, the *Guide to College Programs in Hospitality, Tourism, and*

Culinary Arts (8th ed.) listed 170 baccalaureate degree-granting institutions in the United States alone. Further, there were more than 800 programs listing either a professional certificate in hospitality management or an associate-level/2-year degree, or both. It appeared that hospitality education offerings were attempting to keep pace with the burgeoning growth in the number of available hospitality management positions.

Although the numbers are increasing, many senior managers currently employed in the hospitality industry do not possess baccalaureate degrees with specific study of hospitality management (Ricci, Tesone, & DiPietro, 2004). Quite simply, the programs did not exist at the time of study for these individuals.

One observes that in over 80 years since the creation of the first program at Cornell University (Cornell University School of Hotel Administration, 2007) in 1922, hospitality education at the university level has greatly expanded. The true growth occurred mainly since the period 1975–2004 when the number of baccalaureate-level hospitality management programs quadrupled (Guide to College Programs, 2004). While these education offerings have greatly increased in number, the number of available hospitality industry positions has far outpaced the number of course and degree offerings (Travel Industry Association of America, 2006). As either *the* largest industry worldwide, or one of the largest, depending on defining criteria, the hospitality industry indeed does not have a sufficient number of programs producing future leaders according to the numbers (Guide to College Programs, 2004; Walker, 2004). Even after years of growth in college-level programs, only 8.46% of college campuses offering baccalaureate degrees had a hospitality management degree program during the 2000–2001 academic year (Digest of Education Statistics, 2002).

Additionally, there is great variety among the hospitality programs in terms of their offerings. Curricula differ significantly depending on the hospitality management program's age, geographic location, specific academic discipline or college within which the program is housed, style of leadership, funding levels, overall goals of the larger university or college, etc. (Guide to College Programs, 2004). Further, there is little consensus in the literature on which type of curriculum design makes for a perfect match based upon industry needs, student needs, and/or educator needs (Brownell & Chung, 2001; Jayawardena, 2001; Woods, Rutherford, Schmidgall, & Sciarini, 1998).

For the HR professional seeking a future manager in the hospitality industry, the variety of college program styles and variances in curricula may be a cause for consternation. Not only are program numbers not sufficient for job offerings, the program variety makes recruiting challenging at best. Instead, recruiting based on specific job competencies may assist HR professionals in their pursuit of good "matches" for the hospitality industry's managerial needs. By relying upon job competencies deemed appropriate and useful for the hospitality industry, an HR professional can narrow the variance exhibited by a program's curriculum, specific training methods and courses, and academic discipline. Reliance upon job competencies may increase the likelihood for success on the part of the HR recruiter in terms of finding suitable applicant matches to the needs of the hospitality industry.

Competency-based education and testing

Criterion-reference education is most often associated with the work of Bloom, Englehart, Furst, Hill, and Krathwohl (1956). A meeting of university examiners attending the 1948 American Psychological Association in Boston ultimately led to the development of a "theoretical framework which could be used to facilitate communication among examiners" (Bloom *et al.*, p. 4). Under the leadership of Bloom, the team created a taxonomy. As editor, Bloom assisted in the development of a taxonomy which contained cognitive knowledge levels with which educators could implement various strategies at differing levels, dependent on the level of learning experience of their respective students. Bloom *et al.* developed a cognitive educational taxonomy with progressing levels of knowledge, comprehension, application, analysis, synthesis, and evaluation. The opinion of this group was that knowledge alone was the lowest level for an educator to instruct. Students were taught nothing but basic facts using rote memorization. The uppermost level of evaluation would imply that the student not only would know and comprehend the information, but also be able to apply it, analyze it, synthesize it, and make an intelligent evaluation of the material. Bloom's *Taxonomy of Educational Objectives, Handbook I, The Cognitive Domain* (1956) remains a mainstay among the legions of American educators.

Later, in 1964, *A Taxonomy of Educational Objectives, Handbook II, The Affective Domain* was put forth further developing Bloom *et al.*'s taxonomy of 1956 (Krathwohl, Bloom, & Masia, 1964). This taxonomy featured a hierarchical learning domain based upon the mental processing of a learner that takes place during the course of the overall learning process. In this taxonomy, the lowest level was receiving; the student is simply "willing to receive to attend" (p. 176) to stimuli. Moving upward in the taxonomy simply receiving is next followed by responding to then valuing to organization and, lastly, to characterization. In this viewpoint, educators were asked to focus on the mental states and processes of a learner versus the cognitive or knowledge focus which comprised the initial handbook and its cognitive domain (Bloom *et al.*, 1956). Hence, in *Handbook II*, the educator is encouraged to move from simply having a learner attend to his or her stimuli being demonstrated to higher levels where students have characterized their own personal values about life, the universe, etc. Students' attitudes and ideas are assumed to fit into a pattern of internal consistency. The individual has a fully encompassed mental thinking system within himself or herself rather than strictly focusing on facts and knowledge given from an outsider.

Moving into the latter part of the 20th century, educators have moved more toward a criterion-based learn process. Information and material is presented to the student or learner dependent on where one is learning from within the broader structure of a taxonomy. The testing and giving back of expected knowledge and/or the ability to synthesize knowledge and make overall evaluations is quite evident in today's classrooms. In 1958, McClelland, Baldwin, Bronfenbrenner, and Strodtbeck first proposed looking at talent in society and began to query whether individuals should be tested on specific talents, competencies, or personal ability criteria versus standardized measures of intelligence. To this group of researchers, standardized measures of intelligence appeared vague and unreliable. Their treatise, *Talent and Society* (1958) was largely ignored and overlooked by the educational community of the time as IQ and other standardized measures were still considered the mainstay (McClelland, 1973).

McClelland (1973) vehemently opposed the use of general intelligence and fervently pushed for competence testing. His argument centered on the fact that the testing movement (standardized) was so ingrained in American society that it would take many years to change the system. His research discussed bias against certain socioeconomic groups when tested used standardized methods; however, his report further stated that generalized intelligence testing showed dubious reliability and validity when predicting future business success or general life success for individuals (McClelland). His objective was to "review skeptically the main lines of evidence for the validity of intelligence and aptitude tests" (p. 1). He went so far as to say that most of the general public in the United States was left unaware that intelligence measures were unrelated to most "any other behaviors of importance—other than doing well on aptitude tests" (p. 2). Instead of testing for how well one would perform on an intelligence measure (i.e., IQ test), he instead suggested the notion of testing for specific job competencies, otherwise known as criterion-based testing. McClelland clearly championed criterion-based testing when he remarked: "If you want to know how well a person can drive a car (the criterion), sample his ability to do so by giving him a driver's test. Do not give him a paper-and-pencil test for following directions, a general intelligence test" (p. 7).

Challenged by the instructional community for many years, McClelland (1994) continued his ongoing fight to promote the efficacy of criterion- or competency-based training and education. His more recent research demonstrated that scores on standardized tests, especially intelligence measures, had very little connection, if any, with future success in one's life. Instead, these measures were useful in predicting future scores on other such standardized examinations. Under McClelland's (1973, 1994) paradigm, competency-based education would be worthy for retail store managers, taxi cab drivers, railroad engineers, or teachers. Indeed, one could assume that hospitality managers would also benefit from training and education specific to the field of hospitality management.

The mantra purported by McClelland (1973, 1994) for over 20 years pushed forward the notion of education for specific and necessary competencies, dependent on the specific industry or job function on hand. McClelland (1994) suggested designing tests that would measure "threshold competencies" (p. 68) whereby trainers could design examinations with minimum scores to test for specific job positions and duties. In his development of a competency testing measure for the Civil Service Commission in Massachusetts, the resultant instrument correlated significantly with the specific criterion needed for a job as a human service worker (HSW). He identified a "cutting score on the test battery that would ensure that most of the people at that score or above would be classified as 'outstanding'" (p. 68).

Popham and Husek (1969) discussed competency-based learning as well. The remarked that "a criterion-referenced test is used to identify an individual's status with respect to an established standard of performance" (p. 1). Individuals are compared with some established competency rather than with other individuals as would an IQ type of examination. As the reader, you can envision an admissions director of a university or college wishing to possibly see where an applicant falls in comparison to other applicants on a norm-referenced or criterion-referenced examination such as the Scholastic Aptitude Test (SAT). Yet, a hiring manager for a hospitality company would more probably want to know whether or not an applicant possesses specific knowledge, ability, or values (competencies) as demonstrated on a competency-referenced measurement tool.

Future managers and leaders in industry are often now subject to competency-based testing. It appears to have come of age. A review of literature indicates that job competency testing is used to determine a good match for future employees in a wide variety of industries. A non-exhaustive list includes: trucking (Mele, 1993), banking, sports, parcel delivery, emergency road service (Jaffee, 2000), tour operators, restaurants (Agut & Grau, 2002), and club management (Perdue, Woods, & Ninemeier, 2001). Weatherly (2004) went so far as to say that "work now requires more knowledge and skills than ever before" (p. 1). Job competency testing is a more exact method to locate successful and appropriate employee matches. Similarly, Taylor (2004) stated "Now that the economic tide is slowly turning, forward-looking companies are employing the use of tests to identify core competencies and specific behaviors they're looking for in new hires and future leaders" (p. G1).

Competency-based training and testing certain appears a viable resource for those seeking future hospitality employees, managers, and leaders. In comparison to more traditional norm-referenced testing of general intelligence, one can create testing focused and targeted for the specific needs of today's hospitality industry.

The hospitality industry and job competencies

"Although the selection and training of good administrators is widely recognized as one of American industry's most pressing problems, there is surprisingly little agreement among executives or educators on what makes a good administrator" (Katz, 1955, p. 33). The above statement from Katz is as current today as it was in the middle of the 20th century. In his seminal work, *Skills of an Effective Administrator*, Katz discussed migration toward a more competency or skill-based competency approach when recruiting and selecting executive talent. Instead of general personality characteristics or traits, one should instead focus on what these individuals could *do* in terms of their job abilities or skills. A skill would be something able to be taught, learned, and comprehended—not inborn as a personality characteristic (Katz).

Katz (1955) suggested a "three-skill approach" (p. 34). These three basic skills were technical, human, and conceptual.

Technical skills are most important at the lowest levels—specialized knowledge. Human ability is useful at all levels within an organization—in today's business jargon this is referred to often as interpersonal skills. Conceptual skills would be used at the highest levels of management. This skill sets includes the ability to integrate and think globally. Katz broke ground on initial researcher focus in terms of skills or competencies for executives.

Stull (1974) commented, "Through practice and research, management work is being identified, classified, and measured. As a specialized skill, management work is transferable, can be taught, and can be practiced in terms of recognized principles and an emerging common vocabulary" (p. 6). Throughout the 1970s, a competency-based learning and testing system for hiring talent emerged in the literature. The first known hospitality industry competency-based study was conducted in Las Vegas, NV by Sapienza (1978). Hotel executives were invited by Sapienza to "assess the outlook in terms of what industry leaders think hospitality students ought to study" (p. 12). While naïve in its format and deployment, it was nonetheless a bold step forward into the realm of competency-based testing for hiring in the hospitality industry. In this primitive study, course titles from the University of Nevada's College of Hotel Administration were listed and managers considered executives by the researcher were asked to rank order the course listings in terms of importance using a Likert-style five-point continuum. Competencies, then, were inferred indirectly through the ranking of the course listings. Confined geographically to Las Vegas with a convenience sample of 30 participants, the study was quite limited in its usefulness; nonetheless, it was a valiant step forward in terms of competency-based education and testing within the hospitality industry. Indeed, Sapienza only considered these recommendations as expert opinions. Reading this article today indicates that many of these so-called opinions still remain highly regarded competencies for tomorrow's hospitality leaders.

Guglielmino and Carroll (1979) replicated the earlier work of Katz (1955) by looking, instead, at skills necessary for mid-level managers. Whereas Katz focused on the executives, Guglielmino and Carroll focused on the skills that would be even more important for those recruiting out of college and university programs. Their findings "provided a clear indication that there appears to be a definite *hierarchy of management skills* [sic] in the development of an effective manager" (p. 342). Their findings were similar to Katz in that conceptual skills were the most important at the highest levels of management with technical skills most important at the lower levels of management.

The work of Mariampolski, Spears, and Vaden (1980) emphasized hospitality competencies specific to food service managers. "Despite the large number of institutions offering programs in hospitality management—and the continuing debate about what subjects hospitality curricula should emphasize—the authors' literature search uncovered no competency statements developed specifically for food-service managers" (p. 77). It is interesting to note that even in 1980 the authors felt that there were a large number of institutions offering programs in hospitality management, yet no consensus on hospitality competencies. Using a sample of past executives from the National Restaurant Association (NRA), the authors identified three broad competency areas almost identical to those discussed by Katz (1955) two and a half decades prior. These competencies included: knowledge/technical, attitude/human/, and ability/conceptual.

The first overarching effort at competency study in the hospitality industry was focused in the lodging arena by Tas (1983). In agreement with previous studies (Guglielmino & Carroll, 1979; Katz, 1955; Mariampolski et al., 1980) human relationship or interpersonal skills were deemed not only important, but essential. Tas stated "no previously prepared instrument is suitable for the collection of data needed for this study. Hence, a multi-stage endeavor is used to develop the appropriate instrument" (pp. 31–32). Hence, a job competency skills assessment for future lodging managers was born. Seven distinct competency categories emerged: accounting procedures, hotel sales and promotions, housekeeping, hotel front office, personnel (now termed HR), food and beverage, and managerial responsibilities (pp. 32–33). "The study sample was composed of 229 hotel general managers with active members in the American Hotel and Motel Association. A total of 75 (33%) general managers returned the instrument" (p. 82).

Tas (1983) found that hotel managers rated the importance of job competencies different and made suggestions for competencies useful in hospitality management curricula at the university level. Consistent with previous studies (i.e., Katz, 1955) conceptual competencies were considered the least vital among entry-level managers. In 1988, Tas expanded his work. He now looked at whether or not specific area competencies had been attained by his sample. As evidenced in the literature of the time, an exhaustive list of specific competencies was nowhere to be found. Tas remarked, "Unfortunately, a specific list of these competencies has not been compiled before now" (p. 41). Having developed an initial list of 70 competencies that "might be needed by hotel-manager trainees" (p. 42), Tas eventually narrowed the list to 36 after using expert review panels.

Using a stratified format, Tas (1988) administered the categorization to members of the American Hotel and Motel Association. Tas used the following scale: 4.50 importance or higher on a 5-point Likert-type scale would translate to an *essential* competency for a would-be hotel-manager trainee. A *considerably important* competency would have a score on the same scale from 3.50 to 4.49. Those scoring 2.50–3.49 would be considered *moderately important*. Any item scoring lower than 2.50 would not be deemed a core competency whatsoever. "Six competencies were deemed essential for hotel-manager trainees. These six attributes center primarily on human-relations skills" (p. 43).

Getty, Tas, and Getty (1991) furthered the attempt to study hospitality industry practitioner requirements and desires for new hires in terms of job competencies. "The researchers used a research instrument developed and validated by Tas (1983)" (p. 395). In this study, employers rated their general satisfaction level with hospitality management graduates using the 36 competencies identified in the former study by Tas (1988). The purpose of the Getty *et al.* study "...was to assess the quality of the graduates based upon their level of competence in their current management positions and thereby determine if the program's [hospitality management program] mission is being met" (p. 394). As in previous studies by Tas (1983, 1988), human relations, knowledge, and ability competencies were deemed the most important. Getty *et al.* discussed that "to a large extent, the academic program is meeting its mission by providing students with the competencies deemed important by managers" (p. 397).

Rutherford (1987) examined specific competencies for the role of a chief engineer within a hotel operation. His findings identified not only the evolution of the chief engineer role within the hospitality industry, but the matching competencies required for the specific duties of this position. This position has less of a reliance on interpersonal skills than many others found in the hospitality industry and as the findings reported. Okeiyi, Finley, and Postel (1994) focused on food and beverage management competencies. Their top 10 competencies included human relations, knowledge, and conceptual skills. For the entry-level manager, as in previous research efforts, human relations skills emerged as the most important. Okeiyi *et al.* concluded by stating, "Although this study has some limitations due to response rates and sample size, it is apparent that educators in conjunction with industry practitioners need to work together to design curricula...Hospitality educators and students must continue to keep abreast of industry expectations and incorporate them into hospitality management curricula" (p. 40). In 1998, Emenheiser, Clay, and Palakurthi reduced 72 criteria to 12 success attributes and traits for restaurant managers. Also a believer in criterion-based education and testing, Emenheiser *et al.* stated "Hospitality curriculum planners can consider the traits of those most successful in the industry when educating current students and determining curriculum content" (p. 55). Using factor analysis, "the goal of the researchers was to reduce the numerous attributes and traits to a manageable number of components that can be used for further analysis" (p. 57). The result listed five components: management skills, organizational skills, marketing skills, communication skills, and psychomotor skills. Further, these were labeled as leadership, interpersonal, personality, and model attitude (p. 59).

Others have also found competencies to be important for the new hospitality manager. Knight and Salter (1985) honed in on communication skills specifically. Jonker and Jonker (1990) looked more at technical skills, computer skills, and a guest-orientation or guest-focus. Creativity was a key component analyzed by Hanson (1993). Without a doubt, human relations skills continue to be important among a vast variety of the research available (Ashley *et al.*, 1995; Hsu, Gilmore, & Walsh, 1992; Tas, LaBrecque, & Clayton, 1996).

Recently, Lin (2002) explored the relationship between hotel management courses and industry required competencies. A statistically significant regression demonstrated a link between the competencies of "communication skills" and "adaptation to environmental changes" with hospitality industry career success (p. 92). Ricci (2005) further refined the job competencies suggested by Tas (1988) using focus groups of experts in the lodging industry. A sample of lodging managers in the central FL area was queried to see if this group of individuals had higher expectations based upon job competencies for graduates of baccalaureate degrees specific to hospitality management compared to more general degree disciplines. Statistical significance was found in a vast majority of instances. It did appear that a majority of lodging managers expect institutions to be better preparing our future hospitality leaders through training and learning of specific job competencies.

The most recent movement (since the late 1990s) in terms of job competency research within hospitality concerns competency modeling. "A current hot topic in HRD [*Human Resources Development*] is competency modeling" (Mirabile, 1997, p. 73). Competency modeling was defined by Mirabile as "the output from analyses that differentiate high performers from average and lower performers" (p. 75). It was created using a variety of techniques, models help recruiters and employers identify success factors. Such techniques include job-analysis interviews, focus groups, questionnaires, job descriptions, etc. (p. 75). Hospitality venues may identify such success factors after being rank ordered by various expert groups. The venue can then establish minimum levels of competency or proficiency for each factor as determined by the group effort, research literature, or input from educators within the hospitality field. Cautioning that competency models are only as strong as their ingredients, Mirabile states: "The most important point about competency models is that the formats be governed by the collective wisdom of the people that need to build them" (p. 76). Competency modeling is slowly emerging as an area of research within the hospitality management literature (Brownell & Chung, 2001; Lefever & Withiam, 1998; Lin, 2002). Lefever and Withiam emphasized that "curriculum review now involves regular contacts with industry representatives...As a result, we believe industry and academe are now tied more closely together than at any time in the 75 years that colleges have offered formal hospitality-management curricula" (pp. 70–71).

Over the past several decades, competencies deemed significant and useful in the identification of future hospitality industry leaders have been proposed, identified, evaluated, re-tested, and either refined or refuted by multiple hospitality industry researchers (Getty *et al.*, 1991; Hsu *et al.*, 1992; Jonker & Jonker, 1990; Lin, 2002; Okeiyi *et al.*, 1994; Sapienza, 1978; Tas, 1983, 1999; Tas *et al.*, 1996). Emerging from this iterative process are competencies related to knowledge, attitude, and ability of the future hospitality management leaders. These appear quite often as the key drivers or anchors for future success in the hospitality industry.

As a HR professional interested in creating better and stronger work environments of the future, specific job competencies determined relevant and important for hospitality careers must be identified and measured among our future workforce. Our professional assistance in the development and refinement of the various hospitality management curricula found in college-level programs will enhance the future success of the overall industry based upon employee performance. If we match correctly the first time around, our employees are likely to be more satisfied and content in their positions.

Summary and conclusion

From 1950 through the present, job competency use among HR professionals in recruiting, selecting, and interviewing prospective hospitality industry employees has become prevalent in not only the academic literature, but also the hospitality professional's repertoire as an effective and worthy tool for matching applicants with future potential career success. Lodging managers were recently found to expect more from college hospitality management programs than from non-hospitality 4-year degrees In Ricci *et al.* (2004), it was stated that "practicing professionals currently expect more from college graduates who have studied hospitality" (p. 29). Human skills/interpersonal skills were found to be equally important whether students emerged from hospitality programs or non-hospitality programs continuing a decades-long trend within the research that interpersonal skills remain paramount for hospitality industry professional success among employers.

Ricci and Tesone (2007) found consistency between educators and industry practitioners when examining the competencies expected by hospitality managers with hospitality workers. The findings were combined to one large metropolitan statistical area (MSA); yet, the findings were consistent with the broad array of hospitality and business literature over multiple decades (Chung-Herrera, Enz, & Lankau, 2003; Katz, 1955; McClelland, 1994; Tas, 1983, 1988).

With the high expense of employee turnover in the hospitality industry (Hinkin & Tracey, 2000; Simons & Hinkin, 2001), job competency instruments may assist HR professionals in their ongoing pursuit of the "right" employees for the "right" positions. As suggested by Boles, Lawrence, and Johnson (1995), pre-employment application screening and matching of demographics and skills will help reduce employee turnover. In their lodging oriented study, Milman and Ricci (2004) also discussed many variations (of which job competency pre-employment screening could be utilized) of methods to enhance employee retention and reduce employee turnover.

The literature is replete with the discussion of job competency and competency-based education. The hospitality industry has only recently moved toward incorporating competency-based education and pre-employment measurement to improve organizational profitability, employee satisfaction, and to help reduce employee turnover. By matching the "right employees" to the "right jobs" initially, job competencies specific to the hospitality industry can be a key indicator of future success for such new employees in the field. The hospitality industry is wide and varies considerably between segments (i.e., event planning, airline, restaurant management). Nonetheless, it appears that interpersonal skills remain paramount across segments and across time. Job-specific knowledge/skills also appear important. As

HR leaders, we must tailor specific competencies to the nuances of the individualized segment within which we make our professional livelihood. The development of job competency identification instruments specific to our segment, will assist us in honing our perfection in the identification of such individuals possessing these competencies. Further, we shall work alongside those in academia designing curricula and course materials to help foster and communicate these important and necessary competencies to the future leaders.

The reader is encouraged to help develop instruments ideal for their respective hospitality segments. Only through expert panels, focus groups, and continual refinement will these instruments become ubiquitous among hospitality recruiters. We have only touched the surface of job competency research and instrument design in the hospitality industry. The reader is encouraged to peruse the literature specific to his or her discipline and to help identify specific job competencies relevant in today's workplace. The hospitality industry continues to grow and change. Technology, economical, and societal influences are ever-present. With the changing times come changing expectations for our future leaders. Only through ongoing identification and refinement of job competencies can we continue to design instruments to identify the talent our industry needs to continue to flourish and grow.

References

Agut, S., & Grau, R. (2002). Managerial competency needs and training requests; the case of the Spanish tourist industry. *Human Resource Development Quarterly, 13*(1), 31–51.

Ashley, R. A., Bach, S. A., Chesser, J. W., Ellis, E. T., Ford, R. C., LeBruto, S. M., et al. (1995). A customer-based approach to hospitality education. *Cornell Hotel and Restaurant Administration Quarterly, 36*(4), 74–79.

Bloom, B. S., Englehart, M. D., Furst, E. J., Hill, W. H., & Krathwohl, D. R. (1956). *A taxonomy of educational objectives: Handbook I, the cognitive domain.* New York: David McKay Co.

Boles, J. S., Lawrence, E. R., & Johnson, J. T. (1995). Reducing employee turnover through the use of pre-employment application demographics. *Hospitality Research Journal, 19*(2), 19–30.

Brady, J. E. (1988). Development of facilities standards for accrediting baccalaureate degree programs in hospitality management education (Doctoral dissertation, Vanderbilt University, 1988). *Dissertation Abstracts International, 49*, 10A.

Brownell, J., & Chung, B. G. (2001). The management development program: A competency based model for preparing hospitality leaders. *Journal of Management Education*, 25(2), 124–145.

Chung-Herrera, B. G., Enz, C. A., & Lankau, M. J. (2003). Grooming future hospitality leaders: A competencies model. *Cornell Hotel and Restaurant Administration Quarterly*, 44(3), 17–25.

Cornell University School of Hotel Administration. (2007). Retrieved August 17, 2007 from http://www.hotelschool. cornell.edu/about/history

Digest of Education Statistics. (2002). Number of degree-granting institutions conferring degrees, by level of degree and discipline division: 2000–2001. Retrieved June 28, 2004 at http://www.nces.ed.gov/programs/digest/d02/tables/ dt258.asp National Center for Education Statistics: Author.

Emenheiser, D. A., Clay, J., & Palakurthi, R. (1998). Profiles of successful restaurant managers for recruitment and selection in the U.S. *International Journal of Contemporary Hospitality Management*, 10(2), 54–61.

Getty, J. M., Tas, R. F., & Getty, R. L. (1991). Quality assessment of hotel & restaurant management graduates: Are we meeting our mission? *Hospitality Research Journal*, 14(2), 393–404.

Guglielmino, P. J., & Carroll, A. B. (1979). The hierarchy of management skills: Future professional development for mid-level managers. *Management Decision*, 17(4), 341–345.

Guide to college programs in hospitality, tourism, and culinary arts (8th ed.). (2004). Richmond, VA: International Council on Hotel, Restaurant, and Institutional Education.

Hinkin, T. R., & Tracey, B. J. (2000). The cost of turnover: Putting a price on the learning curve. *Cornell Hotel and Restaurant Administration Quarterly*, 41(3), 14–21.

Hsu, C. H., Gilmore, S. A., & Walsh, T. E. (1992). Competencies needed and demonstrated by hospitality management graduates: Perceptions of employers. *National Association of College and University Food Service Journal*, 16, 34–42.

Jaffee, C. S., Sr. (2000). Measurement of human potential. *Employment Relations Today*, 27(2), 15–27.

Jayawardena, C. (2001). Challenges in international hospitality management education. *International Journal of Contemporary Hospitality Management*, 13(4/5), 259–266.

Jonker, P., & Jonker, D. (1990). What do hospitality graduates really need? An industry perspective. *Hospitality and Tourism Educator*, 3(1), 12–13.

Katz, R. L. (1955). Skills of an effective administrator: Performance depends on fundamental skills rather than personality traits. *Harvard Business Review*, 33(1), 33–42.

Knight, J. B., & Salter, C. A. (1985). Some considerations for hospitality training programs. *Cornell Hotel and Restaurant Administration Quarterly*, *25*(4), 38–43.

Krathwohl, D. R., Bloom, B. S., & Masia, B. (1964). *A taxonomy of educational objectives: Handbook II, the affective domain.* New York: David McKay Co.

Lattin, G. W. (1995). *Introduction to the hospitality industry* (3rd ed.). East Lansing, MI: Educational Institute of the American Hotel and Motel Association.

Lefever, M. M., & Withiam, G. (1998). Curriculum review: How industry views hospitality education. *Cornell Hotel and Restaurant Administration Quarterly*, *39*(4), 70–78.

Lin, S.-C. (2002). Exploring the relationships between hotel management courses and industry required competencies. *Journal of Teaching in Travel and Tourism*, *2*(3/4), 81–101.

Mariampolski, A., Spears, M. C., & Vaden, A. G. (1980). What the restaurant manager needs to know: The consensus. *Cornell Hotel and Administration Quarterly*, *21*(3), 77–81.

Marriott, J. W., Jr. (2001). Our competitive strength: Human capital. *The Executive Speaker*, *15*(2), 18–21.

McClelland, D. C. (1973). Testing for competence rather than for "intelligence". *American Psychologist*, *28*(1), 1–14.

McClelland, D. C. (1994). The knowledge-testing-educational complex strikes back. *American Psychologist*, *49*(1), 66–69.

McClelland, D. C., Baldwin, A. L., Bronfenbrenner, U., & Strodtbeck, F. L. (1958). *Talent and society.* New York: Van Nostrand.

Mele, J. (1993, March). Hiring smarter. *Fleet Owner*, *88*(3), 82.

Milman, A., & Ricci, P. (2004). Predicting job retention of hourly employees in the lodging industry. *Journal of Hospitality and Tourism Management*, *11*(1), 28–41.

Mirabile, R. J. (1997). Everything you wanted to know about competency modeling. *Training and Development*, *5*(18), 73–77.

Okeiyi, E., Finley, D., & Postel, R. T. (1994). Food and beverage management competencies: Educator, industry, and student perspectives. *Hospitality and Tourism Educator*, *6*(4), 37–40.

Perdue, J., Woods, R., & Ninemeier, J. (2001). Competencies required for future club managers' success. *Cornell Hotel and Restaurant Administration Quarterly*, *42*(1), 60–65.

Popham, W. J., & Husek, T. R. (1969). Implications for criterion-referenced measurement. *Journal of Educational Measurement*, *6*, 1–9.

Ricci, P. (2005). A comparative analysis of job competency expectations for new hires: The relative value of a hospitality management degree. *Dissertation Abstracts International*, *66* (05), 1855A (UMI No. 3176080).

Ricci, P., & Tesone, D. V. (2007, in press). Hotel and restaurant entry-level job competencies: Comparisons of management and worker perceptions. *FIU Hospitality Review*.

Ricci, P., Tesone, D. V., & DiPietro, R. B. (2004). Job competency expectations for lodging managers: A comparison of college graduates. *Frontiers in Southwest I CHRIE Hospitality and Tourism Research*, *8*(2), 27–30.

Rutherford, D. G. (1987). The evolution of the hotel engineer's job. *Cornell Hotel and Restaurant Administration Quarterly*, *27*(4), 72–78.

Sapienza, D. L. (1978). What university hotel students ought to study: Opinions expressed by a selected group of Nevada hotel executives. *Journal of Hospitality Education*, *2*(2), 11–16.

Simons, T., & Hinkin, T. (2001). The effect of employee turnover on hotel profits: A test across multiple hotels. *Cornell Hotel and Restaurant Administration Quarterly*, *42*(4), 65–69.

Stull, R. A. (1974, June). Profiles of the future: A view of the management to 1980. *Business Horizons*, *17*(3), 5–12.

Tanke, M. L. (1986). Accreditation: Implications for hospitality management education. *FIU Hospitality Review*, *4*(1), 48–54.

Tas, R. F. (1983). Competencies important for hotel manager trainees. *Dissertation Abstracts International*, *43*(03), 151B.

Tas, R. F. (1988). Teaching future managers. *Cornell Hotel and Restaurant Administration Quarterly*, *29*(2), 41–43.

Tas, R. F., LaBrecque, S. V., & Clayton, H. R. (1996). Property-management competencies for management trainees. *Cornell Hotel and Restaurant Administration Quarterly*, *37*(3), 90–96.

Taylor, T. S. (2004, August 18). Gut-feeling bias can be a waste of job talent. *Orlando Sentinel*, G1–G10.

The Merriam-Webster Dictionary (11th ed.). (2003). Springfield, MA: Merriam-Webster.

Travel Industry Association of America. (2006). Retrieved August 17, 2007 from http://www.tia.org/uploads/power-travel/pdf/talkingpoints.pdf

Walker, J. R. (1999). *Introduction to hospitality* (2nd ed.). Upper Saddle River, NJ: Prentice Hall.

Walker, J. R. (2004). *Introduction to hospitality management*. Upper Saddle River, NJ: Pearson Prentice Hall.

Weatherly, L. A. (2004, March). Performance management: Getting it right from the start. *HR Magazine*, *49*(3), 1–11.

Woods, R. H., Rutherford, D. G., Schmidgall, R., & Sciarini, M. (1998). Hotel general managers. *Cornell Hotel and Restaurant Administration Quarterly*, *39*(6), 38–44.

Part Two

Retaining human resources

Organizational culture in the casual dining restaurant industry: the impact that culture has on service quality and customers' intentions to return

Dean A. Koutroumanis, DBA

University of Tampa
Tampa, FL 33606, USA

Introduction

The restaurant industry is a very complex and unique industry, dealing with multiple facets of typical business operations. In essence, restaurateurs are running two critical components of business operations: manufacturing and sales, all under one roof (Biswas & Cassell, 1996). It is one of a few industries that must coordinate these complex tasks within the confines of the same facility. The manufacturing component has to do with kitchen operations. Restaurateurs must coordinate human resource management practices for this component of business, to hire, train, and develop the kitchen staff to produce food items consistently on a daily basis. Secondly, restaurateurs must coordinate proper human resource management practices in hiring, developing, and executing proper salesmanship and service practices to ensure a positive dining experience (Biswas & Cassell, 1996; Smucker, 2001). Therefore, restaurateurs must be concerned with both product quality and the level of service quality provided (Bojanic & Rosen, 1994).

The restaurant industry is the second largest employer in the United States, topped only by the Federal government, and employs 12.8 million individuals. Food and beverage sales are projected to hit approximately $537 billion industry wide in 2007 (National Restaurant Association, 2007).

Employee attitude, behavior, and work effort has a high impact on service quality, satisfaction, and customer retention in the service industry (Stamper & Van Dyne, 2003; Davidson, 2003; Schneider & Bowen, 1993). The theory is especially indicative in the highly competitive full service restaurant industry. The importance of customer–employee interaction in the restaurant industry is magnified because of the high level of contact the employee has with the customer for the duration of the dining experience. Organizational culture has a significant impact on employee service delivery (Davidson, 2003), which in turn could affect customers' behavioral intentions. With organizational culture being the "glue" that allows the organization to sustain its unique identity (Cameron & Quinn, 1999; Creque, 2003), one would believe that building a customer-oriented restaurant would begin with developing the appropriate culture.

In a survey conducted by the National Restaurant Association (2004), restaurateurs stated that 70% of their business base comes from repeat customers. The same survey asked restaurateurs if it was getting more difficult to maintain customer loyalty. Fifty-two percent of the respondents said yes (Sanson, 2004). According to Crook, Ketchen, and Snow (2003), reasons for this difficulty may be attributed to two factors: (1) increased levels of competition and (2) low switching costs, which refers to customers ease in ability to dine at different restaurants if not satisfied with their dining experience. The restaurant business is a very difficult, highly competitive, and complex business with a high failure rate, running at approximately 60% (Sydney, 2003). Additionally, there are high start-up costs associated with opening a restaurant that add to the burden of failure (Crook *et al.*, 2003).

With an increasing number of people dining out today, restaurateurs are focusing efforts on improving levels of service quality, which will in turn help build frequency of dining. As can be seen through the National Restaurant Association study, return patronage has a significant effect on the long-term success of restaurants. By gaining an understanding of how to provide the highest levels of service, organizations will be able to see increases in both brand loyalty and market share (Oh & Parks, 1997). Every business strives to build a high level of brand loyalty and repeat business. The restaurant business is challenged even more so than other businesses because of the tremendous number of choices and competition in the industry (Crook *et al.*, 2003). According to Stevens, Knutson, and Patton (1995), if a restaurant does not provide its guests with the service and value they demand, they will leave it for another. The linkage of service quality to this defecting behavior was initially studied by Zeithalm *et al.* (1996) in a variety of industries.

Service firms still have a lot to learn when it comes to understanding how to execute service delivery, especially in the restaurant industry. Although there has been research examining what constitutes service quality (Parasuraman, Zeithalm, & Berry, 1985, 1988; Parasuraman, Berry, & Zeithalm, 1991a, 1991b), the execution and implementation of the construct is still lacking, and the restaurant industry continues to struggle in implementing appropriate service programs. Service organizations must build strong customer-oriented firms in order to continue to prosper in the future (Reicheld & Sasser, 1990; Seidman, 2001).

Is the key to developing this service orientation grounded in the development of the proper organizational culture? This chapter will look at some of the key elements in organizational culture and their linkage to both service quality and customers intentions to return, in hopes of drawing some conclusions. Based on empirical research conducted by this author, implications of the findings will be discussed and recommendations to practitioners will be made.

Background of constructs examined

The constructs that will be examined in this chapter include Organizational Culture, Service Quality, and Behavioral Intentions as they relate to the restaurant industry. After a review of the literature, linkages will be made as to how the findings of this empirical research can have an impact on the restaurant industry.

Traditionally, the restaurant industry is known for having a highly bureaucratic management style and philosophy (Tracey & Hinkin, 1994). Classical management styles are that of highly defined, routine practices, which have strict adherence to specific rules and regulations (Smucker, 2001). The traditional management philosophy in the hospitality industry does not take into effect the person, or individual doing the job, but focuses more on the job itself. Identifying what the specific tasks and requirements of the job are, and then training the employees to perform these duties has been and remains to be the norm in the restaurant industry (Tracey & Hinkin, 1994). In most cases, the restaurant industry is almost militaristic in nature causing it to be a difficult and demanding industry to those employed within. The classical management style works well when there is little competition and local unemployment figures are high. The alternate seems to be true of the restaurant industry in the United States and Canada. Competition among operators is fierce, and lack of a large labor pool has plagued the industry for a long time. According to David Ulrich (1998), human resource practices and how they are viewed must be radically changed for organizations to optimize the use of their human capital. Human capital is defined as "the belief that the development of workers will add value to an organization" (Tesone, 2005, p. 2). For the transformation to be achieved, organizations must first understand and manage the complexities of their respective organizational cultures (Goodman, Zammuto, & Gifford, 2001) and build stronger levels of commitment. Many organizations divert the blame for failures to other capital assets and neglect to look at the lack of effective human capital as a reason for failure (Tesone, Platt, & Alexakis, 2003). The faulty deduction seems to be the case in the restaurant industry.

Organizational culture

Schein (1990) defines organizational culture as "what a group learns over a period of time as that group solves its problems of survival in an external environment and its problems of internal integration. Such learning is simultaneously a behavioral, cognitive, and an emotional process" (p. 111). Organizational culture is defined by Davidson (2003) as "the shared beliefs and values that are passed on to all within the organization" (p. 206). Employee perspective with regard to the organization has been shown to have positive effects on the success of the organization. Having employees with the right attitude will enhance the probability for success in any company in any industry (Davidson). Firms with a strong sense of customer orientation have also shown greater levels of customer satisfaction (Schneider & Bowen, 1993).

Due to its labor-intensive nature and the high level of interaction between customers and employees, the hospitality industry has a greater likelihood of being impacted by its employees' actions than other industries (Davidson, 2003). Therefore, developing an appropriate organizational culture should be a critical component in the success of a restaurant.

In 2002, Ogbonna and Harris investigated organizational culture in an international five star hotel, a national four-star hotel, and two national restaurants and wine bars in the United Kingdom. This study, conducted between 1999 and 2000, observed the organizations' cultures and the effects of forced changes in culture on the organization. The researchers wanted to see if an organizational change in culture could be used as a management tool to enhance operations. One of the implications of this study related to turnover in the hospitality industry. The study questioned how high levels of turnover affected the overall organizational culture. After a year of research, primarily through interviews with employees and management, the researchers concluded that indoctrination with a specific culture would have a positive impact on the organization. However, the employees that turn over quickly, which are common in this industry, never acclimated to the culture (Ogbonna & Harris, 2002).

Another study by Michael Davidson (2003) examined the linkage between organizational climate and service quality in the hotel industry. Results showed a high correlation between organizational climate and performance. Davidson states, "The culture and climate shape not only employee actions but also their commitment to a service ethic. It is this commitment to service that is of paramount importance if customer satisfaction is to be achieved" (p. 211). The model he postulates discusses organizational culture as the glue between organizational climate, HR practices, and service quality (Davidson, 2003).

Research has helped in the development of empirically tested typologies that would assist in defining different types of organizational cultures that exist. The Competing Values

Framework adapted by Cameron and Quinn (1999), shows a complete evaluation of different culture types. There are four culture types which exist in this typology, including: (a) Clan Culture Type, (b) Adhocracy Culture Type, (c) Market Culture Type, and (d) Hierarchy Culture Type. These culture types are defined as follows, appearing alphabetically:

Adhocracy culture type

This culture breeds a sense of entrepreneurship. The workplace has a sense of urgency in a highly dynamic environment, where creativity is at the forefront (Cameron & Quinn, 1999; Creque, 2003). Such an organizational culture exists in many advertising firms, high-tech software companies, and certain sectors of academia.

Clan culture type

Clan type culture can be defined simply as a "family-type organization" (Cameron & Quinn, 1999, p. 36). This type of culture incorporates a sense of "we" in the organization instead of "I." Clan culture has a high level of autonomy, which is indicative of an organic type of organization. The development of a humane work environment and an environment of loyalty, commitment, and participation is paramount in this type of culture. Examples of such an organization abound in the hospitality industry where so-called Mom and Pop operations still flourish, although decreasingly so.

Hierarchy culture type

This culture type dates back to the work of Max Weber during the late 19th and early 20th centuries. The characteristics of the hierarchal organization include a very distinct authoritarian structure. It is a culture high on rules and regulations, distinct lines of communication and accountability. Maintaining tight control and smooth operations are important in this type of culture. The rules and policies are believed to hold the organization together and increase levels of efficiency and effectiveness (Cameron & Quinn, 1999; Creque, 2003). Arguably, all corporations are pyramid-shaped, hierarchical, and even autocratic structures. The larger they are, the more tyrannical their systems become, where the majority of people essentially mimic what is said and done above them in the organizational hierarchy (Alexakis, Platt, & Tesone, 2006).

Market culture type

The word market concerns itself with the external market environment. This type of culture orientation is goal focused, geared towards market superiority, and highly competitive in nature (Cameron & Quinn, 1999; Creque, 2003). Microsoft Corporation is an extreme example of a market culture type. The people who run the company are highly class conscious who see themselves engaged in some kind of bitter class struggle reminiscent of several crude Marxists yesteryear (Couey & Karliner, 1998).

Clan focus

After reviewing the literature, it would seem that a clan culture type would be most representative of what the restaurant industry would want to accomplish. The level of cohesiveness, teamwork, fun and high levels of energy are attributes that draw a "fit" to what restaurants are trying to accomplish from a culture standpoint (Berta, 2002). The ability to build loyalty among customers and build bonded relationships in order to grow business is essential to future success (Bowen & Shoemaker, 2003). Cameron and Quinn (1999) state that the clan culture type emphasizes the building of customer "partnerships." Most restaurants would seek to establish those types of relationships with customers in order to promote loyalty. Figure 4.1 depicts these culture types and illustrates the relationships that exist.

Figure 4.1 was adapted from Cameron and Freeman (1991); Quinn and Rohrbaugh (1983); Deshpande, Farley, and Webster (1993); Denison and Spreitzer (1991); Cameron and Quinn (1999); Obenchain (2002); Creque (2003).

Service quality

Lehtinen and Lehtinen (1992) break service into three categories: (a) physical qualities (visible components), (b) interactive service (actual performance of the service), and (c) corporate quality (image). The intangible nature of the construct of service quality makes it difficult to properly measure and analyze (Oh & Parks, 1997; Parasuraman, Zeithalm, & Berry, 1985; Seidman, 2001). The leading researchers in service quality and those primarily responsible for creating the first instrument to measure this construct are Parasuraman, Zeithalm, *et al.* (1985, 1988), (Parasuraman, Berry, *et al.* 1991a, 1991b). In 1985, Parasuraman *et al.* identified ten measurable dimensions

ORGANIC PROCESSES (flexibility, spontaneity)	
HUMAN RELATIONS MODEL	**OPEN SYSTEMS MODEL**
Type: CLAN **DOMINANT ATTRIBUTES** Cohesiveness, participation, teamwork, sense of family **BONDING:** Loyalty, tradition interpersonal cohesion **STRATEGIC EMPHASES:** Toward developing human resources, commitment, moral	**Type: ADHOCRACY** **DOMINANT ATTRIBUTES** Entrepreneurship, creativity, adaptability **BONDING:** Entrepreneurship, risk flexibility **STRATEGIC EMPHASES:** Toward innovation, growth, new resources
INTERNAL MAINTENANCE (smoothing activities, integration)	**INTERNAL POSITIONING** (competition, differentiation)
TYPE: HIERARCHY **DOMINANT ATTRIBUTES** Order, rules & regulations, uniformity **BONDING:** Rules, policies, and procedures **STRATEGIC EMPHASES:** Toward stability, predictability, smooth operations	**TYPE: MARKET** **DOMINANT ATTRIBUTES** Competitiveness, goal achievement **BONDING:** Goal orientation production, competition **STRATEGIC EMPHASES:** Toward competitive advantage and market superiority
INTERNAL PROCESS MODEL	**RATIONAL GOAL MODEL**
MECHANISTIC PROCESSES (control, order, stability)	

Figure 4.1
A model of organizational culture types

of service quality. Further research (Parasuraman *et al.*, 1988) identified levels of overlap among some of the dimensions identified earlier in 1985. They therefore merged the ten dimensions into five: (a) tangibles: facilities, equipment, and appearance of personnel; (b) reliability: ability to perform the promised service; (c) responsiveness: willingness to provide the service promptly; (d) assurance: knowledge and courtesy of employees and their ability to inspire trust and confidence; (e) empathy: caring, individualized attention the firm provides its customers (Parasuraman *et al.*, 1988). The instrument developed to measure this construct was called SERVQUAL. The SERVQUAL model analyzes the level of service quality by evaluating the gaps between customers' expectations and perceptions of service. The smaller the gaps, the higher the level of service quality (Kivela, Inbakaran, & Reece, 1999). SERVQUAL has been validated and tested in a variety of industries including banks, credit card companies, repairs and maintenance firms and long distance telephone companies (Parasuraman, Zeithalm, *et al.*, 1988; Parasuraman, Berry, *et al.*, 1991a, 1991b). Babakus and Mangold studied hospital services in 1991 and research in hospitality using this instrument has been conducted by Saleh and Ryan (1991), Bojanic and Rosen (1994), Seidman (2001). Although altered by subsequent researchers, the SERVQUAL instrument has maintained the fundamental five dimensions and has had high levels reliability and validity throughout all tests (Seidman, 2001).

In 1990, Knutson, Stevens, Wullaert, Patton, and Yokoyama, modified Parasuraman *et al.*'s (1988) original instrument to create a more appropriate measure for the hotel industry. With a factor analysis of the original 36-item scale of SERVQUAL, 10 of the 36 items did not add to the measurement and were dropped (Knutson *et al.*, 1990). The new 26-item scale measuring lodging service quality was called LODGSERV, and again utilized the core five dimensions used by SERVQUAL. Measuring this new instrument across the five dimensions showed that, as in the original instrument, SERVQUAL, the reliability factor was the highest ranking of all. The remaining factors were ranked in the following descending order of relative importance to lodging guests: assurance, responsiveness, tangibles, and empathy (Stevens *et al.*, 1995). LODGSERV was tested both domestically and internationally and proved reliable across cultures.

In 1995, three of the same researchers that developed LODGSERV, Stevens, Knutson, and Patton, developed DINESERV, originally a 40-item scale used to measure what should happen during a restaurant dining experience. After factor analysis of the 40 items, a final 29-item scale was developed. DINESERV was tested in a multitude of different types of restaurants, including both quick service and full service restaurants. The new instrument proved valid, and again results concurred with the dimensionality findings of SERVQUAL. As with LODGSERV, the reliability dimension ranked the highest in importance to guests dining at restaurants. The remaining rankings of dimensions varied from LODGSERV, with tangibles ranking the next most important. The remaining dimensions ranked as follows: assurance, responsiveness, and empathy (Stevens *et al.*, 1995).

Behavioral intentions

Consumers who are dissatisfied with a service experience may take a variety of different actions. They can voice their opinion to management, they can say nothing and just not return to that organization, or they can continue patronizing the organization and not say anything (Susskind, 2002). In an early study of customer retention, Rosenberg and Czepiel (1983) stated that organizations spend a lot of time and money in finding new customers. However, once the organization has the customers, it does not do enough to keep them. Bill Marriott of Marriott Hotels has been quoted as saying that it costs the Marriott company an average of ten marketing dollars to attract a new customer, and just one dollar in "special efforts" to get them to return to the hotel (Stevens *et al.*, 1995).

The study of behavioral patterns and responses can be traced to Ajzen and Fishbein (1980) who state that behavior can be predicted from intentions that correspond to a certain behavior (Baker & Crompton, 2000). Research demonstrated that a dissatisfied customer could tell an average of 10–20 other people (Brown & Reingen, 1987; Shaw-Ching Liu, Furrer, & Sudharshan, 2001; Tax, Brown, & Chandrashekaren, 1996). Other studies report that people discuss both positive and negative experiences (Susskind, 2002). Ultimately, it has been found that the economic impact of customer retention is incredibly significant from a profitability position. The defining study was conducted by Reichheld and Sasser (1990) who showed that a 5% increase in customer retention equated to a net present value increase of 25–125% in profitability (Bowen & Chen, 2001; Reicheld & Sasser, 1990; Shaw-Ching Liu *et al.*, 2001). From a restaurateur's perspective, if the organization is to increase its guest return rate from 76% to 81%, profits would more than likely double (Stevens *et al.*, 1995).

In 1996, Zeithalm *et al.* showed that behavioral intentions are intervening variables between service quality and financial gain or loss of an organization. This study postulated that a positive level of service quality would create favorable behavioral intentions. This behavior increases the probability that customers' relationship to the organization will be strengthened and return patronage will occur. Conversely, low levels of service quality will create unfavorable behavioral intentions, which in turn will decrease relationships with organizations and could cause patrons to not return to the business (Alexandris, Dimitriadis, & Markata, 2002; Zeithalm *et al.*, 1996).

Zeithalm *et al.* (1996) developed the Behavioral Intentions Battery, to help measure customer's intentions to defect or return. The final framework included the following five-dimension model (Bloemer, deRuyter, & Wetzels *et al.*, 1999). The dimensions were as follows: (1) loyalty to company, (2) propensity to switch, (3) willingness to pay more, (4) external response to a problem, and (5) internal response to a problem (Alexandris *et al.*, 2002; Bloemer *et al.*, 1999; Zeithalm and Bitner, 2000). Subsequent research found some variation to Zeithalm *et al.*'s original dimensions (Bloemer *et al.*, 1999). The Bloemer *et al.* study found that there were different dimensions that were important in predicting behavior including, repurchase intentions, word-of-mouth communication, price sensitivity and complaining behavior (Shaw-Ching Liu *et al.*, 2001). The relationships between service quality and behavioral intentions were also found to differ across a variety of industries (Alexandris *et al.*, 2002; Athanassopoulos, Gounaris, & Stathakopoulos, 2001; Shaw-Ching Liu *et al.*, 2001). The researchers found varied levels of importance with regard to the intentions dimensions across industries. For example, in the entertainment industry, behavioral intentions were highly weighted by responsiveness and tangibles, whereas in the food industry, it was assurance and empathy (Alexandris *et al.*, 2002). The Alexandris *et al.* study of the hotel sector in northern Greece found that the tangible factors of service quality did not affect the intention factors. Other research has also shown that the tangibles were not significant in determining behavioral intentions in some industries (Zeithalm & Bitner, 2000; Alexandris *et al.*, 2002). One reason posited by Alexandris *et al.* for this effect is that in the hospitality industry today tangible factors have become a prerequisite, and have become expected by customers (Alexandris *et al.*, 2002).

Although some variations of the dimensions have been found across studies, the overall reliability and validity of Zeithalm *et al.*'s (1996) model is clearly indicated. The theoretical model has been supported in all studies conducted since 1996 with its inception (Bloemer *et al.*, 1999; Baker & Crompton, 2000; Zeithalm & Bitner, 2000; Athanassopoulos *et al.*, 2001; Shaw-Ching Liu *et al.*, 2001; Alexandris *et al.*, 2002).

Study methodology

This study sought out to investigate the relationship between organizational culture type, specifically clan type culture as defined by Cameron and Quinn (1999); to service quality as defined by Parasuraman, Zeithalm, and Berry (1985, 1988) Parasuraman, Berry, and Zeithalm (1991a, 1991b); Bojanic and Rosen (1994); Stevens *et al.* (1995) and behavioral intensions as defined by Zeithalm *et al.* (1996), Gounaris and Stathakopoulos (2001), and Alexandris *et al.* (2002). The research instrument used in this study was a compilation of DINESERV (Stevens *et al.*, 1995), the Behavioral Intentions Battery (Zeithalm *et al.*, 1996) and the organizational culture type scale developed by Yeung, Brockbank, and Ulrich (1991). All scales have shown high levels of reliability in previous research.

This research study attempted to answer the following questions:

1. Is organizational culture, specifically clan type culture, related to service quality in the casual dining restaurant industry?
2. Are organizational culture values, specifically clan type culture, related to customers' future intentions in the casual dining restaurant industry?
3. Does service quality impact customers' future intentions in the full service, casual dining restaurant industry?

The research questions and their respective relationships were tested through the Pearson correlation analysis.

Data collection and response rate

A total of six, independently owned and operated restaurants were utilized in this study. Independent restaurants were used in the study because the cultural dynamics lend themselves better to the clan type dimensions because of how the companies are structured. Independents tend to be more organic in structure lending themselves better to the clan type dimensions (Robbins & Decenzo, 2003).

Three restaurants were located in the Tampa, FL area and three restaurants in the New Haven, CT area, providing a cross section of the population. A total of 310 questionnaires were distributed to customers dining in the participating restaurants. The surveys were distributed to every 10th customer over the age of 18 dining in the restaurants. Additionally, the customers participating in the study had to have dined in the restaurant at least once before the study in order to be eligible for the study. In order to increase response rate a complimentary dessert was offered to participants. A small percentage of those participants accepted the offer. Fifty surveys were collected in five of the six restaurants, and 60 surveys were collected in one of the Florida restaurants where data collection was received extremely well. Of the 310 surveys distributed, 17 were returned incomplete and were not included in the sample. The final sample included 293 usable surveys, which were analyzed for the results of this study.

Table 4.1 Means, Standard Deviations, Correlations, and Reliabilities of Study

	Mean	Standard Deviation	Clan	Service Quality	Behavioral Intentions
Clan	5.67	1.03	(0.81)		
Service quality	6.22	0.59	0.56**	(0.92)	
Behavioral intentions	5.56	0.74	0.50**	0.62**	(0.62)

$N = 293$. Figures in parentheses on the diagonal indicate Cronbach's alpha reliability for the variables.
* Correlation is significant at the 0.05 level.
** Correlation is significant at the 0.01 level.

Results of the study

Table 4.1 shows the means, standard deviations, correlations, and reliabilities for the study variables. The reliabilities (Cronbach's alpha) in Figure 2 show that all scales have 0.70 or higher reliability except for behavioral intentions (0.62). The correlations found in Figure 2 were used to examine the research questions.

The results of this study showed several points of interest and adds to the hospitality literature that currently exists regarding the constructs examined. To begin, clan type cultural characteristics were detected in the independent restaurants studied. There was a positive correlation between clan culture type and service quality ($r = 0.56$, $p < 0.001$) in this study. Additionally, in analyzing the effect of clan culture type on customers' behavioral intentions, the results in Figure 2 show a positive correlation between the two variables ($r = 0.50$, $p < 0.001$). Finally, as in past studies in various industries a strong positive relationship exists between the perception of service quality received and customers' intentions to return to that business (Alexandris *et al.*, 2002; Athanassopoulos *et al.*, 2001; Baker & Crompton, 2000; Shaw-Ching Liu *et al.*, 2001). This also holds true in this study of the casual dining restaurant industry. The results in Figure 2 show there is a strong positive correlation between service quality and behavioral intentions ($r = 0.62$, $p = <0.001$).

Application

This study provides empirical evidence that strong relationships exist between organizational culture, specifically clan culture type, service quality, and behavioral intentions in the independent, casual dining restaurant industry. The findings of this study have a significant relevance and great importance to both academicians and practitioners. From an academic perspective the literature for all of the constructs studied, as well as the hospitality literature has been extended. The results of this study hold many ramifications for practitioners in the casual dining restaurant industry. Organizational culture (clan) showed a positive relationship to both service quality and behavioral intentions in this study. According to Cameron and Quinn (1999), the characteristics of this culture type include developing an environment of loyalty, commitment, and participation. It is a culture type where a sense of belonging and family create the essence and foundation of the organization. The restaurants in this study showed a significantly high level of service quality, with a dominant clan culture evident. Practitioners might want to consider developing an organizational culture that captures the elements of the clan culture in order to improve service delivery systems and help reduce factors that negatively influence service delivery. This study shows that having good service programs in place and improving service levels will help increase repeat business. Previous studies have shown that customers in all segments of the restaurant industry have high expectation levels, when it comes to service (Stevens *et al.*, 1995). Meeting and exceeding those expectations is of paramount importance to restaurants if they want to increase the frequency of repeat customers.

Limitations

Although there were several limitations to this study, the most significant, is that the sample for this study included only independently owned and operated restaurants. National chain restaurants were not included in this study. The findings of this study could very well be different if national chains were included in the sample. In most cases, independently operated restaurants are not managed the same way national chains are. Therefore, the importance of the dominant clan culture could be because the sample included only independently owned restaurants. The question remains as to what culture type would dominate in the national chain environment, and to what respect does that impact service quality and customers' intention to return.

Conclusions

In the service industry, service quality, and customers' intentions to return are the cornerstones to organizations success. Many variables affect the service delivery process that the likelihood of error is extremely great.

The restaurant industry is a unique and complex business. Restaurateurs need to be concerned with both product quality and service quality (Bojanic & Rosen, 1994). The execution of proper service delivery is magnified even more in this industry because of the high level of employee interaction with the customers. For example, a customer may be completely satisfied with the food they ordered, but not satisfied with their overall dining experience. Slow, rude, or inattentive service from the server may lead to negative behavioral consequences leading to loss of return customers.

With the complex nature of the restaurant industry, it is the hope of this researcher that the findings of this study can be of benefit to restaurateurs. People play a big role in this industry, from both customer and employee perspectives. In order to build repeat business restaurateurs need to be able to develop the appropriate culture, build proper service programs, and successfully execute these tasks simultaneously. The findings of this study can be used as a starting point to help restaurateurs develop these systems.

References

Ajzen, I., & Fishbein, M. (1980). *Understanding attitudes and predicting social behavior.* Englewood Cliffs, NJ: Prentice Hall.

Alexakis, G., Platt, A. R., & Tesone, D. V. (2006). Appropriating biological paradigms for the organizational setting to support democratic constructs in the workplace. *Journal of Applied Business and Economics, 6*(1), 17–28.

Alexandris, K., Dimitriadis, N., & Markata, D. (2002). Can perception of service quality predict behavioral intentions? An exploratory study in the hotel sector in Greece. *Managing Service Quality, Bedford, 12*(4), 224.

Athanassopoulos, A., Gounaris, S., & Stathakopoulos, V. (2001). Behavioural responses to customer satisfaction: An empirical study. *European Journal of Marketing, 35*(5/6), 687–707.

Baker, D., & Crompton, J. (2000). Quality, satisfaction and behavioral intentions. *Annals of Tourism Research, 27,* 785–804.

Berta, D. (2002). Sexual harassment remains nagging issue for food service industry. *Nations Restaurant News, 36*(50), 1, 16.

Biswas, R., & Cassell, C. (1996). Strategic HRM and the gendered division of labor in the hotel industry: A case study. *Personnel Review, 25*(2), 19–28.

Bloemer, J., deRuyter, K., & Wetzels, M. (1999). Linking perceived service quality and service loyalty: A multi-dimensional perspective. *Journal of Marketing, 33,* 1082–1106.

Bojanic, D. C., & Rosen, L. D. (1994). Measuring service quality in restaurants: An application of the SERVQUAL instrument. *Hospitality Research Journal, 18*(1), 3–14.

Boulding, W., Kalra, A., Staelin, S., & Zeithaml, V. A. (1993). A dynamic process of service quality: From expectations to behavioral intentions. *Journal of Marketing Research, 30,* 2–27.

Bowen, J. T., & Chen, S. L. (2001). The relationship between customer loyalty and customer satisfaction. *International Journal of Contemporary Hospitality Management, 13*(4/5), 213–218.

Bowen, J. T., & Shoemaker, S. (2003). Loyalty: A strategic commitment. *Cornell Hotel and Restaurant Administration Quarterly, 39*(1), 12–25.

Brown, J. J., & Reingen, P. H. (1987). Social ties and word-of-mouth referral behavior. *Journal of Consumer Research, 14*(3), 350–362.

Cameron, K. S., & Quinn, R. E. (1999). *Diagnosing and changing organizational culture based on competing values framework.* Reading, MA: Addison Wesley.

Cameron, K., & Freeman, S. (1991). Organizational culture and organizational development: A competing values approach. In R. W. Woodman & W. A. Pasmore (Eds.), *Research in organizational change and development* (pp. 25–38). London: JAI Press.

Couey, A., & Karliner, J. (1998). Noam Chomsky on Microsoft and corporate control of the internet. *CorpWatch.* Retrieved June 24, 2004, from http://www.corpwatch.org/article.php?id=1408

Creque, C. A. (2003). *Organizational culture type and business process orientation congruence in buyer seller relationships.* UMI: Unpublished Dissertation, Nova Southeastern University.

Crook, T. R., Ketchen, D. J., & Snow, C. C. (2003). Competitive edge: A strategic management model. *Cornell Hotel and Restaurant Administration Quarterly, 44*(3), 44–53.

Davidson, M. C. (2003). Does organizational climate add to service quality in hotels? *International Journal of Contemporary Hospitality Management, 15*(4), 206–213.

Deshpande, R., & Webster, F. E., Jr. (1989). Organizational culture and marketing: Defining the research agenda. *Journal of Marketing, 53,* 3–15.

Fisk, R. P., Brown, S. W., & Bitner, M. J. (1993). Tracking the evolution of services marketing literature. *Journal of Retailing, 69,* 61–103.

Fornell, C., & Wernerfelt, B. (1987). Defensive marketing strategy by customer complaint management: A theoretical analysis. *Journal of Marketing Research, 24,* 337–346.

Goodman, E. A., Zammuto, R. F., & Gifford, B. D. (2001). The competing values framework: Understanding the impact of organizational culture on the quality of work life. *Organizational Development Journal, 19*(3), 58–68.

Gronroos, C. (1993). Towards a third phase in service quality research: Challenges and future directions. In T. A. Swahrtz, D. Bowen & S. W. Brown (Eds.), *Advances in services marketing management* (Vol. 3, pp. 49–64).

Kivela, J., Inbakaran, R., & Reece, J. (1999). Consumer research in the restaurant environment, part 1: A conceptual model of dining satisfaction and return patronage. *International Journal of Contemporary Hospitality Management, 11*(5), 205–225.

Knutson, B., Stevens, P., Wullaert, C., Patton, M., & Yokoyama, F. (1990). LODGSERV: A service quality index for the lodging industry. *Hospitality Research Journal, 14*(2), 27–43.

Lehtinen, U., & Lehtinen, J. R. (1992). *Service quality: A study of quality dimensions.* Unpublished. Service Management Institute, Helsinki.

National Restaurant Association. (2004). Retrieved May 5, 04, from http://restaurant.org

National Restaurant Association. (2007). Retrieved January 9, 07, from http://restaurant.org

Obenchain, A. (2002). *Organizational culture and organizational innovation in not-for-profit, private and public institutions of higher education.* UMI: Unpublished Dissertation, Nova Southeastern University.

Ogbonna, E., & Harris, L. (2002). Managing organizational culture: Insights from the hospitality industry. *Human Resource Management, 12*(1), 33–54.

Oh, H., & Parks, S. (1997). Customer satisfaction and service quality: A critical review of the literature and research implications for the hospitality industry. *Hospitality Research Journal, 20*(3), 36–64.

Parasuraman, A., Berry, L. L., & Zeithalm, V. A. (1991a). Refinement and reassessment of the SERVQUAL scale. *Journal of Retailing, 67*(4), 420–450.

Parasuraman, A., Berry, L. L., & Zeithalm, V. A. (1991b). Understanding customer expectations of service. *Sloan Management Review, 32*, 39–48.

Parasuraman, A., Zeithalm, V. A., & Berry, L. L. (1985). A conceptual model of service quality and its implications for further research. *Journal of Marketing, 49*, 41–50.

Parasuraman, A., Zeithalm, V. A., & Berry, L. L. (1988). SERVQUAL: A multiple item scale for measuring consumer perceptions of service quality. *Journal of Retailing, 64*(1), 12–40.

Parasuraman, A., Zeithalm, V. A., & Berry, L. L. (1994, September). Moving forward in service quality research: Measuring different levels of customer expectations, comparing alternative scales, and examining the behavioral intentions link. *Marketing Science Working Paper, report # 94-114.*

Quinn, R., & Rohrbaugh, J. (1983). A special model of effectiveness criteria: Towards a competing values approach to organizational analysis. *Management Science, 29*, 363–377.

Reicheld, F., & Sasser, W. E. (1990). Zero defections: Quality comes to services. *Harvard Business Review, 68*, 105–111.

Reichers, A., & Schneider, B. (1990). Climate and culture: An evolution of constructs. In B. Schneider (Ed.), *Organizational climate and culture* (pp. 5–39). San Francisco, CA: Jossey-Bass.

Robbins, S. P., & Decenzo, D. A. (2003). *Fundamentals of management: Essential concepts and applications* (4th ed., Rev.). Upper Saddle River, NJ: Pearson Prentice Hall.

Rust, R. T., & Zahorik, A. J. (1993). Customer satisfaction, customer retention, and market share *Journal of Retailing, 69*(2), 193–215.

Rust, R. T., Zahorik, A. J., & Keiningham, T. L. (1995). Return on quality (ROQ): Making service quality financially responsible. *Journal of Marketing, 59*, 58–70.

Saleh, F., & Ryan, C. (1991). Analyzing service quality in the hospitality industry using the SERVQUAL model. *The Service Industry Journal, 11*(3), 324–343.

Sanson, M. (2004). Revved and ready. *Restaurant Hospitality, 88*(2), 41–49.

Schein, E. (1990). Organizational culture. *American Psychologist, 45*(2), 109–119.

Schneider, B., & Bowen, D. E. (1993). The service organization: Human resources management is crucial. *Organizational Dynamics, Spring,* 39–52.

Seidman, A. (2001). *An investigation of employee behavior on customer satisfaction in the quick service restaurant industry.* UMI: Unpublished dissertation, Nova Southeastern University.

Shaw-Ching Liu, B., Furrer, O., & Sudharshan, D. (2001). The relationship between culture and behavioral intentions toward services. *Journal of Service Research*, 4(2), 118–130.

Smucker, J. (2001). *Employee empowerment and self-direction in a family dining restaurant chain: A case study.* UMI: Unpublished dissertation, Walden University.

Solomon, M. R., Suprenant, C., Czepiel, J. A., & Gutman, E. G. (1895). A role theory perspective on dynamic interactions: The service encounter. *Journal of Marketing*, 49, 99–111.

Stamper, C. L., & Van Dyne, L. (2003). Organizational citizenship: A comparison between part-time and full-time service employees. *Cornell Hotel and Restaurant Administration Quarterly*, 44(1), 33–43.

Stevens, P., Knutson, B., & Patton, M. (1995). DINESERV: A tool for measuring service quality *Cornell Hotel and Restaurant Administration Quarterly*, 36(2), 56.

Susskind, A. M. (2002). I told you so!: Restaurant customers' word-of-mouth communication patterns. *Cornell Hotel and Restaurant Administration Quarterly*, 43(2), 75–85.

Sydney, G. (2003). Restaurant failure rates recounted. *Restaurant Start-up and Growth, January*, 36.

Tax, S., Brown, S., & Chandrashekaren, M. (1996). Customer evaluations of service complaint experiences: Implications for relationship marketing. *Working paper: Center for Service Marketing and Management.* College of Business, Arizona State University, Tempe, AZ.

Teas, R. K. (1993). Expectations, performance evaluation and consumer's perceptions of quality. *Journal of Marketing*, 70, 18–34.

Tesone, D. V. (2005). *Human resource management in the hospitality industry.* Upper Saddle River, NJ: Prentice Hall.

Tesone, D. V., Platt, A. R., & Alexakis, G. (2003). The human capital factor: Strategies for dealing with performance challenges in business and sports management. *Journal of Applied Management and Entrepreneurship*, 9(3), 22–33.

Tracey, J. B., & Hinkin, T. R. (1994). Transformational leaders in the hospitality industry. *Cornell Hotel and Restaurant Administration Quarterly*, 35(2), 18–25.

Ulrich, D. (1998). A new mandate for human resources. *Harvard Business Review*, 76(1), 125–134.

Yeung, A., Brockbank, J., & Ulrich, D. (1991). Organizational culture and human resource practices: An empirical assessment. In R. W. Woodman & W. A. Pasmore (Eds.), *Research in organizational change and development* (pp. 59–82). London: JAI Press.

Zahorik, A. J., & Rust, R. T. (1992). Modeling the impact of service quality on profitability: A review. *Advances in services marketing and management* (pp. 247–276). Greenwich, CT: JAI Press.

Zammuto, R., Gifford, B., & Goodman, E. (2000). Managerial ideologies, organizational culture, and the outcomes of innovation. In N. Ashanasy, C. Wilderon & M. Peterson (Eds.) *Handbook of organizational culture and climate* (pp. 261–278). Thousand Oaks, CA: Sage.

Zeithalm, V. A., Berry, L. L., & Parasuraman, A. (1996, April). The behavioral consequences of service quality. *Journal of Marketing, 60,* 31–46.

Zeithalm, V. A., & Bitner, M. J. (2000). *Services marketing: Integrating customer focus across the firm.* New York: McGraw-Hill.

Ethical principles and practices in human resources management

Frank J. Cavico and Bahaudin G. Mujtaba

H. Wayne Huizenga School of Business and Entrepreneurship
Nova Southeastern University
Ft. Lauderdale, FL 33314, USA

Human resource management centers on fairness, justice, and advocacy for a company's most critical resource, its human resources. In other words, human resource management is about ethics, ethical principles, and ethical practices. For ethics to be taken seriously by people in modern organizations, it must be related to business and management activities and, most importantly, to a competitive advantage and successful business performance. Otherwise, ethics, at "best," will be perceived as nothing more than a mere "academic" exercise and at worst as an impediment to success. The challenge is to strategically link ethics, most specifically business ethics, to a firm's competitive advantage and overall performance. The purpose of this chapter, therefore, is to discuss ethics, ethical principles, and the requirements of morality in conjunction with claims of business, management, and personal self-interest. The perceived conflict between morality and self-interest lies at the heart of ethics; and this relationship is addressed in this chapter, as it must be in any true "ethical" endeavor. Overall, basic ethical practices and discussions regarding ethics, values, law, and why business professionals need to focus on morality, are examined in this chapter.

The foundations of ethics and philosophy[1]

When one initially encounters the field of ethics, one is confronted with some confusion due to a lack of an agreed-upon terminology and set of definitions. Yet, if one is going to understand how ethics works, there must be some agreement on, and some insight into, the structure within which ethics works. There is, therefore, a need for words, terms, and definitions with precise meaning. Definitions can function as the first ethical principles of moral reasoning. If one defines terms carefully at the start or knows the appropriate definitions and one applies them consistently, one can draw moral conclusions deductively from these incontrovertible first ethical principles. One, therefore, can use definitions and terms to decide what to do in particular cases.

Philosophy is the study and analysis of such deeply problematical and fundamental question, such as the nature of reality, conduct, and thought. The field of philosophy traditionally is

---

[1] This material is an overview from the authors book entitled "*Business Ethics: Transcending Requirements through Moral Leadership*," 2005; authored by Frank J. Cavico and Bahaudin G. Mujtaba.

divided into three parts: the metaphysical, the political and ethical, and the philosophy of knowledge.

Metaphysics is philosophy in the "macro" sense. It is the attempt to understand and to explain the ultimate nature of the world in which human beings live. Political and ethical philosophy is philosophy in a more practical and "micro" sense. It is the study of human beings, their nature, place in the world, and their relations with others. It is an attempt to formulate systematic doctrines to determine the best way of living. The philosophy of knowledge is the attempt to determine what knowledge is, what it is ultimately based on, and what correct mental processes. A philosopher is a person with the conviction that beneath the apparent chaos, multiplicity, confusion, and change in the universe, there exists an underlying permanence, unity, stability, identity, and fundamental truth that reason may discover. A philosopher is a person who seeks this truth.

Moral philosophy is the philosophical study of morality; it is the application of philosophy to moral thinking, moral conduct, and moral problems. Moral philosophy encompasses various theories that prescribe what is good for people and what is bad, what constitutes right and wrong, and what one ought to do and ought not to do. Moral philosophy offers ethical theories that provide a theoretical framework for making, asserting, and defending a moral decision.

There is not one determinate set of ethical theories. Moral philosophy embraces a range of ethical perspectives and spends a great deal of time in analyzing the differences among these ethical views. Each ethical theory, however, does underscore some ultimate principle or set of principles that one is obligated to follow to ensure moral behavior and the good life.

The philosophical study of morality is distinguished by the general, systematic, and logical nature of the endeavor. It is the effort to systematize ethically moral judgments and to establish and defend ethically moral beliefs and standards. Moral philosophy develops ethical frameworks for evaluating the merits of asserted moral positions. Moral philosophy attempts to establish logical thought processes that will determine if an action is right or wrong and seeks to find criteria by which to distinguish good from bad conduct. Moral philosophy endeavors to prove its claims through ethical arguments that can demonstrate that the ideal thought, conduct, life, and morality are in fact ideal. The ultimate aim of moral philosophy is to answer Socrates fundamental question: how *should* one live?

Specifically, moral philosophy attempts to answer the following questions: What is the nature of morality and the meaning of good and bad and right and wrong in human conduct? How is one to know the good from the bad? How can moral judgments be established or justified? Can they be justified at all? What is the nature of the good life? What should one seek in life? Is there a highest good for human beings? What are one's moral obligations? Why should one be moral?

A study of moral philosophy also reveals the question as to just how far purely rational inquiry can take one in answering the preceding questions.

Values

Values are rankings or priorities that a person establishes for one's norms and beliefs. Values express what the chief end of life is, the highest good, and what things in life are worthwhile or desirable. According to Values Theory, deeply held values drive behavior.

One very difficult problem is placing values in proper relation to one another. Values often are controversial because the norms and beliefs that one person holds in high esteem conflict with different norms and beliefs that another person holds in equally high esteem. Moral values are the rankings or priorities that a person establishes for one's moral norms and moral beliefs.

A distinction is made between two types of values: instrumental and intrinsic values. Instrumental (or extrinsic values) are good because of their consequences. They are desired as a means to an end. Their worth is not in their own right, but because of what they can bring in the way of other values, for example, economic values. Intrinsic values are good in and of themselves. They are an end in themselves and desired for their own sake. They are values that claim appraisal in their own right. They are, or claim to be, of absolute worth, such as pleasure (to a hedonist), power (to a Machiavellian), knowledge, or self-realization. Moral values are generally held to be intrinsic.

There are theories of ethics that depend on some theory of intrinsic value. That is, in order to determine if something is good or right, one first must determine which things are worth seeking without regard to their consequences. Whose intrinsic good, however, should be promoted? To an egoist, one should promote one's own greatest good; but to a utilitarian, one should promote the greatest good for everyone.

Ethics

Ethics is the theoretical study of morality. Ethical theories are moral philosophical undertakings that contain bodies of formal, systematic, and ethical principles that are committed to the view that an asserted ethical theory can determine how one should morally think and act. Moral judgments are deducible from a hierarchy of ethical principles. It is the moral philosopher's task to articulate such ethical principles and to insist upon their proper application. Ethics is the sustained and reasoned attempt to determine what is morally right or wrong. Ethics is used to test the moral correctness of beliefs, practices, and rules. Ethics necessarily involves an effort both to define what is meant by morality and to justify the way of acting and living that is being advocated.

Ethics proceed from a conviction that moral disagreements and conflicts are resolvable rationally. There is one "right" answer to any moral dispute, and this answer can be reached through reasoning. The purpose of ethics is to develop, articulate, and justify principles and techniques that can be used in specific situations where a moral determination must be made about a particular action or practice.

There are, of course, problems in this ethical attempt to formulate principles to resolve concrete moral problems. To what extent is ethics a source of objective, determinate, and reasoned principles rather than merely personal, political, cultural, legal, or religious "answers" to moral questions? Presuming ethical principles are objective and reasoned, how are they justified? Is there some independent, overarching, principle, or mechanism that can arbitrate among various moral philosophies and validate the correctness of ethical principles? Even if people agree on general ethical principles, the application of those principles to specific moral problems also causes controversy.

Morals and morality

There is, of course, a relationship between ethics and morals in the conduct of human affairs. When something is judged good or bad, right or wrong, or just or unjust, the underlying standards on which the judgment is based are moral standards. Moral standards include not only specific moral rules but also the more general ethical principles upon which the moral rules are based. When a decision involves a moral component, the decision necessarily encompasses moral rules and ethical principles.

Morals are beliefs or views as to what is right or wrong or good or bad. Moral norms are standards of behavior by which people are judged and that require, prohibit, or allow specific types of behavior. Moral rules are action-guiding or prescriptive statements about how people ought to behave or ought not to behave.

Ethics deals with matters that are of serious consequence to human beings. Ethics affects human welfare and fulfillment in significant ways. People will be positively or negatively affected by moral decisions. Ethics, therefore, is concerned with conduct that can benefit or harm human beings.

Morals fundamentally convey norms to human life. Moral standards enable resolution of disputes by providing acceptable justification for actions. If one bases a decision on a moral rule, and if the moral rule is based on and derived from an agreed-upon ethical principle, the decision should be publicly acceptable. Ethics then can identify certain behaviors as better or worse than others by endowing these determinations with normative moral force. Ethics and morality thus perform a directive role, encouraging or discouraging ways of conduct, living, thinking, and choosing. People can then pursue their conception of the good life in such a way as not to conflict with the ways of life of others. There obviously must be constraints on the manners in which people pursue their chosen ways of life; morality emerges as an important delimiting factor.

Although ethical theories and ethical principles are propounded principally by moral philosophers, morality is not an invention of philosophers; rather, it is part of the make-up and outlook of almost all people. A moral judgment, however, is a particularly important type of deliberation. It is a reasoned ethical conclusion directed toward what one ought or ought not to do. Morality, therefore, properly and accurately should be understood as a development and application of ethical theories and principles.

Application of values, ethics, and morals

Due to socialization in the society, each professional probably has had a good amount of reading on the basics of ethics, leadership, stewardship, morality, and social responsibility. As such, he or she has already formed a good understanding of these values based on his or her experiences and thoughts. However, most people do not really take the time to understand the true meaning of values, ethics, and morality because of their busy schedules. Accordingly, let us start with the basics by defining values, ethics, and morals in a practical manner.

Values are core beliefs or desires that guide or motivate our attitude and actions. What one values drives his/her behavior. Some people value honesty or truthfulness in all situations while others may value loyalty to a higher degree in certain situations. *Ethics* is the branch of philosophy that theoretically, logically, and rationally determines right from wrong, good from bad, moral from immoral, and just from unjust actions, conducts, and behavior. Some people define ethics simply as doing what you say you would do or "walking the talk." Overall, ethics establishes the rules and standards that govern the moral behavior of individuals and groups. It also distinguishes between right and wrong conducts. It involves honest consideration to underlying motive, to possible potential harm, and to congruency with established values and rules. *Applied ethics* refers to moral conclusions based on rules, standards, code of ethics, and models that help guide decisions. There are many subdivisions in the field of ethics and some of the common ones are descriptive, normative, and comparative ethics. *Business ethic*, more specifically, deals with the creation and application of moral standards in the business environment. *Morals* are judgments, standards, and rules of good conduct in the society. They guide people toward permissible behavior with regard to basic values. Consider the following dilemma and how the terms values, ethics, and morals actually apply here.

A thief, named Zar, guarantees that you will receive the agreed-upon confidential information from your competitor in 5 days. Zar is professing a *value*—he will deal with you honestly because you as the customer are very important to his/her business. When Zar has delivered the proper documents within the agreed-upon time (5 days), one can say that Zar has behaved *ethically* because he was consistent with his/her professed values. The following year you ask Dar, who is a competitor to Zar, and he makes the same promise as Zar by professing the same values, to get the same information from your competitor for this year. Five days later, Dar only delivers part of the information which is not totally accurate, and in the meantime Dar is blackmailing you for more money. If Dar does not get more money then he will be going to the authorities and to the competitor to report this business dealing. Now, one can say that Dar has behaved *unethically* because his actions were not consistent with his professed values. Finally, one can conclude that all three parties involved in stealing inside information have acted *immorally* as judged by majority of the population. Overall, values are professed statements of one's beliefs, ethics is delivering on one's professed values; and morals are actions of good conduct as judged by the society that enhance the welfare of human beings.

Understanding values, ethics, and morals while using ethical principles, each organization can form a framework for effective decision-making with formalized strategies. The willingness to add ethical principles to the decision-making structure indicates a desire to promote fairness, as well as prevent potential moral problems from occurring.

Corporate ethics programs initiated and updated by human resource managers and professionals are part of organizational life; and organizations can use such sessions to further discuss the meaning of values, ethics, and morals in the context of their businesses. Organizational codes of ethics should protect individuals and address the moral values of the firm in the decision-making processes. Corporate codes of ethics are not merely some manuals for how-to-solve problems. They are tools which can empower everyone in the organization to say, "I am sorry that is against our policy, or that would violate our company's code of ethics." This ethical foundation also will increase personal commitment of employees to their companies because people do take pride in the integrity of their corporate culture.

Ethics and the law

Ethics attempts to resolve difficult and contentious moral issues by methods that resemble scientific methods. Ethics is based on theories of moral philosophy. Ethical principles and moral rules are used to establish and explain particular decisions. Principles and rules can be tested by appealing to moral determination that certain actions are right or wrong.

The scientific world, however, is amenable to observation, testing, and resolution in a way that the moral world is not. Ethics is not accurate in the same sense that a scientific theory must be accurate if it is to be accepted. An ethical theory is not necessarily, or even usually, confirmed or disproved by clear and indisputable evidence.

Consequently, many moral questions do not have clearly demonstrable "correct" answers; and many moral issues are highly controversial. Competent moral philosophers may disagree even about fundamental moral matters. Yet, if ethics is not scientific, how does one ultimately resolve moral disputes? Are there any agreed-upon, objective ethical truths to be discovered? If there are objective ethical principles, can they be used to formulate moral rules governing conduct? Some moral philosophers, such as Plato, emphasized the scientific objectivity of moral judgments. They posited a "moral order" in the world waiting to be discovered. The faculty of reason will disclose immutable "moral facts" that will enable one to discover what is good and bad and thus to regulate one's life accordingly.

For most moral philosophers, however, it is sufficient that an ethical theory, and the set of more or less general principles that compose it, is acceptable for the most part, on the whole, and in actual experience.

Since there is little in ethics that is analogous to scientific methodology, nothing in ethics is known in a scientific sense. Ethics, therefore, has not made any definite "advances" in the sense of ascertainable and provable discoveries. One, for example, can say definitely that Aristotle's commentary on astronomy is wrong; but one cannot say, in the same sense, that Aristotle's ethical views are right or wrong. One advantage, however, to this lack of scientific ethical advancement is that an ancient treatise on ethics is not necessarily inferior to a modern one.

Ethics is not morally neutral. A moral philosopher is not content to merely state the facts; he or she also attempts to obtain worth and value. Ethics asks not only what is the good, but also how one can be good. Ethics not only describes the world but also evaluates the world and represents it the way one wants it to be. Moral judgments are the core of ethical analysis.

Managers should be comfortable with scientific methods. Gathering data, analyzing data, corroborating data, and arriving at a conclusion are standard managerial practices. A manager should be more sure of himself or herself when making a provable factual statement.

Managers, however, may not be so comfortable with resolving moral issues. While managers certainly recognize the necessity of confronting moral issues and making moral determinations, a manager may find it difficult to analyze ethically and to justify a moral decision. Most managers simply are not trained to conduct an ethical analysis and to argue about morality in a reasonable "scientific" manner.

Ethics vs. law

Law is the set of public, universal commands that are capable of being complied with, generally accepted, and enforced by sanctions. Law describes the ways in which people are required to act in their relationships with others in an organized society. One purpose of the law is to keep people's ambitions, self-interest, and greed especially in a capitalistic society, in check and in moderation.

Positive law is the law of a people's own making; it is the law laid down by legislative bodies, courts, and other governmental organs. Whenever any mention of "law" is made, the term customarily refers only to positive law, unless clearly stipulated otherwise. This is so because law also may mean "natural" law. Consequently, there are two theories of ethics that claim that morality depends on law: positive law and a natural law theory.

Law must be declared publicly. It must be published and made accessible in advance to all so that people can know that they are bound. Trained professionals, however, may be necessary to interpret and explain law.

Law must treat equally those with similar characteristics who are similarly situated.

There is an aura of insistency and inevitability to law. It must define what one must do and forbear from doing. The law is not composed of expectations, suggestions, and petitions to act in a certain way. The law requires one to act in a certain way. Most laws, however, are negative; that is, they require one not to act in a certain way.

Law must be accessible to the people who are to be bound by it. Laws are not legitimate if they neither can be found nor understood by people. Laws, moreover, are not legitimate if they do not clearly specify in advance what actions lie under the domain of those laws.

Law cannot be so incomprehensible that no one can obey it. It also cannot be inconsistent. Legal requirements, for example, that contradict each other cannot be termed "law" because people obviously cannot obey both.

Law generally must be obeyed. It cannot be so contrary to dominant public opinion that virtually no one will either obey or enforce the law. Most members of a society must voluntarily obey the law.

Law consists of commands enforced by sanctions, political, physical, and economic, that the officials of the state are able to, and disposed to, inflict on those who fail to comply. The essence of law is coercion. The law also relies on persuasion, but ultimately on force.

The purpose of legal sanctions is to motivate compliance. People must be made to understand that they will be compelled to obey the law or suffer some loss. If law is not enforced, or enforced so rarely that people forget about it, the law degenerates into a mere "trap" for the unwary or unlucky.

As ethics is based predominantly on rationality, and excludes force, ethics relies on persuasion to "enforce" moral rules. The characteristic "sanctions" in a moral system encompass blame, loss of esteem, and disassociation, as well as first-person reactions such as guilt, self-reproach, and remorse.

Many business practices, for example, bribery, can be cast as either legal or moral questions, or both. Managers probably are more comfortable with such questions posed as legal issues, since managers have familiarity with, experience with, and access to the law, the legal system, and lawyers. The problem, of course, is how and when the manager decides whether it is best to formulate a question as a legal issue and turn it over to the legal department to decide or to formulate it as a moral issue and turn it over to the ethics department, perhaps, to decide.

Ethics and religion

A religious ethics theory defines morality in terms of God's will. What is morally right is commanded by God; what is morally wrong is forbidden by God. Moral standards, therefore, are the set of laws or commands sanctioned by God. What ultimately makes an action right or wrong is its being commanded or forbidden by God. Religion once had, and still does in some spheres, the authority to regulate people's affairs, including their business activities, in accordance with their spiritual welfare.

Atheists obviously would not accept a religious-based standard for ethics. Questions about religious ethics are interesting and useful only if one believes in God; if not, any important moral issues must involve human beings.

A serious problem, even for the believer, is how to establish "the" convincing truth. How can one claim to have a conduit to a divine being so that one can be an authoritative spokesperson for revealed truth and a definitive interpreter of scripture? A religious theory of ethics is certainly a triumph of faith. It takes the world on trust, but diminishes human thought and endeavor. Why should the faith of any being, even God, in and of itself make an act right? Are God's commands to be regarded as arbitrary because God could have given different commands? If good is "good" or honesty is "right" because God commands it, then God could have commanded the opposite. There is, then, for God, no difference between right and wrong. Thus, it is no longer an accurate and significant statement to say that God is good; all one can say is that God is God and likes himself or herself the way he or she is, which then seems rather trivial.

A theologian would defend a religious ethics standard by declaring that God is good and that God desires worship and obedience since He or She is morally perfect. God's decrees, moreover, are not arbitrary because they are inspired by God's goodness. God's will constitutes whatever moral qualities there are to an act.

Does God, however, command what is good and right because it is good and right, or is an act good and right because God commands it? The problem with the theologian's defense is that it implies a standard of goodness independent of God. That is, the defense makes sense only if one understands the concept of moral perfection before one relates it to God. There then must be some notion of goodness antecedent to God's decrees that has led God to make these decrees rather than any others. Socrates asserted that God wills an action because it is right. The standard of right and wrong, therefore, logically is independent of God. Goodness and rightness exist prior to God's commands, and the goodness and rightness in and of themselves are the reasons for God's commands. Yet, if goodness is good, and God merely recognizes this fact, the logical conclusion is that morality does not depend on God, but rather on ethics.

Ethics is an autonomous discipline, depending solely on reason that can be studied, discussed, and applied without any reference to religious beliefs and without any reliance on religious supports. The moral determinations that prevail are the ones with the best reasons on their side.

The Socratic Method

Socrates' philosophy focused attention on the problems of human life as opposed to the speculations about the nature of the physical world that had been prevalent in Greek philosophy. Socrates stressed the importance of comprehending what it means to be a human being, how one should live in the world, and for what purpose.

In making the change from natural to moral philosophy, Socrates confronted a great deal of confusion in the moral thought of his time, particularly the wide variety of general terms used that purported to express moral notions. Socrates' main contribution to philosophy was to "bring it down from the skies"; that is, to demand precise, workable definitions, and to enunciate a procedure for formulating such definitions.

Socrates believed it was extremely harmful for people to use continually a wide variety of very general terms, especially terms intending to describe moral ideas. Even more dangerous were the Sophists, who taught an extreme personal relativism. Socrates deplored the Sophists' declaration that moral terms, such as "justice," had no basis in reality and that whatever any person thought was just was "just" for him or her. Yet, if one really needed a definition of "justice" the Sophists could supply one: "Justice is the will of the strong." The lack of any fixed meaning, the inability of people to provide proper explanations, the individualistic, expedient decision-making, and the Sophists' emphasis on rhetoric and persuasion engendered relativism, skepticism, and a great deal of confusion, particularly in the meanings attached to moral terms.

Perhaps the Sophists were right and the terms had no meaning; but if so, then people should not use them. Yet, if the terms do have permanent, objective meaning, then the people who do use them ought to be able to say what they mean. It is not only wrong but also quite unhelpful to discuss whether a person's conduct was just or unjust, moral or immoral, or good or bad unless there is some agreement as to what justice, morality, and goodness are. If there is no agreement, people are using the same words to mean different things. They then will be talking at cross purposes and their discussions will make no progress, either intellectually or morally. Only confusion, skepticism, chaos, and perhaps even conflict will ensue.

The Sophists maintained that knowledge was impossible; they viewed life as a contest in which one must be prepared to win. Socrates held that knowledge was attainable; he viewed life as a positive, common search for knowledge, but one that could begin only if the confusing, misleading, and dangerous tendencies were eliminated and people understood the right way to achieve the goal. The Sophistic outlook was for Socrates not only intellectually incorrect but also morally harmful. He would make it his life work to combat such "Sophistry." He would seek the clear meanings and shape them into definitions, principles, and rules, always for a moral purpose; and life would be better for knowing and acting by these definitions. "Goodness is real; and reality is good," declared Socrates.

The Socratic Method • • •

Socrates realized that many people have strong opinions on moral issues; but he also recognized the serious problem caused by the fact that most people are capable neither of adequately justifying their opinions nor of defining their essential terms. For Socrates, morality must be subject to a rigorous scientific method that would reveal ultimate knowledge and universal truth.

Yet before this scientific philosophical inquiry can commence, one must question one's own beliefs. Socrates consistently maintained that he knew nothing. The only way in which he was wiser than others was that he was conscious of his own ignorance, while other people were not.

An essential aspect of the Socratic Method was to convince people that although they think they know something, in fact they do not. The conviction of ignorance is the necessary first step to the acquisition of knowledge; because no one is going to seek knowledge on any subject if one is under the delusion that one already possesses it.

Socrates did not think knowledge was unobtainable, and he thought the search for knowledge is of the utmost importance. Socrates is remembered, however, not primarily for any philosophical positions, but for the primacy he accorded reason in philosophical reflection and for a method of philosophical analysis that bears his name.

How is one to go about acquiring this knowledge, for example, of what justice and morality are? Not by playing the role of an advocate, seeking to persuade others of the correctness of one's opinions, but rather by questioning people and examining the ways in which they use words, such as "just" and "unjust," and in the process progressing from particular instances to universal definitions.

The Socratic Method is a means of obtaining knowledge in three stages: questions and answers, inductive argument, and general definitions. Socrates asks a general question, for example, "What is justice?" The answer provided by the respondent will be an instance where justice was or was not present. Socrates then proceeds to refute each instance by offering a counterexample designed to show that the respondent's answer was too narrow or broad, uninformed, or wrong. Once the answer is negated, a new, more precise answer must be given to cover this instance.

The next step is to collect the instances where the parties can agree that the word under consideration, "justice," for example, can be applied. The collected instances, of "just" actions, for example, are examined to discover in them some common quality or essence by virtue of which they have that name. This common quality, or group thereof, constitutes their nature as "just" acts. A general definition of justice can be abstracted from the shared characteristics that belong to each of the examined just acts individually.

By means of questions and answers and inductive reasoning, one's mind is "led on" from the observation of individual instances, assembled and examined collectively, to grasp a general characteristic shared by all members of a class, and finally to comprehend a common, general definition. Learning, therefore, is the bringing into full consciousness the knowledge that a person already possesses but has been unable to formulate or use.

To arrive at a general meaning and to express it in a definition is to make explicit the standards by which one previously had been unconsciously or imperfectly acting. To define a term is to express one's understanding not only of what it is but also of what it is not. Definition is the remedy for confusion, relativism, and skepticism. One's life will be for the better by one's acting pursuant to known, explicit, and reasoned standards.

Problems with Socrates • • •

Even assuming one can obtain true knowledge of the good, there is no guarantee that one will act on it and thereby do what is right. There are many irrational forces assaulting people that combat reason, such as emotions and instincts. One may recognize the right way to act, but be unwilling or unable to do so because of a superseding desire or a weakness of will.

Although part of Socrates' "mission" was to convince people of their ignorance, he was markedly different from the Sophists by holding that knowledge was possible. Once people cleared their heads of misleading notions, and once they understood the proper method to attain the goal, he was ready to embark on a common search for true knowledge. For underlying Socrates' emphasis on methodology, procedure, and reasoning is the conviction that knowledge exists, that goodness is real, and that reality is good.

The Categorical Imperative

The main text for the study of "Kantian" ethics is the German philosopher Immanuel Kant's seminal 1785 work—*Groundwork (or Foundation) of the Metaphysics of Morals*. Kant called the supreme ethical principle the Categorical Imperative. This principle is a necessary element of human reason and the foundation upon which rest all moral judgments.

Before examining the Categorical Imperative, it is necessary to differentiate categorical from hypothetical imperatives. An imperative is a command; it gives instructions about how one ought to act. A hypothetical imperative prescribes the necessary means for attaining certain ends; that is, one must do X if one wishes to achieve Y. The imperative or command (X) is "hypoethical" because it is binding only insofar as one accepts the end (Y); if one rejects the end (Y), then the command (X) has no force.

A categorical imperative prescribes certain kinds of actions as objectively and absolutely necessary, without any regard to any end or any particular desire. One must do X, period! One, for example, categorically must keep promises, and not merely because one ought to keep promises if certain results are to be obtained; rather, one ought to keep promises without qualification and condition. There is, moreover, a moral obligation to keep promises even in the absence of any desire to keep promises. The rational moral rules that govern conduct are of this categorical kind. They are absolutely binding and unqualified.

The Categorical Imperative is not a principle of action itself; instead, it ethically lays down the form a moral maxim must take. Thus, said Kant, reason indicates that a moral action must have a certain form. The ethics "test" is a formal test. An action is morally right if it has a certain form, and morally wrong if it does not have that form.

The Form, the Categorical Imperative, is the first, supreme, fundamental principle in ethics. It is the form a moral action must have; it provides the ultimate standard by which one can test actions, rules, beliefs, and standards to determine if they are moral.

There are three aspects to the Categorical Imperative. Kant claims they amount to the same thing, providing the form, matter, and complete characterization of morality. The three formal conditions that an action must have to be a moral action are: (1) the action must be possible to be made consistently universal; (2) it must respect rational beings as ends in themselves; and (3) the action must stem from and respect the autonomy of rational beings and be acceptable to rational beings. If an action or rule passes all three, it is moral; if it fails one, it is immoral.

One must be moral, regardless of circumstances, consequences and regardless of whether one wants to achieve a particular end. Acting morally is a command of reason. Since morality is derived from reason, and there is a presumption that all people are rational, a moral action is one that must be done.

Duty, therefore, is a central concept in Kant's ethical theory. He places a premium on the obligation, the "ought," in ethics. One ought to perform an action, regardless of self-interest, personal desires, or consequences, because it is one's duty to do so. Morality is possible for rational beings because only rational beings have the power to act according to the idea of a moral duty. Moral worth, moreover, exists only when a person acts from a sense of duty. An act possesses only moral merit when it is performed because duty demands it. A morally good person, therefore, is one who acts conscientiously from duty.

Morality often arises as a duty or constraint because people are human beings who are subject to self-interest and personal desires. The demands of morality, however, should not be viewed as external constraints, but as self-imposed and acceptable restrictions decreed by the very autonomous and rational beings who are subject to them.

Utilitarianism: Basics and principles

Utilitarianism refers to a systematic theory of moral philosophy developed by the British philosopher Jeremy Bentham (1748–1832), and elaborated on and refined by his primary disciple, John Stuart Mill (1806–1873). Bentham was one of the earliest and the most influential utilitarians. He was trained in law and he originated utilitarianism from a general and intense disenchantment with the British legal system. He made very little distinction between morality and law, basing both on utilitarianism.

The utilitarians were more than moral philosophers; they were social reformers too. They regarded utilitarianism as an objective, scientific system of ethics, not merely as abstract ethical theory.

Bentham and the utilitarians rejected any theory of natural rights, which they viewed as discredited by the excesses of the French Revolution and which served as a "license" for the masses to overturn the political order. Locke's natural law theory was viewed as a meaningless generality, which only supplied an elaborate rationalization for the privileged classes to maintain the status quo. Bentham also rejected any intuitive basis for ethics. Intuition or conscience merely reflected irrational sentiments, which lacked any objective basis. The English common law was ancient, ossified, and harshly punitive. The true purpose of the law, for Bentham, is to promote the welfare of the people, not to impose severe punishments.

In place of these erroneous beliefs and in order to reform the law, Bentham offered a new, fundamental, universal principle of ethics to determine morality and to justify changes. Bentham's doctrine would cut through the abstractness, irrationality, and partiality of the status quo. Bentham's ethics was "scientific"; it supplied an external, objective standard for morality, which is mathematically calculable and proven by empirical means. Utilitarianism was aimed at the English middle class, who were searching for a doctrine, other than natural law or natural rights, to serve as a basis for effectuating legal and political changes.

Bentham realistically took hedonism as the governing principle of human conduct. He viewed pleasure and pain as the "sovereign masters" of human beings. From this foundational principle, Bentham derived the ethical theory known as utilitarianism.

Bentham's goal was to create as much happiness as possible, and accordingly his ethics was an attempt to bring about this happiness. The moral course of human conduct, therefore, is the one that promotes the greatest amount of happiness for the greatest number of people. Bentham's objective was to create the greatest degree of benefit for the largest number of people, while incurring the least amount of damage and harm.

Utilitarianism, therefore, determines morality by focusing on the consequences of actions. Actions are not good or bad in themselves; they are judged right or wrong solely by virtue of their consequences.

A utilitarian, after identifying the action for ethical evaluation, determines those people directly and indirectly affected by the action. The utilitarian then attempts to ascertain consequences of the action, good and bad, on the affected parties. In the most challenging aspect of this ethical theory, the utilitarian then strives to measure and weigh the good as compared to the bad consequences. If the good consequences outweigh the bad, the action is moral; if the bad outweigh the good, the action is immoral.

A utilitarian analysis of an action, private employment surveillance or monitoring, for example, would proceed as follows: Does the sum of the good attained by these actions outweigh the sum of the bad that results from them? The people and groups affected by such an action include the employer, the employees, shareholders of the employer, customers, the competition, and society. A utilitarian would require that an employer contemplating surveillance and monitoring consider the consequences not only to itself and its direct "stakeholders," but also to the interests of society. Accordingly, surveillance and monitoring at the workplace negatively can affect society as a whole because such practices may violate the right to privacy of its individual members. If employers, however, implement such practices in part to advance recognized societal agendas, such as eliminating incompetent, dishonest, or impaired employees from the workforce, one can say that society benefits.

A utilitarian would attempt to measure and weigh all the preceding consequences. To illustrate this step, one could argue that benefits or pleasure of surveillance and monitoring as outlined above may outweigh the costs or pain. If this were true, it would be moral based on the ethical principle of utilitarianism for an employer to artificially and electronically monitor and observe its employees.

Measuring pleasure and pain • • •

Utilitarianism assumes that one can measure on a common numerical scale the quantities of pleasure and pain produced by an action. Once one adds up the quantity of pleasure and then subtracts from it the quantity of pain, one thereby can determine whether the action produces more pleasure than pain; and when comparing actions, one can determine which produces the greatest total good (or perhaps the lowest total pain). How this numerical measuring is to be done and, indeed, whether it can be accomplished at all are highly controversial theoretical and practical ethical issues.

Bentham certainly wanted ethics to be a scientific and mathematical subject matter capable of quantitative measurement. He naturally assumed that pleasure and pain could be measured in numerical terms. In Bentham's bookkeeping or accounting approach to ethics, all one has to do is add up the good and bad consequences of an action to determine its morality.

Yet is it really possible to measure quantities of pleasure and pain? There are certainly problems with Bentham's moral accounting. There is, for example, the improbability of accurate measurement. If the greatest happiness principle is to work, pleasures and pains must be capable of exact measurement, so as to be weighed against one another. Exact mathematical measurement and quantification, however, either seems to be out of the question or so long to perform as to be impractical for determining what ought to be done in daily life.

Attempts to measure pleasure and pain and to quantify utility also unavoidably involve arbitrary and subjective assessments. How safe is it to assume that the person doing the weighing desires to promote the common good, as opposed to furthering his or her own private pleasure? Can the person doing the weighing be adequately supervised and controlled? There is, moreover, the distinct possibility of rationalization. One can act for purely selfish reasons and then conveniently (and perhaps even unconsciously) weigh the consequences in such a way so as to justify the action one desires.

The utilitarians would reply that people make utilitarian-type calculations everyday, weighing present against future utilities. In so doing, people rely on their intelligence, common sense, and past experience. The utilitarians, moreover, do not demand precise mathematical calculations. One can approximate outcomes and include these approximations in the calculations. In many cases, the consequences are sufficiently obvious; the good and bad predominate so clearly that great precision is not necessary. In difficult cases, where the calculation is not clear, and one is not sure if one is correct in moral measurement, one must be ready to revise one's calculations. Ultimately, however, all one humanly can do is to "satisfy," which means to provide a reasonable predictability and assessment, and not perfect predictability or computer-like calculations.

The value of morality: the utilitarian approach ● ● ●

According to Richard DeGeorge, in his 2006 book, *Business Ethics*, value can be quantified using the Utilitarian approach. In order to determine the morality of an action, practice, rule, or law pursuant to the ethical theory of Utilitarianism, and with reference to the DeGeorge Utilitarian Model, one can use the following steps

- Accurately and narrowly state the action to be evaluated (e.g., is it moral for a particular company to…?)
- Identify all stakeholders who are directly and indirectly affected by the action (including the company's constituent groups as well as society).
- Ascertain whether there are some obvious, dominant considerations that carry such weight as to predominate over other considerations.
- Specify for each person or group that is affected directly or indirectly all the reasonably foreseeable good—pleasurable and bad—painful consequences of the action, as far as into the future as appears appropriate, and consider the various predictable outcomes, good and bad, and the likelihood of their occurring.
- For each person and group, including society as a whole, measure and weigh the total good consequences against the bad consequences.
- Quantify the good and bad consequences for each person and group on a numerical scale (e.g., -5, -4, -3, -2, -1, 0, $+1$, $+2$, $+3$, $+4$, $+5$) representing units and extremes of pleasure and pain.

Sum up all the good and bad consequences.

If the action results in a positive number, it produces more good than bad and is a morally right action; and if the action results in a negative number, it produces more bad than good and is morally wrong.

A utilitarian analysis • • •

Since utilitarianism assumes that the pleasures and pains of an action can be measured and weighed on a common numerical scale, and then added and subtracted from each other, the following detailed, "mathematical" utilitarian analysis of most challenging human resource management problem is offered.

The action A utilitarian analysis first requires identification of the action to be evaluated. Here, the action is random, observed, urinalysis drug testing and the subsequent discharge of employees who test positive. The second step is to identify parties affected by the action. This action directly affects employers and employees. Those indirectly affected are employees' families, shareholders of the employers, customers and consumers, suppliers, local communities, and society in general.

The consequences The final step in a utilitarian analysis is to weigh the positive and negative consequences of any action. This step of balancing necessarily implies that good and bad are capable of measurement in some quantitative manner. Although there is disagreement regarding whether values can truly be quantified and compared, people make numerous such evaluations in a fashion every day. Further, the utilitarian process of identifying alternatives and estimating their consequences may be of use to decision makers faced with ethical judgments. The purpose of assigning numbers to units of pleasure and pain is to underscore the "scientific" spirit of the utilitarian ethical philosophy to demonstrate one potential practical application of an ethical theory, and to encourage the reader to actually apply this ethical measuring procedure. The figures used in this article are not to be taken as revealed "truth," but as an illustration of applied ethics. This analysis assigns hypothetical numerical values to the relative benefit or pain for each category of person affected. These values fall on a suggested numerical scale from -5 (most pain) to $+5$ (most benefit). Accordingly, $+1$ or -1 would represent a negligible amount of benefit or pain, respectively, with $+5$ or -5 simplifying a considerable amount.

Employers Positive consequences for employers who randomly test employees for drugs result from the reduction and gradual elimination of drug use from the workplace and ultimately the workforce. If employees were to become drug-free, many problems now associated with the use of drugs would be lessened. Considerable decreases, for example, in tardiness, absenteeism, poor performance, on- and off-the-job accidents, and medical costs would be likely, with a final result of more productive employees and overall enhanced profitability. Negative consequences are a diminished level of trust between employers and employees, a decrease (at least short-lived) in employee morale, and a loss of some "good" employees (drug using, privacy-threatened, or both). Overall, the good consequences appear to weigh heavily against the bad, resulting in a value of +4 for the employer.

Employees   Employees are negatively affected in that they lose some privacy rights as a consequence of the testing program. Urination is a private bodily function; drug testing is an invasive procedure. Compelling employees to undergo the actual physical act of collecting urine under observation for analysis strains the bounds of decency.

An obvious negative consequence of drug testing to those employees who test positive is the possibility of losing their jobs. Employees who do not use drugs also may feel violated if treated as though they are under suspicion for the drug use and subject to testing. Finally, employees may believe that if they do their jobs properly, then what they do outside the company is none of the employer's business.

Positive consequences for employees are the identification of impaired individuals and their removal from the workplace, thereby providing a safer working environment for all personnel. The eliminated drug user may be a friend to many, but coworkers will no longer have to worry about drug-induced substandard performance. Another good consequence of a drug testing program is the early identification of employee drug users. Early identification helps in the eventual rehabilitation of some individual users, especially if an employer's program allows for assistance to the impaired employee. Discharging the possibly good effects of drug screening for the sake of argument, employees are assigned −4 units of pain.

Families of employees   Discharging employees for testing positive may adversely impact their families. The families must deal not only with the loss of income but also with the emotions of the discharged employees. These negative consequences, however, can be tempered if an employee, as a result of the drug testing policy, does become drug-free. An employee who is compelled to receive help, perhaps through an employee assistance program, may be able to achieve a more balanced life not only at work, but also at home. Nonetheless, due to the foreseeable consequence of loss of family income, the families of employees are assigned a −3 pain designation.

Shareholders of employees Shareholders benefit from the imposition of the testing due to the resulting elimination of poorly performing drug users. The company will reduce its liability from accidents caused by impaired employees. Diminished liability and healthier employees translates into enhanced performance, possible higher market share, and presumably a higher rate of return for the shareholders' investments. Although shareholders could be affected negatively from wrongful discharge litigation or adverse publicity stemming from a drug testing program, the overall benefit is +4.

Customers and consumers Purchasers and users of the employer's products and services gain substantially through surveillance and monitoring. Because employees will be more likely to perform their duties at optimum capacity, customers can expect to receive better products and services. The customers, however, may have to pay for the drug testing program, if the employer passes along costs. The result is an over all measurement of +4.

Suppliers Suppliers also would benefit from an employer's drug testing program. They would be protected against dealing with drug-impaired employees. Suppliers would gain, for example, in not incurring unnecessary absenteeism costs and by meeting with capable representatives of the employer. The employer's drug testing program should lead to safer, more harmonious, and economically more productive relationship with its suppliers. As an employer's costs decrease, and its efficiency and economic growth increase, suppliers will benefit from the employer's concomitant rise in purchasing power. Overall, the employer should find abundant support from its suppliers for the company's drug testing program. Consequently, because the drug testing program will effectuate better and more profitable relationships with "stakeholders," such as suppliers, who interact with and depend on the employer, suppliers represent +4 units on the scale.

Local communities The benefits to local communities rise from the decrease in the number of drug users in the workforce, including those employed in critical positions. These benefits are reduced, however, by the possibility that the community may have to support terminated employees' families through the use of public assistance. Local communities are assigned a +3.

Society Society will experience pain due to the diminution of privacy rights of the individual employees who must undergo testing. Society will gain, however, because elimination of drug users will reduce the possibility of defective products and negligent services, which in turn enhances public safety. Drug testing will also improve employers' productivity. As productivity increases, society's standard of living should correspondingly improve. If such a blanket program does in fact help produce a drug-free work force, it would contribute to a drug-free society, thus giving other social programs a better chance of working. There admittedly is a price to be paid for the further loss in privacy rights, but the resulting societal good outweighs the pain. Society is assigned a value of +3.

Weighing the consequences The consequences expressed in the assigned units of pleasure and pain are as follows: Employers +4; employees −4; families of employees −3; shareholders +4; customers and consumers +4; suppliers +4; local communities +3; and society +3. The result is −7 units of pain and +22 units of pleasure. Because the random drug testing program produced more good than bad, the action is moral under the ethical doctrine utilitarianism.

Although not "scientific" doctrine, utilitarianism can be a useful tool for making moral determinations. Individuals would benefit from familiarity with the central tenets of this ethical theory—foreseeing, measuring, and weighing the consequences of actions. A person who does focus on consequences usually is concerned with the impact of the consequences on himself. Utilitarianism, however, asks that a person expand the scope of analysis and objectively anticipate the consequences of an action on others.

Despite the problems inherent in utilitarianism, several strong arguments favor the use of this ethical theory. Utilitarianism accords with the criteria people actually do employ when making practical decisions. At the level of theory, Bentham's "science" may appear imprecise and even crude, but at the level of practice, the principle of utility is not foreign to ordinary ways of thinking and acting. It is perfectly natural that people seek pleasure and happiness and avoid pain. It also seems quite sensible to try to foresee pleasure and pain, to balance pleasure and pain against one another, and to bear a certain amount of short-term pain in order to achieve greater long-term pleasure. People, consciously or unconsciously, do make utilitarian-type calculations on a daily basis. They realize that the consequences of actions are important, they strive to foresee these consequences, they draw up a balance sheet of pleasures and pains or "pros" and "cons," and they then choose the actions that produce the most happiness. It is important to note, however, that when people choose these "good" actions, they predominantly are choosing actions that promote the most good for themselves.

Utilitarianism, moreover, accords with practical, governmental decision making. The theory matches the way government operates when deciding public policy issues and allocating public pleasures and pains. The principle of utility has had a strong influence upon the view of how a government should legislate. One purpose of present day legislative hearings, for example, is for the legislators to hear various opinions on how much happiness or unhappiness a proposed law will cause. The principle of utility itself, moreover, provides a criterion to judge legislation, law, and government. Utilitarianism measures actions against a standard of usefulness. Its values for the purposes of public policy are obvious. The doctrine shifts attention from the origin of law and government to its operation, and from precedence to consequence. The implication of this thinking is that obedience to government and law is required only if government and law are useful in producing pleasure.

The utilitarians were reformers; they wanted societal and legal reforms. They wanted their moral philosophy to be a "live," efficacious, contemporary public policy option, not simply an arcane, abstruse, theoretical relic. The utilitarians understood that reforms require more than mere "talk"; they require appropriate action on the part of those who want them. The utilitarians wanted their ethics to be judged by its efficacy as an instrument of reform. They wanted to make goodness a matter of genuine concern in the practical affairs of human beings; and, in fact, their influence was great and on the whole positive.

Utilitarianism does supply ethics with an objective component. By advancing utility as a standard, the theory substantially lessens the danger of incorporating dogma, irrationality, and pure subjectivism into ethics. Utilitarianism, consequently, may justify actions that are contrary to many peoples' feelings, intuitions, or moral beliefs.

Utilitarianism seeks to give to ethics a precise content that can be defined concretely, measured scientifically, and determined objectively. Utilitarianism is a comparatively clear, coherent, and comprehensible ethical theory that can be translated into practical terms.

Utilitarianism, moreover, is an ethical theory that places human beings at the center of morality. It is a universal, impartial, egalitarian theory that stresses the importance and equality of all human beings, not merely one person, group, or class. Utilitarianism underscores the shared capabilities of all human beings to experience pleasure and pain. No one's pleasure or pain is overlooked; nobody is excluded as unworthy. The amount of pleasure and pain is considered without favoritism.

By affording all human beings an equal moral importance, utilitarianism serves as a reminder that law, government, and the social order exist for everyone and that the general well-being and happiness always are relevant considerations. The theory embodies generous, enlightened, and humane tendencies, and it instills feelings of benevolence toward all humanity.

Although Bentham and Mill and their adherents may not have persuaded all that utilitarianism is the "right" ethical theory or a "scientific" one, they did establish utilitarianism as permanent and very influential ethical position. They also expanded dramatically the moral intelligence and sensitivity of people by drawing attention to the full consequences of actions and by emphasizing the vital happiness of all sentient beings capable of feeling pleasure and pain.

Being a moral professional?

One must recognize that life necessarily presents conflict between moral ways of acting and other types of conduct. All people will be tempted to cast aside moral concerns in favor of allowing non-moral reasons. Even ethically well-demonstrated moral assertions will be resisted when their acceptance threatens peoples, or one's own, self-interest.

The question, therefore, as to why one should act morally, emerges as a fundamental question of moral philosophy and the ultimate problem of moral justification. Why should a rational person do what is right? Why should one recognize any distinction between right and wrong? How can the moral way of life rationally be justified, particularly since a moral way of life may conflict with self-interest? Why should one act on moral reasons rather than legal reasons, conventional reasons, or reasons of self-interest? Even if one can determine ethically what one morally ought to do, why one ought to do what is morally required? Perhaps rational people can be persuaded by reasons of self-interest to adhere to moral rules, but then their "moral" reasons to do things are ultimately reasons of self-interest. Is there an unresolvable tension between morality and self-interest?

How are moral rules justified? If one is an Ethical Relativist, one ought to be moral because that is what is approved by society. Societal rules are necessary if people are to coexist, cooperate, and prosper in a society. If one is a Legal Positivist, one ought to be moral for the same reason that one ought to obey the law, which ultimately is in order to avoid punishment. If one is a Utilitarian, one must be moral so as to achieve the greater good. One thus will set aside any egoistic motives in favor of moral rules that promote the general welfare. If one is a Kantian, one ought to be moral and do the moral act for no other reason than it is "moral." The "ought" in morality, therefore, has in itself an unconditional obligation for a Kantian.

Why else be moral? A moral person, said Socrates, is happier than an immoral one. Acting morally produces certain harmonious results—inner peace, satisfaction, and happiness. The moral person sets goals that fit into the scheme of human development and at the same time satisfy one's own desires. The achievement of goals creates a feeling of satisfaction and pleasure, which is characteristic of happiness. Achieving goals produces new goals and thus a happy life. The moral person, moreover, does not blindly rush at every object, but sees the necessity of acknowledging limits to his or her actions and objectives. He or she progresses steadily along a demarcated path toward definite, attainable objectives. The moral person recognizes that "limits" are used in the sense of a guide, not a restraint; and that he or she will be happier for acknowledging such moral guidelines. Even if the moral person suffers through moments of disappointment, bitterness, and despair, even if he or she escapes the notice of the world or is misjudged by the world, even if he or she suffers from injustice, and even if he or she meets an untimely end, nonetheless, the moral person will be at peace with himself or herself.

Acting immorally, moreover, can be argued as acting imprudently against one's self-interest. Perhaps the immoral person can win some temporary short-term advantage; but ultimately immorality brings on social censure and sanctions, such as rejection, isolation, and ostracism. A prudent person realizes that acting morally will obviate many of the disadvantages that one would be forced to encounter if one acted immorally, not only societal sanctions, but also the incurring of personal costs such as guilt, remorse, and other psychological discomforts.

In order to convince a person to act morally, he or she must be able to envision a way of life that not only provides a satisfying life for himself or herself as an individual, but also contains the conditions necessary for a meaningful, satisfying, social way of life. The conditions for such a life for people living in social groups requires morality. Morality, therefore, has a social source and a social function. It is, moreover, to one's advantage to live in a society in which morality is accepted. One will be able to rely on people obeying certain norms; and one will feel safe and confident by knowing so. One's own compliance with moral standards, however, is the "price" one must pay to secure the compliance of others.

Even presuming that society needs and requires morality, and even if it is in one's advantage to have others act in a moral manner, does it follow that one should adopt a moral way of life, and does it follow that one always should act morally? Can it be demonstrated to a prudential person that it always and certainly will be advantageous for him or her to act in a thoroughly moral manner? Why should not the pragmatic person instead encourage and persuade others to be moral; and then take advantage of that fact; and at the same time avoid his or her own moral responsibilities? It may not be a satisfactory answer that one is not likely to get away with acting immorally. In all honesty, it must be admitted that there will be at least some circumstances where one can act immorally with impunity, perhaps without even detection, and quite efficaciously. Surely, if one is a Machiavellian, it would be advantageous for everyone else to be constrained by morality and for one to escape any moral sanctions by pretending to act morally, or, if one has the power, simply to flout moral standards. The Machiavellian goal is to succeed in making one's self-interest paramount, and this goal can be attained in part by inducing others to make the demands of morality paramount in their lives. Does not this Machiavellian scenario appear to be the best possible world for oneself? To this question, it is difficult to provide a completely satisfying answer of any kind.

In selecting a course of conduct, moral reasons and prudential ones not always will coincide. It is necessary, therefore, to demonstrate to people that morality is required for the well-being of people in general, and that morality demands that people to some extent and at some times act in ways that they cannot perceive as presently egoistically prudential. The challenge of explicating a way of life that both secures the agreement of rational egoistic individuals and provides the conditions necessary for a social life is a daunting one. One good way is to create a way of life that helps to make the advancement of one person's self-interest consistent, as far as possible, with the success of other people.

The moral human resource manager

The moral human resource manager will habitually manifest the following virtuous characteristics:

1. *Prudent self-interest*. A moral manager manages the business with prudent self-interest. No one can make the conscientious manager do what he or she thinks is not in best interest of shareholders and other stakeholders. Society, of course, needs material wealth for the exercise of freedom and attainment of the "good life." Adam Smith, in *The Wealth of Nations*, however, noted that the freedom only can come from an intelligent and humane use of the free-market system.

2. *No self-exoneration*. Moral managers must be very careful in exonerating themselves from amoral attitudes or morally dubious practices on the basis of business "survival." The moral business manager avoids the placing of blame for moral failings on others, for example, society, government, the legal system, or the marketplace. Business ethics has no future if it is gradually suffocated by moral "compromises" of individual managers.

3. *Practical reason*. The moral manager is one who predictably can be trusted to act reasonably under the circumstances. The best approach is for business managers to conceive of their task as attempting to reach the most reasonable result under the circumstances (which includes, but is not limited to, the facts of the case, the law, ethics, and economics). "Reasonableness" can be used as a standard for moral rightness. It is an appropriate substitute for other standards of absolute moral rightness. It is not a pipe dream, but a rational standard and attainable with effective commitments.

4. *Impartiality*. Fundamental impartiality and a consideration of others when making decisions are attributes of the moral

manager. Ethics naturally become more relevant as managers make business decisions that affect human beings in significant ways. There must be a recognition that managers make judgments not only about the future of a business, but also about the future of society.

5. *Management ethics.* Morality in business must be seen as a management responsibility. Moral questions must be effectively dealt with by business managers in order to develop an ethical philosophy that is sound; and in order to develop managers who are capable of thinking that can produce high ethical standards.

    A firm philosophical foundation already exists for the moral development of business. A moral business manager, for example, can use the Doctrine of the Mean to determine moral standards. He or she can use inductive reasoning and work from current business practices. He or she then can use Utilitarianism to determine if the "mean" standard promotes greater good, and he or she can use Kant's Categorical Imperative to ensure that an action is not unjust to persons. If the act passes all three tests, the moral business manager can frame it as a rule and promulgate it in a code of ethics for the business.

6. *Moral accountability.* Management must not only incorporate morality into business decision making, but also must hold itself accountable to standards of moral conduct. Managers must make a commitment to a moral course of conduct, and once they make the commitment, not abandon it lightly. A manager cannot do what he or she judges or thinks should not be done ethically.

7. *Codes of ethics.* Managers must promulgate and adopt codes of ethics. A code of ethics is a set of just laws, ethical principles, and fundamental moral rules, governing how business and management are to treat one another, stakeholders, and society, and a set of subsidiary, supplemental moral rules that business people will agree to accept for their mutual benefit on condition that others follow those rules as well.

8. *Trust.* Management must be viewed as more than mere "business"; rather, as a trust. Business managers must take collective action to ensure that goods and services are available and accessible to all. They must take responsibility for management's moral behavior and do so seriously enough so as to monitor, discipline, and even remove business managers when standards of morality are violated.

9. *Moral leadership.* A human resource professional, staff member, and manager must be a moral leader. He or she must be a paradigm of morality and raise level of conventional

morality by example. He or she must use moral power to build and sustain the moral community. He or she must implement moral concerns throughout management and business. He or she must give recognition to the fact that a business manager's task is fundamentally moral in nature. The moral manager must be an instrument of character formation. He or she must demonstrate that moral integrity and competence are inseparable, and that demonstrating that moral character and trust are indispensable traits of business management as a profession.

Such a manager can bring about good in the world, in his or her own life as well as in others. He or she can touch the better aspects of his or her own or another's human nature. By demonstrating enthusiasm, cooperativeness, self-discipline, and dedication, the moral manager can build teamwork and a moral business entity.

10. *Why should human resource professionals and managers be moral?* Human resource professionals, staff members, and managers have considerable discretion. If moral, human resource managers will be able to increase their discretion by adhering to moral standards and thus winning the trust of public. As a result, management will gain greater freedom from external interference. If business managers want the freedom to conduct affairs with a minimum of outside interference, they must see themselves as moral agents and act accordingly.

If business managers act in an immoral or amoral manner, the public will not trust management to take its interests into account. Consequently, any moral dimensions to management decision making will be pursued by others, who will take action to shape management and business behavior. Government regulation, for example, will continue to be relied on to promote moral and social values. To abandon the moral debate to others is an irresponsible act by business managers; it is an abdication of responsibility.

Summary

Modern ethical efforts to moralize business are radically different from those of religion. Moral philosophers derive their authority from neither revelation nor godly commandments; rather, ethical appeals are based on rational argumentation. Moral philosophers attempt to answer ethically moral questions that theologians may have answered religiously.

If one views morality as not to be intuited, but to be rationally ascertained, then one must determine what moral standards to adopt. The moral conclusions reached will reflect one's ethical reasoning and also may encompass any moral conscience or intuition. Moral beliefs, if urged by conscience and sensed by intuition, may provide a starting point for the application of a principled ethical theory. One's conscience, for example, could present a person with a number of proscriptions against unconscionable behavior. One would then reflect on these insights in a critical ethical manner and apply a principled ethical theory to insure that one's intuited moral beliefs are really right.

Human resources management and a service culture

Denver E. Severt and Catherine Curtis

*Rosen College of Hospitality Management,
University of Central Florida
Orlando, FL 32819, USA*

Introduction

Two complex factors are responsible for an organization's service culture, the external and internal customer service alignment (Cannon, 2002; Varoglu & Eser, 2006; Seibert & Lingle, 2007) and respect for an internal service profit chain (Paraskevas, 2001). Offering internal service quality (i.e., meeting the expectations of employees across important dimensions) is a critical element that sustains business in successful companies by enhancing company employee relationships (Varoglu & Eser, 2006). From the employee perspective and in keeping with the consumerism movement in American, employees expect satisfying work situations that are fair in procedures, fair in people interactions, and fair in levels of pay and work expected. Further employees expect internal service strengthening initiatives. From the employer's viewpoint such internal service quality initiatives are important for company long-range success in that internal service leads to satisfied employees that intend to stay and tell others about the company and that at high levels generate employee loyalty (Seibert & Lingle, 2007). From the researcher's viewpoint, this is important because studying various companies and relationships between these variables can yield support for theoretical models, which can lend themselves to industry application.

This paper presents a brief definition of organizational culture and climate suggesting that a company define the type of culture that best matches the natural organizational life both from the internal and external stakeholder perspective. For a service culture to be realized, the organizational climate must be aligned and fit the organizational culture. Next, actions that HR can take towards solidifying and maintaining a service culture are presented including but not limited to staffing, values, trust, functions of HR, types of HR, and steps HR can take to foster an internal service climate. After that, a brief discussion of literature on service culture and human resources is discussed. Finally, a summary and conclusions section finalizes the chapter by offering an overview of the material along with some limitations of the chapter.

Organizational life and culture

The life of the organization is the culture of the organization (Martin, 1992; Schein, 2004; Tower & Rodrigues, 2007). Schein (1983) defined organizational culture as:

"The pattern of basic assumptions that a given group has invented, discovered, or developed in learning to cope with its problems of external adaptation and internal integration. A pattern of assumptions that has worked well enough to be taught to new members as the correct way to perceive, think and feel in relation to those problems." (p. 14)

Further Schein (1985, 2004) acknowledges invisible and visible features of a culture. Invisible features guide the company while the visible features of culture include artifacts, beliefs, and values. The artifacts include visible processes. The beliefs include strategies, goals, and philosophies of the company. Values refer to the way that people are treated and the way things are handled in general and include but are not limited to honesty, integrity, and hospitableness.

Various schemes exist for the culture classification across companies. Goffee and Jones (as cited in Varoglu & Eser, 2006, p. 34) comprised one such classification scheme for organizational culture. They categorized low and high levels of solidarity and sociability into four culture types including networked, mercenary, fragmented, and communal. Solidarity deals with the employees' ability to see the organizations tasks and goals, while sociability deals with the friendliness among the members of the organization. Networked culture has high sociability and low solidarity and is the culture where people know one another quickly and feel part of a group. Mercenary culture is the opposite of a networked culture and has low sociability and high solidarity. It is a culture that may believe in the individual winning at all costs and may be present in organizations where closing the sale is critical and pay is based on commission. Fragmented culture is a culture whereby employees feel more identification with their profession rather than their organization so low sociability and high solidarity. The last type of culture is communal, where employees get along personally and professionally, making the difference between work and nonworking times indistinct and is exemplified by high sociability and high solidarity (Varoglu & Eser, 2006). Various companies will optimize their culture by providing the culture most conducive to the natural state of business transactions in that firm. It is important to understand an organization's culture in relation to the organization's climate. For the hospitality business, a communal culture matches best with organizational goals including hotels, restaurants, and any hospitality business that is consumer experience based.

While organizational culture is derived from shared values and beliefs passed throughout the organization, Davidson (2003) defined organizational climate as a more conceptualized, individualized psychological approach that seeks to understand the cognitive processes and behavior of a company (Davidson, 2003). Organizational climate is "an experientially based description of the work environment" reflective of employee perceptions of the workplace (Schulte, Ostroff, & Kinicki, 2006). Organizational climate takes a snapshot of current happenings, whereas organization culture probes for deeper reasons for company occurrences (Davidson, 2003). Research has typically supported the mediating role of organizational climate between human resources management, employee satisfaction, and customer satisfaction (Rogg, Schmidt, Shull, & Schmitt, 2001).

Johnstone and Johnston (2005) defined four dimensions of organizational climate including: coworker cohesion, supervisor support, work pressure, and involvement. Coworker cohesion is a sense of belonging and peer support. Supervisor support is the assistance the company provides the employee. Higher levels of assistance create greater acceptance and value. Work pressure was defined as the stress associated with job accomplishment. High levels of work pressure can lead to employee burnout, but high levels of work pressure can be also be balanced by a culture of coworker cohesion and supervisory support. Finally, involvement can be defined as the buy-in of the employee. Generally speaking, higher levels of employee involvement leads to higher levels of employee satisfaction (Johnstone & Johnston, 2005).

Research by Schneider, Gunnarson, and Niles-Jolly (1994) has shown that there should be three types of organizational climate present to ensure success and on-going quality improvement: (1) a climate for service, (2) a climate for innovation, and (3) a climate for human resources (as cited in Davidson, 2003, p. 208). The climate for service suggests that hospitality employees possess the right attitude to serve customers. The climate for innovation suggests that new events, including ideas, happen continuously. The climate for human resources suggests that employees are kept linked to the other facets of organizational climate as well as leadership and empowerment (Davidson, 2003). This climate plays a vital role in shaping employee's perceptions of their jobs and the overall organization, and has been shown to exude both positive and negative consequences on a firm's operations (Chen & Huang, 2007; Fleet & Griffin, 2006). Finally, since this chapter is written within the context of a hospitality and leisure business, a fourth type of organizational climate is suggested and that is a climate of hospitableness. This climate is different from service. Hospitableness involves a climate filled with competent ladies and gentlemen behaving with hospitableness towards all other ladies and gentlemen inside and outside the company. These components of organizational climate are necessary in a hospitality and leisure business. If these four dimensions are present, it is easier for the employees to transfer the climate to guests.

In Figure 6.1 below, and in keeping with our discussion that climate is more personalized and that culture can be a direct outflow of climate. Thus, a service culture begins with organizational climate, which starts smaller with the individual and must have the components of service, innovation, human resources, and hospitableness. From the climate of service, innovativeness level, human resource style, and hospitableness, flows the organizational culture. The classification mentioned above form the rest of the figure with a display of the four culture types as they vary between sociability and solidarity: networked, mercenary, fragmented, and communal. For example, a communal service culture creates the cornerstones for the culture. Human resources management can be pivotal in this role by attracting, interviewing enough and then selected the folks that match. After this process, human resources can assist in motivating, retaining, remunerating properly and developing innovative, service-oriented and hospitable employees that are satisfied or have a high level of internal service quality.

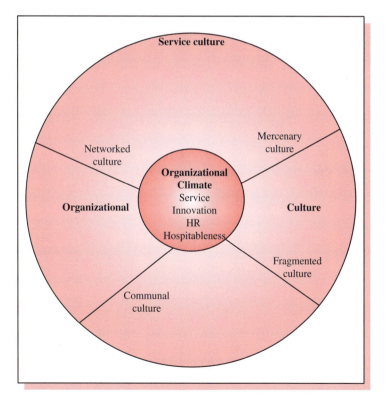

Figure 6.1
Service culture diagram.

Service culture

Service culture defined

A service culture is defined as a business that places service at the center of their organizational culture (Teare, 1993). This should apply to external customers and in our context, to internal customers or employees dealing with leaders, managers, or other employees. Externally, Enz and Siguaw (2000) have suggested that in order for a lodging operation to have successful service quality, it must possess four characteristics: (1) a service culture, (2) an empowered service-delivery system, (3) a "customer listening" orientation, and (4) a responsive service guarantee. A commitment to service quality that sets and maintains service standards is necessary from the organization (Enz & Siguaw, 2000). Employees are the internal customers who also have needs, wants, and problems (Cannon, 2002; Varoglu & Eser, 2006). If these desires are met internally throughout an organization, the external customer is more likely to be satisfied, thus benefiting from an internal service chain (Seibert & Lingle, 2007; Paraskevas, 2001). The development of an internal service chain must be derived through each department within a hospitality organization, as one department serves another (Paraskevas, 2001). Human resources can perform a vital role by insuring that employee issues are heard and responded to in at least the same manner that service failures are heard and then responded to hopefully in the form of a correction and recovery.

Inter-departmental relationships

Successful inter-departmental relationships are critical for internal service. Research in inter-departmental relationships has shown more tension than ease of communication. This tension can easily eat away at any climate and culture. Some possible factors may include: departmental loyalty rather than organizational loyalty, different knowledge levels concerning procedures, goals and rules between departments, and difference in priorities between departments (Paraskevas, 2001). Frequent communication or listening systems between human resources and other departments can aid in detection and resolve in such misaligned situations. Workflow type service encounters are internal service encounters in which one department is dependent upon another's accomplishments in the service chain, such as housekeeping and the front desk of a lodging facility whereby the guest is an internal guest (Paraskevas, 2001).

These departments may receive internal as well as external pressure to perform in a certain manner, and to prevent animosity between these departments, it is necessary for managers to demonstrate a successful internal service culture (Seibert & Lingle, 2007; Varoglu & Eser, 2006). This affect of inter-departmental communication was highlighted in Zeithaml, Parasuraman and Berry's (1998) *Gap Four* of why guests' perceptions differ from expectations. Gap Four stated that horizontal and vertical communication's in the company created a propensity to over promise. In turn, this creates internal friction with organizational employees. This friction may be viewed by inter-departmental failures which must be recovered from. Again, the human resources department can perform a vital role in helping to keep inter-departmental miscommunications resolved by applying various recovery schemes and by continued measurement and monitoring for situations of inter-departmental conflict. Finally, the same can apply to intra-departmental conflicts with the conflict being in one department.

The involvement of human resources with service culture

Human resource involvement in business has been categorized into four areas by Buyens and DeVos (as cited in Raub, Alvarez, & Khanna, 2006) including value-driven, time involvement, executive and reactive human resource management. Value-driven HRM, involves HR professionals in decision-making processes from the early stages of problem identification; timely involvement of HRM, involves the inclusion of HR professionals in the processing of solution development and in the creation of tools for implementation. Executive HRM involves the implementation of a solution to an internal problem that has been solved by other members of the organization. Reactive HRM involves the minimal use of HRM in the decision making process possibly in the monitoring stages, or to watch for problems during implementation.

In the hospitality and leisure industry, the work is labor intensive, the conditions are less than ideal, and there is much diversity in education, qualifications, and cultural backgrounds (Raub et al., 2006). Human resources is not completely trusted by the lower levels of hospitality organizations (Tracey & Charpentier, 2004). For some it may be viewed as nothing more than a cost center, where practices are informal and efficiency driven (Tracey & Nathan, 2002; Francis & D'Annunzio-Green, 2005). For the human resources department that is going to be instrumental in sustaining, monitoring, and creating a service culture throughout the organization, the value-driven HRM must be implemented so that HRM can be monitoring for various employee, inter-departmental or intra-departmental issues.

A trust proposition

The importance of managers displaying the same focus on employees as they do to customers validates the internal service profit chain (Varoglu & Eser, 2006). The acceptance and trust of management by the staff is critical to effective operations. Trust is significantly related to sales, profits, and employee turnover in the restaurant industry, for instance, and trust is dependant on management's ability as perceived by the staff (Davis, Schoorman, Mayer, & Tam, 2000). Thus, for human resources to be valuable in enforcing a culture of service and hospitality, it is important that top management supports HR in this role both symbolically and formally.

When managers and supervisors feel supported by the organization during the leader–leader exchange (LLX), they are more apt to positively relate to frontline employees during the leader–member exchange (LMX) (Tangirala, Green, & Ramanujam, 2007). When frontline employees feel supported by management, they transfer those perceptions back to the entire organization through interactions with other employees and into the marketplace based on their interactions with consumers (Shanock & Eisenberger, 2006).

An HR emphasis on company traits/values

Human resource departments may aid in the implementation of a service culture by developing a structure for an internal service culture by addressing five categories of traits that lend themselves towards an excellent culture: professionalism, dependability, conscientiousness, communication, and consideration. Professionalism consists of having the knowledge and/or experience to perform the required tasks, providing correct level of service, and using resources efficiently. Dependability is the likelihood for doing a task correctly the first time. Conscientiousness is the process of enacting prompt service, flexibility, and responsiveness to the special needs of the internal customer. Conscientiousness offers a greater likelihood for good performance under stressful circumstances. Communication is listening to the internal customer and reporting progress of actions taken to resolve situations. Finally, consideration deals with how internal customers are treated (Paraskevas, 2001). As much internal justice research has proven, employees should be treated with the highest levels of interactive, distributive, and procedural fairness essentially fairness in interpersonal interaction, in pay and promotion issues and in issues of process which can be as simple as the timing of smoke breaks or as complex as processes for on-going employee evaluation. When and if fairness has not been delivered to employees, a recovery process should begin to restore fairness. The human resource function can serve as an objective department to which such issues are handled.

Four HR functions supporting a service culture

To better understand human resources and its role in creating, implementing, and monitoring change in organizational culture, it is necessary to understand the functions of human resources. According to Ulrich (1998), there are four capabilities that human resources possess including as a partner in strategy execution, an administrative expert, an employee champion, and a change agent. All of these capabilities must be enabled for HR to be instrumental in promoting the culture of the organization.

As a *partner in strategy* execution, HR is contributing by enforcing strategic human resources management by implementing new plans, organizational audits, renovating necessary changes, and setting reward systems that are aligned with the operation's performance. As an *administrative* expert, HR professionals must manage their routine processes quickly and efficiently while monitoring the company's guidelines. HR should also step into the role as an internal consultant to save money and enhance competition.

As an *employee champion*, today's workers' jobs have become more enlarged than ever, and due to current job demands, with many workers rarely investing more than their required time helps in the development of transactional relationships. This type of employer–employee relationship rewards worker behaviors through an exchange system without building a sense of cohesion or organizational support (Fleet & Griffin, 2006). To avoid transactional relationships, HR must engage employees in social activities such as parties and picnics to foster employee commitment. Activities such as these create an environment of social suppllort, which can act as a buffer against workplace stress, while encouraging positive employee interactions and enhancing a sense of coherence (Wong & Lin, 2007).

With higher levels of trust and commitment, the company–employee relationship strengthens potentially enhancing employee involvement. Involvement in the company has a significant effect on enjoyment of work (Johnstone & Johnston, 2005). In addition, they must continually offer programs that encourage employee morale beginning with orientation, moving on to workshops, reports, and employee surveys. Strong orientations allow for HR to educate the employee on climate and culture, and to allow the employee to experience the current organizational climate. As a result, when employees are familiar with the company's organizational values, practices, and goals, the employee has the necessary knowledge and tools to make quick, responsible decisions that reflect the organization's mission and encourage eventual customer satisfaction.

HR must also take an integral role in repairing morale when it is low. This improved overall morale also translates into increased employee productivity, and ultimately, the organization's bottom line (Prince, 2007). To ensure that HR is working properly as an employee champion, HR must be an employee advocate. Employees should be informed of the involvement HR takes in the decision making process and must represent employee rights. This relationship will result in the communication of needs of the employee from the employee to HR.

Finally, as *Change Agent*, the human resources department makes sure that organizational change occurs smoothly by planning the transition. This planning includes defining and explaining the cultural change to employees. HR must communicate why the change is integral to the company's success, review the current state of culture and proposed new culture, and prepare alternative solutions to implement desired change. Finally, on-going assessment of the culture is critical for smooth transitions from one type of culture to another type of culture. These changes typically only occur a few times and are more likely to occur with changes in company leadership. Likely, the best assessment is rounding or management by walking around so that the sentiment of the change and the climate can be sensed.

Folaron (2005) proposed three considerations when implementing change: general readiness, emotional readiness, and capability vs. desire to change (Folaron, 2005). General readiness to change is affected by previous organizational changes, influenced by the level of success of those changes. To assess general readiness, a well-constructed plan must be presented, implemented, and evaluated. Once general readiness is determined, emotional readiness must be addressed. Employees must be given time to digest the change and mourn for the loss. Finally, the difference between the capability to achieve the change and the desire to change must be recognized. Employees must have the desire to change for change capabilities to overcome challenges (Folaron, 2005).

The importance of HR staffing to organizational culture

Given the nature of the business in the hospitality industry, there are many uncertain variables within the organization in matters relating to customers and service. The hospitality industry must train and allow their employees to accommodate customers at the discretion of the employee (Bowen & Ford, 2004). In order to produce this type of service and hospitality climate, the procedure must begin in human resources with staffing. According to Rowley and Purcell (as cited in Collins, 2007) the hospitality industry has been known to implement poor hiring practices. According to Collins (2007), recruitment is an area where there is a collapse in meeting the needs of the hotel with the hiring specifications. Prior research suggests that that service quality may be improved if proper employee selection occurs. Personality becomes an important trait in selecting a person for a customer service position (Bowen & Ford, 2004). In addition to personality, consideration to the match of employee–guest demographics must be given. Sacco and Schmitt (2005) studied the effects of service provider demographics on turnover and profitability. Through the study, the researchers illustrated the necessity for demographic matching, though not necessarily identical matches are warranted. Linkages were established between racial diversity of the staff and turnover rates, which in itself contributes to profitability. Second, disparity in demographics, including racial composition and socio-economic status, between the customer and service provider affected sales and profitability (Sacco & Schmitt, 2005).

Presently, human resources has become "gatekeepers for whom and how many to hire," although the immediate supervisor will probably understand which candidate would work best in a position (Tracey & Nathan, 2002). According to Dickson (2007), human resource managers need to talk to five people for every one person they hire to be staffing with folks that are aligned with an organization's strategy. Specifically, Dickson (2007) said The HR function is integral to maintaining the service culture in any hospitality organization. Perhaps the most important task is the acquiring of the right talent for service and to fit a company's culture. Not everyone has the ability to function in the hospitality industry and from those that do, not all can function within a specific company culture. Thus, selection of talent becomes a major imperative for the human resources department in helping to maintain a certain organizational culture and climate.

One of the major areas where HR lets the operators down is in gaining a large enough pool of applicants from which to choose. Unless there is at least a 5:1 interview to hire ratio; HR has not done its job and the organization cannot be selective enough to provide the operator with the service-oriented talent necessary to maintain the culture.

After the potential employees are identified, a screening process should begin. In a study conducted by Hickman and Mayer (2003) in a Florida theme park, hiring managers are asked to inspect applicants for six qualities: (1) a team player attitude, (2) guest service orientation, (3) business savvy, (4) leadership potential, (5) personal and professional style, and (6) communication skills. After the right people are selected, it is necessary to begin proper training. In order to develop a successful service culture, an internal marketing program must be implemented and managed by the human resources department. George and Groonroos (as cited in Bowen & Ford, 2004) described internal marketing as the philosophy for managing the organization's human resources department centered from a marketing perspective. This includes the front line employees that handle customers and their back of the house support employees. It is critical for all employees to understand the impact they have on the external customer and the effect that they have on each other internally (Bowen & Ford, 2004). To begin this process and immersion into an organization's culture, training programs should begin with an orientation led by the human resources department (Tracey & Nathan, 2002). Adequate training and development of technical skills add value to human assets.

Conversely, deficiencies in the staff can be detrimental to profitability and overall unit success (Ebster, Wagner, & Valis, 2006). Beyond selection, HR needs to incorporate the service mission in every aspect of orientation and training in the organization. Then they need to use appropriate metrics to insure that the service mission is being represented rewarding and recognizing employees modeling exemplary service mission behavior. When a member of the organization is not living the service mission, HR must intervene quickly by correcting the individual, reassigning the individual to a role that better fits their talents, or by separating from the individual through termination in cases of recurring inappropriate behaviors (Dickson, 2007).

Further training should continue from the new employees' department managers (Tracey & Nathan, 2002; Hickman & Mayer, 2003). Training must begin in this manner so that a climate for service is well established and an employee can receive an introduction into an organization's culture (Bowen & Ford, 2004). The effect of the employee's personal experience on the job can affect the quality of the onsite experience for customers (Bowen, 1990).

In hospitality organizations, the managerial functions of motivation, leadership, and command differ as the service being delivered is more intangible in nature. The nature of the business and the service situations that arise is reason enough for employees to become empowered or self-managed (Hickman & Mayer, 2003; Bowen & Ford, 2004). There are benefits to both the employee and customer when an employee has decision-making ability. A front line service provider will know and understand a customer's needs and will be able to anticipate the customer's needs and know what to do to satisfy each specific need. It can also act as a buffer against job-related stress and tension creating situations because it gives employees the confidence to use their experiences to create problem solutions. This type of service culture can influence an employee's motivation to satisfy the tension (Ramlall, 2004).

Human resource departments have an obligation to the company to recruit, select, hire, train, and retain the best employees. Current research has shown positive relationships between good human resource practices and increased financial performance (Hinkin & Tracey, 2000). According to research conducted by Delery and Doty, (as cited in Hinkin & Tracey, 2000), results-oriented performance appraisals, employment security, and profit sharing are three human resource practices that have demonstrated these effects.

Service culture development

Though in some form presented above, there are many steps or strategies possible for developing service culture within hospitality organizations which minimize internal service gaps for HR departments when developing a service culture within their organizations. A summary of some of the actions that can be made as suggested by Cannon (2002) includes the following seven steps. First, establish an organizational culture that values employees as essential contributors to the success of the company and continuously display the notion that quality internal service leads to quality external service. Second, enhance the support from the executive leaders for a work environment that is collaborative featuring empowered, respected, and trusted employees. Third, recruit and select employees that are enthusiastic about service. Fourth, maximize performance for employees by providing the tools necessary for success. Fifth, encourage open communication with employees and understand individual needs relating to their work place needs and quality of life. Sixth, institute a plan for development of employees for the present and the future and let them become active in the participant management approach. Seventh, create programs through the training of managers that acknowledge and reward quality internal and external service. These steps will help reduce the potential onset of service errors while creating an innovative culture of service that can be consistently employed throughout the entire organization.

Other literature concerning service culture and human resource management

Finally, if we were to consider emergent themes and literature review relevant to this specialized subject, Lucas and Deery (2004) conducted a human resource literature review over five prominent hospitality journals showing the importance of culture and climate. The linkages to service quality and human resource management come up again and again over only 2 years. They found many articles surrounding the topic and suggested that more specific and theory building work begin rather than just a mimicking of previous generic human resource work. It was clear that the research is vast concerning employee satisfaction, motivation, and human resource management across many industry segments including theme parks, hotels, restaurants, state parks, and many other venues. An extension of this literature review is suggested to update the current literature but is beyond the scope of this chapter which covers possible organizational culture types and actions human resource managers can take to further improve service climate and culture within an organization as written by human resource and service scholars.

Future studies regarding the perceptions of human resource departments regarding their responsibility in creating a service culture as compared with the rest of the organization may prove helpful as well as studies demonstrating top management's expectation for the human resource management office as compared with human resource's expectation followed by a surveying of employees. In the literature it is typical for many employees and management teams to express frustration with the human resource department which lends towards poor internal customer service and leads to a poor organizational climate. Qualitative interviews to probe deeper into people's thoughts and reactions to observe whether service culture perceptions have changed, stayed the same, or are indifferent before, during and after service initiatives have been activated by a human resource department. Finally, case studies across companies of different sizes and HR structures could be helpful for further specifying roles of HR in fostering and maintaining a service culture.

A longitudinal research approach within one company may help gain understanding of how employees' needs may change over time in a service culture. This longitudinal approach could develop a set of internal and external service standards that are company specific and investigate whether standards and employee expectations change over various spans of employment. Finally, service culture research across different hospitality organizational structures may not be generalizable leaving room for service culture research as it relates to the human resource management function. The Lucas and Deery (2004) article suggested as one area related to service climate and human resource management as the role of HR in impacting employee and family quality of life due to unusual work schedules. Beyond this suggestion, the importance of employee emotions at work and how that influences other employees whether as LLX or LMX may prove beneficial in strengthening the research stream. For example, a recent study by Wall and Berry (2007) investigated customer's perceptions of three types of clues in a restaurant with the humanic clue being the perceived demeanors and emotional aspects of servers while other clues were more physical or visual in nature. A similar study used internally in an employee-to-employee exchange may provide helpful insight into perception of service climate across human and physical dimensions.

Conclusions and summary

This chapter suggests many different approaches to develop service cultures within hospitality organizations sharing only a brief review of the literature on the subject but focused on prescriptive actions that HR can take to develop a service culture and climate. First a suggestion of matching the culture to the job environment was suggested by using high and low levels of sociability and solidarity. Further, the type of culture that aligned best with most hospitality and leisure businesses was suggested to be the communal service culture environment. Once the culture type is decided, four traits within service climate were identified. Together, these traits make service climate. Due to the importance of hospitality, authors' added hospitableness as a fourth dimension. The alignment of the climate and the culture was shown as crucial for accomplishing the desired culture in an organization. From the organizational climate, an organizational culture is developed through the culmination of how individuals in an organization act and react.

Next, the authors focused on the potential role of HR in developing and maintaining a service culture. The importance of inter-departmental communications to service culture was presented suggesting HR as a champion for the improvement of inter-departmental communication. Next, the types of HR intervention, HRs representation of company values and traits was proposed, the specific functions of HR were presented including staffing from recruitment to retraining. Finally, steps that HR can take towards ensuring a culture of internal service for employees were detailed.

Certainly the human resource intervention will vary with structure of organization with large corporate restaurant chain human resources management functions differing from human resources in a small one-city restaurant chain. Since our discussion centered on the roles of HR roles in achieving a service culture, a limitation of this chapter is that various industry structures were not considered yet the information presented here can be adapted to different HR structures.

However, gaining an insight of each role HR portrays, as detailed in the example by Ulrich (1998) offers a better understanding to an organization's cohesion. Within these roles, human resource practitioners are asked to perform their job functions efficiently while observing, maintaining, and reacting to the organization's culture. The strategy begins with recruiting and selection, moves forward to training that includes an introduction to the organization's culture through orientation, continues with departmentalized training by managers, and empowers employees with decision-making abilities in relation to guest service. In summary, the approach to creating a service culture can be achieved by several different methods. Different strategies on how to develop and attain a culture have been addressed along with the suggestion to minimize gaps from the human resources department.

References

Bowen, D. E. (1990). Interdisciplinary study of service: Some progress, some prospects. *Journal of Business Research*, *20*(1), 71–79.

Bowen, J., & Ford, R. C. (2004). What experts say about managing hospitality service delivery systems. *International Journal of Contemporary Hospitality Management*, *16*(7), 394–401.

Cannon, D. F. (2002). Expanding paradigms in providing internal service. *Managing Service Quality*, *12*(2), 87–99.

Chen, C., & Huang, J. (2007). How organizational climate and structure affect knowledge management—the social interaction perspective. *International Journal of Information Management, 27*(2), 104–118.

Collins, A. B. (2007). Human resources: A hidden advantage. *International Journal of Contemporary Hospitality Management, 19*(1), 78–84.

Davis, J., Schoorman, D., Mayer, R., & Tan, H. H. (2000). The trusted general manager and business unit performance: Empirical evidence of a competitive advantage. *Strategic Management Journal, 21*(5), 563–576.

Davidson, M. C. G. (2003). Does organizational climate add to service quality in hotels? *International Journal of Contemporary Hospitality Management, 15*(4), 206–213.

Dickson, D. (2007). Interview with Dr. Duncan Dickson, March 8, 2007, University of Central Florida.

Ebster, C., Wagner, U., & Valis, S. (2006). The effectiveness of verbal prompts on sales. *Journal of Retailing and Consumer Services, 13*, 169–176.

Enz, C. A., & Siguaw, J. A. (2000). Best practices in service quality. *Cornell Hotel and Restaurant Administration Quarterly, 41*(5), 20–29.

Fleet, D., & Griffin, R. (2006). Dysfunctional organization culture: The role of leadership in motivating dysfunctional work behaviors. *Journal of Managerial Psychology, 18*(8), 698–708.

Folaron, J. (2005). The human side of change leadership. *Quality Progress, 38*(4), 39–43.

Francis, H., & D'Annunzio-Green, N. (2005). HRM and the pursuit of a service culture. *Employee Relations, 27*(1/2), 71–85.

Hickman, J., & Mayer, K. J. (2003). Service quality and human resource practices: A theme park case study. *International Journal of Contemporary Hospitality Management, 15*(2), 116–119.

Hinkin, T., & Tracey, J. B. (2000). The cost of turnover. *Cornell Hotel and Restaurant Administration Quarterly, 41*(3), 14–21.

Johnstone, A., & Johnston, L. (2005). The relationship between organizational climate, occupational type, and workaholism. *New Zealand Journal of Psychology, 34*(3), 181–188.

Lucas, R., & Deery, M. (2004). Significant developments and emerging issues in human resource management. *International Journal of Hospitality Management, 23*(5), 459–472.

Martin, J. (1992). *Cultures in organizations.* Oxford University Press New york,.

Paraskevas, A. (2001). Internal service counters in hotels: An empirical study. *International Journal of Contemporary Hospitality Management, 13*(6), 285–292.

Ramlall, S. (2004). A review of employee motivation theories and their implications for employee retention within organizations. *The Journal of American Academy of Business, Cambridge, 5*(1/2), 52–63.

Raub, S., Alvarez, L., & Khanna, R. (2006). The different roles of corporate and unit level human resources managers in the hospitality industry. *International Journal of Contemporary Hospitality Management, 18*(2), 135–144.

Rogg, K., Schmidt, D., Shull, C., & Schmitt, N. (2001). Human resource practices, organizational climate, and customer satisfaction. *Journal of Management, 27*(4), 431–449.

Sacco, J., & Schmitt, N. (2005) A dynamic multilevel model of demographic diversity and misfit effects. *Journal of Applied Psychology, 90*(2), 203–231.

Schneider, B., Gunnarson, S., & Niles-Jolly, K. (1994). Creating the climate and culture of success. *Organizational Dynamics, 23*(1), 17–30.

Seibert, J., & Lingle, J. (2007). Internal customer service: Has it improved? *Quality Progress, 40*(3), 35–40.

Schein, E. H. (1983). The role of the founder in creating organizational culture. *Organizational Dynamics, 12*(1), 13–28.

Schein, E. (1985). *Organizational culture and leadership.* Jossey-Bass, San Francisco, CA.

Schein, E. (2004). *Organizational culture and leadership*, Wiley.

Schulte, M., Ostroff, C., & Kinicki, A. (2006). Organizational climate systems and psychological climate perceptions: A cross-level study of climate-satisfaction relationships. *Journal of Occupational and Organizational Psychology, 79*, 645–671.

Shanock, L. R., & Eisenberger, R. (2006). When supervisors feel supported: Relationships with subordinates' perceived supervisor support, perceived organizational support, and performance. *Journal of Applied Psychology, 91*(3), 689–695.

Tangirala, S., Green, S., & Ramanujam, R. (2007). In the shadow of the boss's boss: Effects of supervisors' upward exchange relationships on employees. *Journal of Applied Psychology, 92*(2), 309–320.

Teare, R. (1993). Designing a contemporary hotel service culture. *International Journal of Service Industry Management, 4*(2), 63–73.

Tower, D., & Rodrigues, S. (2007). An investigation into whether organisational culture is directly linked to motivation and performance through looking at Google, inc. An unpublished extended essay, 1–31.

Tracey, J. B., & Charpentier, A. (2004). Professionalizing the human resources function. *Cornell Hotel and Restaurant Administration Quarterly, 45*(4), 388–397.

Tracey, J. B., & Nathan, A. E. (2002). The strategic and operational roles of human resources: An emerging model. *Cornell Hotel and Restaurant Administration Quarterly, 43*(4), 17–26.

Ulrich, D. (1998). A new mandate for human resources. *Harvard Business Review, 76*(1), 124–134.

Varoglu, D., & Eser, Z. (2006). How service employees can be treated as internal customers in the hospitality industry. *The Business Review*, 5(2), 30–35.

Wall, E., & Berry, L. (2007). The combined effects of the physical environment and employee behavior on customer perception of restaurant service quality. *Cornell Hotel and Restaurant Administration Quarterly*, February, 48(1), 10–22.

Wong, J., & Lin, J. (2007). The role of job control and job support in adjusting service employees' work-to-leisure conflict. *Tourism Management*, 28(3), 726–735.

Zeithaml, V., Parasuraman, A., & Berry, L. (1988). Delivering service: Balancing expectations and perceptions. New York, NY: The Free Press.

CHAPTER **7**

Employee relations: a problem-solving approach

R. Thomas George

Hospitality Management Program
The Ohio State University
Columbus, OH 43210-1295, USA

Introduction

The establishments of the hospitality industry employ a wide variety of individuals, each having a unique experience, skill set, and motivational pattern. A high level of employee turnover is not only costly but also highly inconvenient when attempting to deliver a consistent level of quality product and high level of service. Hinkin and Tracey (2000) found that employee turnover runs into the thousands of dollars and has a negative affect on moral and service quality. They also suggest that poor supervision is a contributor to the problem. It is to the advantage of the unit manager to have a variety of tools to assist employees to perform at a high level.

This chapter presents a discussion of employee relations from a problem-solving orientation. The set of activities of employee relations will be defined and discussed. The nature of employee performance problems: causes and approaches to correction will be presented in a problem-solving manner. The concept of progressive discipline as well as two approaches to counseling employees will be discussed. The corrective interview and employee-centered counseling, will be presented as means of assisting employees who may be having problems that may have an affect on job performance. The goal is to develop strong employee relationships by taking a positive approach to correcting problems.

Employee relations

Employee relations may be described as a wide variety of activities all designed to improve and maintain quality relationships within the organization. Lucas (1995) suggests that employee relations is about the management of employment and work relationships. In general, it may include those functions related to the recruitment, hiring, training, and career development of employees. It might also include the communication activities related to the management of organization–employee, manager–employee, and employee–employee relationships. The development of a productive work environment may be included in the domain of employee relations as well as the administration of compensation and benefits programs. The employee relations department is involved in assisting employees settle in to the work environment and preventing and resolving problems arising out of the relationship. Formal employee assistance programs may fall under this umbrella. Tesone (2005) refers to employee relations as "Maintaining rapport with workers while satisfying their needs." (p. 14)

In some organizations the employee relations department may be chiefly concerned with the development of the organization–union relationship. This would include the negotiation of the contract, the administration of the ongoing contract, and the procedures involved in the maintenance of the grievance process. In non-union situations, it may be involved in conflict resolution and performance problem solving. Jerris (1999) suggests that in non-union organizations the concern of employee relations is promoting more effective communications without the involvement of a union. These may include the administration of coaching to improve performance, counseling to help resolve personal and job-related issues, and, when necessary, the steps involved in progressive discipline.

Depending on the size and degree of centralization, these activities may be organized into departments located at a central or regional office or they may be vested in the individual operating unit and its management. The overall function may be referred to as: the Department of Employee Relations, Human Resources, or as Personnel. Each of these may be further subdivided as: employment, training and development, benefits and compensation, and health and safety. All of these may fall under a variety of names and structures. In highly decentralized organizations, individual unit managers will often be responsible for the implementation of many of these programs at the local operating level.

Just as the manager must be skilled in interviewing job applicants and skilled in training new jobholders, they must be skilled in working with employees who are having performance problems. The ability to communicate with those seemingly distracted or not mentally with the job performance is also important.

The remainder of this chapter will address the activities involved in employee relations and working with the problem employee. Included will be the identification of the problem employee, progressive discipline, and employee counseling.

The nature of the problem employee

The individual labeled as a "problem employee" is often one who is doing something that the supervisor is displeased with, not doing what the supervisor feels he or she should be doing, or not doing the tasks well enough. The problem behavior may be related to the present job performance of the employee, such as not getting orders correct or not completing the job function according to specifications. It may be that he or she is chronically late or often absent. The employee might also be expressing what often falls under the heading of "bad attitude," a term having many interpretations. These individuals are often described as being lazy or having no ambition. In essence, the individual seems to have a poor outlook on all or part of his or her environment. This feeling is often manifested through speaking negatively of others or the company, presenting an appearance of sullenness, or lack of courtesy to others. There are other times when the capable employee is distracted or not giving the job his or her full attention. The result of this "problem" behavior is often reduced productivity, increased costs, and poor service. It may affect other employees by contributing to a reduction of morale.

At this time the supervisor may take any one of several approaches to dealing with the individual. Avoiding the situation in hoping that it will either correct itself or go away will not work. Quite often the undesired behavior will get worse and quite possibly be contagious, with others seeing the behavior as being acceptable. Complaining is often a path taken by many supervisors. In addition to inner grumbling, they may complain about the problem employee to other supervisors and often to other employees. Complaining often increases the tension and leads to additional problems and bad feelings. The supervisor must be both willing and able to confront the situation and work for a successful resolution. Rather than avoid confrontation, many will overreact. They will become excited, raise their voice, gesture wildly and often say something not desirable, sometimes regrettable. A process guaranteed to bring abut a loss of respect and ridicule. Lecturing the "problem" employee on the desirability of quality performance often leads to negative feelings on the part of the employee. Who enjoys being lectured to, especially if the real issue is not addressed? None of these approaches work to resolve the problem issue on a long-term basis.

When thinking of employee performance problems, it is necessary to examine the performance of the employee and the end result of that performance. What is it that causes you to be less than completely satisfied with the performance of the employee? What should the employee be doing or not doing for you to feel there is not a problem? Then asking what may have a negative influence on the performance of the employee. What might be contributing to the problem as you see it? The questions must be specific and seek observable evidence. While a "gut" feel might cause you to believe that something is not right, it is not enough to make a formal determination that there is a problem. Additional observation and discussion are necessary to formulate a plan to determine the nature of the uneasy feeling and plan of corrective action, if necessary. Formal comparison of the individual's actions against the job performance standards is necessary to determine if there is a performance problem. A central question to be asked "is this performance problem related to a skill deficiency or is there something else getting in the way of successful performance"? It is also important that the manager/supervisor examine their own behaviors to determine if they might, in some manner, be contributing to the problem behavior of the employee. Is the supervisor giving sufficient information, the tools, and the time need for proper task performance?

The approaches to arriving at solutions to these issues are quite different and mixing the process, or not implementing them correctly, may lead to additional problems.

Responding to employee problems: progressive discipline

By definition, discipline is both a punishing activity and a learning activity. Discipline may be seen as an act that is taken to punish wrong behavior. It might also be seen as an opportunity to be education-focused in that the purpose is to assist the individual to develop the knowledge and skills to perform in a more proper manner.

Progressive discipline is a form of "discipline" that takes place over time. It seeks to set guidelines and eliminate any surprise actions by the employer. The actions are taken incrementally to correct the more serious "problem" behaviors. The actions will typically include: an oral warning, followed by a written warning of the problem behavior, time off without pay, and termination. There may be several meetings with the employee to assess progress in overcoming the "problem" behavior. The employee handbook will outline the process and the conduct subjected to a form of progressive discipline.

Any form of discipline must fall within the guidelines of the union contract, if a union is present. It should also utilize the formal grievance or appeals process in instances in which the employee disagrees with the definition of the problem or the form of discipline. Coaching, the use of the corrective interview and employee-centered counseling are some of the actions that may be used to help in seeking to correct problem behavior. Documentation by the supervisor is important to demonstrate that the actions were not somewhat arbitrary or illegally discriminatory.

Should all attempts to correct the problem behavior or skill deficiency, a form of punishment may be necessary.

Punishment may include: termination, suspension, demotion, loss of wages, or formal reprimand placed in the individuals personnel file. While punishment may demonstrate that the offensive behavior is not acceptable, it often does not bring about performance correction.

The problem with traditional discipline is that it may lead to disrespect of supervisor or employee, resentment, and no guarantee that the behavior will change for the better. The attempts to correct the problem behavior and punishment given will be noticed by other employees. Others observing the process will draw conclusions as to the fairness of the actions taken. Often referred to as procedural justice and fairness. This decision may affect future work relationships.

John Huberman, writing in the Harvard Business Review (1964), suggested an approach to discipline without punishment. Believing that punishment does not always do what it is designed to do, Huberman presents an approach that does not include demotion, suspension, or other forms of punishment. In place are a series of reminders and discussions, and time off (with pay) to think about the behavior. The employee is given opportunity to make the decision to change or to seek other employment. Should the improper behavior be repeated, termination is initiated. The approach is designed to demonstrate regard for the employee while reinforcing the need to change.

In a union situation, the manager/supervisor must document all actions taken and demonstrate that attempts to assist the employee to correct the problem behavior. In the case of a labor–management impasse, the decision may go to arbitration.

Blancero and Bohlander (1995, p. 619) have identified six instances in which arbitrators have overturned or modified disciplinary actions. These include: lack of evidence, mitigating circumstances, rules violations, due process and industrial justice, severe punishment for misconduct, and management contributed to employee offence.

Believing that the traditional concept of progressive discipline is ineffective, Osigweh and Hutchison (1989) describe what they call positive discipline in seeking to respond to individual employee unacceptable behavior. The approach is one that seeks to make progressively serious contacts while eliminating hastiness in using punishment. In this approach the authors suggest an oral warning, a written warning, and then a decision-making leave. At this time the employee is to make a decision to make a total commitment to correcting the unacceptable performance or to leave and seek employment elsewhere. They believe the approach is useful in developing responsibility and self-discipline. Grote (2001) also endorses the paid leave time to reexamine feelings. He states it generates additional benefits as: good faith, transforms anger into guilt, reduces hostility, and reinforces your values.

While some offenses (i.e., theft, substance abuse on the job, or destruction of property) suggest immediate discharge, the above approaches to progressive discipline and punishment are often directed toward giving the employee an opportunity to change.

The following three methods may be used to help retain employees while seeking to correct the problem behavior. The methods examine both the problem behavior and the employee. All are development oriented rather than punishment oriented. Each is unique in that it seeks to involve the employee in arriving at acceptable solutions to present or potential performance problems.

Performance problems and coaching

When it is determined that the individual is not performing as desired, several questions must be asked to determine the causes of the poor performance. Does the individual know how to do the job? Has he or she performed according to the specifications in the past? Making the assumption that additional training is necessary is often not the answer.

Quite often the individual knows how to do the job and could do it properly if he or she had to. In this instance of a demonstrated performance deficiency, the supervisor assumes the role of a coach in assisting the employee to improve the performance or removing obstacles to proper achievement. While coaching may be used in conjunction with formal performance reviews (Wexley & Latham, 2002), it may also be used whenever the employee is deviating from the preferred practice. Pointing out errors in performance that the employee may not be aware of or explaining how to work more efficiently may be considered as coaching. Buzzotta, et al. (1977) suggest that coaching is a feedback process designed to assist the employee to become more proficient in the job.

There are some skills the supervisor must exhibit when doing performance coaching. Among these are the ability to listen, the ability to watch to determine the real performance deficiency, and the ability to give instructions in a manner that both respects the employee and reinforces the desired behavior.

There are times when the employee is able to do the job and does it quite well. The employee has demonstrated the necessary skills and the ability to use them. There are other issues getting in the way of successful performance. Consequently, a different approach to working with the problem employee is called for. The approaches discussed here are outside of the formal employee assistance programs and are seen as communication techniques easily mastered by managers and supervisors.

Employee counseling

The term "counseling" evokes many individual definitions and connotations. Then adding the "manager/supervisor" to the mix, additional feelings of concern arise. Should managers and supervisors engage in this activity called counseling? What about ethics and confidentiality? Many feel that counseling is working with people who have emotional problems and the workplace is no place for this activity.

Counseling differs from psychotherapy in that psychotherapy deals with more deep-seated personality problems, while counseling in the workplace becomes more of a supportive process in which the manager or supervisor helps an employee define a problem and arrive at a solution to that problem. The method by which the manager or supervisor communicates with the employee will have an impact on the success of the process and individual productivity. Counseling as described by Hansen, Stevic, and Warner (1972) is helping people adjust to life situations and make decisions to become more fully functioning. It does not deal with personality reorientation. In essence, counseling is a self-examination process by which a person examines a problem and arrives at a decision as to how to meet the situation. The counselor is there to act as a facilitator in the process.

When discussing the counseling process, two approaches are most often mentioned. Each has its place in maintaining a productive workplace. The first, known most often as directive counseling, is one in which the manager/supervisor takes a strong role in the process. The counselor structures the interview and is active in the search for a solution, often suggesting solutions. The second approach, known as non-directive counseling, is more employee-centered and the manager/supervisor takes a supportive role. The employee is responsible for the definition and solution to the perceived problem or concern. A concern that is or has the potential to interfere with job performance.

Directive counseling and the corrective interview

When coaching for skill improvement is not needed, a different approach is called for. An approach that is confronting the problem issue but problem solving and not seen as punitive. One that calls for different forms of communication. The corrective interview is a form of counseling that is more directive in nature. It involves the manager/supervisor in the definition of the problem and its solution, while involving the employee in the process.

The corrective interview is a face-to-face meeting to come to an understanding of what happened and what is to be done. It is an attempt to change the behavior of an employee so that the undesirable behavior or performance deficiency may be eliminated. It is an opportunity to demonstrate that you, the supervisor, do care about the employee and are interested in him or her as a member of the organization. The corrective interview is a problem-solving process easily implemented to improve performance and retain an employee.

The process may be useful when there are performance problems not related to a skill deficiency or a lack of ability. Often there are other issues inhibiting the desired performance and additional training or coaching is not appropriate. The issues may be related to lateness, absenteeism, not completing work on time, complaining, or not presenting a desired approach to guest service. It might also be related to interpersonal relations with other employees.

Stages of the corrective interview

The corrective interview has three stages. In the first stage the manager/supervisor prepares for the interview. Identifying the performance-related deficiency and being able to identify positive behavior change goals for the employee. Identifying the desired behavior changes for each goal is next. It is important to identify the areas where the employee is performing effectively. Being able to give specific examples of positive behavior will help take away the negative feelings of the interview. All of this is done by the supervisor to help set direction and a positive atmosphere for the discussion. Setting sufficient time for the interview and having a location lacking in distractions are important.

The second phase is conducting the interview. In conducting the interview, the supervisor states the reason for the interview and presents the issues as he or she sees it. The employee is asked for his or her opinion. At this time the supervisor demonstrates active listening and attempts to understand the feelings and reasoning of the employee. Through the discussion there must be an agreement that the issue is a problem and that it must be remedied. The manager/supervisor seeks information from the employee as to the contributors to the problem. This helps to set ownership of the problem and future solutions. Agreement of the causes is sought. A decision on an action is next. The employee is encouraged to suggest potential corrective actions. What the supervisor will do and what the employee will do to correct the undesirable behavior is identified. Again there must be an agreement on the actions to be taken. An integral part of the discussion is the provision for a follow-up activity. This is necessary in order to demonstrate the importance of the correction. Agreements on the action and the check on performance are mandatory. All through the corrective interview, the coming to agreement is central to the success of the process. If one party does not agree on the problem, the causes, the corrective action, or the follow-up, the potential for failure is increased. Positive statements regarding the employee's performance might be given at the beginning to help bring about a positive atmosphere or at the end to reinforce the feeling the employee is a valued contributor to the organization.

Follow-up then becomes the third phase to the corrective interview. This formal process is necessary in that it lets the employee know there must be correction and it gives the supervisor an opportunity to review the activity with the employee and that progress has been noted. The follow-up interview is an opportunity to determine if the agreed upon approach to solving the performance problem is working. This is an opportunity for the supervisor to demonstrate a sincere concern for the employee and the job performance of that employee. The time of the discussion should have been agreed upon during the corrective interview and be sufficient that improvement in performance be evident over a reasonable timeframe.

During the follow-up, one of several scenarios may play out. The employee has made significant progress and the undesired behaviors have disappeared. This is time for a statement of appreciation and positive reinforcement. It may be that the employee has worked hard and made some progress but work needs to be done to meet the standard. The supervisor may offer suggestions for continued improvement and encouragement. A third possibility is that the employee either has not made much progress or there is no change in behavior. The supervisor must make the decision that the prospects for desired change are low and a more severe action must be taken. In this case the supervisor has documented evidence that the opportunity to change has been given and the employee has not made use of the opportunity.

Throughout the corrective interview process, the need for acceptance of responsibility and agreement on action has been stressed. The supervisor and employee have identified a problem behavior and a process for correcting the undesired behavior. The corrective interview is a communication process in which the supervisor and employee have come together to solve a non-skill related performance problem. However, there are times when the employee is confronted by concerns that may have an affect on future performance. Coaching or the corrective interviewing process may not resolve these concerns. A different form of communication is called for in this instance.

Employee-centered counseling

There are often times when other issues become obstacles to proper and consistent performance by the otherwise proficient employee. These issues may have the potential to interfere with desired performance and may reduce the effectiveness of the employee. If the employee knows how to do the job and has done it successfully in the past, additional training or coaching is not the answer to working with this potential "problem employee."

A high quality worker may seem distracted or does not seem to be him/her self. The person is not exhibiting their usual behavior. They are doing the job, but not to their usual standard of performance. Level of attention, facial expressions, or tone of voice are not what is usually expected of that employee. They may be avoiding others or seem to be distracted or "moody". Something seems to be getting in the way of the desired performance, a performance they have demonstrated in the past. In this case additional training or performance coaching is not the answer nor is the corrective interview appropriate.

These issues may relate to personal problems stemming from home relationships, financial concerns, or health-related issues. There may be issues relating to relationships with coworkers or supervisors, or possibly career concerns. The individual may have substance abuse problems or be demonstrating apathy toward the job stemming from many directions. Employees have often been told to leave their personal problems at home and concentrate on the job while at workplace. However, when we hire the individual, we hire the whole person and not just a part of the individual.

Supervisors must be aware of employee behaviors as those behaviors have an impact on the quality of service provided to the guest. A distracted employee may not give the quality expected with the result being a potentially dissatisfied guest.

In all of these situations, the role of the supervisor changes from a coaching situation to one of counseling. While the role of the coach is to point out performance problems and to suggest corrections, the role of the supervisor in counseling is quite different.

Two situations are described below.

You, the supervisor, notice that an employee seems to be other than his or her usual upbeat self. There has been a gradual or quite possibly a sudden change in behavior. You are concerned that this change in behavior will affect the employee's work performance. What will you do?

Or perhaps the individual comes to you, the supervisor, and wants to talk about a problem. The "problem" turns out to be of a personal nature. It is important enough that it may have the potential to affect work performance. What will you do?

In response to the valued employee, you have a variety of response options. You might seek to ignore the employee's concerns by stating, "it's your problem—you solve it" or "don't worry, it will work out in time." You might use a directive counseling approach that is strong on advice giving: tell the employee what to do. Another response is to use a nondirective or employee-centered approach to counseling. Many supervisors are reluctant to use this counseling approach, as they are uncertain of how to proceed using this method or that solving personal problems of employees is not in their job description. However, the employee-centered approach is a communication process that may be mastered by nearly all supervisors. It is a natural to the trust building and communication processes necessary in effective supervision and the development of quality employee relations.

In each of the situations described above, you must be aware of the present and future feelings of the employee as well as the placement of responsibility for solving a problem that is not yours. In the first instance you may have told the employee that you do not care about them as individuals, or that their problem is not important. Nothing is done to help the employee over a stressful period. The performance could get worse or the employee loses respect for the supervisor. In the second option, the supervisor has accepted the responsibility for the presented solution and consequently for the outcome. As we often do not have all of the information necessary to give sound advice, we give advice on only the part we know. If the advice does not workout, the employee is tempted to blame the supervisor for the "bad" advice given. Employee relations, in these two options, have the possibility of deteriorating. The organization may lose a valued and productive employee. Other employees will notice what is happening and form opinions as to what extent the organization or the supervisor cares about them as people.

The option of acting in a counseling situation is often one that is not practiced due to a lack of knowing what to do. However, when utilized with skill and understanding, the process has the ability to help the employee identify potential solutions, but also to develop additional problem-solving skills and confidence. It also helps identify the supervisor as one who cares about employees and sees them as more than hired hands. In a time of strong competition and high employee turnover this relationship may help to increase the effectiveness of the business.

Employee-centered counseling and the supervisor

A working definition of employee-centered counseling is that it is a meeting between a manager or supervisor and an employee in which the employee attempts to better understand a problem and successfully identify approaches to successfully deal with the concerns. The manager/supervisor acts as a facilitator in the process.

It is important to note that this is not a therapy session. It is the creation of a supporting atmosphere in which an employee is able to express a concern to a supervisor and come to a better understanding of the problem and develop possible solutions. The concern may be affecting the employee's present job performance or have the potential to do so. It may be or may not be job related. The responsibility for the solution remains with the employee.

This is a communication process in which the supervisor is required to listen carefully, to remain non-judgmental, and refrain from being directive. That is, the employee states the problem as he or she sees it. In the process the supervisor does not attempt to diagnose the employee's problem and therefore does not offer a solution, or offer advice as to what to do. Employee-centered counseling also requires that the supervisor be an active listener, be able to reflect feelings of the other person, and to use questioning with care (Ruch, 1973).

The supervisor's purpose is to help the employee arrive at a solution to his or her own problem. The supervisor does not take responsibility for the problem or the solution to it. However, the supervisor is responsible for the productivity of the employee and therefore has a responsibility to help maintain a high level of employee development. This process may be useful when an employee wants to talk about career development, problems with other employees, some personal problems, or is dissatisfied with some aspect of company policy.

This approach to working with the employee requires the supervisor to accept and demonstrate certain views. Views most would agree are representative of effective supervisors. Zima (1971) suggests that the following views are important

- The individual is responsible for himself.
- A person is capable of solving his or her own problems, once he recognizes them.
- People want to be understood, not judged.
- The supervisor must see the employee as an important person.
- The supervisor must project an attitude of acceptance of the employee.
- The supervisor must serve as a facilitator of, or helper, as the employee seeks to work out his own problems.
- The supervisor must not allow the employee to come to depend on him, but must help the employee to come to depend on himself.

If the supervisor is unable to accept the above views, there is the chance that he or she will become more directive in the approach to working with the employee. This could result in additional problems in the future regarding dependency, responsibility, and seeking advice. The approach is consistent with what McGregor (1960) would call Theory Y assumptions about people.

The employee-centered counseling process

There are several planning concerns over the use of the employee-centered approach to working with the employee. These concern both physical and psychological issues. The timing and location of the discussion must be appropriate as the supervisor must be able to concentrate on the discussion and maintain the confidentiality of the discussion while meeting the needs of the employee.

The supervisor must put him or herself in the right frame of mind to hold the discussion with preconceived notions, solutions, and experiences being put aside. The supervisor being mentally prepared will help to put the employee at ease and establish rapport. This may be accomplished by demonstrating interest in the concerns of the employee and by being patient. Not arguing, admonishing, or displaying authority will aid in letting the employee get to the problem. This is not the time to judge or evaluate the employee's concern and displaying authority is a turnoff. The supervisor must listen carefully to words and for feeling. It is important that the supervisor not advice the employee, but may help to clarify courses of action. It is the employee's concern and the employee is responsible for the solution.

Another concern is the skill needed to be effective in this form of problem solving. The supervisor may believe that he or she does not have the needed skills to "counsel" employees who have personal concerns. However, many of the skills necessary in employee-centered counseling are those considered necessary in effective supervision of employees. The desire to not get involved is strong, however the desire to have smiling and productive employees must be stronger. Involvement in the process is limited to being a facilitator and demonstrating interest in the employee. The supervisor does not accept responsibility for the problem and its solution. That is reserved for the employee.

Three phases of the employee-centered interview

The non-directive interview process may be divided into three phases (Benjamin, 1969, p. 19). In each one the employee is exploring the concern and possible approaches to managing that concern. The supervisor is acting as a support and one who values the employee as a person.

Initiation phase • • •

In this phase it may be the employee who initiates the discussion or it may be the supervisor who initiates the discussion by addressing an observed concern and seeking the employee's thoughts. If the supervisor initiates the discussion, it may be by asking how the employee feels today or a statement recognizing that the employee seems to be distracted or not himself or herself. It may be brought up in friendly conversation without a feeling of judgment. The employee may initiate the discussion by stating a desire to talk about a concern or something that is on his/her mind. The concern may be job-related or a personal issue. Directive statements as "What's wrong with you?" are not appropriate. However, openings as: how are you doing, you look distracted is anything wrong, or other casual statements indicating interest in the person are acceptable and invite the employee to talk.

As the employee may seem to be hesitant to speak or may seem to ramble, it is the role of the supervisor is to put the employee at ease, establish rapport, and demonstrate interest. At this time the employee will be determining if you are willing to listen or will take charge of the situation and tell him what to do. The phase ends when there is agreement on the topic for discussion. However, the focus of the discussion may shift during the exploration or development phase as feelings of trust grow and as the employee explores the concerns.

Exploration or development phase • • •

This involves a discussion of the concerns of the employee. The supervisor listens, invites expression of feeling, and seeks to reflect the feelings expressed. In this phase concerns are brought out and potential solutions may be explored. All subjects being introduced by the employee. It is important to permit the employee the opportunity to express all feelings, as the initial feeling expressed may not be the real concern. At this time it is also important to remember the iceberg and that most of it is under water and hidden from view. Often, much of the employee's concern has not been expressed it is still hidden. Giving advice at this time may prove to be disastrous. Also, sharing personal experiences may not be helpful as each experience is personal and may be taken as making the employee's concern seem less important.

In this phase the supervisor may demonstrate active listening skills, those showing interest and that you are seeking to understand the employee's concern. Facial expressions and head nods are important. They convey a message of attentiveness to the employee, however overdoing it is distracting. The supervisor may demonstrate an acceptance of the feelings of the employee. This is not to be confused with agreement or approval. It means that you have accepted the feelings of the other as being important to that person. This permits the other to continue without fear of judgment. Reflecting feelings may be important in demonstrating acceptance.

During the discussion the employee may bring up a possible approach to a means of addressing the concern. The supervisor may ask "what do you think would happen if you did that"? This is an opportunity for the employee to determine, for him/herself, if this is a possible course of action. The question is posed in a non-judgmental or evaluative manner.

When the concern is future job development or career-related the supervisor might give information helpful to the employee in making a decision. This is information the employee might not have immediate access to or not be aware of. The information may stimulate additional discussion and thought regarding potential training or education to assist in career advancement.

If the concern is of a more deep-seated personal nature the supervisor may ask if the employee has considered other avenues of assistance. It is important for the supervisor to know his or her limitations and be able to refer to those with additional resources. At this time there may be possible referrals to other sources of help given. Being able to list a variety of options is helpful, such as financial or legal counseling. Perhaps there is another more skilled in assisting the working through of the employee's concerns. None of these are suggested; all are offered as possibilities for the employee to consider and are offered only after demonstrations of acceptance of the employee's concern have been expressed. Statements as: have you considered … or what about … may be useful in the referral process. When the concern involves emotional or psychological difficulties and issues related to alcohol or drug abuse, referral is needed. The phase winds down when the employee seems satisfied with a potential course of action or a referral is made.

Closing phase • • •

This is an ending of the discussion with no new information being introduced. It may include a summary statement of the concerns of the employee and the employee's solution and process for implementation. The purpose is to reinforce support for the employee and the decision he or she made. This closing will have an effect on the feelings of the employee and an overall impression of the value of the discussion. Was there some measure of relief or greater understanding and future action?

Counseling tools

There are many additional tools the supervisor might employ in the non-directive counseling session. At times the supervisor may want to reflect the feelings of the employee. Here only expressed feelings should be reflected. A statement as "I can see that you are really concerned about this," may demonstrate acceptance of the employee and the importance of the concern. The supervisor might restate the employee's expressed ideas in their own words. This lets the employee hear what he or she has said and permits additional individual reflection. When restating remarks, place them as statements and not as questions.

While it is acceptable to ask questions for clarification, care must be taken to not be judgmental or attempt to redirect the discussion. Probes may be used to explore specific issues the employee expresses. These must be used with care. Give time for the person to pause and reflect on their thoughts. Silence is a valuable technique allowing the employee time to think about what is happening. It is common that many feelings and thoughts will be expressed. There may be some ambivalence on the part of the employee as to what to do. Reflection of feelings, restatement of thoughts, and questions for clarification may assist the employee to be able to more clearly examine his or her concerns. At this time the supervisor must not diagnose or give advice. Often we will want to assume we know the problem, however what appears is often not the real issue. Avoid being solution-minded. The solution must come from the employee's own thoughtfulness. It is the employee who must implement and live with the outcome.

In this process it is important that the supervisor restrains from saying, "I know how you feel." or "That happened to so-and-so and they did ..." Each concern is unique to the individual and has an emotional component. Playing amateur psychologist and diagnosing the problem will not be appreciated. Supervisors must be careful to not be persuaded to give advice. Advice giving is usually based on our own experience and not that of the other.

There are times when the coaching and counseling efforts have not been successful and the behavior of the employee has not changed. The supervisor is required to take a more formal approach to demonstrating the need for the employee to change his or her behavior.

Should the need for termination of the employment relationship occur, the documentation of the coaching and corrective interview is important. However, when speaking with an employee concerning personal problems, confidentiality is of the utmost importance. Documentation of the content of this discussion is not appropriate, nor is it ethical to relate the discussion to others.

Application to hospitality managers

The management of employee relations is a function of all hospitality managers requiring a variety of individual skills and approaches. In operations not having onsite human resource professionals, the individual manager and first line supervisor have the responsibility of performing many of the employee relation functions, but also to maintain quality relations with all employees.

The managers and supervisors in hospitality operations work with a variety of employees, each having their own approach to the work environment. They come with a variety of backgrounds and experiences and each relates to the work environment in their own way. Not only do skill levels vary, but willingness to use them also varies. They bring their own unique personality, needs, and motivations to work. None of these are left at home.

It is the manager and first line supervisor who must work with these individuals. Individuals who at times have job skill problems and at times performance problems that are not related to skill. They also have personal concerns that may interfere with performance. Each of these situations requires a different type of problem-solving skill. The more tools managers are available for working with the employees, the greater the opportunity for success of the business.

The use of coaching, the corrective interview, and employee-centered counseling are three tools that may be mastered to work with employees in a problem-solving mode. The skills are essentially communication skills, those necessary to successful supervision. They can be mastered and used to benefit all. In most instances they are not restricted to the work setting, but may used in a wide variety of settings.

Desired outcomes

The ability of the manager or supervisor to work with those individuals having performance problems will often significantly contribute to the success of the business. It is believed that the proper use of coaching for performance improvement, the corrective interview for correcting non-skill issues, and employee-centered counseling to help employees deal with a distraction will result in several desired outcomes.

Use of these techniques may result in reduced employee turnover by helping employees demonstrate a higher level of performance on the job. Employees feel better about their job skills and are more willing to do the job as desired. The techniques may result in the employee's having higher levels of self-esteem resulting in greater confidence. As the supervisor was willing to take the extra time and demonstrate interest in the employee, there may be higher levels of feeling about the company and respect for the supervisor. The manager/supervisor may gain increased levels of self-confidence in working with employees. Other employees may perceive increased fairness in company treatment of employee that may result in lower personnel costs. Increased levels of productivity and higher levels of service may result in greater profits.

Summary

The over arching goal of this chapter was to discuss the topic of employee relations from a problem-solving approach. In doing this we sought to define our terms and to identify causes of potential employee performance-related problems. We then outlined approaches to working with the problem employee. Coaching for performance improvement related to job skills. The corrective interview for working through non-skill problems was described. Then an approach to employee-centered counseling was outlined. The application to hospitality operations then discussed. All were given as added tools for the supervisor in maintaining quality employee relations.

References

Benjamin, A. (1969). *The helping interview*. Boston, MA: Houghton Mifflin Company.

Blancero, D., & Bohlander, G. W. (1995). Minimizing arbitrator "Reversals" in discipline land discharge cases. *Labor Law Journal, 10*, 616–621.

Buzzotta, V. R., Lefton, R. E., & Sherberg, M. (1977). Coaching and counseling: How you can improve the way it's done. *Training and Development Journal, 11*, 50–60.

Grote, D. (2001). Discipline without punishment. *Across the Board*, Sept./Oct., 52–57.

Hansen, J. C., Stgevic, R. R., & Warner, R. W., Jr. (1972). Counseling: Theory and process. Boston, MA: Allyn and Bacon, Inc.

Hinkin, T. L., & Tracey, J. B. (2000). The cost of turnover. *The Cornell Hotel and Restaurant Administration Quarterly, 41*(3), 14–21.

Huberman, J. (1964). Discipline without punishment. *Harvard Business Review, 42*(4), 62–70.

Jerris, L. A. (1999). *Human resources management for hospitality*. Upper Saddle River, NJ: Prentice-Hall, Inc.

Lucas, R. E. (1995). Managing employee relations in the hotel and catering industry. London: Cassell.

McGregor, D. (1960). *The human side of enterprise*. New York: McGraw-Hill.

Osigweh, C. A. B., & Hutchison, W. R. (1989). Positive discipline. *Human Resource Management*, *28*, 367–383.

Ruch, W. A. (1973). The why and how of nondirective counseling. *Supervisory Management*, *18*(1), 13–19.

Tesone, D. V. (2005). *Human resource management in the hospitality industry*. Upper Saddle River, NJ: Prentice-Hall, Inc.

Wexley, K. N., & Latham, G. P. (2002). *Developing and training human resources in organizations*. Upper Saddle River, NJ: Prentice Hall.

Zima, J. P. (1971). Counseling concepts for supervision. *Personnel Journal*, 50, 482–485.

Human resource management's role in ethics within the hospitality industry

Jalane M. Meloun

School of Adult and Continuing Education
Barry University
Miami Shores, FL 336161,
USA

Stephen E. Sussman

School of Adult and Continuing Education
Barry University
Palm Beach Gardens, FL 33410,
USA

Introduction

Ethics is an inherently challenging part of life. Humans are faced with ethical decisions on perhaps an hourly basis and the results of such decisions may be far-reaching and/or unintended. Executives in manufacturing, financial service, food service, and retail firms reported that ethics is a subject of concern in the workplace (Conaway & Fernandez, 2000). When looking specifically at the hospitality industry, it is easy to see how especially important it is to have ethical decisions made by employees. Often, a customer's perception of the entire organization stems from a single encounter with a sole front-line employee (FLE). Compounding the problem, oftentimes these interactions are unsupervised which can allow for greater temptations encouraging the employee to make unethical decisions.

Organizations are beginning to realize the importance of ethics and how it can impact not only the bottom line, but also employee satisfaction, retention, and productivity. That being said, the one part of the organization that is typically tasked with being responsible for the ethics of the employees is the human resources department. This may be because human resources deals with not only leadership and staffing in the organization, but also handles the employee training and development. Thus, this chapter's purpose is to shed some light on ethics, ethical decision-making, and the human resource department's role, as it relates to the hospitality industry.

Prevalence and impact of ethics

Current national state of affairs

Approximately every 2 years, the Ethics Resource Center (ERC) implements the National Business Ethics Survey (NBES) of employees across different sectors in the United States. The point of these surveys is to learn about employees' perceptions of ethics and compliance in the workplace. The most current survey was done in 2005. Since the NBES tracks employee perceptions over time, trends emerge. Unfortunately, ethical outcomes are showing a stagnant or declining trend. For example, during the range of 1994–2005, there was little change in percentage of employees who observed at least one type of misconduct during the past year; the percentage hovers at 52%. Thirty-six percent of those employees observed two or more violations. Further, of those employees who observed wrongdoing, barely over half (55%) reported it to a manager, which constitutes a 10 percentage point *decrease* since 2003 (NBES,

2005). In terms of how frequently employees feel pressure to compromise their own personal standards, 10% of employees reported they feel this way fairly often or always, which is comparable to levels reported in the 2003 survey (NBES, 2005). Taken together, the findings are astounding and suggest a fraying of the national moral fabric.

Ethics in the hospitality and tourism industries

The above results are from a commingling of employees from both the private and public sector. Let's turn attention to the hospitality industry. The industry as a whole lends itself to many instances of unethical behavior as the most common position in hospitality and tourism is the FLE. Cook *et al.* (2002) emphasized the importance of the FLE's behavior, specifically the attitude and demeanor during the service encounter. And it is this service encounter on which the hospitality and tourism organizations depend on for their very survival (Pizam & Ellis, 1999). Thus, if a FLE displays any behavior construed by the customer as unethical, then there is a chance that the customer will generalize the encounter to assume that the employing organization condones the behavior and is likewise unethical.

As a means of illustration, one of the authors has personal knowledge of a restaurant that has a counter where regulars come in every morning and only order coffee, totaling less than a dollar. Most patrons leave a dollar to cover the coffee and tip. The early morning crew of waitresses do not ring up the coffee, but pocket the entire dollar. This is such a typical behavior at this restaurant that it would be difficult to see how management is unaware of this frequent, daily standard, albeit unethical, operating practice. In this circumstance, the waitresses are clever, although not upstanding, to pocket the money from the coffee sales. The waitresses know that coffee refills to paying customers are free and thus quantity of coffee consumed by restaurant patrons on any given day is not traceable and therefore does not suggest impropriety. Carried further, nobody counts used coffee mugs either.

Risk of financial unethical practices can logically increase when the employees are dealing directly with money. On July 13, 2007, the Florida Highway Patrol charged three toll collectors at the Florida Turnpike with grand theft for stealing between $742 and $7400 each (3, 2007). Because the man who skimmed $7400 also violated a current probation, suspicion was cast upon his employer for having weak screening processes (Three, 2007). Several things may be learned from this.

First, it again illustrates that when FLE's are dealing with the public in an unsupervised manner, there is a potential for misconduct. Second, perhaps mere exposure to massive sums of cash provides too much temptation to some. And third, this incident shows that bad apple employees can cast a bad shadow on their employers.

Sometimes, the state of the industry itself or even the economy will set the stage for unethical behavior. For example, let's look at the lodging industry. It routinely deals with employee turnover rates as high as nearly 160% for some employees and has also had to deal with the downturn in revenues attributed to the economy's sluggishness and the terrorist attacks (Poe, 2003). The lower revenues can apply a downward pressure on wages, which negatively impacts turnover, which snowballs to poorer customer service from newly hired employees, etc. Sometimes hiring is done on the basis of getting a "warm body" to fill the position and other requirements are relaxed. To illustrate, in the aftermath of Hurricane Katrina, it was (and still is) difficult to get employees. "In the hospitality industry, for example, according to Troutman (a New Orleans attorney) and Perkins (VP and general counsel at an HR organization), a relaxed attitude toward drug testing is now becoming even more lenient in the Gulf Coast region. 'In some parts of the hospitality industry, drug testing wasn't prevalent even before the storm,' Troutman said" (Cadrian, 2006, p. 1). Thus, difficult circumstances may negatively impact ethical judgment.

Values and ethics

"Everyone operates from a set of values, whether they are established by family history, community imperatives, religious tradition, principles of the golden rule, or the values, all differences rule" (Williams, 1995, p. 65). This quote reminds us specifically that all employees are making their decisions on the basis of some moral philosophical system, whatever that may be. Each individual holds a set of values dear to his/her heart and these values become a governing force. The only problem is that employers typically are not privy to such employee values and may assume that employees have no basis whatsoever for their choices. Let's take an example of a McDonald's employee who is entitled to purchase any food or beverage product at a 50% discount. Let's further say that this employee chooses, instead of paying the reduced rate, to simply sneak some snacks into the restroom and consume them safely away from the security cameras. A McDonald's manager might come to the conclusion that the employee has stolen merchandise and that his decision to steal was wrong. The employee, on the other hand, may perceive that he is severely underpaid for the work he produces and he cannot afford to even pay the discounted rate for the food. He may feel he is righting the wrong of inequity of payment for his work productivity. The value that colored his choice to not pay for the snacks was his sense of fair treatment. Thus, the employee feels he "fixed" the unfair treatment that McDonald's dealt to him, and likewise, the manager thinks the employee has been unfair in violating an otherwise fair reduced employee rate policy. The bottom line is that it is crucial to realize that all people who have a certain minimum level of cognitive functioning are often operating on the basis of their value system.

At times, the ethical framework of decisions made by their employing organizations may impact employee perspectives, which, then, in turn, influence the ethical decisions made by those employees. For example, in a federally funded quality of employment study by the Family and Work Institute, a national sample of nearly 3000 wage and salaried employees was undertaken. Employees were surveyed on a multitude of issues, ranging from relationships with their bosses to household chores. Forty-two percent of the respondents had experienced downsizing in their corporations; 28% had watched management cutbacks in their corporations, suggesting that promotions were a thing of the past; and 20% feared being fired by the organization (Williams, 1995). With such drastic personal observations of management's behavior toward its workers, it is not difficult to understand that the survey's results suggested that American workers have become less loyal than the two previous generations.

Definitions

Ethics may be defined as a system of morals of a particular person, religion, or group. It may also be considered the rules that define right and wrong conduct. As alluded to above, ethics is based on an individual's perspective. Across people, there are several standard moral systems that govern moral thought, which then shows up as behaviors. There are numerous moral philosophies and to mention them all would be beyond the scope of this chapter. However some of the more common ones will be addressed in a hospitality context.

Moral philosophies

Perhaps the easiest moral philosophy to grasp is the *Rule of Conscience*. This philosophical system simply holds that one's own conscience is one's guide, as the old adage states. In theory, this is an excellent system as each individual self-polices, and this relieves others of the obligation of moral enforcement. However, in practice, this moral system falls short of being ideal as individuals have a wide range of behaviors that they can easily live with. A positive example is seen in the recent move by Steve Jobs, CEO of Apple. It is suspected that Mr. Jobs did not feel ethically comfortable making such a high profit (approximately 55%) on the Apple's iPhone and made an announcement that those who purchased the product within a certain number of weeks prior were either entitled to a partial refund or a voucher for other Apple products. In this case, the rule of conscience appears to have compelled Mr. Jobs to act in a manner beneficial to his customers. But, as mentioned, the rule of conscience does not always yield positive results. For example, one would hope that an employee who works at a weight-guessing booth at an amusement park would not make snide comments about those who were on the higher end of the scale. However, an employee in this position could simply be working for a paycheck and not feel a responsibility to be nice as she works for an hourly wage and customer satisfaction does not factor into her behavior. Thus, her conscience may be perfectly comfortable with her disrespectful comments.

Relativism is another common moral philosophy. This standard moral system holds that what is determined to be moral comes from what is normative in the culture in which the thought or behavior occurs. For example, in some cultures, it may be considered standard business practice to bribe the host of a restaurant for a table when no reservations have been made or to get a table that offers a better view. In other cultures, this may be considered bribery and unfair as others had enough forethought to call ahead and make a reservation and otherwise followed the standard "rules" of obtaining a table.

There is a category of moral philosophical systems called *Consequentialism* or *Teleology*. Aptly named, this division of systems places emphasis on the outcomes. An easy way to conceptualize these systems is to think of the phrase *the end justifies the means.* Let's take a look at general consequentialism before we get into the subtypes. Consequentialism is seen in the use of Electronic Performance Monitoring (EPM) which is "the use of electronic instruments, such as audio, video, and computer systems to collect store, analyze, and report individual or group performance" (Ambrose, 1998, p. 62). Organizations utilize EPM to observe, record, and report a wide range of worker activities with or without the employees' knowledge. Proponents of EPM state that monitoring is similar to other widely accepted managerial practices, and if implemented properly, will not create the abuses feared by critics. Proponents further argue that monitoring is an important tool that organizations can use to increase productivity, improve quality and service, heighten safety, and reduce costs. Advocates also suggest that electronic monitoring increases employee satisfaction and morale by resulting in more objective performance appraisals and improved performance feedback (Ambrose, 1998). For example, casinos typically use EPM to observe both employee and customer behavior to ensure rules are abided by and that no employee steals money. Thus the focus is on the end (i.e. rule following and money saving) to justify the means (i.e. monitoring of every employee movement). So, from the casino's perspective, the use of EPM is fully justified and stands on high moral ground. On the other hand, casino employees may feel differently as it enables employers to track how often and for how long employees make trips to the restroom, which could be construed as a violation of privacy.

As mentioned, consequentialism has subtypes, one of which is *Utilitarianism*. This moral philosophy is quite common and thus easily understood. Essentially, decisions are based on the perceived end result that offers the greatest good for the greatest number of people. Now, this begs the question of what constitutes the "greatest good" but this is solved by each individual's own perception of the greatest good in any given decision. Also, please take note that the greatest number of people does not award status differences to individuals; it simply implies that all people potentially affected by the decision are equal or interchangeable. An example should serve to clarify the concept.

Several years back, a national restaurant chain sent out a memo to all waitresses explaining that the new policy was to ask each customer who requested water whether a lemon slice was also desired. The memo further explained that each lemon slice cost the company one cent and with the approximated number of waters with lemon served to customers who did not want the lemon, this cost the company a sizeable loss of revenue annually. This decision could have been justified from the utilitarian perspective. The number of people inconvenienced (i.e. number of servers) was far outweighed by the number of people who benefited (e.g. customers who did not want lemon polluting their water, the prep cooks who sliced the lemons, the bussers who did not have to throw away unwanted lemon slices, and hypothetically the restaurant owners and stockholders who would enjoy increased net profits though cost savings).

Another subtype of consequentialism is *Egoism*. Again, the focus is on the outcome and not the means of obtaining it. However, egoism, as the name implies benefits one's self. Egoism itself subdivides into *Psychological Egoism* and *Ethical* or *Enlightened Egoism*. Psychological egoism suggests that individuals do act in manners that promote their own best interest. For example, let's say that a small hotel has no vacancy and a couple wanders in and bribes the front desk clerk into giving them a room someone else reserved. This becomes an ethical choice on the part of the front desk clerk and the couple who offered the bribe. This sounds counter to what we generally think is right and wrong; however, the basis on which we are making our decision is psychological egoism, not our own particular value system. Thus, the front desk clerk profits by pocketing some cash and the couple benefits by obtaining a room for the night. Each party served him/themselves. There is less initial consideration for others (i.e. the poor schmucks who took the time to make the reservation) from this moral system.

Ethical or enlightened egoism changes the focus from what some people *tend* to do (psychological egoism) to what people *ought* to do. To be clear, ethical egoism *recommends* that individuals make decisions that benefit them. At first glance, this seems counter to what is general thought of as moral advice. However, if we take a step back and look at the outcome of all individuals making their decisions on this basis, then each person ensures the best outcome for him/herself and with everyone individually bettered, then in aggregate, the group is bettered, as well. In addition, ethical egoism does inherently suggest that one would take into consideration the interests of others, when doing so would lead to more self-benefit, as is often the case. This aspect also makes this ethical perspective a little more palatable. For example, servers in a restaurant generally want to maximize the cash they take home at the conclusion of their shifts. Ethical egoism says that they should care about this as it increases their consumer purchasing power, ability to meet their financial obligations, etc. The moral system continues by suggesting that their self-interest in money will lead them to look for ways of augmenting their tips. The most obvious way to do so is to better please the customer. Thus, although it is a selfish interest that drives the service to improve, both the server and the customer benefit in the end.

Quite opposite to consequentialism is *Universalism*. Whereas consequentialism dispenses with the means to focus on the end, universalism does not care so much about the ending result because the emphasis is placed on the means. Essentially, universalism involves upholding certain values regardless of their immediate consequence. To revisit an earlier example, when Steve Jobs decided to lower the prices of the iPhone and refund money to those who were willing to pay the higher price, it is suspected that his action was propelled by his sense that he was choosing the right course of action. The concern was on the means of returning the money, not the negative effect it might have on the tremendous number of people who purchased their iPhones between their release date and 2 weeks before his announcement. Those affected individuals would be doubtless angry that they spent an additional $200 on a product that others got so much cheaper by waiting a relatively short time. Such an action also sets a bad precedent for any future Apple product as people will want to wait to see if the price drastically drops after it has been available for a while or people may continue to be late adopters of the product. In the worst case scenario, some people may never actually get around to purchasing the product because any day the price might drop and they never wish to purchase it before that happens. In essence, they are paralyzed from ever making the purchase.

Deontology is also easily contrasted with utilitarianism. Whereas utilitarianism regards each individual as equivalent to each other individual and the emphasis is on the greatest number of individuals impacted, deontology focuses on the rights of an individual. Each individual has rights and each one is to be respected. Following these lines, if there is an action that would benefit many, but would trample on the rights of one, it would not be considered as a viable, ethical option. For example, in this day and age when so many companies (e.g. Enron, Tyco, Adelphia, WorldCom) are in the headlines for scandals, it becomes tempting for a company that is suspected of wrongdoing to quickly name a scapegoat and expeditiously put the matter to bed. While this action may curry favor with the suspicious public and save many innocent employees' positions, such behavior would not be considered ethical under the deontological moral system as the scapegoat's rights have been violated. To aid your understanding, the same example *would* be considered an ethical choice according to utilitarianism because the greatest good for the greatest number of people was served.

Difficulties with ethical systems between people

This contradiction brings to light one of the problems with ethics in the workplace or elsewhere. If employees are making their decisions on the basis of their values and moral systems, then the differences between values/moral systems between people can be what causes problems. Typically what moral system an employee subscribes to is unknown, so even when the individual is basing decisions on one philosophical system, if it does not comport with someone else's system, then the individual's behavior, and thus the individual, is deemed unethical. This is compounded by the fact that ethics is one of those subjects that people rightfully feel they know about from experience (Ciulla, 1998). Such confidence in familiarity with the topic encourages people to feel justified that their particular philosophical system is *the right one*. Thus, it is important to understand that the differences between moral systems cause countless problems.

Human resource departments' responsibilities for ethics

With the knowledge that having sound ethics is important in the workplace, the next logical question is: Who should be responsible for the organizational ethics? Many point to the human resources department. Driscoll and Hoffman (1998), explain why HR departments should be responsible for implementing a company's ethics program. They make a case for the view that business has a social responsibility, and also suggest seven basic questions to help establish objectives for a company's ethics program, including establishing a set of standards, implementing these standards, and reevaluating the program efficiency and timeliness. They explain that "successful programs increase employee morale and foster a corporate culture that values honesty and integrity" (Driscoll & Hoffman, 1998, p. 123). They conclude that human resource departments are capable of establishing and implementing a successful ethics program. Mees and Bonham (2004) also suggest that corporate social responsibility and organizational ethics belongs to HR because this department can cut across all departments and systematically implement positive change.

Vickers (2005) also weighs in on the subject of HR's role in cultivating an ethic-friendly corporate environment. To be more specific, Vickers suggests that HR has four broad responsibilities

1. HR professionals must help ensure that ethics is a top organizational priority. Monitoring is a good start but alone will not suffice. HR executives must either take on the mantle of ethics champion or ensure that some other capable person in the organization does so. Such a champion will need to be highly experienced and respected, having enough organizational clout to make a difference.

2. HR must ensure that the leadership selection and development processes include an ethics component. After all, leaders at all levels of the organization need to both model ethical behavior and communicate ethical standards to employees. Selection procedures must filter out people who, despite making their numbers, are known for cutting ethical corners. Leadership development should include not only ethics theory but also real-life examples, perhaps from mentors, on how managers have handled ethical dilemmas in the past. Among the most difficult aspects of this may be convincing top management, perhaps including board members, that they too should receive ethics training. Promoting gender diversity among top leadership might also have a positive impact on ethics.

3. HR is responsible for ensuring that the right programs and policies are in place. HR professionals should, of course, be aware of legal guidelines and how they are evolving.

4. HR must be aware of ethics issues. This does not mean just following legislation, which tends to be reactive rather than proactive. It means looking at the entire social and business environment and spotting conflicts of interest and other ethics problems before they develop into full-blown scandals. A combination of tools can help with this. Obviously, employers need to pay close attention to the questions and concerns that are flagged via employee hotline services. Surveys or focus groups may also helpful in spotting potential ethical conflicts in the workplace. To gauge what is happening outside the company, HR can turn to environmental scanning techniques to imagine how new trends could result in large problems down the road (Vickers, 2005).

While human resource departments are suggested to be ultimately responsible for ethics, it is important to know who actually holds this accountability. A national survey found 8 out of 10 HR professionals claimed they were responsible for ethical leadership in their organization. Further, a full 95% of these respondents said that the HR staff should be responsible for ethical leadership in the organization (SHRM/CCH survey, 1991, as cited in Klingner and Nalbandian, 2003, p. 301). It is important to note that it was the HR professionals themselves who agreed that their own departments should shoulder this responsibility. In a time when employees are working more hours and handling more work during that time, it is somewhat refreshing to know that these professionals are not shirking this weighty duty.

Increasing organizational ethics

Training as a solution

Given that human resources departments are often tasked with handling the ethics in the organization and typically these departments are also ultimately responsible for the training and development of employees, these two responsibilities may be married, producing ethics training.

"If one accepts the premise that nonethical or unethical people can learn to behave ethically, then training can be a valuable tool for enhancing such learning. It is our premise that people are not born with values and standards. They are learned (or not learned) at home, in church, synagogue, or mosque, at school, and in the workplace. Inappropriate standards can be replaced with their own values. Voids in standards can be filled"

(Sims, 1994, p. 150).

Although the training may be performed either in-house or externally, it is becoming typical for organizations to conduct their own ethics training, using training specialists. If the objective of ethics training is ethical awareness, then the initial effort to increase ethical awareness should occur at the orientation session for new employees, another task that typically falls to the HR department. Providing basic information on the ethical practices of the organization is critical in helping new employees begin their work experience in the organization with the understanding and confidence that will support their making ethical decisions (Sims, 2002).

While ethics training is becoming more common in the workplace, it is important to note that there are problems and myths associated with teaching ethics (The importance of business ethics, 2001). One myth is that it is impossible to teach ethical behavior in the workplace. "The truth: Teaching ethical behavior in the workplace involves giving employees the opportunity to discuss relevant dilemmas in a non-threatening, supportive environment" (Importance, 2001, p. 17).

Reinforcing the ethics training

Let's say new employees at a national hotel chain are run through an ethics training session. If those individuals observe unethical behaviors on the job as commonplace, then the training was useless and will be perceived as a waste of time. Employees tend to pay more attention to what goes on and is accepted business practice rather than what was stated in a formalized ethics training program (NBES, 2005). Thus, it becomes important for leaders and current employees to put sound ethical principles into practice. Sims (1994) opines that

"the development of sound ethical practices becomes a realistic possibility when those who hold positions of leadership at all levels acquire an understanding of how ethical reasoning changes as individuals mature, how organization culture supports or inhibits the practice of sound ethics, and how to strengthen and reinforce decision making that supports highest standards of ethical reasoning and conduct" (p. 84).

When organizational leaders themselves display ethical behaviors, this leads to the organization being perceived as an ethical organization, which reaps advantages. "Organizations that have strong ethical values and consistently display them in all their activity derive other benefits, too: improved top-management control, increased productivity, avoidance of litigation, and an enhanced company image that attracts talent and earns the public's goodwill" (Sims, 1994, p. 5).

Beyond training

Having the HR department provide ethics training goes a way toward increasing the ethics in the organization, but it is not everything (NBES, 2005). Another way to augment the prevalence of better ethical choices is to examine what causes individuals to make the "wrong" choice in the first place. The Ethics Officer Association conducted a survey of 213 members from 150 different companies and found that the most commonly stated reason for contacting the ethics office was simply conflicts of interest. A whopping 74% of respondents mentioned this reason, demonstrating how pervasive and prevalent these conflicts are (Ethics Officer Association, 2000, as cited in Vickers, 2005).

Of all possible conflicts, it appears that management is at the core of the most cited, according to a 2003 study jointly conducted by the Society of Human Resource Management (SHRM) and the ERC. Specifically, when SHRM members were asked to rank sources of workplace conflict, the most often cited was the "need to follow boss's directive." This was cited by nearly half of respondents. The next two common responses were "meeting overly aggressive business objectives" (48%) and "helping the organization survive" (40%) (Joseph & Esen, 2003, as cited in Vickers, 2005). Looking at the commonality across all three popular responses, it is apparent that employees feel pressured from above to do what is construed as necessary to directly keep their positions or indirectly by keeping the organization afloat. Other research supports this supposition.

Numerous British HR professionals and accountants were interviewed about ethical dilemmas experienced in the workplace. Interestingly enough, results implied that "ethical behavior was only infrequently a function of personal values." This suggests that people inherently want to behave ethically. On the other hand, ethical concerns were more often cited as being founded by "externally generated pressures, but most notably the fear of jeopardizing one's current or future employment prospects ad the consequences of this for the individual's dependents" (Lovell, 2002, as cited in Vickers, 2005). The study went on to report that the combination of employees' fear of losing their jobs combined with their loyalty to their fellow employees, supervisors, and the organization at large, led to many of them essentially turning their heads when they observed unethical behavior. Let's examine the experienced fear. When perception of losing one's position, for example, is involved, it may be that this is a realistic impression based on something written, such as an outrageously high sales goal for someone selling timeshares, or it may be voiced by a supervisor. However, the other possibilities are that the threat is implied or simply imagined by the employee. Regardless, the pressured feeling experienced by the employees is tangible.

A culture of ethics

Code of ethics • • •

It helps to have a culture of ethics. This can begin with a code of ethics. In 2000, only 50% of respondents in a survey reported their organization had either a code of ethics in place or one in progress (Conaway & Fernandez). However, a 2003 SHRM survey shows that nearly 80% of respondents report having an ethics policy (Business ethics, 2003) and a 2005 ERC survey showed 86% (NBES, 2005).

Beyond a simple code of ethics, it is important to create a strong culture of ethical behavior. According to recent research, employees in organizations with strong ethical cultures and formal ethics programs are 36 percentage points less likely to observe misconduct than employees in organizations with weak culture and full formal programs (NBES, 2005). This national study also revealed a strong relationship between formal programs and cultures, leading to the conclusion that, where cultures are strong, it is in part because a formal ethics program is in place (NBES, 2005).

Creating an ethical environment • • •

Connecting employee satisfaction/productivity and HR through the ethical environment can affect employee satisfaction and productivity. Individual beliefs and corporate beliefs need to be on the same track for a relationship to take hold and grow. A difference of opinion about core issues can ultimately force the relationship to fail (Pava, 1999, p. 20). Research shows that when employees perceive that others are held accountable for their actions (i.e. an ethical environment), their overall satisfaction scores increase by 32 percentage points (NBES, 2005). Knowing satisfaction factors into retention, which is typically a challenge in many hospitality jobs, this is significant.

Driscoll and Hoffman (1997) use a four-part framework-pyramid (see Figure 8.1) to visualize the ethical environment. *Ethical awareness* is the basic level of the ethical environment. Here, human resource professionals ask whether employees recognize ethical problems as they occur. "Some employees concentrate on their duties so intently that they miss an obvious ethical situation when it happens" (Driscoll & Hoffman, 1997, p. 1). The following real-life example happened in a large restaurant chain in the Cleveland area. A man walked in and asked the hostess to give him ten $20 for the $200 of $5 and $10 bills he had in a sealed envelope he handed her. Eager to please the customer, she complied. The man rapidly exited as she opened the envelope to put the money into the cash register. To her shock, she found only folded paper napkins in the envelope. Although this example demonstrates lack of ethical

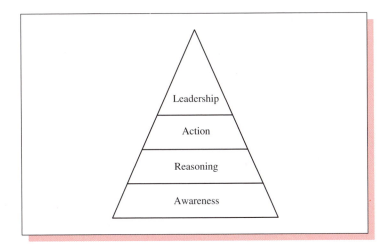

Figure 8.1
Ethical environment.

awareness, there is evidence that suggest many employees do have this characteristic. Fifty-two percent of employees in a national survey admitting that they observed at least one wrongdoing at work in the past year (NBES, 2005).

Ethical reasoning recognizes that employees should be equipped to think through ethical problems (Driscoll & Hoffman, 1997). Pava (1999) explains that most business curricula teach students to view decisions almost exclusively as opportunities to maximize self-interest. This is the *rational model* of decision-making. From the ethical perspective, decision-making provides opportunities to explore issues of individual and group identity, and to seek personal and communal meaning. Understanding corporate decision-making and searching for better ways to resolve these decisions can improve business decisions. Ethical dilemmas are never well defined and rarely well understood. Treating ethical dilemmas as normal decisions is often tantamount to ignoring them, and ignoring them can lead to business ethics failures. Pava concludes that is necessary move beyond the exclusive use of the rational model of decision-making. However, the rational model of decision-making is an extremely important tool for business managers, and needs to be viewed in its proper context (Pava, 1999). Using the rational model of decision-making is an excellent starting point to ethical reasoning; it is one tool of decision making among others.

Ethical action emphasizes that managers must provide the tools to allow employees to solve ethical questions (Driscoll & Hoffman, 1997). Research shows that ethics-related actions of coworkers can increase employee willingness to report misconduct, by as much as 10 percentage points (NBES, 2005). Examples of tools to aid employees in their ethical quandaries may include an anonymous hotline for reporting wrongdoing or perhaps an ethics officer or ombudsperson who could act as a sounding board.

At the top of the ethical pyramid is the *Ethical leadership*. Ethical leadership relies on an individual or organization to be the moral compass for others. These are people who walk the walk and talk the talk. Research shows that where top management displays certain ethics-related actions, employees are 50 percentage points less likely to observe misconduct in others, suggesting they, and others in their organizations are affected by the leadership's behaviors (NBES, 2005).

Stakeholders

When we discuss all four levels of the pyramid, it is important to understand that we are all stakeholders, including businesses, executives, managers, supervisors, employees, customers, clients, suppliers, competitors, and the community. At one time or another, ethical decision-making involves all of these constituents and affects all aspects of a business including satisfaction and morale.

Inherent in the term "business ethics" is an unavoidable tension: Managers must continuously balance the needs of the organization and its stockholders with the needs of other stakeholders. Managers must also balance their personal needs and desires against those of their organizations. These disparate pulls in different directions speak to the conflicts of interest expressed earlier. However, despite this tension between competing interests, today's business leaders can model behaviors and create a corporate culture that supports ethical business practices even while making their firms more competitive in the marketplace (Vickers, 2005).

Conclusion

Ethical issues are a daily component of business, and they are more important today than ever before. Ethics are involved in all aspects of a business, including decision-making, marketing and sales, financial reporting, personnel, appraisal, and leadership. Managers and other employees must be able to see the ethical issues in the choices they face, make decisions within an ethical framework, and build and maintain an ethical work environment (Sims, 1994, p. 4). This is especially important in the hospitality industry where FLE's are interfacing with the customers in an often-unsupervised environment.

The U.S. business culture is going through a period of change during which ethics has become a higher priority, and with this comes some important roles for HR. This change goes beyond merely following the letter of new laws and regulations. It includes a general feeling among many workers that the ethics environment is improving and that many of their leaders are "walking the talk" (Vickers, 2005). Although, there is still much research that suggests incidents of misconduct are not decreasing (NBES, 2005). It is also important to note that although there are rampant conflicts of interest, some of the pressure is caused by entities such as stockholders who are pushing organizations to make ethical decisions, such as to abort animal testing. In general, organizations are becoming more transparent, and the most progressive of them are adopting a complementary array of ethics programs to help them avoid the types of scandals that have lately tarnished the reputations of many (Vickers, 2005). Hopefully, these HR driven measures will lead to greater responsibility, accountability, and an overall raising of the ethical bar.

References

3 turnpike toll collectors accused of stealing cash. (2007, July 14). *Miami Herald*, p. B3.

Ambrose, M. L. (1998). Chapter four electronic performance monitoring: A consideration of rights. In: M. Schminke (Ed.), *Managerial ethics: Moral management of people and processes* (pp. 61–77). Mahwah, NJ: Lawrence Erlbaum Associates. Retrieved September 12, 2007, from Questia database: http://www.questia.com/PM.qst?a=o&d=47612023

Business ethics. (2003). Alexandria, VA: Society for Human Resource Management.

Cadrian, D. (2006). Employers turning their backs on drug testing. Alexandria, VA: Society for Human Resource Management.

Ciulla, J. B. (Ed.). (1998). *Ethics: The heart of leadership*. Westport, CT: Praeger Publishers. Retrieved September 12, 2007, from Questia database: http://www.questia.com/PM.qst?a=o&d=28028053

Conaway, R. N., & Fernandez, T. L. (2000). Ethical preferences among business leaders: Implications for business schools. *Business Communication Quarterly*, *63*(1), 23. Retrieved September 12, 2007, from Questia database: http://www.questia.com/PM.qst?a=o&d=5001210452

Cook, L. S., Bowen, D. E., Chase, R. B., Dasu, S., Stewart, D. M., & Tansik, D. A. (2002). Human issues in service design. *Journal of Operations Management. 20*(2), 159–174.

Driscoll, D.-M., & Hoffman, W. M. (1997). *Ethics matters: How to implement values-driven management*. Waltham, MA: Bentley College Center for Business Ethics.

Driscoll, D.-M., & Hoffman, M. (1998). HR plays a central role in ethics programs. *Workforce, 77*(April), 121–123.

Klingner, D., & Nalbandian, J. (2003). *Public personnel management, contexts and strategies* (5th ed.). Upper Saddle River, NJ: Prentice Hall/Simon & Schuster.

Mees, A., & Bonham, J. (2004). Corporate social responsibility belongs with HR. *Canadian HR Reporter, 7*(April 5), 11–13.

Pizam, A., & Ellis, T. (1999). Customer satisfaction and its measurement in hospitality enterprises. *International Journal of Contemporary Hospitality Management, 11*(7), 326–339.

Pava, M. L. (1999). *The search for meaning in organizations: Seven practical questions for ethical managers*. Westport, CT: Quorum Books. Retrieved September 12, 2007, from Questia database: http://www.questia.com/PM.qst?a=o&d=28991214

Poe, A. C. (2003). Keeping hotel workers. *HR Magazine, 48*(2).

Sims, R. R. (1994). *Ethics and organizational decision making: A call for renewal*. Westport, CT: Quorum Books. Retrieved September 12, 2007, from Questia database: http://www.questia.com/PM.qst?a=o&d=51538565

Sims, R. R. (2002). *Teaching business ethics for effective learning*. Westport, CT: Quorum Books. Retrieved September 12, 2007, from Questia database: http://www.questia.com/PM.qst?a=o&d=101315746

The importance of business ethics. (2001, July). *HR Focus, 78*, 13+.

Three toll collectors on Florida's Turnpike arrested for $13k thievery. Retrieved September 15, 2007 from http://www.tollroad-snews.com/node/3026.

Vickers, M. R. (2005). Business ethics and the HR role: Past, present, and future. *Human Resource Planning, 28*(1), 26+. Retrieved September 12, 2007, from Questia database: http://www.questia.com/PM.qst?a=o&d=5009356449

Williams, L. C. (1995). *Human resources in a changing society: Balancing compliance and development*. Westport, CT: Quorum Books. Retrieved September 15, 2007, from Questia database: http://www.questia.com/PM.qst?a=o&d=28143361

CHAPTER 9

Organisational communication in the hospitality industry: critical issues

Margaret Deery and Leo Jago

*Centre for Tourism and services Research,
Victoria University, Melbourne City
Victoria 8001*

It is a truism to say that good communication is vital to an organisation. What is not so evident is how communication is made effective. Good communication becomes the "central means by which individual activity is coordinated to devise, disseminate, and pursue organizational goals" (Gardner, Paulsen, Gallios, Callan, & Mongahan, 2001, p. 561). It has the effect of mobilizing employees to work for the organisation's goals. Poor communication, on the other hand can produce negative consequences such as distortion of goals, conflict and inefficiency in the performance of duties (Wood *et al.*, 2004). Organisations exist through individuals communicating with each other; equally, organisations can be dysfunctional if the communication channels are not working well. The constant state of change within today's work environments means that the communication process needs to change with the new structures. Communicating organisational changes clearly and accurately is crucial to ensuring a satisfied workforce. Organisational communication presents a number of challenges ranging from the regularity of communication to the medium used for effective communication. Given that the hospitality industry is such a labour-intensive and people centred industry, effective communication is critical to the success of organisations within the industry.

This chapter examines current practices in communication within organisations generally, and in hospitality establishments specifically. The chapter, first, provides a review of these practices as portrayed in academic literature. Second, the chapter focuses on some of the difficult issues associated with effective communication and finally, a case study of a five star hotel is included to illustrate some of the issues discussed in the literature.

Organisational communication: a review of the literature

Models of the interpersonal communication process provide the basis for understanding the complexities of organisation communication. There are any number of variations on the individual communication process and the following one, taken from McShane and Von Glinow (2000) is an example of the way in which the communication process is explained (Figure 9.1).

Communication barriers (noise), can include an individual's perceptions, the filtering of messages, the language that is used including jargon and ambiguous language. In addition, communication researchers discuss the impact that information overload has on the receiver. This issue is particularly relevant

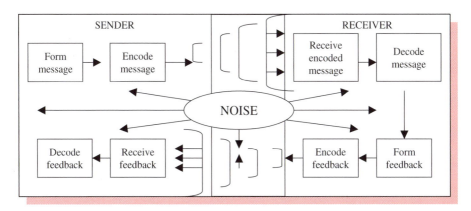

Figure 9.1
The Communication Process Model. *Source*: McShane and Von Glinow (2000, p. 234).

in a work environment that uses electronic means of communication in addition to traditional methods of newsletters, memos, signs/posters and letters. What is interesting with the model above, however, is that there is no feedback loop to the sender to influence the message. Good communication relies on decoding a message and then being able to take that new information into account for the next round of communication.

The ramifications for good and poor communication within organisations are vital for management to understand. Gray and Laidlaw (2004) report research findings that good communication enhances effective working relationships. A number of studies have found a strong positive relationship between communication satisfaction and job satisfaction and Anderson and Martin (1995) argue that communication is a means of satisfying interpersonal needs at work and engenders feelings of inclusion. Poor communication, on the other hand, can reduce employee commitment, increase absenteeism and industrial unrest, promote higher employee turnover and reduce productivity (Hargie, Tourish, & Wilson, 2002). Gray and Laidlaw (2004) also report that poor communication at the individual level can lead to uncertainty about situations, themselves, others and relationships and therefore increase the chances of occupational stress and burnout.

Communication can be viewed from a number of perspectives. Hoofe van den and Ritter (2004, p. 117) argue that the term "organisational communication" refers to

both the communication climate of the organization as a whole (both intensity and experienced quality of organizational communication) and the use of different instruments for communication.

These authors found that having a sound communication climate was crucial to knowledge sharing—both donating and collecting knowledge. Others such as Grudin (1996, p. 171) discuss the term "dialogue" meaning "a reciprocal exchange of meaning ... across a physical or mental space". If we examine the concept from the perspective of the Total Quality Management (TQM) literature, we find that the key elements focus on the levels at which communication occurs. Traditionally, communication in organisations has been top-down, but using the TQM model, three levels are involved, those being top-down, horizontal or lateral and multidirectional. There is also the medium or manner through which communication takes place to be considered. Woerner, Orelikowski and Yates (2004) suggest that face-to-face communication is extremely valuable but can also be very costly. Face-to-face is seen to be the most information-rich, although social influence theories suggest that people will perceive the value of the richness differently. Situational factors will influence these individual perceptions of the value or richness of the communication (Carlson & Zmud, 1999).

The topic of communication has been researched from the perspectives of social psychology, sociology and the political sciences. Jones, Watson, Gardner and Gallois (2004) argue that communication theories are constantly being reviewed, critiqued and new theories developed. They also suggest that communication research needs to use a triangulation method in order to validate the findings. They argue that little research has been undertaken using such validation.

A number of critical issues for effective organisational communication have been identified in the literature. One of these is finding the appropriate methods to deal with the diversity and complexity of stakeholder relationships (Deetz, 2001). Communication has been one of the critical factors in building successful relationships with stakeholders and needs to be made a priority (Tower, 2007). Stakeholders, of course, include employees, suppliers, clients and other organisations involved in business-to-business relationships. The diversity of stakeholders adds to the complexity of sound relationships and research on issues such as gender (Taylor & Trujillo, 2001) and race (Ashcroft & Allen, 2003) illustrate the difficulties in effective communication within the organisational setting.

Within an organisation, communication operates at a number of levels and, to date, much of the research has focused at the micro or operational level (Jones et al., 2004). Allen, Gotcher and Siebert (1993) found that the area of interpersonal relations was the most researched area in organisational communication. In summarizing, Jones et al. (2004,

p. 732) state that "this means too much concentration on positive communication and inadequate attention to problematising communication".

Communication in hospitality organisations

Effective communication provides the basis for best practice in any organisation, but it is especially important in the hospitality industry. Watson, D'Annunzio-Green and Maxwell (2005) report on the findings from a number of studies that found the most important Human Resource Management (HRM) issues facing hospitality enterprises were those of service quality, training and development and staff recruitment and selection. In their study, Watson *et al.* (2005) found that the most critical future HRM issues confronting the hospitality sector were those of gaining employee attitudinal commitment, training and development, service quality, staff recruitment and selection, team-building and management development. In work by Cannon (2005, p. 167) examining the development of employee attitudinal commitment in hospitality organisations, face-to-face communication was found to be most effective and "keeping employees abreast of company information has been related positively to organizational commitment if employees perceive that there is effective and regular communication".

Hospitality work is characterised by part-time and casual work (Jago & Deery, 2004). As such, it is difficult to acculturate staff because of the often disconnected work schedules given to staff and therefore communication is especially important. Baum (2006) discusses the changing patterns of work in the hospitality industry. The insecure and transitory nature of seasonal work in the hospitality industry further reinforces the need for strong internal communication processes to provide information in a timely manner. In addition to the season nature of hospitality work is the high level of employee turnover. Baum (1988) found that managers in Irish hotels changed jobs every 15 months requiring induction processes to be communicated effectively. Varini and Diamantis (2006) have examined the most effective communication channels within hotels in their study on managing hotel revenue. They found that effective communication has the ability to encourage and enforce change and this is best done through face-to-face meetings. The least effective method was through letters followed by email.

The labour-intensive and personal nature of hospitality work brings into focus research undertaken on emotional labour. Chappel (2005) argues that a feature of the hospitality workplace is the exchange or encounter between the person serving and those being served. She suggests that "hospitality employees seek to convey a desirable image designed to pleased the customer" (p. 225). In order to present this image, employees require the correct training and development. In addition, the practices of recruitment and selection come into focus—the role of the HR manager in being able to deliver these desired behaviours is crucial. While the topic of emotional labour is linked closely with that of effective communication, it will not be an area of discussion in this chapter which will focus on the perceptions of employees with regard to what constitutes effective communication.

As stated, the key focus for this chapter is employee perceptions of effective communication in the hospitality sector. The chapter presents the findings from an employee attitudinal study at a five star hotel over a number of years. The aim of the study was to monitor the effectiveness of management changes that were introduced to improve employee satisfaction and commitment. Improving communication within the hotel was one of the key strategies used to make these improvements.

Case study: exploring the communication needs of employees

This study was undertaken at the instigation of hotel management who were keen to understand employee perceptions and attitudes towards their work and the hotel. The HR manager instituted an annual climate survey to examine these issues and approached the researchers to undertake an independent study which began in 1998. Over the years, however, the questions relating to communication varied due to changing conditions and issues and hence only the last 3 years are provided here as they represent the most consistent in terms of the survey items used.

There were three changes in particular that impacted on the hotel during the time of the survey. The first of these was a change in ownership that, over a period of time, left the staff in an uncertain environment. This change occurred during 2005–2006 and the survey results reflect the level of uncertainty that was perceived by staff.

The second change effecting the hotel related to the industrial relations legislation and the introduction of the Workchoices Workplace Relations System. According to the commentary on this legislation, Workchoices introduces a "system which will give Australia a flexible labour market, allowing economic growth and employment opportunities". The legislation was introduced in 2006 and research on the effects of the legislation found hospitality workers to have been substantially disadvantaged by the new laws. A key component of the legislation was the introduction of individual workplace agreement called Australian Workplace Agreements (AWAs). According to work by Van Barneveld (2006)

For award-dependent employees who move to AWAs, the abolition of the No-Disadvantage Test (NDT) "will lead to the loss of important sources of earnings such as overtime/penalty rates and casual loadings—especially in non-union service sector jobs" (Briggs, 2005, p. 4). This prediction has some currency since there is overwhelming evidence that, in some traditionally award-dependent industries such as hospitality, inadequacies in the NDT have already caused some employees to lose these entitlements and fall behind the rates in the relevant award.

The final change during the survey period that needs to be discussed was the impact of labour and skill shortages both generally and in the hospitality industry. This shortage was so difficult to understand and manage that the Australian Government instituted an inquiry through the Parliamentary House of Representatives. These shortages placed organisations in the hospitality industry under a great deal of pressure to be "the employer of choice". As a consequence, places such as the case study hotel needed to improve its practices to merely remain competitive in the labour market.

During this time, hotel management introduced a number of measures to improve communication and employee satisfaction. One scheme that had been introduced was a government funded project, Workplace English and Literacy (WEL) project. This was introduced to assist the large number of non-native English speaking staff, mainly employed in the housekeeping and laundry departments. This program ran over a 4-month period, using a private education provider for 1–2 days a week to enhance the English speaking skills of staff. The course included classes on running meetings and improving the input of staff at meetings. The course appeared to be quite successful but the external funding for it ceased and classes were discontinued.

Hotel management also instituted management and supervisor training using Stephen Covey's "7 Habits" as well as a 360 Degree performance appraisal system for managers and supervisors. All these measures were made in response to feedback from the employee survey and were instituted to improve, among other things, communication. In particular, the employee survey had noted the high level of autocratic management style practiced by managers and department heads. Most staff did not like this style and there was obvious resentment (as shown in the survey responses) at being managed in this way. The 360 Degree appraisal system was introduced to give managers direct feedback from peers, staff in their department and their own managers. While those who were appraised in this system were satisfied with the method and felt they improved their management style as a consequence of the feedback, this level of satisfaction did not necessarily flow to their staff.

The data presented here cover a range of areas that impact on the effectiveness of the organisation's communication—variables such as employee work status and length of tenure will impact on the stability and communication flow of an organisation.

Method

A survey instrument was used to obtain data on, among a number of organisational issues, employee perceptions of the effectiveness of the communication within the hotel. Between 2004 and 2006, employees were asked questions using the following headings

- How well people are informed at the hotel
- Relative importance of various modes of communication (only 2006)
- Communication of job expectations and performance
- Someone to listen to and act on complaints

Each employee received a copy of the questionnaire, together with a reply paid envelope to be sent straight to the researchers. The responses to these questions were analysed using SPSS and are presented below showing the changes in perceptions over the 3-year period. In addition to the quantitative items, employees were invited to provide qualitative responses to open-ended questions relating to communication. These responses were coded into themes and analysed.

Results

In examining the trends over the years from 2004 to 2006, it would appear that both the perceptions of the effectiveness of the hotel communication and the number of staff that were prepared to respond varied greatly over the years. In 2004, 113 employees completed the questionnaire (out of a possible 130), in 2005, only 58 employees responded and in 2006, 81 employees responded to the survey with a total population of 140. Given that completing the survey was a voluntary activity, the lower respondent numbers perhaps reflect a level of disillusionment with the hotel and the follow-up from the survey.

Respondent profile

The following section provides a brief demographic profile of respondents to the survey. In each year, the ratio of male to female respondents was roughly equal, while the age profile tended to get older, in line with general trends in the Australian workforce. In 2006, for example, over 40% of the respondents were in the 40 years or older age categories. During the 3-year period the percentage of those employees between 18 and 24 had decreased as had those in the age group of 30–34. The trends in length of employment appeared to be relatively consistent over the 3 years and illustrate current employee career trends where fewer employees stay within any one organisation for any more than 5 years, for example, 76% of employees in 2006 had been employed at the hotel for 5 or fewer years.

The majority of the respondents were full-time staff with the rest being either part-time or casual. The percentage of respondents working in housekeeping increased substantially in 2006, with those in front office and administration positions seemingly decreasing. It is important to note these changes as they may have some bearing on the overall responses with regard to communication. The majority of the respondents were staff rather than supervisors or management. Finally, respondents were asked to state how long they intended staying at the hotel. The largest percentage was always those who answered that they did not know how long they would stay, but there was a trend for respondents to be staying at the hotel for longer periods of time.

Communication

Respondents were asked a range of questions relating to communication. The first of these inquired about staff perceptions of the effectiveness of the communication flow at the hotel. The percentage of responses is provided in Table 9.1.

Table 9.1 How Well People are Informed at the Hotel

Measure of How Well Informed People are at the Hotel	2004 (%)	2005 (%)	2006 (%)
I am kept up to date with what's going on in my department	73.5	78.9	73.4
New staff receive proper orientation	71.4	67.9	70.1
New staff receive proper induction	59.5	57.9	62.8
I am kept up to date with what's going on at the Hotel	61.9	62.5	55.4
Communication has improved in last 12 months	34.9	45.3	39.0

By and large, respondents felt that they received reasonable communication from the hotel, although it is interesting that the questions relating to improved communication are substantially lower than other responses. The scores for the third and fourth items are relatively low, indicating that the respondents did not consider they were being inducted or trained into the organisation properly, nor were they being kept abreast of the changes such as the new ownership of the hotel. The final item in this group of questions is a very negative result for the hotel and quite possibly relate to the changes in industrial relations legislation as well as the ownership change process. It would appear that measures introduced to improve communication were not seen to have achieved a great deal. For example, one respondent stated

The communication between top levels need to flow down at a faster rate to all other levels. It happens slowly

and

Management should take some time out to talk one on one to staff from each department to see how things are going.

Staff obviously perceive that effective communication is reliant on management being able to communicate with each other as well as to staff—and to take the time to do so.

A new question, which was introduced in 2006, and is included here because it provides a perspective on communication modes, inquires of the relative importance of the different types of communication. Table 9.2 provides the rankings of the responses.

Table 9.2 Relative Importance of Various Modes of Communication

Mode of Communication	Ranking (%)
Team briefings	84
Quarterly staff meetings	78
Memos	78
Staff notice board	76
Newsletter	58
Word of mouth	58
Email	49

The importance of face-to-face communication is evident in the finding that team briefings are the most important means of communication, followed by meetings, memos and the staff notice board. These findings suggest that if staff were unable to attend a meeting or team briefing—perhaps due to being casual or part-time—then they were able to still obtain the information through other means such as the notice boards. Just fewer than half the staff felt that email was a good means of communication, but again, this may be influenced by the percentage of respondents who were in housekeeping where there has traditionally been a problem with English language. These staff are also less likely to have access to email, particularly as they are not in desk-based jobs. As stated above, team briefings are critical to effective communication as perceived by staff and there were constructive comments to improve these

Multiple repeat team briefings. If someone is off on the day a new initiative is brought in, they may not find out for another week before someone tells them things have changed.

One meeting per month where someone from each department is represented. This way problems that arise regarding other departments can be discussed and resolved. Points from these meetings can be discussed in weekly meets.

Staff parties for departments, social clubs, briefings before your shifts, more meetings in reception with everyone together.

The bulletin board also came in for substantial comment

Everyone is responsible to read the staff notice board. Department heads to have active role in dissemination of information.

Improved bulletin boards to each for the information they supply. Visual boards: A tidier message board with more clearly defined sections.

Table 9.3 Communication of Job Expectations and Performance

Level of Clarity About My Job at the Hotel	2004 (%)	2005 (%)	2006 (%)
I understand what is expected from me in my job	95.6	94.7	83.5
I understand what is expected from me to ensure department is successful	92.9	98.2	88.6
I am well informed about job performance	63.7	62.5	59.5
I am well informed about changes that affect me	64.3	60.7	57.0

The next area of inquiry was the level of clarity of job expectations and performance. As Table 9.3 illustrates, most people understand what their job involves.

In each of the items relating to communication about job expectations and performance, however, there has been decrease in the perception of the level of information being provided by the hotel. The responses to information on changes in the 2006 survey reflect the difficult period of time when the hotel changed ownership. The communication of job expectations and performance appears to have decreased in effectiveness and this may be as a result of higher expectations from staff. With the labour shortages that have been critical over the time of the survey, the expectations of what the organisation needs to provide may have increased. Employees now have the opportunity to leave an organisation and find other employment if their expectations are not met. The pressure on organisations to improve this type of communication is immense and the following comments exhibit some of the frustration by staff

Communication will only improve if people become more aware of what each department does and how their role effects others. Perhaps a list of departments and positions with a brief description of their role and duties could be circulated.

Managers, supervisors of each department implement a system that suits each department. A much better follow up system e.g. Diary briefings. Line staff to take more responsibility in passing on messages rather than having a "don't care" attitude.

The issue of whether staff are heard and problems dealt with properly was also examined. In Table 9.4, the figures suggest

Table 9.4 Someone to Listen to and Act on Complaints

There is Someone to Listen to and Act on Complaints	2004 (%)	2005 (%)	2006 (%)
Strongly agree	23	28.6	16.7
Agree	40.7	51.8	38.9
Neither disagree or agree	22.1	10.7	23.6
Disagree	8.8	8.9	11.1
Strongly disagree	5.3	0	9.7

that there was a reasonable level of satisfaction with this element of communication.

Again, the hotel appears to be not performing well on this dimension. Over 20% perceived that there was no one within the organisation to listen to and act on complaints. This is a very important finding for the hotel and one that provides useful information to the hotel executive.

Very easy—everyone should just talk to each other. People should tell each other what is going on and how it should be done.

Email is a good idea—by the way if someone has got a personal problem and dare to talk face to face is a good change. Survey also good because we do not have to indicate out personal identity—make us feel more comfortable.

The hotel obviously needs to take on board the responses that are being provided to management about staff needs with regard to being listened to and having a process for complaints. In another part of the study, it was found that there was an increasing number of staff who were either intending to stay for a short period of time and, more worryingly, that almost half the respondents would not or could not state how long they would stay with the hotel. It is possible that this increased trend for staff turnover could be linked to the perceptions of poor communication.

Conclusions and recommendations

The findings from the case study suggest that effective communication with the hospitality industry is comprised of a number of elements. It is the responsibility of both management and staff to ensure that the communication works and is constantly improved. A proposed framework for effective communication is provided in Figure 9.2. As argued in the literature, face-to-face communication is perceived as the most effective style and is the preferred method whenever possible.

The implications from Figure 9.2 are that communication within the hotel sector is something that requires constant review. It is important to assess whether the messages that are

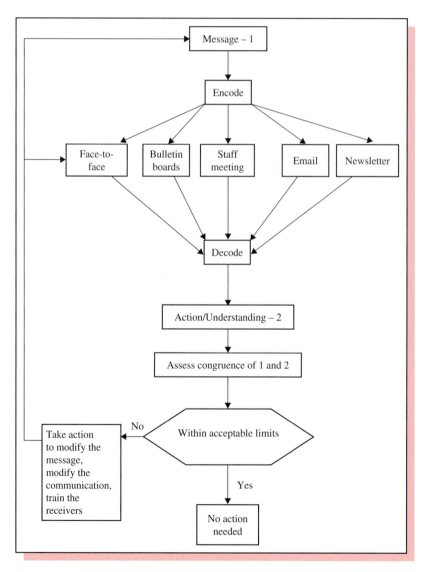

Figure 9.2
A framework for improved communications in the hospitality industry.

being given from the executive or supervisors are being understood and that the implementation of the messages is what was intended. As the framework suggests, the responsibility for clear communication is at three levels: the person with the message (possibly the HR manager or General Manager), the communicator of the message (possibly a supervisor or department head) and finally the receiver of the message (most likely a member of staff). It is incumbent on organisations, particularly those in labour-intensive industries such as the hospitality industry, to ensure that the communication channels and processes have a variety of means of sending and receiving messages and that there be a continual evaluation of the effectiveness of these channels and processes.

References

Allen, M., Gotcher, J., & Seibert, J. (1993). A decade of organizational communication research: Journal articles 1980–1991. *Communication Yearbook, 16*, 252–330.

Anderson, C., & Martin, M. (1995). Why employees speak to coworkers and bosses: Motives, gender, and organizational satisfaction. *Journal of Business Communication, 32*(3), 249–266.

Ashcroft, B., & Allen, B. (2003). The racial foundation of organizational communication. *Communication Theory, 13*, 5–38.

Baum, T. (1988). Towards a new definition of hotel management. *Cornell HRA Quarterly, 29*(2), 36–40.

Baum, T. (2006). *Human resource management for tourism, hospitality and leisure, an international perspective.* London: Thomson.

Briggs, C. (2005). *Federal IR Reform: The shape of things to come.* ACIRRT report commissioned by Unions NSW, University of Sydney, November.

Cannon, D. (2005). Building organizational commitment in international hospitality and tourism organizations. In N. D'Annunzio-Green, G. Maxwell & S. Watson (Eds.), *Human resource management: International perspectives in hospitality and tourism* (pp. 156–173). London: Thomson.

Carlson, J., & Zmud, R. (1999). Channel expansion theory and the experiential nature of media richness perceptions. *Academy of Management Journal, 42*, 153–170.

Chappel, S. (2005). Hospitality and emotional labour in an international context. In N. D'Annunzio-Green, G. Maxwell & S. Watson (Eds.), *Human resource management: International perspectives in hospitality and tourism* (pp. 225–240). London: Thomson.

Daft, R., & Lengel, R. (1984). Information richness: A new approach to managerial behaviour and organizational design. *Research in Organizational Behaviour*, *6*, 191–233.

Deetz, S. (2001). Conceptual foundations. In F. Jablin & L. Putnam (Eds.), *The new handbook of organizational communication: Advances in theory, research and methods* (pp. 3–46). Thousand Oaks, CA: Sage.

Gardner, J., Paulsen, N., Gallios, C., Callan, V., & Monaghan, P. (2001). An intergroup perspective on communication in organizations. In H. Giles & W. Robinson (Eds.), *The new handbook of language and social psychology* (pp. 561–584). Chichester, UK: Wiley.

Gray, J., & Laidlaw, H. (2004). Improving the management of communication satisfaction. *Management Communication Quarterly*, *17*(3), 425–448.

Grudin, J. (1996). The organizational contexts of development and use. *ACM Computing Surveys*, *28*(10), 169–171.

Hargie, O., Tourish, D., & Wilson, N. (2002). Communication audits and the effects of increased information: A follow-up study. *The Journal of Business Communication*, *39*(4), 414–436.

Hoofe van den, B., & Ritter, J. (2004). Knowledge sharing in context: The influence of organizational commitment, communication climate and CMC use on knowledge management. *Journal on Knowledge Management*, *8*(6), 118–134.

Jago, L., & Deery, M. (2004). An investigation of the impact of internal labour markets in the hotel industry. *The Service Industries Journal*, *24*(2), 118–129.

Jones, E., Watson, B., Gardner, J., & Gallois, C. (2004). Organisational communication: Challenges for the new century. *Journal of Communication*, *54*(4), 722–750.

Lengel, R., & Daft, R. (1988). The selection of communication media as an executive skill. *Academy of Management Executive*, *2*, 225–232.

McShane, S., & Von Glinow, M. (2000). *Organizational behaviour*. Boston, MA: Irwin McGraw-Hill.

Taylor, B., & Trujillo, N. (2001). Qualitative research methods. In F. Jablin & L. Putnam (Eds.), *The new handbook of organizational communication: Advances in theory, research and methods* (pp. 161–196). Thousand Oaks, CA: Sage.

Tower, J. (2007). *An analysis of the relationships between sport associations and sport venues in Victoria*. Unpublished Ph.D. thesis, Victoria University.

Van Barneveld, K. (2006). Australian Workplace Agreements under Workchoices. *The Economics and Labour Relations Review*, *16*(2), 165.

Varini, K., & Diamantis, D. (2006). Effective management of hotel revenue. In B. Prideaux, G. Moscardo & E. Laws (Eds.), *Managing tourism and hospitality services. Theory and international applications.* Wallingford, UK: CAB International.

Watson, N., D'Annunzio-Green, G., & Maxwell, G. (2005). *Human resource management: International perspectives in hospitality and tourism.* London: Thomson.

Woerner, S., Orelikowski, W., & Yates, J. (2004). The media toolbox: Combining media in organizational communication. *Proceedings of the Academy of Management*, New Orleans.

Wood, J., Chapman, J., Fromholtz, M., Morrison, V., Wallace, J., Zeffane, R., Schermerhorn, J., Hunt, J., & Osborne, R. (2004). *Organisational behaviour. A global perspective* (3rd ed.). Australia: Wiley.

CHAPTER 10

Employee turnover: calculation of turnover rates and costs

Akin Aksu

School of Tourism and Hotel Management, Akdeniz University, 07058, Arapsuyu Campus, Antalya, Turkey

Literature review

In terms of economic perspective, service industries play critical role in world economy and as an important component of service industry, tourism industry has direct effect on service industry (Varoglu & Eser, 2006, p. 30). Today like other establishments, touristic establishments are trying to survive under conditions of high-level competition. In order to survive they are trying to realize greater economic aims (such as profitability) and social aims (supporting recruitment and raising employee motivation). In this context, employee turnover can be seen as one of the indicators of the touristic establishment's working conditions.

Because of high employee–customer interaction, turnover has special importance in the hospitality industry. In literature it is possible to see a number of publications regarding turnover motives (Robinson, 2005, p. 349). In the hospitality industry, managers must possess an awareness of their employees in terms of their feelings toward the job and satisfaction levels from their working conditions, superiors and peers (Lam *et al.*, 2001, p. 157). Satisfied and motivated employees comprise a major factor for successful competition among rivals. Satisfied and motivated employees may contribute to developing satisfied customers. There is a strong relationship between customer satisfaction and employee satisfaction in tourism industry. The success of organizations is heavily dependent on customer evaluations (Jolliffe & Farnsworth, 2003, p. 312). Customer needs and expectations will be met by providing products and services that meet or exceed their expectations. This requires work activities provided by satisfied and motivated employees. Customer satisfaction yields repeat purchases from customers within an existing establishment, just as employee satisfaction results in increased retention of workers. In other words, from the studies in the literature it can be said that organizations with low employee satisfaction levels will tend to possess higher turnover rates than those with high satisfaction levels (Wright & Bonett, 1992, p. 605). There is a close connection between employee satisfaction and length of service. Generally high levels of turnover occur for the employees with low satisfaction levels for more than 6 months (Lam *et al.*, 2001, p. 159).

In the near future keeping employees who have desired communication and interaction skills with customers will become increasingly more important (Rust *et al.*, 1996, p. 63). Since employee behaviours influence customer satisfaction, managers are realizing the importance of including "personality" factors as part of the recruitment and selection processes (Stone & Ineson, 1997, p. 216). Neither high nor low turnover rates are useful indicators of organizational success for any specific enterprise. Instead, each touristic establishment must determine its own tolerable turnover rates and costs. In the hospitality industry, employee turnover is generally high by comparison with other industries, which may present adverse effects on the morale, motivation and job satisfaction of employees. Employee turnover may be defined as "any permanent departure beyond organizational boundaries" (Cascio, 1995, p. 581). Another definition for employee turnover may be simply stated as employee leaving an organization for whatever reason/reasons.

There are two types of employee turnover: (1) voluntary and (2) involuntary.

If an employee starts to look for a new job, this behaviour reflects his/her intention to leave the establishment, which is referred to as voluntary turnover (Ito & Brotheridge, 2005, p. 7). In this kind of turnover, employees leave establishments based on free choice. In other words, voluntary turnover can be regarded as "avoidable" turnover in some cases (Price, 2001, p. 600). Possible reasons for voluntary turnover are low salary, job dissatisfaction for the people with high expectancy levels, bad relations with superiors and colleagues, lack of job security, educational purposes for students, family purposes especially for females, better job opportunity purposes, experiencing new jobs and alternative job offers especially for skilled employee, etc. With a whole perspective to voluntary turnover, the outcome job satisfaction can be seen as vital. Job satisfaction is defined as how people feel about their jobs and job components. In this context, person-organization fit is important. Person-organization fit can be defined as a balance between individual and organizational values that will result in positive outcomes for all sides. Person-organization fit decreases employee turnover, increases organization commitment. Increasing job satisfaction and thereby decreasing employee turnover are critical tactics. Estimates calculate that separation, replacement and training costs are 1.5 to 2.5 times annual salary for each quitting employee (Rust *et al.*, 1996, p. 63). Voluntary turnover affects organizational effectiveness in reaching their goals. Therefore managers must be aware of the situation and must give support for minimizing the cost of unwanted separations (Price, 2001, p. 601). Some hospitality firms are changing their employee retention strategies and want to benefit from employee retention. After investigating 76 hotels, Simons and Mclean(2001) showed the importance of employee turnover on hotel profitability (Simons & Hinkin, 2001, p. 66).

Tourism industry operations require significant investments in labour. The success of an enterprise depends on feelings and needs of its customers, as well as employees. Hence, managers should understand the expectations of their customers and employees (Lim & Boger, 2005, pp. 59, 61). In the matter of involuntary turnover, the establishment removes employees (examples: poor performance, economic conditions, etc.). Some consider this type of turnover to be "unavoidable" turnover (Price, 2001, p. 600). Adding involuntary turnover cases because of death, illness or retirement are not suggested for inclusion of turnover calculations (Abelson & Baysinger, 1984, p. 331).

In the hospitality industry employee turnover is generally high by comparison with other industries. For example in Taiwan because of long working hours, rush hour stress, and frequent changes in the work shifts there is high employee turnover in the hospitality industry and of course this situation affects quality of goods and services (Huang, 2006, p. 31). According to Horton and Ghiselli (1999) there are 30 different individual factors affecting turnover (Walmsley, 2004, p. 276). In addition to individual factors affecting employee turnover, "outsourcing" and "seasonality" are two important factors affecting employee mobility. According to Center for Economic Policy Research, there is a loss of 8000 jobs per year in Germany and 2000 jobs in Austria because of outsourcing retrieved 03.08.2006 from www.ilo.org/public/english/employment/strat/download/wr04c1en.pdf.Seasonality as a second important factor, influences sector employment and leading to widespread seasonal employment. Seasonal jobs enable non-permanent jobs that will end in the near future (Jolliffe & Farnsworth, 2003, pp. 312, 313). Seasonality in the tourism industry can be defined as fluctuations in terms of demand. The tourism industry has been facing this problem for many years. The seasonality problem not only affects touristic establishments and their employees, but also governments' recruitment policies (Jolliffe & Farnsworth, 2003, p. 312).

Mullins (1992) mentioned that according to HCITB report, turnover rates were identified as 19% for managers, 55% for craftsmen, 65% for operatives and 94% for supervisors; hotels and guesthouses had the highest turnover rate with 86%. As Ladkin and Riley (1996) and Ladkin and Laws (1999) mentioned, hotel general managers change their jobs in every 2–3 years. Another study by Mccabe and Weeks (1999) shows employee turnover rates to be problematic for convention service manager positions in Australia (Mccabe, 2001, p. 494). In the restaurant business approximately half of all separations occur within the first 30 days. So this first period at the job plays an important role in employee turnover. Perceived alienation on the part of the establishment and employee policies and practices within the establishment are important factors affecting the decision of new employee to stay or to leave. According to the Bureau of National Affairs Report for 1987 half of all employees left their jobs in the first year. Drummond (1990) reports that turnover costs can go up to $2000–$3000 for skilled employee such as line cooks and servers. Even for the minimum wages, the replacement cost of a new employee will be approximately $3700 (Lim & Boger, 2005, p. 62). The National Restaurant Association estimates turnover costs per restaurant employee to be $5000. The food-service industry employs many young workers who tend not to stay with a company for long periods of time. It has been reported that 60% of eating and drinking-place workers are 29 years old or younger (Ghiselli *et al.*, 2001, p. 29). Restaurants are generally characterized by high employee turnover rates. This industry has grown so fast (Hjalager & Andersen, 2001, p. 117) that it is faced with the problem of balancing supply and demand in terms of employment. It is not so easy to find well-trained employees. With entry level job possibilities, homogeneity of wages and hard working conditions high levels of employee turnover can be found to be normal (Bills, 1999, p. 587). Generally speaking, the working conditions of chefs' are poor (Robinson, 2005, p. 350). Together with supply and demand problem, working conditions of chefs must be taken into consideration. Another reality for restaurants is related with the image of "serving others" (Wildes, 2005, p. 214). For some employees this can be a problem that affects their leaving or staying decisions. The results of a research conducted in the USA in 1990 indicate that the cost of turn-over for a staff member was between $2900 and $4700; for top management it was between $17,000 and $20,000 (Grandone, 1994, pp. 3–6). Even in Turkey, one of the world's developing countries, employee turnover has been experienced as a problem in terms of costs. Average wages in Turkey have been lower than those in Argentina, Brazil, Greece and South Africa. Especially since 1993, the wages have continuously decreased. Between 1993 and 1998 the decreased rate of real wages was 31.8%. According to the result of one study carried out in Antalya Region of Turkey turnover costs of food and beverage managers (with 3 years' experience) were between $3906 and $11,526 (Aksu, 2004, p. 207). In fact, employee turnover is not only an economic problem; but it is also a social problem, which has become a global scenario for different industry sectors around the world.

Relative to other industries young employees are working in the hospitality industry. They have high expectations from the job and their job satisfaction levels are considered to be low. At the same time younger employees change their jobs more frequently than older workers, retrieved 03.08.2006 from www.ilo.org/public/english/employment/strat/download/wr04c4en.pdf.

Of course, these situations pose negative impacts concerning the topic of employee turnover. Age factors can be seen as the most consistent individual characteristic variable that poses a negative relationship to turnover. According to researches, older employees are more satisfied than younger ones. As a general tendency, people leave establishments because of dissatisfaction with wages, mobbing from peers or superiors, disagreement with human resources management policies, etc. One of the realities in the hospitality industry is that it does not offer attractive working conditions. Tanke (1990) found that the work is physical, hours are long, weekends and holidays are the busiest times and wages are low. These situations together with job stress naturally lead people to re-evaluate their positions in the organization. According to Survey Research Center of Michigan four types of stress are distinguished; resource inadequacy (lack of means to perform a job), role ambiguity (unclear job obligations), role conflict (inconsistent job obligations) and workload (amount of effort required by a job) (Price, 2001, p. 603). According to Kaynak (1996), many other macro (external) factors may contribute to national turnover rates, such as a nation's general economic conditions and political crises, natural disasters, etc. Micro factors (internal) related to establishment's unique conditions would include employee–establishment relations, job dissatisfaction, demoralization, etc.

High levels of employee turnover have adverse effects on the morale, motivation and job satisfaction of employees and on the level of the establishment's performance in customer interaction. The costs of recruiting and integrating new employees are considerable both direct and indirect costs. According to Rutherford (1990), the formal and informal relationships that have been established between worker and supervisor, and among peers are disrupted when someone leaves an establishment and a replacement worker enters.

Experiencing high turnover rates occasionally would not be a big problem for establishments, but having them constantly will be a real problem (Geylan, 1989, p. 87). Employee turnover has a much greater negative impact for operations needing high quality and experience. Especially for management levels, examples can be seen like a manager or responsible person leaving the establishment during the high-season period or the strategically important season for the establishment. In such cases this kind of separation has very negative effects on the employees who continue their employment. Eren (1993) wrote that every separation means the loss of some quality and experience. In all establishments the components of turnover costs vary according to employee types. There is always a big demand for qualified and experienced employees in the hospitality industry. According to Aytek (1978), turnover of unqualified or semi-qualified employee is not a big problem for countries having an excess of human resources like in the current situation in Turkey. The costs of employee turnover are important even in entry-level positions for simple jobs. Turnover costs change according to the different positions because of the complexities of positions (Hinkin & Tracey, 2000, p. 20).

In some instances establishments may want to benefit from employee turnover. For example, they can support voluntary separation for the sake of employee savings. Or they may want to replace employees who have performed poorly. Generally, employee turnover can be viewed as a positive factor for the establishment when poor performers or dissatisfied employee leave (Geylan, 1989, p. 88).

Although it will change according to the applications of establishments and fluctuations in demand for workforce in the hospitality industry, neither high nor low turnover rates are beneficial for touristic establishments. Each organization must determine its tolerable turnover rate. In detailed research on employee turnover, some important questions can be asked (PGF, 1991, p. 9) like:

- What are the main reasons for leaving the work?
- When do the employee leave?
- Which kind of staff in the hospitality industry has the highest turnover rate?

The answers to these questions will help to understand employee turnover and will direct us to new strategies. It must be remembered that every establishment will give different answers to these questions according to their applications. If turnover reasons are carefully examined, it is possible to see that most of the reasons can easily be handled and be solved. In this context for every establishment stating the reasons and trying to solve them can become the first two steps in managing turnover. Especially human resource management practitioners must identify the reasons why people leave so that appropriate actions may be taken. In voluntary turnover defining and trying to solve the problems by establishments is important for the rest of the employees who are in continue employment.

Related to leaving time, there is not any certain time of leaving, but in high season the rate of voluntary turnover and in low season the rate of involuntary turnover are generally high. Employee turnover can be easily experienced in every kind of staff position in the tourism industry. Both skilled, semi-skilled or non-skilled employees can be viewed as possible candidates for turnover. Skilled and semi-skilled employees always have the chance of finding other job opportunities with better conditions and non-skilled employee are generally at the top of the removing employee list during times of economic recession.

A close look to employee turnover process

According to the related literature employee turnover (voluntary or involuntary) can be seen as a physical separation and most of the studies investigated demographic aspects as important factors in the turnover process (Mobley, 1982, p. 111). Morrell *et al.* (2004) classified turnover studies in two groups: (1) labour-market school and (2) psychological school studies.

Labour-market school studies are mainly concentrated on external variables (like job alternatives, performance) affecting turnover and assume that all employees are homogeneous. With different perspective, the psychological school studies are focused on explaining of employees' behaviours (like job satisfaction, organizational commitment).

In practice, possible employee turnover process starts with selection of new employees. The first day at job is always important for the new employees. It is possible that a wrong candidate might have been selected for a position and that he/she will not be successful in the very near future. In order to facilitate correct selection decisions, practitioners should seek referrals from existing staff members. Since present employees know the current working conditions and expectations of their managers, they can help to potential employees in translating the realities about the establishment. If managers confirm referrals of present employees, there is a possibility of decreasing the number of new hires that will not assimilate to the organization (Linnehan & Blau, 2003, p. 256).

Regarding turnover, the interview process alone plays an important role in right or wrong decisions for new employees.

Unsuccessful hiring decisions may be based on the following deficiencies:

- Defining the individual characteristics in an incorrect manner.
- Having a time limitation for selecting the right employee.
- Failure to afford enough time and interest in performing recruitment and selection processes.

Assuming that appropriate selection processes are in place, there are other factors that may influence possible turnover rates. For instance, a new employee may perceive an unfavourable impression of the establishment. As it was stated before, the impression and feeling of new employees starting from the first day to last day concerning the establishment will define a stay or leave decision. An external factor that influences employee turnover is known as the "opportunity" to seek positions with alternate organizations or industries. The term "opportunity" refers to the availability of alternative jobs in the local vicinity. If the employee perceives alternative jobs are better than his/her current position, he/she might resign to pursue those opportunities (Price, 2001, p. 601). Job related factors from other perspectives giving the first job to new employees is important and affects each employee directly. Giving a first job after a reasonable orientation period can be done. The first job must be easy to do and new employee must be ready for the first job. In order to reach this aim; on the job training, in-house training or orientation programmes might be suggested. In current times, many organizations are trying to improve their existing orientation programmes. A successful orientation programme must be updated, written and have standards according to the rules of the establishments and status of new employees. Together with establishment presentations, a manual (showing vision, mission and important values of the establishment) must be given. During and just after orientation periods possibly bad impressions could occur and affect stay or leave decisions of employees. Carefully organized orientation programmes enable two positive developments in the organizations; (1) turnover rates of new employees decrease and (2) the number of stayers in the establishment increases. Figure 10.1, the study of Werther and Davis (1996), shows effects of short- and long-term orientation programmes on turnover rates.

With the help of orientation programmes, new employees can learn more things in an easy way. At the same time they can understand the expectations of their management. In reality orientation programmes provide unique opportunities for new employees to understand accepted behaviours, rules and ceremonies in their new work places. In current organizations, especially in service industries, in order to cope with employee turnover, establishments must combine organizational and individual targets. In this context, leaders must communicate their expectations to employees personally. Another thing is related with matching individual characteristics with the job requirements. For most cases in the tourism industry, the practice of recruitment of new employees in the absence character analysis can easily be witnessed.

Employee turnover can be seen as a final step of job/establishment dissatisfaction. If an employee perceives dissatisfaction he/she will have three possible steps:

1. He/she will go on obeying the rules and norms of the establishment.
2. He/she leaves the establishment.
3. He/she limits his/her performance (İncir, 1989, p. 50).

Robbins (1993) found that individuals show their dissatisfaction in different ways, as shown in Figure 10.2.

Leaving work: Means leaving of work and establishment at the same time.

Giving suggestion: Means suggestions coming from the employee in order to improve working conditions.

Loyalty: Means waiting of employee in a passive way for having an improvement in working conditions.

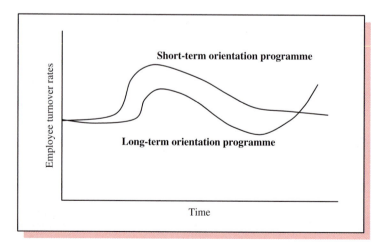

Figure 10.1
Effects of short and long term orientation programmes on turnover rates.

No interest: Watching the negative developments in the establishment in a passive way. In this situation there will be continuous absenteeism and work accidents. Employee retention is based on agreements between employees and employers. There must be idea of maintaining employment relations (Dalton *et al.*, 1982, p. 118). Both sides must make the decision of stay employed in order to continue their partnerships.

The disadvantages of turnover for establishments

According to Manley (1996), there are advantages and disadvantages of employee turnover and in order to manage turnover, developing a suitable organizational surrounding is necessary (Deery, 2002, p. 52). Despite some advantages like changing poorer performers with better ones or coming of new employees with fresh and innovative ideas (Werbel & Bedeian, 1989, p. 275), mostly employee turnover has disadvantages. Generally, high employee turnover has more disadvantages for establishments than for employees. The disadvantages for establishments are:

*High turnover increases employment costs. Here for employee costs, separation costs of terminated employees, replacement costs and training costs and productivity loss of new employees during new employee orientation period must be considered. In turnover calculations generally it is assumed for the new employees that there is a standard performance level to reach, but in practice reaching this level can change

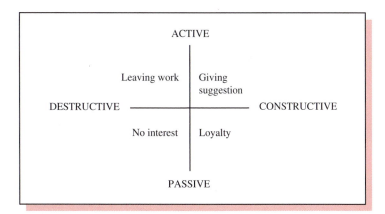

Figure 10.2
Different ways of showing dissatisfaction.

according to the position and skills of the new employee (Staw, 1980, p. 259).

*Although turnover periods can be seen as suitable during times for changing of organizations, especially high turnover increases the incidents of work accidents. Statistics show that especially during the orientation period of new employees, rate of work accidents are high.

*It means wasting of time, effort and money. Because employee turnover covers recruiting and selecting new employees, this topic includes all necessary works and training expenses. If an organization faces continuous high levels of turnover, the leadership may have to consider recruiting full time experts for selection and recruitment processes.

*It has an adverse effect on the morale, motivation and job satisfaction of the other employees (Sabuncuoğlu, 1988, p. 41). Touristic establishments must have positive images in their external and internal environments. High turnover rates will damage these positive images. It is well known that "mouth-to-mouth publicity" is widely used in the tourism sector worldwide. The positive image of an establishment can be mentioned by customers as well as among employees. In this context, the practices of managers can be a subject impact to customers (external customers) and employees (internal customers).

*Establishments that have high turnover rates and negative image on labour will always have problems in finding new and qualified employee. Possibly, they will have to offer much more salaries than sector salary standards to persuade workers to join the organization.

*Turnover decreases the level of social relations between individuals (Geylan, 1989, p. 90). Both voluntary and involuntary turnover will interrupt formal and informal relations of organization members. For every new employee, an orientation process will start new relations between the new employee and the rest of employees in the organization. This will have an adverse effect on building continuous and strong relations among the employees and establishment-customer long-term relations.

*Employee turnover affects learning levels of organizations in a negative way. In the learning process of any organization, retaining knowledge and experiences in the organizations and transmitting them to new employees will enable organizational learning. In employee turnover cases, if organizations have no written rules or specialization and knowledge transmitting mechanisms, they will probably suffer from negative effects of employee turnover (Rao & Argote, 2006, pp. 77, 78). Every separation will result as loses in terms of knowledge and experience.

*In the cases of unexpected turnover in high season periods, usually there will not be enough time to select, recruit and train the new employees (Darmon, 2004, p. 291). Reactions to staff shortages could result in increased short-term recruitment and reoccurring of turnover during crucial business periods.

The disadvantages of turnover for employees

The disadvantages of turnover for employees are:

*In voluntary turnover, the employee will lose his/her legal payment rights. Here legal payment rights means severance pay and leave compensation. If an establishment decides to terminate a person, it has to pay both severance pay and leave compensation.

*A terminated employee will look for new recruitment opportunities until finding a new job, he/she may have economic and social problems. Some people suggest that finding a new job and adjusting to it takes a period of approximately 1 year (Holtom *et al.*, 2005, p. 339). In addition to this, it can be thought that finding new job may take a long period of time during low season periods, generating the potential for economic crisis on the part of the unemployed worker.

*Voluntary departure results in loss of promotion opportunities. In addition to this, after finding a new job new employee has to show great effort to guarantee the retention of his/her new position.

*Terminated employees might become demoralized and may feel uncomfortable until finding a new job (Sabuncuoğlu, 1988, p. 41). In the next organization the new employee may miss the last working conditions or atmosphere when he/she makes a comparison between the previous and new organization. In addition to this another problem can be like; finding a new job in certain establishments may not fully guarantee the process of rebuilding former levels of self-confidence for employees. Retrieved 03.08.2006 from www.ilo.org/public/english/employment/skills/download/displacement.pdf.

*Turnover problem must be thought both for leavers and stayers. For leavers, changing of establishment and/or job can be stressful and for stayers this situation can decrease their satisfaction levels (Wright & Bonett, 1992, p. 603).

Short-term prescriptions for turnover

From a human resource managers' perspective, forecasting organizational labour supply and demand is important.

Especially at management levels when the costs of turnover reach high levels, monitoring and auditing of turnover are needed. Accurate forecasting, planning and applying short- and long-term prescriptions can be helpful in reducing turnover (Terborg & Lee, 1984, pp. 793–794).

Mullins (1992) wrote that according to Woods and Macaulay (1989), in reducing employee turnover establishments can follow short- and long-term prescriptions.

*Identifying the nature and character of the organization. This will be helpful in showing the possible qualification gaps between employees and the work requirements.

*Finding out why employees leave or stay. The performance of exit interviews is important. From exit interviews the working condition problems of employees or leaving reasons of employees can be identified regarding voluntary separations. According to the information learned from exit interviews, related precautions may be taken by hotel/travel agency managers. Of course, organizations cannot solve every type of problem, but at least they can reduce number of separations.

*Asking employees what they want from their jobs and providing formal opportunities for employees to voice opinions about their work.

*Developing effective recruitment, employment interviewing and orientation procedures. This will have a positive impact on new employee's image about his/her new organization.

Long-term prescriptions for turnover

*Establishing effective socialization, training and career-path development programmes. This will be helpful in combining individual and organizational targets. Also these applications make employee to be loyal to their organization.

*Developing profit sharing and incentive schemes. Motivating employees with both financial and non-financial support systems are important.

*Establishing child-care facilities and support services to attract older workers. Giving employees meaningful work is also needed. Currently, working employees are interested in social, non-financial benefits, as well as financial benefits associated with employment in their organizations. They may compare applications of their establishments with other establishments in the same or different sector.

*Maintaining competitive pay scales. This has two import-ant benefits. One benefit is important for an organization by enabling continuous work performance of employees and the other benefit is needed for employees to be recognized for superior performance.

*Culture of belonging must be created for the employees (Deery, 2002, p. 52). If employees feel themselves as part of organizations, they will try to do their best.

Short-term prescriptions can be evaluated within a year and long-term prescriptions can be thought for a period of more than 1 year. Both short- and long-term prescriptions will help to find out the current working conditions in an establishment and will help to decrease the employee turnover rate.

In the literature on employee turnover, Katz (1964) argues that turnover can be a measure of organizational productivity. The higher the overall job dissatisfaction, the higher the turn-over (Bass & Edward, 1979, p. 73). Beside this view, some other research can be given on employee turnover for the hospitality industry covering such topics as the rate, cost and causes of turnover. Regarding various strategies for managing turnover, Wasmuth and Davis (1983) collected data through interviews with 200 general managers, executive assistants and manag-ers in a sample of 20 large national and international hotels in North America and Europe. For investigating the magnitude and underlying causes of absenteeism and voluntary turnover a pilot study was conducted among 62 hotel human resources managers in Central Florida (Pizam & Thornburg, 2000, p. 211). Related to the turnover subject in the tourism area, short period of hotel work and temporary positions must be taken into consideration. For short period of hotel work, an example can be thought as temporary request of employee for working for some time in tourism industry and for tem-porary leaving. For example, the temporary work of a female employee in a sector might be intended until her child/chil-dren grow up can be given. This situation can easily occur since the industry has not been successful in providing good working hours, etc. Both examples play important roles in turnover in tourism industry.

Calculation of turnover rates

In calculation of employee turnover rates, there are different methods in related literature. Having different methods com-ing from different ways of looking various aspects of turnover. One common calculation of turnover rate is based on number of separated employees. According to this calculation rate of turnover can be seen as:

$$\text{Employee turnover rate} = \frac{\text{Number of separated employees}}{\text{Average number of employees}} \times 100$$

Note: Here separations include quits, lay-offs, etc.

Average number of employees (for wholeyear working establishments) can be calculated as:

$$\text{Average number of employees} = \frac{\text{Number of employees in the first day of the year} + \text{number of employees in the last day of the year}}{2}$$

(Sabuncuoğlu, 2000, p. 40).

From the calculation it can be asked that what will be the calculation of average number for seasonally working touristic establishments? Then the answer will be,

$$\text{Average number of employees} = \frac{\text{Number of employees in the first day of season} + \text{number of employees in the last day of season}}{2}$$

Another common calculation of turnover rate is based on number of recruited employees. According to this calculation rate of turnover can be seen as:

$$\text{Employee turnover rate} = \frac{\text{Number of recruited employees}}{\text{Average number of employees}} \times 100$$

Here the vital question is which of the calculation method will be used for turnover rates. The answer will be change according to the situation of the establishment. By months if the establishment has the same number of employees/increase in the number of employees then it will use the calculation for recruited employees. If the establishment has a decrease in the number of employee then it will use the calculation for separated employees. Every establishment can make this comparison in terms of employee numbers on a monthly or yearly basis. In literature it is possible to see other different calculation methods for turnover, but the most practical ones are those that calculate recruited/separated employees.

Generally, calculating of employee turnover rates use easy and systematic formulas to provide valuable information to the establishments. Having continuous calculation on a monthly or yearly basis give the opportunity of comparing rates with other establishments and tourism sector averages. In addition to the calculation of turnover rates, knowing types of turnover (voluntary or involuntary turnover) will give more accurate results.

Simpler calculation of turnover rates may not provide meaningful information for establishments. For example having 15% turnover can be evaluated as; 15 terminations out of 100 or, 1 termination out of 100 for 15 times. In order to have meaningful results, beside calculation of turnover rates, calculation of stability indexes are also needed for human resource managers of establishments.

Stability index is based on the number of stayers (employees) in one work period. It can be calculated as follows:

$$\text{Stability index} = \frac{\text{The number of employees working for last year}}{\text{The number of employees recruited one year ago}} \times 100$$

Normally this index does not give information about new employees, but human resource managers can benefit from this information together with turnover rates. Another stability index can be given as follows:

$$\text{Stability index} = \frac{n}{\text{Number of average employees}} \times 100$$

Here n means: the number of employees working for one or more years in the same establishment.

Based on turnover rates, indexes and costs every, touristic establishment may define its tolerable figures. In this context, there must be optimal turnover when separation, replacement and training efforts were evaluated. From Figure 10.3 optimal turnover details can be seen.

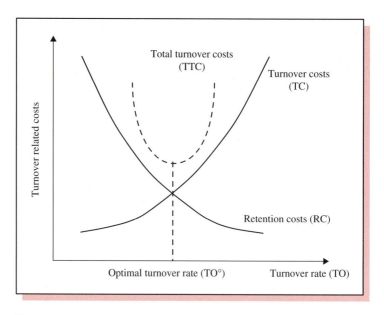

Figure 10.3
Optimal turnover (*Source*: Abelson & Baysinger, 1984, p. 333).

Figure 10.3 shows costs of turnover (separation, replacement and training) which was symbolized with (TC). In addition to this, retention costs (like increasing compensation) in order to decrease turnover was symbolized with (RC). If managers want to decrease turnover, it means increasing of retention costs. Therefore retention costs and turnover costs can be evaluated in opposite poles. Defining optimal costs is vital for the organizations. In Figure 10.3, total turnover costs were symbolized with (TTC). As shown, TTC was a U-shaped function.

Calculation of turnover costs

Before determining costs of employee turnover, it will be better to mention training and turnover relation in details. According to literature; there is a positive connection between employee turnover and investment in training in two ways: (1) an organization with high turnover will invest more in training in order to replace the skills of outgoing employee or to increase employee loyalty in the future and (2) an organization experiences higher turnover because the trained employees leave the organization for better paid jobs or working conditions where they can use their capacity better. When we determine costs of employee turnover, there are three main components according to Cascio (1995, pp. 582, 583).

1. Separation costs
2. Replacement costs
3. Training costs

Note: As a general information, it will be better to mention that both for voluntary and involuntary turnover most of the cost components are the same. Only for voluntary turnover separation pay (see "Separation pay") will be omitted from the calculations. Separation pay can be severance pay and/or leave compensation. This payment will change according to country's legal applications.

The sum of these three cost components represents the total turnover costs. Benefiting from Cascio (1995), turnover costs can also be showed in formulas.

Separation costs

1. Exit interview
2. Administrative functions related to termination (example removal of the employee from the payroll, termination of benefits, etc.)
3. Separation pay
4. Increased unemployment tax

Exit interview • • •

$$\text{Cost of interviewer's time} = \left[\begin{array}{c} \text{Time required of} \\ \text{interviewer prior} \\ \text{to interview} \end{array} + \begin{array}{c} \text{Time} \\ \text{required} \\ \text{for interview} \end{array}\right]$$
$$\times \text{interviewer's pay rate}$$

$$\text{Cost of time for terminated employee} = \begin{array}{c} \text{Time required for terminated} \\ \text{employee's interview} \\ \times \text{Pay rate of employee} \end{array}$$

Administrative functions • • •

$$\text{Cost of administrative functions} = \begin{array}{c} \text{Time required for administrative} \\ \text{functions} \\ \times \text{Pay rate of responsible person} \end{array}$$

Separation pay • • •

> All legal payments by establishments to terminated employee.

Increased unemployment tax • • •

Replacement cost analysis formulas

1. Communicating job availability
2. Preemployment administrative functions (accepting applications and checking references)
3. Entrance interview
4. Testing and/or other types of assessment procedures
5. Employee meetings
6. Travel and moving expenses (travel for all applicants and travel plus moving expenses for all new hires)
7. Postemployment acquisition and dissemination of information (all the activities associated with in-processing new employee)
8. Medical examinations

Communicating job availability • • •

> It changes according to the communication methods used. For newspaper advertisements it can be limited with advertisement fee and for direct applications it will have no cost.

Preemployment administrative functions • • •

$$\text{Preemployment administrative functions} = \begin{array}{l} \text{Time required for preemployment} \\ \text{administrative functions} \\ \times \text{Pay rate of responsible person} \end{array}$$

> In some establishments preemployment administrative functions like accepting applications and checking references can be done simultaneously with the entrance interviews.

Entrance interview • • •

$$\text{Entrance interview} = \left[\begin{array}{l} \text{Time required} \\ \text{of interviewer} \\ \text{prior to interview} \end{array} + \begin{array}{l} \text{Time required} \\ \text{for interview} \end{array} \right] \\ \times \text{Interviewer's pay rate}$$

Generally human resources manager and related department manager are responsible for entrance interviews.

Testing and/or other types of assessment procedures • • •

$$\text{Testing costs} = \frac{\text{Time required for testing}}{\times \text{Pay rate of responsible person}}$$

Testing costs can change according to the testing methods.

Cost of employee meetings • • •

$$\begin{array}{l}\text{Cost of employee} \\ \text{meetings}\end{array} = \begin{array}{l}\text{Time required for responsible} \\ \text{employee for meeting} \\ \times \text{Pay rate of responsible employee}\end{array}$$

For employee meetings human resources manager and related department manager come together in order to accept applicant to the job.

Travel and moving expenses • • •

Travel and moving expenses may change according to the travel options. If there is an invitation for the applicant out of city then establishment must pay his/her travel and moving expenses.

Postemployment acquisition and dissemination of information • • •

$$\begin{array}{l}\text{Postemployment} \\ \text{acquistion and} \\ \text{of information}\end{array} = \begin{array}{l}\text{Time required for the process} \\ \times \text{Pay rate of responsible employee}\end{array}$$

It means all the activities associated with in-processing new personnel.

Medical examinations • • •

$$\begin{array}{l}\text{Medical} \\ \text{examinations}\end{array} = \begin{array}{l}\text{Time required for medical examinations} \\ \times \text{Pay rate of responsible person}\end{array}$$

The total cost of medical examinations for new employee is paid by the establishment.

Training costs (orientation)

1. Informational literature
2. Instruction in a formal training programme
3. Instruction by employee assignment (on-the-job training)

Total training costs for new employee include both inside and outside the establishment.

Note: In calculating the turnover costs for establishments, the gross monthly wages of employees must be divided by 30 to find the daily figures. Then the daily figures must be converted to hourly wages. In formulas hourly wages can be used for calculations.

Conclusion

As Lynn (2002) stated, giving the causes, rates and costs of turnover, managers of touristic establishments will understand the importance of turnover problems and can make their decisions according to the priority of the subject.

Although the same cost components exist, different turnover costs can occur for the establishments because of their wages, human resource policies and applications. Calculating only the turnover costs is insufficient. For detailed information, establishments must have statistics related to their monthly and yearly turnover costs, the reasons for turnover and turnover rates according to departmental distribution. Having accurate and detailed figures about turnover and then making correct applications drawn from them, unsatisfactory turnover rates can be avoided and/or decreased.

Especially for involuntary turnover organizations must be very careful, because this kind of turnover generally serves as a red flag to potential or current employees of a company. For organizations having constantly high involuntary turnover rates, recruitment of new employee could become a serious problem in the future.

The hospitality industry was not perceived as an attractive industry to work in by employee because of its long working hours, lack of job guarantees, poor communication possibilities between colleagues, low wages and limited training possibilities. Of course these negative aspects affect employees directly or indirectly. One example can be given for limited training opportunities. Sometimes these kinds of applications may lead employees to seek skills in other establishments (Deery & Shaw, 1998, p. 376). Responsible managers and governments have to re-check human resource policies at micro and macro levels appropriate to the needs and expectations of employee.

In the process of involuntary turnover, managers of touristic establishments must orient the employees starting from pre-layoff step to layoff step. This effort must be seen as social responsibility of management teams.

At macro and micro levels, labour unions can promote stability of employees by using their social dialogue opportunities with governments and employers' unions/representatives. As is generally known, union employees earn more than average and they have better working conditions retrieved 03.08.2006 from www.ilo.org/public/english/employment/strat/download/wr04c4en.pdf.

By time, with the increase in the number of labour unions will be resulted with a decrease in employee turnover rates.

Voluntary turnover can be seen as a final step of dissatisfied employees and separation of these employees will affect productivity of organizations in a negative way. In this context the human resource policies, regulations, quality of work life, job-employee balance in hotels become important in attaining employee satisfaction. Establishments should give the same value to their employees as they do to their customers. Especially in the tourism industry, managers must see "taking care of people" as same process for customers, as well as for their present employees.

New employees must identify themselves with the other employees and must obey the rules and values of their new organizations. If they can manage accepting new organizations as part of himself/herself, this will bring possible success in their future careers (Dick *et al.*, 2004, p. 352).

Within human resources management perspective, every touristic establishment must have suitable recruitment policies in terms of quality and quantity. If an organization wants to survive for a long time then it must orient all its policies like investment, recruitment, innovation, etc. in order to reach this aim. With labour-intensive aspect, employees play a very important role in the success of organizations. With current technology in the tourism industry, still it is not possible to give service to customers with 100% technology. This means organizations must still cooperate with human beings.

In evaluating the results and causes of employee turnover, managers/owners of touristic establishments generally think that every separation has different reason. In fact, in some of turnover cases it is possible to find common reasons of turnover. In this context, managers must have collective studies to find common reasons. Common reasons can show right ways in managing turnover problems.

As a retention strategy, a new trend initiated by certain employers is to provide family-friendly policies towards employees. It is possible to see financial support for child care (Batt & Valcour, 2003, p. 190) and different forms of social activities. Establishments have already reported the benefits of these policies and have increased the number of family-friendly activities.

Regarding job possibilities in tourism industry may be it will be better to investigate current jobs in terms of employee expectations. Are current jobs useful for individual development of employees? Did they meet expectations of employees in general? The tourism industry is developing new job opportunities to new/potential employees on an annual basis. But the general images of some current jobs and working conditions can be discussed.

Finally, tourism managers must separate avoidable and unavoidable (in other words; voluntary and involuntary) turnover (Holtom *et al.*, 2005, p. 338) and always compare the costs of retaining employees.

References

Abelson, M. A., & Baysinger, B. D. (1984). Optimal and dysfunctional turnover: Toward an organizational level model. *Academy of Management Review, 9*(2), 331–341.

Aksu, A. A. (2004). Turnover costs: Research among five-star hotels in the city of Antalya, Turkey. *Tourism Analysis, 9*(3), 207–217.

Aytek, B. (1978). *İşletmelerde insangücü planlaması.* Ankara: İktisadi ve İdari İlimler Akademisi.

Bass, B. M., & Edward, C. R. (1979). *Organizational psychology* (2nd ed.). Boston, MA: Allyn and Bacon.

Batt, R., & Valcour, P. M. (2003). Human resources practices and predictors of work-family outcomes and employee turnover. *Industrial Relations, 42*(2), 189–220.

Bills, D. B. (1999). Labor market information and selection in a local restaurant industry: The tenuous balance between rewards, commitments, and costs. *Sociological Forum, 14*(4), 583–607.

Cascio, W. F. (1995). *Managing human resources productivity, quality of worklife, profits* (4th ed.). New York: Mc Graw-Hill, Inc.

Dalton, Dan R., Todar, William D., Krackhardt, David M. (1982). Turnover overstated: The functional taxonomy. *The Academy of Management Review, 7*(1), 117–123.

Darmon, O. R. (2004). Controlling of sales force turnover costs through optimal recruiting and training policies. *European Journal of Operational Research, 154*, 291–303.

Deery, M. (2002). Labour turnover in international hospitality and tourism. In: N. D. Green, *et al.* (Eds.), *Human resource management international perspectives in hospitality and tourism.* London: Continuum Publishing.

Deery, M. A., & Shaw, R. N. (1998). An exploratory analysis of turnover culture in the hotel industry in Australia. *International Journal of Hospitality Management, 16*(4), 375–392.

Dick, Rolf V., Christ, Oliver., Stellmacher, Jost, *et al.*, (2004). Should I stay or should I go? Explaining turnover intentions with organizational identification and job satisfaction. *British Journal of Management, 15*, 351–360.

Drummond, K. E. (1990). *Human resource management for the hospitality industry.* New York: Van Nostrand Reinhold.

Eren, E. (1993). *Yönetim psikolojisi.* İstanbul: Beta Basım.

Geylan, R. (1989). *Yüksek personel devir oranının süreklilik gösterdiği bir ortamda ortaya çıkan sorunları en aza indirme yolları* (pp. 87–90). Anadolu Üniversitesi İ.İ.B.F. Dergisi.

Ghiselli, Richard F., La Lopa, Joseph M and Bai, Billy. (2001). Job satisfaction, life satisfaction, and turnover intent. *Cornell Hotel and Restaurant Administration Quarterly, 42*(2), 28–37.

Grandone, V. (1994). Tourism and employment-policy initiatives in tourism labour markets. Paper presented at the OECD Seminar.

Hinkin, T. R., & Tracey, J. B. (2000). The cost of turnover. *Cornell Hotel and Restaurant Administration Quarterly, 41*(3), 14–21.

Hjalager, A. M., & Andersen, S. (2001). Tourism employment: Contingent work or professional career? *Employee Relations, 23*(2), 115–123.

Holtom, B. C., Mitchell TR, Lee TW & Inderrieden, EJ. (2005). Shocks as causes of turnover: What they are and how organizations can manage them. *Human Resource Management, 44*(3), 337–352.

Horton, B. W., & Ghiselli, R. (1999). Identification of variables influencing food and beverage employee turnover. In: K. S. Chon (Ed.), *In the practice of graduate research in hospitality and tourism.* New York: Haworth Hospitality Press.

Huang, H. I. (2006). Personality traits reflect employee job attitudes in the workplace. *Consortium Journal of Hospitality and Tourism, 10*(1), 31–43.

İncir, G. (1989). Çalışanların örgütsel gereksinimleri ve iş doyumu. Paper presented at the 1989 2. Ulusal Ergonomi Kongresi MPM. Ankara.

Ito, J. K., & Brotheridge, C. M. (2005). Does supporting employees' career adaptability lead to commitment, turnover or both? *Human Resource Management*, *44*(1), 5–19.

Jolliffe, L., & Farnsworth, R. (2003). Seasonality in tourism employment: Human resource challenges. *International Journal of Contemporary Hospitality Management*, *15*(6), 312–316.

Katz, D. (1964). The motivational basis of organizational behavior. *Behavioral Science*, *9*, 131–146.

Kaynak, T. (1996). *İnsan kaynakları planlaması*. İstanbul: Alfa Basım.

Ladkin, A., & Laws, E. (1999). *A career profile of hotel managers in Australia*. UK: International Centre for Tourism.

Ladkin, A., & Riley, M. (1996). Mobility and structure in the career paths of UK hotel managers: A labour market hybrid of the bureaucratic model? *Tourism Management*, *17*(6), 443–452.

Lam, T., *et al.* (2001). An investigation of employees' job satisfaction: The case of hotels in Hong Kong. *Tourism Management*, *22*, 157–165.

Lim, E., & Boger, E. (2005). Management requires leadership. *Consortium Journal of Hospitality and Tourism*, *9*(1), 59–66.

Linnehan, F., & Blau, G. (2003). Testing the impact of job search and recruitment source on new hire turnover in a Maquiladora. *Applied Psychology: An International Review*, *52*(2), 253–271.

Lynn, M. (2002). Turnover's relationship with sales, tips and service across restaurants in a chain. *Hospitality Management*, *21*, 443–447.

Mccabe, V. (2001). Career paths and labour mobility in the conventions and exhibitions industry in Eastern Australia: Results from a preliminary study. *International Journal of Tourism Research*, *3*, 493–499.

Mccabe, V. S., & Weeks, P. (1999). Convention services management in Sydney four to five star hotels. *Journal of Convention and Exhibition Management*, *1*(4), 67–84.

Mobley, W. H. (1982). Some unanswered questions in turnover and withdrawal research. *Academy of Management Review*, *7*(1), 111–116.

Morrell, Kevin., Loan-Clarke, John and Wilkinson, Andrian. (2004). The role of shocks in employee turnover. *British Journal of Management*, *15*, 335–349.

Mullins, L. J. (1992). *Hospitality management a human resources approach*. London: Pitman Publishing.

PGF. (1991). *Labour turnover*. England: Group Project, MSTHI University of Surrey.

Pizam, A., & Thornburg, S. W. (2000). Absenteeism and voluntary turnover in Central Florida hotels: A pilot study. *International Journal of Hospitality Management*, *19*(2), 211–217.

Price, J. L. (2001). Reflections on the determinants of voluntary turnover. *International Journal of Manpower*, *22*(7), 600–624.

Rao, R. D., & Argote, L. (2006). Organizational learning and forgetting: The effects of turnover and structure. *European Management Review*, *3*, 77–85.

Retrieved August 3rd, 2006 from http://www.ilo.org/public/english/employment/skills/download/displacement.pdf

Retrieved August 3rd, 2006 from http://www.ilo.org/public/english/employment/strat/download/wr04c4en.pdf

Retrieved August 3rd, 2006 from http://www.ilo.org/public/english/employment/strat/download/wr04c1en.pdf

Robbins, S. (1993).*Organizational behavior*. Englewood Cliffs, NJ: Prentice-Hall Inc.

Robinson, R. N. S. (2005). Tradeperson or artist? A critical exploration of chefs' job satisfaction and turnover. *Tourism*, *53*(4), 347–355.

Rust, Roland T., Stewart, Greg L., Miller, Heather and Pielack, Debbie. (1996). The satisfaction and retention of frontline employees a customer satisfaction measurement approach. *International Journal of Service Industry Management*, *7*(5), 62–80.

Rutherford, D. G. (1990). *Hotel management and operations*. New York: Van Nostrand Reinhold.

Sabuncuoğlu, Z. (1988). *Personel yönetimi-politika ve yönetsel teknikler*. İstanbul: Teknografik Matbaası.

Sabuncuoğlu, Z. (2000). *İnsan kaynakları yönetimi*. Bursa: Ezgi Kitabevi.

Simons, T., & Hinkin, T. (2001). The effect of employee turnover on hotel profits test across multiple hotels. *The Cornell Hotel and Restaurant Administration Quarterly*, *42*(4), 65–69.

Simons, T., & Mclean J. P. (2001). Beyond the service-profit chain: The impact of managerial integrity on customers and profits. Paper presented at the 2001 Asian Hospitality Conference, Hong Kong.

Staw, B. M. (1980). The consequences of turnover. *Journal of Occupational Behaviour*, *1*(4), 253–273.

Stone, G. J., & Ineson, E. M. (1997). An international comparison of personality differences between hospitality and other sector managers. *International Journal of Selection and Assessment*, *5*(4), 215–228.

Tanke, M. L. (1990). *Human resources management for the hospitality industry*. USA: Delmar Publishers.

Terborg, J. R., & Lee, T. W. (1984). A predictive study of organizational turnover rates. *Academy of Management Journal, 27*(4), 793–810.

Varoglu, D., & Eser, Z. (2006). How service employees can be treated as internal customers in hospitality industry. *The Business Review, 5*(2), 30–35.

Walmsley, A. (2004). Assessing staff turnover: A view from the English Riviera. *International Journal of Tourism Research, 6,* 275–287.

Wasmuth, W. J., & Davis, S. W. (1983). Managing employee turnover: Why employees leave. *Cornell Hotel and Restaurant Administration Quarterly, 24*(1), 10–18.

Werbel, J. D., & Bedeian, A. G. (1989). Intended turnover as a function of age and job performance. *Journal of Organizational Behavior, 10*(3), 275–281.

Werther, W. B., & Davis, J. R. K. (1996). *Human resources and personnel management* (3rd ed.). Singapore: McGraw-Hill.

Wildes, V. J. (2005). Stigma in food service work: How it affects restaurant servers' intention to stay in the business or recommend a job to another. *Tourism and Hospitality Research, 5*(3), 213–233.

Woods, R. H., & Macaulay, J. F. (1989). RX for turnover: Retention programs that work. *Cornell Hotel and Restaurant Administration Quarterly, 30*(1), 79–90.

Wright, T. A., & Bonett, D. G. (1992). The effect of turnover on work satisfaction and mental health: Support for a situational perspective. *Journal of Organizational Behavior, 13*(6), 603–615.

The role of conflict management in human resource development in the hospitality industry

Larry A. Rice

Johnson & Wales University,
Miami, FL 33181, USA

Claire Michele Rice

Department Conflict Analysis & Resolution
at the Graduate School of Humanities
and Social Sciences, Nova Southeastern
University, Fort Lauderdale, FL 33314, USA

Introduction

Cliques are quite common in the hospitality field. Many industry professionals can identify with the lines of separation between the "front-of-the-house" and "back-of-the-house." The front-of-the-house is comprised of areas visible to or in direct contact with the guests. Such are the cashier, dining room, front desk, concierge, reception desk, and bars. On the other hand, the back-of-the-house areas are behind the scenes and not as visible to guests. These are areas such as the kitchen, housekeeping, accounting, and engineering departments. In the hospitality industry, while most workplace conflicts are interpersonal (Babin & Boles, 1998), such disputes between employees are often symptoms of much larger problems—inter-departmental conflicts (Bittner, 1995; Cybulski, 1997; Friedman, 2006). On a broader level, workplace conflicts are rooted in departmental disputes and lines of divisions between departments that sprout micro-level conflicts between staff members belonging to different departments.

If for example, the dining room staff in the restaurant shows little regard for the kitchen staff and vice versa, the net result will be a climate of disrespect between both departments. Consequently, disrespect that transcends the larger communities becomes manifested in the social discord between the staff members when they interact. Inter-departmental conflicts are derived from departmental cliques or cohorts which form from departmentalized sub-cultures within the organization. To move beyond the symptoms of interpersonal disputes, it is important to address the inter-departmental issues (Lorenzini & Johnson, 1995; Cybulski, 1997; Sills, 2006; Rosenbloom, 2007). Resolution at the departmental levels requires de-socialization (removing counterproductive values) and re-socialization (teaching productive values) (Thompson & Hickey, 2004). De-socialization in the context of the workplace is simply creating awareness of how these types of divisions are formed and integrating systems through conflict resolution and community building training techniques to develop a more positive workplace. Divided sub-cultures have become a socialized method for how organizations unknowingly build counterproductive communities (Folger, Poole, & Stutman, 2001; Rice, 2004). This type of community building is a social construct linked to a phenomenon we have dubbed, "The Recess Effect" (Rice & Rice, 2005).

Within the context of the hospitality industry, this chapter will first address points of conflict as popularly discussed in hospitality industry literature. Then, the phenomenon known as "The Recess Effect" will be discussed in light of trends in the hospitality workplace and alternative approaches to building productive teams within workplaces that are able to effectively manage conflict.

Workplace conflict in the hospitality industry

The service sector constitutes a significant segment of the U.S. economy, and it is estimated that 8 out of 10 people are employed in the service economy. Therefore, problems arising out of customer service, particularly in the hospitality industry cannot be underemphasized. Service orientation discrepancy results from differing views of what constitutes effective customer service among managers and their employees (Cha, 1995).

In an industry where workers are already receiving low wages, these differing perceptions can quickly result in role ambiguity and job dissatisfaction (Babin & Boles, 1998). Consequently, extreme employee frustration and job stress lead to conflict, blame-shifting, and the resulting high turnovers (Jesitus, 1992; Haynes & Fryer, 2000; Hsieh & Yen, 2005; Ross, 1995; Pryor, 2006).

Part of the problem with conflict among employees—whatever their rank within the organizational structure—is that they engage in *HR self-deception* (Pryor, 2006). This is when the individual sees himself or herself as the *solution* while others are seen as the *problem*. The organization can quickly develop a *Blame Culture*, as Pryor, R. (2006) proposes. This shifting of blame may result in an organizational paralysis. If managers and their employees have not learned to examine what roles they play in conflict (Barrow, 2006; Pryor, 2006; Rice & Hunt, 2004, 2005), they are correspondingly unable to come to terms as to how to fix customer service problems (Haynes & Fryer, 2000). All the while, dissatisfied customers take their business elsewhere, thus impacting the bottom line.

Some conflicts between employees and managers even escalate to violence. The U.S. Centers for Disease Control and Prevention identified workplace violence as a national contagion and hazard to public welfare. In the U.S., workplace violence represented the primary and third cause of death among women and men, respectively. A 1997 study from National Institute for Occupational Safety & Health found that each week, on average, 15 people are killed at work, with 1 of these being a restaurant worker. Each year, on average about 50 restaurant workers are killed due to workplace violence. These figures underscore the importance of dealing with conflict before it escalates. Consequently, Myer and Bosner (1999) propose that hospitality industry supervisors should receive conflict resolution training that will enable them to anticipate and recognize workplace conflict in order to address it before it escalates.

Conflicts within the workplace, however, are not just limited to verbal exchanges between employees and their managers. Some result from poor customer service and the attendant lack of professional behavior that employees demonstrate toward their customers, which spurs serious conflicts. Professionalism relates to one applying a learned skill at an occupational level. However, professional decorum, the essence of professionalism, means having the conventions of cultured behavior and mannerisms (Rice, 1996). When employees fail to behave themselves in a professional manner, they drive away valuable customers. While isolated conflicts between employees and customers may seem insignificant; if U.S. hotels were known to offer poor customer service, this perception would be devastating to the whole industry in terms of tourism revenue (Rice, 1996).

Not everyone is able to provide professional service and this represents another source of conflict between hospitality workers and their customers. If hosts are uneasy in rendering service to their guests perhaps due to their own prejudices, the guests will also sense their unease. Speaking to professionals who operate lodging facilities, Stankus admonishes hosts with "strong intolerance for certain people, for whatever reason" to not serve as hosts. He cites an example in which a reservation service agency makes specific provisions in its contract regarding this issue: "If you have any irreconcilable differences regarding race, creed, color, or national origin, we strongly advise you not to become a host" (Stankus, 1997, p. 5). Customers are often perceptive, and many of them can recognize when a server or a host is genuinely interested in making their lodging or eating experiences, or any other type of service enjoyable and comfortable. They also realize when their hosts and service providers offer them a deceptive mask of courtesy. Effective customer service training and conflict resolution management would ensure that the customer's needs are genuinely attended to with a positive and polite attitude. Furthermore, training employees on professional decorum is the key to a more holistic training experience, which encompasses theoretical knowledge, practical experience, and the less tangible but compelling power of moral and ethical values in the workplace (Rice, 1996). These elements would go a long way in stemming conflict arising from poor customer service.

In devising human resource (HR) solutions, it is incumbent upon line managers and HR professionals to partner in order to develop strategies in conflict management that will inevitably impact the bottom line (Haynes & Fryer, 2000; Peacock, 1995). As an example, in restaurants, cooks, servers, hosts, and restaurant managers must work together as a team to ensure that customers receive what they order in a professional manner. Each group of restaurant workers forms their own units and sometimes can easily clash due to lack of communication and mistakes in performing transactions at peak time. If the server takes the wrong order, the cook cannot produce the desired item for the customer; and if the cook poorly presents a dish, the server may face the wrath of the customer (Lorenzini & Johnson, 1995). With more open and effective communication between managers and their employees, the vision of managers and their teams align concerning what represents success in customer service (Peacock, 1995; Ross, 1995). As employees learn to get along with management and each other, everyone can feel a greater sense of belonging in their organization, less frustration, and customer service will improve (Haynes & Fryer, 2000; Ross, 1995).

Beside the broader issues surrounding customer service incidents that may cause clashes among co-workers, tempers may collide over individuals who are considered to have difficult personalities. Regardless of the industry, people have different personal realities, experiential baggage, and family concerns that shape their personalities (Sills, 2006). Some of this historical and experiential baggage produces employees that psychologists refer to as "difficult people." These individuals often exude negativity and complain about assigned tasks. They are often abrasive, verbally abusive, and uncompromising in their resolve—generally cantankerous (Rosenbloom, 2007). Solutions to dealing with people who are clearly abusive may be more clear-cut than with average employees facing difficult life circumstances who may display such characteristics. For instance, a supervisor might fire a known abrasive employee because he shouted at him in the heat of the moment. However, that supervisor may be more patient in dealing with an employee that is perceived as a good worker, but who happens to be having a bad day.

So much of what hospitality workers do is performed through departmental teams that enable dichotomies or lines of division—for example, cooks versus servers, servers versus hosts, housekeeping versus front desk; in short, front-of-the-house versus back-of-the-house. Consequently, team building strategies that incorporate the management and mediation of conflictual situations should be at the top of the list. In the hospitality industry in particular, conflict management in teams can serve as an effective resource in combating service orientation discrepancies, resulting in employee turnover (Cha, 1995; Haynes & Fryer, 2000) and poor service to clients (Hsieh & Yen, 2005; Swain, 2006). To avoid developing a blame-shifting atmosphere in the workplace, however, the greatest tool in teaching employees how to manage conflict is assisting them in understanding first, how they build teams, then, how to work within teams. Based upon that knowledge, people can determine what they may have contributed to a conflict and devise solutions to address these shortcomings more specifically (Rice & Hunt, 2004).

Clique formation and The Recess Effect: contributing factors to conflict in the hospitality industry

Clique formation within the hospitality industry is a common phenomenon, particularly inter-departmentally. As noted earlier, in the restaurant industry, servers, cooks, hosts, managers, and supervisor all have their respective working groups, and some of the disputes that arise among these groups of workers are partly based on a lack of understanding for the work demands and the kind of load that each group bears (Lorenzini & Johnson, 1995). Hotels have various departments, each responsible for the overall functioning of the facility as well. Housekeeping workers may clash with front desk workers as it pertains to deadlines for room turnover (Bittner, 1995). Such rifts occur if the training and orientation for workers within different departments takes place within a vacuum such that employees are not exposed to what others actually do. While some organizations do cross training and allow a cook, for instance, to spend a day in the life of a server (Lorenzini & Johnson, 1995), these efforts at true enlightenment for employees across departments are limited. This disconnect makes it difficult to mitigate conflict and nurture a culture of team building. Thus, it is important to understand how cliques form within a business context and how the development of cliques versus that of true teams can exacerbate the kinds of conflicts in the hospitality industry that have been previously discussed.

It is notable here that a distinction is drawn between cliques and teams. While cliques are exclusionary in nature, true teams work in a collaborative fashion to perform their allotted tasks (Napier & Gershenfield, 2004). Exclusionary cliques do not suddenly appear as college or high school graduates enter into the world of work. Rather, they emerge from years of socialization from childhood. If left unchecked, this social learning produces a phenomenon related to team building, which we have dubbed, "The Recess Effect" (Rice & Rice, 2005). During recess at school, children quickly learn to form cliques on the playground. Most children fall into three essential categories when playing games, sports, and other team activities: the Pickers, the Picked, or the Benchwarmers. As with children, most adult employees may identify themselves as belonging to one of these categories. Consequently, they may take on roles in work groups that match these labels and influence their level of productivity (Napier & Gershenfield, 2004).

Following a similar description as those of the children of *The Recess Effect* (Rice & Rice, 2005), the following describe the three categories of workers: the Pickers, the Picked, and the Benchwarmers. The Pickers are the popular employees in an organization, and they almost always participate in company activities. Consequently, they quickly gain opportunities to select whom they want in their work groups for departmental projects or duty assignments. The Pickers generally have outstanding qualities that position them in the forefront, including the following: assertiveness, aggressiveness, self-confidence, courage, and enthusiasm. The Pickers are often of above-average statue, more charismatic, and extroverted. Employees who exude these qualities normally emerge as team leaders (Dubrin, 2004; Hasselbein, Goldsmith, & Beckhard, 1996).

The Picked are employees who, for the most part, are held in nearly as high esteem as the Pickers and are next in line. These individuals are either friends of the Pickers or are perceived as being skillful at their jobs. Depending on how often they are selected and who chose them, the Picked are usually quite content and always proud to be on "A" teams at work. Because the Picked are often less outspoken or driven than the Pickers, they choose to follow the leaders. However, it is not uncommon for the Picked to become Pickers as they acquire more skill or popularity (Rice & Rice, 2005).

The Benchwarmer category is comprised of the most interesting group of employees, as they tend to be marginalized by others in the team selection process. These employees are often not included in groups because they are seen as less desirable or perhaps they are perceived as possessing personalities and quirks that make them not a good fit for the team. If personality is not an issue but skill is a factor, the Benchwarmers might be seen as possessing fewer skills than other more seasoned employees, and less aptitude or training for group tasks. It is notable, however, that some employees might be left out of social cliques, yet may be included in group tasks that require their expertise (Rice & Rice, 2005).

Consequently, Benchwarmers might be seen as a liability to the successful completion of a task. The Benchwarmers are usually the passive ones in the departments and begin to develop a lackadaisical attitude about work since they are labeled as being underperforming employees. This constant labeling then becomes a self-fulfilling prophesy (Thompson & Hickey, 2005). They do not tend to make waves when left out during the team selection process. In the rare cases when the Benchwarmers do have the opportunity to participate, it is often because of a departmental mandate or intervention from supervisors (Rice & Rice, 2005).

For the most part, the most dominating figures in departments are Pickers. Not only are Pickers learning how to assert themselves, they are also learning how to position themselves to play the game of survival of the fittest. In some instances, *The Recess Effect* phenomenon can limit a Picker's ability to view the Picked and the Benchwarmer as equals in the department. Such perceptions invariably result in an elitist attitude in dealing with others. While not all team leaders (Pickers) set out to marginalize particular employees, their ability to select team members is overshadowed by their inability to be inclusive and empathetic during the selection process (Dubrin, 2004; Hasselbein *et al.*, 1997). Demands of time and profit may also cause Pickers to cut corners and avoid dealing with employees they feel will need to be mentored or require more attention. Employees who feel marginalized experience the stresses and conflicts noted earlier, far more than their counterparts who seem to be well received in the workplace (Napier & Gershenfeld, 2004). Sometimes, they unwittingly become the difficult personalities described by Sills (2006).

After the selection process, when teams are formed, members can be categorized in the following manner: there are the worker-bees, the dominators, the socializers, and the slackers. Most people, who have ever had a group project, whether on the job, at school, or on a committee, can relate. Each member of the team—whether they play the role of the dominators, the worker-bees, and the slackers—will contribute to group success or failure, particularly as they strive to meet deadlines, grades, or dollars attached to the assignments or tasks of the group. Even within formed groups, The Recess Effect continues to play out, and the cycle of exclusion may follow. The dominators described in the group dynamics literature share characteristics common to Pickers; the worker-bees behave like the Picked; and those who often slack in groups have done so as a result of having experiences similar to those of the Benchwarmers (Rice, 2005; for a more detailed discussion on personality traits and group dynamics, see Folger *et al.*, 2001; Napier & Gershenfeld, 2004). The more outgoing individuals may emerge as socializers and also thwart progress. Invariably in restaurants, hotels or other venues, there are employees, who fall into the mold of the Benchwarmers. Their full potentials are not well developed because cliques formed by the Pickers and the Picked prohibit them from learning, growing, and excelling in the workplace.

Contributing factors such as the experiential baggage that team members bring with them may spur a latent counterproductive culture that manifests when these individuals work with others. If each group member carries his or her own personal baggage and biased expectations about the nature of the group's interactive dynamic, these intangibles may result in conflict and non-productive teams (Napier & Gershenfeld, 2004). Orientation and icebreaker exercises should be used to cut across the veil of unfamiliarity among co-workers. With greater sensitivity and understanding about the past challenges of individual team members, groups can work together to create a more productive trajectory.

Thus, conflict management strategies and training for teams, which consider issues of inclusion in the workplace are key. Hunt and Rice (2005) note that an important quality for inclusive community builders (or team builders in our parlance) is inclusiveness, which is accompanied by complementing values that yield winning teams: sharing, caring, trusting, and respecting. According to the Inclusive Community Building (ICB) Model, if the workplace is seen as a community of people, these values can be emphasized in training sessions during the orientation process and transmitted through mentoring, role modeling, and conflict resolution preparation.

Implementing conflict management strategies in light of The Recess Effect

Managers, leaders, HR professionals, trainers, and line employees in the hospitality industry each can benefit from understanding The Recess Effect. A strategy for dealing with both the internal and external conflicts resulting from problems within teams is instituting conflict resolution training that incorporates team building exercises as a strategy for conflict management. Such preparation would enable workers to understand the vectors of conflict that tend to divide employees across departments.

Conflict resolution must be seen as a process and not just a static occurrence. Resolution strategies vary depending on company culture, resources available for implementation, and other situational factors. Conflict resolution workshops may include training on alternative dispute resolution strategies such as anger management, effective communication, stress management, mediation, and negotiation. Furthermore, the training spectrum should move from the level of the individual and interpersonal conflict to the level of the group. First, at the level of individuals, employees must learn to look at conflict as a unitary process (Rice & Hunt, 2004). That is, they must be willing to discern what part they play in any given problem or argument in order to find sustainable solutions or resolution. This introspective approach reduces the likelihood of defensiveness and encourages problem-solving. Secondly, the unitary (introspective) conflict resolution process discourages people from shifting blame to others (Rice, 2005; Rice & Hunt, 2004). The danger in blame-shifting is that the individual always sees him or herself as the victim and, therefore, cannot move beyond self-pity and denial of fault. Once their own defensive mechanisms have been disarmed, they can more constructively resolve conflict with others (Black, 2006; Pryor, 2006; Rice & Hunt, 2004).

In an article dealing with negotiation and conflict, Ury and Weiss encourage, "going to the balcony" the process by which one can examine a conflictual situation by taking themselves out of it and replaying the issues from an observer's perspective. In this way, one can flesh out the other party's perspective as well as his/her own (Black, 2006). These introspective approaches reduce the likelihood of defensiveness and encourage problem-solving. The danger in blame-shifting is that the individual always sees him or herself as the victim and, therefore, cannot move beyond self-pity and denial of fault. Once the employees' own defensive mechanisms have been disarmed, they can more constructively dialogue and find solutions to disputes with others.

Teaching employees to listen to each other carefully in times of conflict is another critical step towards conflict management (Bolton, 1979; Nichols, 1995; Pryor, 2006). With lines of communication open, they can better diagnose, understand, and analyze problems. Once, they discern key elements of the conflict, they can devise solutions (Freidman, 2006). As the employees agree to the solutions, they develop a sense of ownership for resolving the conflict. In some hospitality organizations such as Hooters restaurants and the Marriott hotels, peer review systems are used to mediate solutions to workplace conflict. The peer review system allows trained workers to review cases between the employers and employees. Essentially employees are tried by a jury of their peers (Cybulski, 1997; Lorenzini & Johnson, 1995).

At the level of teams and departments, conflict management and resolution strategies may be prescriptive, elicitive, or both. In a prescriptive approach, conflict resolution trainers may be asked to provide a strategy or process to manage the hot spots within the organization. They also teach employees how to manage conflict within their own environment as well through workshops and seminars. On the other hand, the resolution process may be elicitive. That is, although a conflict resolution trainer facilitates problem-solving sessions and provides guidance for all parties, the solutions to conflict and problems emerge from the parties involved within the company (Augsburger, 1992; Avruch, 1998). Some of the peer review processes utilized by some hospitality organizations engage this elicitive approach (Cybulski, 1997; Lorenzini & Johnson, 1995). The community tables, used in community organizing in the non-profit sectors, serve as great examples of elicitive approaches to conflict management and resolution. These problem-solving forums would be beneficial as mediums for brainstorming that would not only spur the employees' creativity at problem-solving, but would also enhance employee cohesion (Gitell & Vidal, 1998; Homan, 2004; Rice, 2004).

While conflict resolution trainers often consult with organizations to determine the kind of approach that would be more appropriate for their company; we propose that a combination of the two approaches, the prescriptive and elicitive, would be most beneficial. The onus should be placed on training employees with a distinct conflict management framework that serves as a spring board for future resolution strategies. Brainstormed strategies can be utilized to create environments that promote positive team building within the employees' own workplaces (Gitell & Vidal, 1998; Homan, 2004). If employees own their conflict resolution processes, they can more easily embrace the outcomes.

Applying lessons from The Recess Effect to hospitality leadership and conflict management

Strategies for dealing with workplace conflict are supported only when management and employees alike are willing to implement the solutions. Subsequently, these solutions must be monitored and evaluated to insure that the remedies are sustainable (Rice & Hunt, 2005). This requires effective leadership. The Drucker Foundation addresses the phenomena of natural born leaders (the Pickers described in The Recess Effect), stating that "when leadership is viewed as a nonlearnable set of character traits or as equivalent to an exalted position, a self-fulfilling prophesy is created that dooms societies to having only a few good leaders. It is far healthier and more productive for us to start with the assumption that it is possible for everyone to lead" (Leithwood, Jantzi, & Steinbach, 1999, p. 115).

The problem starts with leaders who are more concerned about meeting the bottom line than servicing people's needs (Dubrin, 2004; Hesselbein *et al.*, 1997). In the hospitality industry, which is a service-oriented industry, servant-leadership is particularly important (DePree, 1989). As managers exhibit the proper examples of servant-leadership within their own organizations, their employees may follow suit. Many people learn best by observation. The phrase, "You've got to walk the walk, not just talk the talk" is a clarion call from individuals who are weary of hearing "smooth words" from people in positions of authority. These people are ready to see the words transformed into action. Servant-leaders who command respect are willing to demonstrate genuine care for their employees and encourage inclusion in the team building process. In turn, this encourages their employees to do the same not only in their work groups, but also for management and for their customers. Ultimately, the organization's customers will benefit.

To counter The Recess Effect, management must make a concerted effort to promote a culture of servant-leadership (DePree, 1989). Supervisors, managers, and team leaders alike within this paradigm, will be placed into action-oriented roles wherein they will serve as mentors and coaches to all of their constituents. Mentoring and coaching entail putting the terms *sharing* and *caring* into action (Rice & Hunt, 2005). Essentially, the Pickers can teach the Picked and the Benchwarmers how to themselves become leaders. To promote respect and solidarity between managers and their employees, management will take the time to institute sustainable team building and conflict management training programs that instruct them on how to develop invaluable traits—a higher tolerance for frustration, humility, trustworthiness, passion, and self-awareness (Peacock, 1995; Rice & Rice, 2005)—all of which are necessary to assist them in managing and resolving conflict and ultimately, sustain winning teams.

References

Augsburger, D. W. (1992). *Conflict mediation across cultures pathways and patterns*. Louisville: Westminster/John Knox Press.

Avruch, K. (1998). *Culture and conflict resolution*. Washington, DC: United States Institute of Peace Press.

Babin, B. J., & Boles, J. S. (1998, April). Employee behavior in a service environment: A model and test of potential differences between men and women. *Journal of Marketing*, *62*(April), 77–81.

Bittner, R. (1995, July). How to handle conflict. *Hotels*, p. 22.

Black, E. (2006). Going to the balcony. *Office Pro*, *6*(7), 26–28.

Bolton, R. (1979). *People skills: How to assert yourself, listen to others and resolve conflict*. New York: Simon & Schuster.

Cha, S. K. (1995). *Service orientation discrepancy between managers and employees and its impact on the affective reactions of employees: A case study of casual restaurant segment*. Doctoral Dissertation, Virginia Polytechnic Institute & State University. Dissertation Abstracts International (UMI No. 9544238).

Cybulski, A. (1997). People's court. *Restaurant Business*, *96*(18), 43.

DePree, M. (1989). *Leadership is an art*. New York: Dell Publishing.

Dubrin, A. J. (2004). *Leadership research findings, practice and skills*. New York: Houghton Mifflin Company.

Friedman, R. (2006, September 11). Knock out on-the-job conflicts, complaints with six simple steps. *Nation's Restaurant News*, p. 30.

Folger, J. P., Poole, M. S., & Stutman, R. D. (2001). *Working through conflict: Strategies for relationships, groups, and organizations*. New York: Addison Wesley Longman, Inc.

Gitell., & Vidal, A. (1998). *Community organizing building social capital as a development strategy*. Thousand Oaks, CA: SAGE Publications.

Hasselbein, F., Goldsmith, M., & Beckhard, R. (1997). *The leader of the future*. New York: Jossey-Bass.

Haynes, P., & Fryer, G. (2000). Human resources, service quality and performance: A case study. *International Journal of Contemporary Hospitality Management*, *12*(4), 240–248.

Homan, M. S. (2004). *Promoting community change: Making it happen in the real world*. Belmont, CA: Brooks/Cole-Thompson Learning.

Hsieh, A., & Yen, C. (2005). The effect of customer service participation on service providers' job stress. *The Service Industries Journal*, *25*(7), 891–905.

Jesitus, J. (1992). Hotels hunger for stable workforce. *Hotel and Motel Management*, *297*, 48–50.

Leithwood, K. A., Jantzi, D., & Steinbach, R. (1999). *Changing leadership for changing times*. Philadelphia, PA: Open University Press.

Lorenzini, B., & Johnson, B. A. (1995, May 1). Restaurant wars. *R&I: The Staff*, pp. 150–158.

235 • • •

Myer, P., & Bosner, K. (1999). Violence in the workplace: What operators can do to help prevent it. *Nation's Restaurant News*, *33*(33), 20.

Napier, R. W., & Gershenfeld, M. K. (2004). *Groups theory and experience*. Boston, MA: Houghton Mifflin Company.

Nichols, M. P. (1995). *The lost art of listening: How learning to listen can improve relationships*. New York: The Guilford Press.

Peacock, M. (1995). A job well done: Hospitality managers and success. *International Journal of Contemporary Hospitality Management*, *7*(2/3), 48–51.

Pryor, R. (2006, November 14). Expert's view: Conflict in the workplace. *Personnel Today*, p. 29.

Pryor, R. (2006, November 14). How to win the war at work. *Personnel Today*, p. 29.

Rice, C. M. (2005). The Ellison's Inclusive Community Building Model: A Functional System's Approach. *FEF Journal of Interdisciplinary Studies*, *1*(1), 100–139.

Rice, C. M., & Hunt, D. G. (2004). The Ellison Unitary Model in Conflict Resolution Training. *Peace and Conflict Studies*, *2*(11), 35–54.

Rice, L. A. (1996). Desperately seeking professionalism. *The Epicurean*, *1*, 4–7.

Rice, L. A., & Rice, C. M. (2005). The recess effect. Life lessons on organizational teambuilding. Manuscript submitted for publication.

Rosenbloom, S. (2007, January 17). *Conflict in the workplace: Help, I'm surrounded by jerks*. The New York Times, p. G1.

Ross, G. F. (1995). Interpersonal stress reactions and service quality responses among hospitality industry employees. *The Service Industries Journal*, *15*(3), 314–331.

Sills, J. (2006). When personalities clash. *Psychology Today*, *39*(6), 60–62.

Stankus, J. (1997). *How to open and operate a bed & breakfast* (5th ed.). Old Saybrook, CT: The Globe Pequot Press.

Thompson, W. & Hickey J. (2005). *Society in focus: An Introduction to Sociology*. 5th Edition, Boston: Allyn & Bacon.

Work-family conflict and facilitation: implications for hospitality researchers

Osman M. Karatepe

School of Tourism and Hospitality Management, Eastern Mediterranean University, Gazimagusa, Turkish Republic of Northern Cyprus Via Mersin 10, Turkey

Introduction

The hospitality industry is a service-oriented business and is one of the largest employers in many tourism destinations. Many of the individuals employed in the hospitality industry have frequent face-to-face or voice-to-voice interaction with customers and are regarded as strategic weapons in the acquisition and retention of profitable loyal customers. Individuals working in back-of-the house and having limited or no face-to-face or voice-to-voice interaction with customers help frontline employees achieve the abovementioned goal.

The hospitality industry, however, is plagued with a number of problems emanating from poor human resource management practices. For instance, employees are often confronted with role stress, heavy workloads, long work hours, irregular work schedules, and job insecurity (Cannon, 1998; Deery & Shaw, 1999; Rowley & Purcell, 2001). They are devoid of effective continuous training programs, empowerment, and rewards. Apart from these problems, employees are susceptible to conflicts in the work-family interface (Karatepe & Baddar, 2006; Karatepe & Sokmen, 2006; Namasivayam & Mount, 2004). *Work-family conflict* and *family-work conflict* are the two forms of interrole conflict (Frone, Russell, & Cooper, 1992). Work-family conflict refers to "a form of interrole conflict in which the general demands of, time devoted to, and strain created by the job interfere with performing family-related responsibilities"; and family-work conflict refers to "a form of interrole conflict in which the general demands of, time devoted to, and strain created by the family interfere with performing work-related responsibilities (Netemeyer, Boles, & McMurrian, 1996, p. 410).

Individuals involved in multiple roles experience work-family conflict and family-work conflict and report negative outcomes such as job and life dissatisfaction. Researchers have used various theoretical frameworks (e.g., scarcity and conservation of resources perspectives) to explain the complexities of the interrelationships between work and family roles and negative outcomes (Aryee, Srinivas, & Tan, 2005; Grandey & Cropanzano, 1999; Netemeyer, Maxham, & Pullig, 2005).

A careful examination of the extant literature demonstrates that there are only few studies examining the underlying factors that may promote positive interaction between work (family) and family (work) domains. Participation in multiple roles may produce a number of benefits for employees, and these benefits may help to overcome the difficulties and costs associated with both domains (Aryee *et al.*, 2005; Demerouti, Geurts, &

Kompier, 2004; Grzywacz & Marks, 2000; Wayne, Musisca, & Fleeson, 2004). This notion is consistent with the expansion-enhancement perspective (Aryee *et al.*, 2005). Types of facilitation in the work-family interface are *work-family facilitation* and *family-work facilitation*. In this context, Frone (2003) suggests a fourfold taxonomy of work-family balance that consists of two types of conflicts and facilitation and defines work-family facilitation as "the extent to which participation at work (or home) is made easier by virtue of the experiences, skills, and opportunities gained or developed at home (or work)" (p. 145). Employees who have the opportunity to participate in decision-making in the workplace and develop decision-making skills may also use these skills and experiences to deal more effectively with family issues. And also, resources such as family/spouse support may enable employees to work long hours and pursue advancement opportunities in the workplace.

Against this backdrop, the purpose of this chapter is to identify significant gaps in the research regarding the antecedents, outcomes, and moderators of both directions of conflict and facilitation and present key issues that have received scant attention in the hospitality management literature. Since it is impossible to provide a detailed review of the interrelationships between work and family roles in one chapter, we have focused on a selective review of the relevant literature. Specifically, as mentioned earlier, work-family conflict and work-family facilitation have bidirectional dimensions. Thus, the overwhelming majority of the peer-reviewed papers we have used in this chapter have assessed work-family conflict and family-work conflict and/or work-family facilitation and family-work facilitation.

This chapter is divided into three parts. In the first part, we review the antecedents, outcomes, and moderators pertaining to work-family conflict and family-work conflict. The second part consists of the review of the antecedents, outcomes, and moderators of two directions of facilitation. Finally, in the third part, we respond to the question "where do we go from here?" in order to present key issues that deserve to be studied more in the hospitality management literature.

Work-family conflict and family-work conflict

Antecedents

As stated before, work-family conflict (also called "work-to-family interference", "work-to-family conflict", and "work interfering with family") and family-work conflict (also called "family-to-work interference", "family-to-work conflict", and "family interfering with work") are the two directions of conflict. Consistent with the recent reviews conducted by Byron (2005), Frone (2003), and Poelmans, O'Driscoll, and Beham (2005), our review of the extant research is based on two major groups of antecedents: (1) work- and family-related variables and (2) individual/personality variables.

Work- and family-related variables • • •

A synthesis of the extant research indicates that work-related variables such as work demands and work stressors are significant determinants of work-family conflict, while family-related variables such as family demands and family stressors are significant predictors of family-work conflict. These findings are actually supported by Frone's (2003) recent review of work-family balance. He stated "… the role antecedents of work-to-family conflict reside in the work domain, whereas the role-related antecedents of family-to-work conflict reside in the family domain" (pp. 151–152).

In empirical terms, Frone *et al.* (1992) found that job stressors were positively related to work-family conflict, while family involvement and family stressors were positively associated with family-work conflict. Aryee, Fields, and Luk (1999) tested Frone *et al.*'s (1992) conceptual model of the work-family interface using a sample of married Hong Kong employees and found similar results. Broadly speaking, they demonstrated that work-family conflict was a significant outcome of job conflict, whereas family conflict was a significant predictor of family-work conflict. In addition, Frone, Yardley, and Markel (1997) reported that work overload and work time commitments intensified work-family conflict. According to their findings, work distress increased work-family conflict, whereas family distress, family overload, and family time commitments intensified family-work conflict. Similar to the above-mentioned findings, Carlson and Kacmar (2000) reported that government employees' work-family conflict increased due to work time demands and job involvement. They further reported that family-related variables such as family involvement, family role conflict, and family role ambiguity increased employees' conflict between family and work domains.

Consistent with the early work of Greenhaus and Beutell (1985), Carlson, Kacmar, and Williams (2000) developed and validated a scale, which measures three forms of work-family conflict and family-work conflict, namely time-based conflict, strain-based conflict, and behavior-based conflict. Using data from a Hong Kong university sample consisting of both academic and nonacademic staff, Fu and Shaffer (2001) examined the relationships of work- and family-related variables with three forms of work-family conflict and family-work conflict. Their findings showed that role overload and hours spent on paid work significantly predicted time- and strain-based work-family conflict, whereas role conflict significantly predicted time-, strain-, and behavior-based work-family conflict. They further emphasized that parental demands were positively linked to time-based conflict between family and work domains, while hours spent on household work were positively related to behavior-based family-work conflict. In a large Dutch study, Peeters, Montgomery, Bakker, and Schaufeli (2005) reported that job demands increased individuals' work-home interference, and individuals being confronted with higher home demands experienced higher home-work interference.

The aforementioned findings based on North American, European, and Hong Kong samples are congruent with Frone's (2003) assertion that work-related antecedents reside in the work domain, while family-related antecedents reside in the family domain. Although these results appear to be convincing, there may be several antecedents affecting both work-family conflict and family-work conflict, even in North American, European, and Hong Kong samples. For example, in a study of employed parents in Hong Kong, Aryee, Luk, Leung, and Lo (1999) found that work overload intensified both work-family conflict and family-work conflict. They stated "… for Hong Kong Chinese employed parents, taking on more responsibilities at work may be indicative of one's commitment to ensuring the financial security of one's family and, therefore, represents a blurring of the family and work domains" (p. 273). As such, Aryee et al. (2005) demonstrated similar findings for a sample of Indian employed parents.

Furthermore, Frye and Breaugh (2004) showed that having supervisor support in the workplace diminished employees' both work-family and family-work conflicts. Karatepe and Kilic (2007) found similar results for a sample of frontline hotel employees in Northern Cyprus. Although spousal support is an effective resource to alleviate family-work conflict, these findings clearly reveal that supervisor support may also reside in the family domain. For instance, a supportive supervisor in the workplace may provide employees with permission so that they may deal more effectively with family-related responsibilities such as meeting with child's teacher, taking the child to medical appointments on time, and spending some time for shopping.

Individual/personality variables • • •

A careful review of the extant research indicates that as an individual variable, gender appears to influence work-family and family-work conflicts, with men experiencing more conflict between work and family domains and women having difficulty in carrying out family and work responsibilities (Poelmans *et al.*, 2005). Yet, empirical evidence based on the samples of the affluent Western countries generally demonstrates no significant impact of gender on two directions of interference (Byron, 2005; Grandey & Cropanzano, 1999; Kinnunen & Mauno, 1998).

In contrast, Fu and Shaffer (2001) found gender differences. Specifically, women experienced greater time- and strain-based conflict between family and work domains, whereas men reported higher time- and behavior-based conflict between work and family domains. They discussed that these findings could be attributed to gender role expectations in Chinese culture. Explicitly, women are still expected to be responsible for family-related issues such as childrearing and homemaking, while men are still expected to be the primary breadwinners.

In a recent empirical study, Karatepe and Sokmen (2006) reported that female frontline employees in the Turkish hotel industry were susceptible to more work-family and family-work conflicts. Although women are now more educated and participate more in the Turkish workforce, they are still expected to set priorities to fulfill family and home duties. Also, Karatepe and Baddar (2006) found that female frontline employees in the Jordanian hotel industry reported higher conflict between family and work domains. They discussed this finding on the basis of masculinity and gender inequalities, stating "men are still considered as the primary breadwinners of the family and are responsible for the well-being of the family, while women are still responsible for home and family duties such as motherhood." (p. 1025).

These findings pertaining to gender differences based on samples from the affluent Western and non-Western countries as well as from developing countries remain inconclusive.

Of the dispositional personality variables studied in the extant research, negative affectivity appears to be an antecedent of work-family conflict and family-work conflict. Negative affectivity is an individual's tendency to experience discomfort across time and situations (Watson & Clark, 1984). However, the relationship of negative affectivity with both directions of conflict has not received much empirical attention. Limited empirical evidence suggests that negative affectivity is significantly and positively related to time-, strain-, and behavior-based work-family conflict (Carlson, 1999). Similar to Carlson's (1999) study, Bruck and Allen (2003) illustrated that individuals high in negative affectivity experienced elevated levels of strain-based conflict between work and family domains. Using a sample of senior civil servants in Hong Kong, Stoeva, Chiu, and Greenhaus (2002) found that negative affectivity had significant positive effects on both directions of interference. It can be deduced from the abovementioned findings that individuals high in negative affectivity experience substantial conflicts between work (family) and family (work) domains.

Positive affectivity is another dispositional personality variable that "reflects the extent to which a person feels enthusiastic, active, and alert" (Watson, Clark, & Tellegen, 1988, p. 1063). However, researchers generally have not examined the impact of positive affectivity on work-family conflict and family-work conflict. This may be due to the fact that positive affectivity has failed to predict stressors and stress outcomes (Stoeva *et al.*, 2002).

Extraversion, agreeableness, conscientiousness, neuroticism, and openness to experience are the 'Big Five' personality variables (Barrick & Mount, 1991). Although limited in number, there is empirical evidence that some of these personality variables play a protective or vulnerability role in both directions of interference. Specifically, in a sample of British female employees, Noor (2003) demonstrated that extraversion mitigated family-work conflict, while neuroticism heightened both work-family and family-work conflicts. In another empirical study, neuroticism was positively linked to both work-family and family-work conflicts (Wayne *et al.*, 2004). In the same study, conscientiousness diminished conflicts in the work-family interface, while agreeableness was negatively associated with conflict between work and family domains. In a recent Finnish longitudinal study, Rantanen, Pulkkinen, and Kinnunen (2005) indicated that as a vulnerability factor, neuroticism was positively related to work-family conflict and family-work conflict for both male and female samples, while as a protective factor, openness to experience was positively related to family-work conflict in men.

Based on the findings of the empirical studies discussed above, it can be asserted that on the whole, the relationships of personality variables with work-family conflict and family-work conflict have not been largely studied in the relevant literature. Although there is some evidence that negative affectivity intensifies two forms of conflicts in the work-family interface, there is no convincing evidence that individuals high in positive affectivity are confronted with low levels of work-family and family-work conflicts. It can also be inferred from the abovementioned findings that not all 'Big Five' personality variables are significantly associated with work-family conflict and family-work conflict, leading to anomalous results.

Outcomes

Consistent with the recent reviews of Allen, Herst, Bruck, and Sutton (2000), Frone (2003), and Poelmans *et al.* (2005), our review of the extant research focuses on three major groups of outcomes of work-family conflict and family-work conflict entitled: (1) work- and family-related outcomes, (2) stress-related outcomes, and (3) other outcomes.

Work- and family-related outcomes • • •

A synthesis of the relevant literature demonstrates that job performance, job satisfaction, career satisfaction, organizational commitment, absenteeism, and turnover intentions are among the work-related consequences of work-family conflict and/or family-work conflict, while family satisfaction and marital satisfaction are among the family-related outcomes of work-family conflict and/or family-work conflict.

Specifically, Netemeyer, Brashear-Alejandro, and Boles (2004) conducted a cross-national study examining the effects of work role and family role variables on job outcomes of salespeople. They found evidence in the United States, Puerto Rico, and Romania samples that salespeople having difficulty in balancing problems between family and work domains reported lower job performance. Their study findings provided empirical support for the positive relationship between work-family conflict and turnover intentions. Similar results also hold true for hospitality settings. For example, Karatepe and Sokmen (2006) found that both directions of conflict had detrimental impacts on service recovery performance and turnover intentions. They also reported that only one direction of conflict, namely, family-work conflict amplified feelings of dissatisfaction with the work role. In another study, Karatepe and Kilic (2007) showed that family-work conflict diminished frontline employees' job performance, while work-family conflict did not. They further illustrated that of the two directions of conflict, only work-family conflict exerted detrimental effects on job satisfaction and turnover intentions.

Aryee, Luk *et al.* (1999) showed that family-work conflict diminished employed parents' job satisfaction, whereas their findings did not lend any empirical support to the negative relationship between work-family conflict and job satisfaction. Neither did their study find significant negative relationships between conflicts in the work-family interface and family satisfaction. On the contrary, Carlson and Kacmar (2000) indicated that work-family conflict reduced family satisfaction. However, their study failed to find a significant negative relationship between family-work conflict and job satisfaction. Namasivayam and Mount (2004) reported that work-family conflict was significantly and negatively related to hotel employees' job satisfaction. Interestingly, they found that family-work conflict positively influenced job satisfaction. They speculated that hotel employees might have perceived work as a resource to handle problems associated with family conflicts, and thus work might have been a source of satisfaction.

In another empirical investigation, work-family conflict reduced job satisfaction, while family-work conflict did not (Wayne *et al.*, 2004). In this study, both directions of conflict also had adverse effects on family satisfaction. Based on data derived from a sample of full-time professional employees in Canada, Mcelwain, Korabik, and Rosin (2005) found that conflict between work and family domains mitigated both male and female employees' family satisfaction, while family-work conflict diminished only male employees' job satisfaction. Karatepe and Baddar (2006) found that family-work conflict was significantly and negatively related to family satisfaction, while work-family conflict was not. According to their findings, both work-family and family-work conflicts escalated employees' turnover intentions.

It is interesting to note that little is known about the relationships of work-family conflict and family-work conflict with career satisfaction, and the individual study results regarding the relationship of work-family conflict with career satisfaction are mixed (Allen *et al.*, 2000). Broadly speaking, Parasuraman, Purohit, Godshalk, and Beutell (1996) found that only family-work conflict had a significant negative impact on entrepreneurial career success. However, Aryee and Luk (1996) did not find any significant effect of work-family conflict on career satisfaction for a sample of dual-earner couples in Hong Kong.

In an empirical research in Finland by Kinnunen and Mauno (1998), family-work conflict was reported to have a detrimental impact on marital satisfaction. Using data from a national family research project in the Netherlands, Kinnunen, Vermulst, Gerris, and Mäkikangas (2003) found that conflicts in the work-family interface affected employed fathers' marital satisfaction deleteriously. As such, employees had marital dissatisfaction because of conflicts between work (family) and family (work) domains (Hill, 2005). In a study of Turkish bank employees conducted by Aycan and Eskin (2005), marital dissatisfaction increased due to work-family conflict.

Carlson *et al.* (2000) indicated that strain- and behavior-based work-family conflicts were significantly and negatively related to family satisfaction, whereas only strain-based form of family-work conflict had a detrimental effect on family satisfaction. They further found that only behavior-based family-work conflict predicted organizational commitment, while only strain-based family-work conflict predicted job satisfaction.

Also, using a sample of professional employed mothers, Casper, Martin, Buffardi, and Erdwins (2002) found that work-family conflict was significantly and positively related to continuance organizational commitment. They, however, found no significant relationship between work-family conflict and affective organizational commitment. Namasivayam and Mount (2004) examined the effects of work-family and family-work conflicts on hotel employees' affective, normative, and continuance organizational commitment and demonstrated that work-family conflict had a significant negative effect on employees' normative commitment. Yet, they failed to find support for the rest of the relationships. In a recent scale development and validation study, a significant negative association between negative home-work interaction and organizational commitment was observed for five Dutch samples (Geurts *et al.*, 2005).

Prior work suggests that work-family conflict is a significant determinant of employees' intentions to leave public accounting, while family-work conflict is not (Greenhaus, Parasuraman, & Collins, 2001). However, recent work indicates that conflicts in the work-family interface trigger turnover intentions of employees in a local government organization in New Zealand (Haar, 2004). Although limited in number, there is empirical evidence that work-family conflict and/or family-work conflict influence absenteeism. For instance, according to the earlier research findings, work-family conflict intensifies employees' absenteeism (Goff, Mount, & Jamison, 1990). Recent research, on the other hand, shows that family-work conflict increases absenteeism, whereas work-family conflict heightens turnover intentions (Anderson, Coffey, & Byerly, 2002).

According to Anderson *et al.* (2002), employees having continuous and unresolved problems between work and family domains would be more interested in intending to find another job, while employees experiencing conflict between family and work domains would display absenteeism to meet family demands.

In his recent review of work-family balance, Frone (2003) suggests that work-family conflict influences family-related variables, whereas family-work conflict influences work-related variables. For example, using data from a sample of employed mothers of adolescents, Frone, Barnes, and Farrell (1994) showed that work-family conflict was significantly and positively related to family dissatisfaction, while family-work conflict had a significant positive impact on job dissatisfaction. Frone *et al.* (1997) found that work-family conflict decreased family performance, while family-work conflict had an adverse impact on work performance. Wayne *et al.* (2004), however, state "… when one role interferes with the other, it may result in poor role quality or performance in the role being inter-fered with" (p. 124). This finding is not congruent with Frone's (2003) assertion that role-related outcomes of work-family con-flict reside in the family domain, while role-related outcomes of family-work conflict reside in the work domain.

Stress-related outcomes ● ● ●

Our review of the relevant literature shows that researchers have examined the relationships of work-family conflict and family-work conflict with such stress-related outcomes as job stress, burnout/emotional (job) exhaustion, psychological strain, depression, poor physical health, and substance use.

Specifically, salespeople had job stress because of the fact that they were confronted with both work-family and family-work conflicts (Netemeyer *et al.*, 2004). Likewise, in a study of employees in the Norwegian food and beverage industry, con-flicts in the work-family interface increased job stress (Hammer, Saksvik, Nytrø, Torvatn, & Bayazit, 2004). However, Netemeyer *et al.* (2005) found that work-family conflict was signifi-cantly and positively associated with job stress, while family-work conflict was not. As such, Karatepe and Baddar (2006) reported similar findings for the Jordanian hotel industry.

There are empirical studies, which have found significant relationships between conflicts in the work-family inter-face and burnout/emotional (job) exhaustion. For example, Kinnunen *et al.* (2003) showed that both work-family con-flict and family-work conflict escalated employed fathers' job exhaustion. Posig and Kickul (2004) reported that work-family conflict was a significant predictor of emotional exhaus-tion for male employees, while both work-family conflict and family-work conflict were significant determinants of emotional exhaustion for female employees. Recently, Peeters *et al.* (2005) demonstrated that both work-home and home-work interferences triggered burnout.

In a study of police department in Canada, MacEwen, and Barling (1994) reported that work-family conflict and family-work conflict were significant determinants of anxiety and depression for men, while only work-family conflict was a significant predictor of anxiety and depression for women. Frone *et al.* (1992) indicated that family-work conflict had a significant positive effect on depression, whereas work-family conflict did not. However, Kinnunen *et al.* (2003) found that work-family conflict and family-work conflict positively affected depression. In addition, O'Driscoll, Ilgen, and Hildreth (1992) illustrated that work-nonwork interference positively affected psychological strain. Brough and Kelling (2002) found evidence in New Zealand that female employees' perceptions of work-family conflict and family-work conflict had significant positive impacts on their psychological strain.

Using data from the National Comorbidity Survey, it was shown that work-family and family-work conflicts triggered mood disorder, anxiety disorder, and substance dependence disorder (Frone, 2000). Conflicts between two domains also increased distress (Noor, 2003). Recently, in a study of employees of the Dutch Postal Service, Demerouti *et al.* (2004) found that negative work-home interaction triggered both fatigue and health complaints, whereas negative home-work interaction increased only fatigue. A more recent empirical study by Geurts *et al.* (2005) concluded that work-home and home-work interferences were significantly and positively associated with fatigue.

Using survey data from two random community samples of employed parents, Frone, Russell, and Barnes (1996) found that depression, poor physical health, and heavy alcohol use were significant outcomes of work-family conflict and family-work conflict in the first sample. Two exceptions in the second sample were that work-family conflict was not significantly associated with poor physical health, while family-work conflict was not significantly associated with heavy alcohol use. In their 4-year longitudinal study of employed parents, Frone, Russell, and Cooper (1997) reported that family-work conflict had significant positive effects on depression, poor physical health, and the incidence of hypertension. They further reported that work-family conflict was related to only heavy alcohol use.

As can be deduced from the abovementioned findings, our review of the relevant literature demonstrates that work-family conflict and family-work conflict appear to have consistent relationships with stress-related consequences such as job stress, burnout, psychological strain, and depression.

Other outcomes • • •

There are empirical studies that demonstrate the relationships of conflicts in the work-family interface with life satisfaction. Specifically, empirical evidence indicates that work-family conflict reduces employees' life satisfaction (Adams, King, & King, 1996; Hill, 2005). Aryee, Luk *et al.* (1999) found that family-work conflict portrayed a negative relationship with life satisfaction, while work-family conflict did not. In another empirical study, Aryee, Fields *et al.* (1999) demonstrated that only work-family conflict weakened life satisfaction. Carlson *et al.* (2000) also showed that strain- and behavior-based work-family conflict had detrimental impacts on life satisfaction, whereas only strain-based form of family-work conflict was negatively related to life satisfaction.

Individuals who cannot establish a balance between work (family) and/or family (work) domains display dissatisfaction with life. This is generally supported by the findings we have discussed above.

Moderators

A careful review of the extant research demonstrates that gender, support from supervisor, coworker and spouse, negative affectivity, and several 'Big Five' personality variables were used as moderators. For example, as mentioned earlier in this chapter, Peeters *et al.* (2005) tested the impacts of work-home and home-work interferences on burnout. They also tested the moderating role of gender on the relationships between work-home and home-work interferences and burnout. In their study, gender moderated the impact of work-home interference on burnout such that the relationship was stronger for women than for men and discussed that such a finding is congruent with gender socialization theory.

Mcelwain *et al.* (2005) demonstrated that high levels of family demands resulted in heightened family-work conflict for women than for men. They also indicated that the negative relationship between family-work conflict and job satisfaction was stronger for men than for women. However, they reported no significant moderating impact of gender on the relationship between work demands and work-family conflict and the

• • •

relationship between work-family conflict and family satis-faction. In another empirical study, Posig and Kickul (2004) assessed the differences between men and women in the strength of the relationships between two directions of conflict and emotional exhaustion and demonstrated that the relation-ship between family-work conflict and emotional exhaustion was stronger for women than for men. Additionally, in a recent study, gender moderated the relationship between family-work conflict and psychological well-being in a way that the detrimental impact of family-work conflict on psychological well-being was stronger for women than for men (Aycan & Eskin, 2005).

Stoeva *et al.* (2002) examined negative affectivity as a mod-erator in the pattern of the relationships between job stress and work-family conflict and between family stress and family-work conflict. In light of their findings, the relationship between family stress and family-work conflict was stronger for employ-ees with high negative affectivity than for employees with low negative affectivity. However, negative affectivity did not mod-erate the impact of job stress on work-family conflict.

In another study, emotional stability moderated the impact of work-family conflict on job exhaustion and depression (Kinnunen *et al.*, 2003). Agreeableness also had a moderating role on the relationship between family-work conflict and mar-ital satisfaction such that employees were less satisfied with their marriage under conditions of high family-work conflict and low agreeableness.

Aryee, Luk *et al.* (1999) found that spousal support had a buffering effect on the relationship between parental overload and family-work conflict. It was also observed that emotion-focused coping behaviors buffered the impact of family-work conflict on job satisfaction. Fu and Shaffer (2001) reported that supervisor support moderated the effect of role conflict on strain- and behavior-based forms of work-family conflict. However, they found no empirical support for the moderat-ing role of coworker support on the relationships between the work-related determinants and various types of work-family conflict. Neither did they find a significant moderating effect of spouse support on the relationship between the family-related determinants and various types of family-work con-flict. Interestingly, domestic support had a positive moderating effect on the relationship between parental demands and time-based family-work conflict. They discussed that individuals having no children or older children perceive domestic help-ers as a source of conflict rather than as a source of support, due to the fact that they are likely to spend time for making the contractual agreement or setting up a plan for daily or weekly work.

Both colleague support and family support serve as moderators in the work-family nexus. Specifically, in a longitudinal study, colleague support buffered the impact of work-family conflict on both psychological strain and family satisfaction for employees in different manufacturing and service industries (O'Driscoll, Brough, & Kalliath, 2004). However, the moderating role of family support on the relationship between family-work conflict and psychological strain and physical health outcomes was inconclusive.

In accordance with the recent reviews of Eby, Casper, Lockwood, Bordeaux, and Brinley (2005), Parasuraman and Greenhaus (2002), and Poelmans *et al.* (2005), our review of the relevant literature indicates that minimum research attention has been devoted to the examination of the roles of moderating variables such as negative affectivity, 'Big Five' personality traits, and gender.

Work-family facilitation and family-work facilitation

Antecedents

Although very limited in number, there is evidence that variables such as gender, several 'Big Five' personality traits, spouse support, and autonomy are among the antecedents of both work-family facilitation and family-work facilitation. The following studies we will discuss have used data from the 1995 National Survey of Midlife Development in the United States.

As one of the 'Big Five' personality variables, neuroticism reduced women's positive spillover from work to family and positive spillover from family to work, whereas extraversion increased positive spillover from work (family) to family (work) for both men and women (Grzwaycz & Marks, 2000). Extraversion positively influenced both work-family and family-work facilitation, and agreeableness and conscientiousness positively influenced only family-work facilitation (Wayne *et al.*, 2004). In the same study, it was reported that neuroticism decreased work-family facilitation, while openness to experience increased facilitation between work and family domains. Also, gender was found to be an antecedent of work-family facilitation. Specifically, women had greater work-family facilitation. Other antecedents such as job autonomy, work pride, sense of community, and support from friends were reported to increase work-family facilitation (Voydanoff, 2004). In another study, Voydanoff (2005) reported that marital disagreements and household demands were significantly and negatively related to family-work facilitation, whereas spouse support, household and parental rewards, and kin support were significantly and positively related to family-work facilitation.

Using a sample of nonprofessional dual-earner couples, Butler, Grzywacz, Bass, and Linney (2005) showed that daily control and skill at work were related to increases in daily levels of facilitation between work and family domains, while the levels of daily demands at work diminished work-family facilitation. Aryee *et al.* (2005) reported that family involvement reduced work-family facilitation, while family support increased family-work facilitation. They noted that job involvement was positively linked to work-family facilitation, whereas proactive personality increased work-family facilitation, and neuroticism weakened family-work facilitation. They further reported that female employees experienced higher work-family facilitation and family-work facilitation. Also, based on data from the National Study of the Changing Workforce in the United States, antecedents such as child care hours, flexible benefits, work group support, supervisor support, work-at-home, and free hours triggered work-family facilitation, while family-supportive supervisor, work-at-home, and stay-at-home spouse increased facilitation between family and work domains (Hill, 2005). However, supervisor support (job) diminished family-work facilitation.

Demerouti *et al.* (2004) found that job control and job support increased positive work-home interaction. They also reported that job support triggered positive home-work interaction. In another recent study, Geurts *et al.* (2005) demonstrated that job support was significantly and positively associated with positive work-home interaction.

Outcomes

As with the antecedents of work-family facilitation and family-work facilitation, very little research attention has been devoted to the role- and stress-related outcomes of work-family facilitation and family-work facilitation. Since there is not much research and evidence regarding the aforementioned relationships in the extant literature, this part does not include the classification of the outcomes into sub-groups such as work- and family-related outcomes, stress-related outcomes, and other outcomes.

Empirical research reveals that for a sample of academic and nonacademic university staff, both positive spillovers from work and home are positively correlated with such work- and family-related outcomes as job satisfaction, satisfaction with home, quality of marriage, and overall life satisfaction (Sumer & Knight, 2001). Recent empirical research illustrates that work-family facilitation increases job satisfaction and job effort, but decreases family effort, while family-work facilitation increases job effort, family satisfaction, and family effort (Wayne *et al.*, 2004). In another recent empirical study, a significant negative relationship between positive work-home interaction and fatigue was observed (Demerouti *et al.*, 2004). In a more recent study, both positive work-home and home-work interactions were positively associated with organizational commitment (Geurts *et al.*, 2005). Using data from the 1995 National Survey of Midlife Development in the United States, Grzywacz and Bass (2003) found that family-work facilitation lessened depression and problem drinking.

Another empirical study found a significant positive relationship between employees' perceptions of work-family facilitation and their job outcomes such as job satisfaction and organizational commitment (Aryee *et al.*, 2005). Beside these findings, job satisfaction and life satisfaction were shown to be significant consequences of work-family facilitation, while family-work facilitation increased family satisfaction, life satisfaction, and marital satisfaction (Hill, 2005). However, it was found that family-work facilitation was negatively related to organizational commitment. Hill (2005) gives a statement for this intriguing finding "… if one is open to influence from family to work, it may be one's connection to family is preeminent and one may be more likely to look for a different job when it does not meet family needs." (p. 811).

Consistent with Frone's (2003) review of work-family balance, our review of the extant literature reveals that there is a lack of empirical research about the role-related consequences of work-family facilitation and family-work facilitation. One interpretation of the aforementioned findings is that role-related outcomes of work-family facilitation and family-work facilitation do not necessarily reside in the family domain and work domain, respectively.

Moderators

Our review of the extant literature shows that evidence concerning the moderating effects in the field of work-family facilitation and family-work facilitation is scanty. Limited evidence in this context is given below.

In a recent empirical study, support from friends moderated the positive relationship between job autonomy and work-family facilitation, and a sense of community moderated the positive impact of work pride on work-family facilitation (Voydanoff, 2004). In a more recent empirical study, friend support was shown to have a positive moderating role on the relationship between spouse support and family-work facilitation (Voydanoff, 2005). In addition, Aryee *et al.* (2005) demonstrated that gender moderated the impacts of optimism and job involvement on family-work facilitation in a way that the relationships were stronger for men than for women.

Research implications

Although the results of the aforementioned empirical studies in the extant literature have made great contributions to our understanding of the complexities of the interrelationships between work and family roles, very little is known about the antecedents, consequences, and moderators of work-family conflict and family-work conflict in the hospitality management literature. The hospitality management literature is devoid of research pertaining to the antecedents, outcomes, and moderators of work-family facilitation and family-work facilitation. With this recognition, we will provide a number of implications for future research in order to respond to the question "where do we go from here?".

Our review shows that the antecedents of work-family conflict and family-work conflict have received very little research attention in the hospitality management literature. There are some important questions to be studied. For example, are front desk agents working in hotels confronted with heightened two forms of conflicts, when they have work overload and work time demands? When they are highly involved in family-related issues, do they experience higher family-work conflict? Do work-related antecedents reside in the work domain, and do family-related antecedents reside in the family domain? These questions are waiting for answers in the hospitality management literature.

Our review points to another important research issue. That is, the preponderance of past and recent empirical evidence based on data derived from affluent Western countries appears to demonstrate no gender differences in the experience of work-family conflict and family-work conflict. Therefore, due to the changing nature of the workforce and changes in gender-role norms, hospitality researchers should examine the impact of gender on both directions of interference using data, especially from the samples of affluent non-Western and developing countries so as to evaluate whether female employees experience greater conflict between family and work domains and male employees experience higher conflict between work and family domains.

Personality variables may decrease or increase individuals' work-family conflict and family-work conflict. Our review reveals that evidence pertaining to the effects of 'Big Five' personality variables on both directions of interference is not consistent, and thus additional research is needed. Also, the relationships of dispositional personality variables with work-family conflict and family-work conflict need more research attention. Since employees having boundary-spanning roles in hospitality organizations are expected to deal with a number of customers' requests and complaints, it is of great importance to understanding what personality variables intensify work-family and family-work conflicts and what personality variables can be used as a coping mechanism to minimize problems stemming from two directions of interference.

Our review also shows that evidence regarding the work- and family-related outcomes of both directions of interference is meager. We have much evidence about the work-related consequences of conflicts in the work-family interface in the extant research. There are, however, several cases where the relationships of in-role and extra-role performance with conflicts in the work-family interface are not obviously clear cut, and evidence concerning the effects of work-family and family-work conflicts on career satisfaction is not abundant. For instance, food servers spending additional time in their work may not be able to fulfill their responsibilities in the family domain and have work-family conflict. In this case, do they display lower job performance or higher job performance? Not surprisingly, the relationship between work-family conflict and job performance should be negative. However, Van Dyne, Jehn, and Cummings (2002) found that two types of strain (work and home strains) amplified sales performance. They stated "… strain may have caused the employees in our sample to focus on their work, thus producing high sales performance (a well-defined work behavior) with increased efficiency." (p. 69). Once employees display higher performance in the workplace when they are prone to heightened work-family conflict, they may not be willing to get involved in additional duties relating to extra-role behaviors and thus display lower extra-role performance (cf. Allen *et al.*, 2000). Future research in the hospitality management literature can shed light on these relationships where empirical evidence is at best mixed.

In addition, it is important to test the relationships of two directions of interference with nonattendance behaviors.

For example, cooks in hotels may be late for work or display absenteeism, when they know that they should deal with a number of family responsibilities. As such, reservations agents in hotels may not attend to work on time or be absent for work due to various family responsibilities. Since there is not enough evidence regarding these relationships, future research should also be addressed to the effects of work-family conflict and family-work conflict on nonattendance behaviors such as absenteeism and tardiness.

In accordance with the recent review conducted by Eby *et al.* (2005), our review illustrates that there is relatively little empirical research associated with the effects of conflicts in the work-family interface on family-related variables. For example, the differential impacts of work-family conflict and family-work conflict on family satisfaction and marital satisfaction as well as on various work-related outcomes need to be tested using various samples from the hospitality industry. By doing so, it is possible to further provide evidence whether the role-related outcomes of work-family conflict reside in the family domain, and the role-related outcomes of family-work conflict reside in the work domain.

Although not discussed in this chapter, an undeniable gap in hospitality research is related to the examination of the cross-over effects (Hammer, Allen, & Grigsby, 1997). Specifically, investigating the effects of male and female employees' work and family variables on their spouses' work-family conflict and family-work conflict in the hospitality industry would be fruitful in understanding the complexities of the interrelationships between work and family domains.

As discussed earlier, negative affectivity intensifies both directions of interference. However, more empirical research is needed concerning the moderating role of negative affectivity on the relationship between conflicts in the work-family interface and work- and family-/nonwork-related outcomes. For example, does negative affectivity moderate the impact of work-family conflict on family satisfaction such that the relationship is stronger for food servers high in negative affectivity than for food servers low in negative affectivity? Also, the examination of gender as a moderating variable deserves future research attention, especially in developing countries where the participation of women in the workforce is steadily rising, and conflict between work (family) and family (work) domains can be expected due to the transition from traditional family structures to dual-earner family structures (Poelmans *et al.*, 2005).

As discussed in the preceding parts, Carlson *et al.* (2000) developed and validated an instrument that measures the three types of work-family conflict and family-work conflict. Our review demonstrates that the effects of various work- and family-related variables as well as the individual/personality variables on three types of work-family conflict and family-work conflict have not been largely studied in the extant literature. In addition, evidence relating to the differential effects of three forms of work-family conflict and family-work conflict on work- and family-/nonwork-related outcomes as well as stress-related outcomes is not abundant. On the basis of this recognition, we suggest that the abovementioned relationships may be examined using samples of various hospitality settings.

As highlighted in a recent review (Frone, 2003) and recent empirical studies (Aryee *et al.*, 2005; Wayne *et al.*, 2004), very little empirical attention has been devoted to investigating the antecedents, consequences, and moderators of work-family facilitation and family-work facilitation. Thus, based on strong theoretical frameworks, developing and testing a research model that examines the antecedents, outcomes, and moderators of conflicts and facilitation in the work-family interface would help understand whether two directions of interference and facilitation have common and unique antecedents, outcomes, and moderators. We suggest that these relationships be assessed using data from the hospitality service settings, especially in developing countries.

In agreement with the recent review conducted by Poelmans *et al.* (2005), there is very little research pertaining to the antecedents, consequences, and moderators of work-family conflict and family-work conflict both cross-nationally and cross-culturally in the extant literature. The situation is also same for work-family facilitation and family-work facilitation. Developing and testing hypotheses regarding cross-national or cross-cultural differences through the use of samples from the hospitality industry would be much beneficial for making useful additions to the relevant literature.

Another important implication for future research is associated with a methodological limitation. The overwhelming majority of the empirical studies we have reviewed have used cross-sectional designs in order to test the hypothesized relationships among a number of variables. Based on cross-sectional designs, it is very difficult to make inferences pertaining to the causal relationships among various variables, and this is an important limitation of the extant research. Based on this realization, hospitality researchers may study the antecedents, outcomes, and moderators of conflicts and facilitation in the work-family interface by using longitudinal research designs.

The last implication for future research is associated with the qualitative research. The overwhelming majority of the findings on the interrelationships between work and family roles are based on quantitative studies. We believe that using various forms of qualitative research would be an important move in making useful additions to the hospitality management literature.

In the scope of this chapter, we have focused on a selective review of the relevant literature. We did not go through every peer-reviewed paper in detail. We tried to show the general picture of what we have in this field and provide a number of suggestions for future research in the hospitality management literature. We hope that various suggestions we have made for future research would be beneficial to hospitality researchers in their efforts to develop and test research models that examine the antecedents, outcomes, and moderators of two directions of conflict and facilitation.

References

Adams, G. A., King, L. A., & King, D. W. (1996). Relationships of job and family involvement, family social support, and work-family conflict with job and life satisfaction. *Journal of Applied Psychology*, *81*(4), 411–420.

Allen, T. D., Herst, D. E. L., Bruck, C. S., & Sutton, M. (2000). Consequences associated with work-to-family conflict: A review and agenda for future research. *Journal of Occupational Health Psychology*, *5*(2), 278–308.

Anderson, S. E., Coffey, B. S., & Byerly, R. T. (2002). Formal organizational initiatives and informal workplace practices: Links to work-family conflict and job-related outcomes. *Journal of Management*, *28*(6), 787–810.

Aryee, S., Fields, D., & Luk, V. (1999). A cross-cultural test of a model of the work-family interface. *Journal of Management*, *25*(4), 491–511.

Aryee, S., & Luk, V. (1996). Work and nonwork influences on the career satisfaction of dual-earner couples. *Journal of Vocational Behavior*, *49*(1), 38–52.

Aryee, S., Luk, V., Leung, A., & Lo, S. (1999). Role stressors, interrole conflict, and well-being: The moderating influence of spousal support and coping behaviors among employed parents in Hong Kong. *Journal of Vocational Behavior*, *54*(2), 259–278.

Aryee, S., Srinivas, E. S., & Tan, H. H. (2005). Rhythms of life: Antecedents and outcomes of work-family balance in employed parents. *Journal of Applied Psychology*, *90*(1), 132–146.

Aycan, Z., & Eskin, M. (2005). Relative contribution of child-care, spousal support, and organizational support in reducing work-family conflict for men and women: The case of Turkey. *Sex Roles*, *53*(7/8), 453–471.

Barrick, M. R., & Mount, M. K. (1991). The big five personality dimensions and job performance: A meta-analysis. *Personnel Psychology*, *44*(1), 1–26.

Brough, P., & Kelling, A. (2002). Women, work & well-being: The influence of work-family and family-work conflict. *New Zealand Journal of Psychology*, *31*(1), 29–38.

Bruck, C. S., & Allen, T. D. (2003). The relationship between big five personality traits, negative affectivity, type A behavior, and work-family conflict. *Journal of Vocational Behavior*, *63*(3), 457–472.

Butler, A. B., Grzywacz, J. G., Bass, B. L., & Linney, K. D. (2005). Extending the demands-control model: A daily diary study of job characteristics, work-family conflict and work-family facilitation. *Journal of Occupational and Organizational Psychology*, *78*(2), 155–169.

Byron, K. (2005). A meta-analytic review of work-family conflict and its antecedents. *Journal of Vocational Behavior*, *67*(2), 169–198.

Cannon, D.F. (1998). Better understanding the impact of work interferences on organizational commitment. *Marriage and Family Review*, *28*(1/2), 153–166.

Carlson, D. S. (1999). Personality and role variables as predictors of three forms of work-family conflict. *Journal of Vocational Behavior*, *55*(2), 236–253.

Carlson, D. S., & Kacmar, K. M. (2000). Work-family conflict in the organization: Do life role values make a difference? *Journal of Management*, *26*(5), 1031–1054.

Carlson, D. S., Kacmar, K. M., & Williams, L. J. (2000). Construction and initial validation of a multidimensional measure of work-family conflict. *Journal of Vocational Behavior*, *56*(2), 249–276.

Casper, W. J., Martin, J. A., Buffardi, L. C., & Erdwins, C. J. (2002). Work-family conflict, perceived organizational support, and organizational commitment among employed mothers. *Journal of Occupational Health Psychology*, *7*(2), 99–108.

Deery, M. A., & Shaw, R. N. (1999). An investigation of the relationship between employee turnover and organizational culture. *Journal of Hospitality and Tourism Research*, *23*(4), 387–400.

Demerouti, E., Geurts, S. A. E., & Kompier, M. (2004). Positive and negative work-home interaction: Prevalence and correlates. *Equal Opportunities International*, *23*(1/2), 6–35.

Eby, L. T., Casper, W. J., Lockwood, A., Bordeaux, C., & Brinley, A. (2005). Work and family research in IO/OB: Content analysis and review of the literature (1980–2002). *Journal of Vocational Behavior*, *66*(1), 124–197.

Frone, M. R. (2000). Work-family conflict and employee psychiatric disorders: The National Comorbidity Survey. *Journal of Applied Psychology*, *85*(6), 888–895.

Frone, M. R. (2003). Work-family balance. In: J. C. Quick & L. E. Tetrick (Eds.), *Handbook of occupational health psychology* (pp. 143–162). Washington, DC: American Psychological Association.

Frone, M. R., Barnes, G. M., & Farrell, M. P. (1994). Relationship of work-family conflict to substance use among employed mothers: The role of negative affect. *Journal of Marriage and the Family*, *56*(November), 1019–1030.

Frone, M. R., Russell, M., & Barnes, G. M. (1996). Work-family conflict, gender, and health-related outcomes: A study of employed parents in two community samples. *Journal of Occupational Health Psychology*, *1*(1), 57–69.

Frone, M. R., Russell, M., & Cooper, M. L. (1992). Antecedents and outcomes of work-family conflict: Testing a model of the work-family interface. *Journal of Applied Psychology*, *77*(1), 65–78.

Frone, M. R., Russell, M., & Cooper, M. L. (1997). Relation of work-family conflict to health outcomes: A four-year longitudinal study of employed parents. *Journal of Occupational and Organizational Psychology*, *70*(4), 325–335.

Frone, M. R., Yardley, J. K., & Markel, K. S. (1997). Developing and testing an integrative model of the work-family interface. *Journal of Vocational Behavior*, *50*(2), 145–167.

Frye, N. K., & Breaugh, J. A. (2004). Family-friendly policies, supervisor support, work-family conflict, family-work conflict, and satisfaction: A test of a conceptual model. *Journal of Business and Psychology*, *19*(2), 197–220.

Fu, C. K., & Shaffer, M. A. (2001). The tug of work and family: Direct and indirect domain-specific determinants of work-family conflict. *Personnel Review*, *30*(5), 502–522.

Geurts, S. A. E., Taris, T. W., Kompier, M. A. J., Dikkers, J. S. E., Van Hooff, M. L. M., & Kinnunen, U. M. (2005). Work-home interaction from a work psychological perspective: Development and validation of a new questionnaire, the SWING. *Work and Stress*, *19*(4), 319–339.

Goff, S. J., Mount, M. K., & Jamison, R. L. (1990). Employer supported child care, work/family conflict, and absenteeism: A field study. *Personnel Psychology*, *43*(4), 793–809.

Grandey, A. A., & Cropanzano, R. (1999). The conservation of resources model applied to work-family conflict and strain. *Journal of Vocational Behavior, 54*(2), 350–370.

Greenhaus, J. H., & Beutell, N. J. (1985). Sources of conflict between work and family roles. *Academy of Management Review, 10*(1), 76–88.

Greenhaus, J. H., Parasuraman, S., & Collins, K. M. (2001). Career involvement and family involvement as moderators of relationships between work-family conflict and withdrawal from a profession. *Journal of Occupational Health Psychology, 6*(2), 91–100.

Grzywacz, J. G., & Bass, B. L. (2003). Work, family, and mental health: Testing different models of work-family fit. *Journal of Marriage and Family, 65*(February), 248–262.

Grzywacz, J. G., & Marks, N. F. (2000). Reconceptualizing the work-family interface: An ecological perspective on the correlates of positive and negative spillover between work and family. *Journal of Occupational Health Psychology, 5*(11), 111–126.

Haar, J. M. (2004). Work-family conflict and turnover intention: Exploring the moderation effects of perceived work-family support. *New Zealand Journal of Psychology, 33*(1), 35–39.

Hammer, L. B., Allen, E., & Grigsby, T. D. (1997). Work-family conflict in dual-earner couples: Within-individual and cross-over effects of work and family. *Journal of Vocational Behavior, 50*(2), 185–203.

Hammer, T. H., Saksvik, P. Ø., Nytrø, K., Torvatn, H., & Bayazit, M. (2004). Expanding the psychosocial work environment: Workplace norms and work-family conflict as correlates of stress and health. *Journal of Occupational Health Psychology, 9*(1), 83–97.

Hill, E. J. (2005). Work-family facilitation and conflict, working fathers and mothers, work-family stressors and support. *Journal of Family Issues, 26*(6), 793–819.

Karatepe, O. M., & Baddar, L. (2006). An empirical study of the selected consequences of frontline employees' work-family conflict and family-work conflict. *Tourism Management, 27*(5), 1017–1028.

Karatepe, O. M., & Kilic, H. (2007). Relationships of supervisor support and conflicts in the work-family interface with the selected job outcomes of frontline employees. *Tourism Management, 28*(1), 238–252.

Karatepe, O. M., & Sokmen, A. (2006). The effects of work role and family role variables on psychological and behavioral outcomes of frontline employees. *Tourism Management*, *27*(2), 255–268.

Kinnunen, U., & Mauno, S. (1998). Antecedents and outcomes of work-family conflict among employed women and men in Finland. *Human Relations*, *51*(2), 157–177.

Kinnunen, U., Vermulst, A., Gerris, J., & Mäkikangas, A. (2003). Work-family conflict and its relations to well-being: The role of personality as a moderating factor. *Personality and Individual Differences*, *35*(7), 1669–1683.

MacEwen, K. E., & Barling, J. (1994). Daily consequences of work interference with family and family interference with work. *Work and Stress*, *8*(3), 244–254.

Mcelwain, A. K., Korabik, K., & Rosin, H. M. (2005). An examination of gender differences in work-family conflict. *Canadian Journal of Behavioral Science*, *37*(4), 283–298.

Namasivayam, K., & Mount D. J. (2004). The relationship of work-family conflicts and family-work conflict to job satisfaction. *Journal of Hospitality and Tourism Research*, *28*(2), 242–250.

Netemeyer, R. G., Boles, J. S., & McMurrian, R. (1996). Development and validation of work-family conflict and family-work conflict scales. *Journal of Applied Psychology*, *81*(4), 400–410.

Netemeyer, R. G., Brashear-Alejandro, T., & Boles, J. S. (2004). A cross-national model of job-related outcomes of work role and family role variables: A retail sales context. *Journal of the Academy of Marketing Science*, *32*(1), 49–60.

Netemeyer, R. G., Maxham, J. G., & Pullig, C. (2005). Conflicts in the work-family interface: Links to job stress, customer service employee performance, and customer purchase intent. *Journal of Marketing*, *69*(April), 130–143.

Noor, N. M. (2003). Work- and family-related variables, work-family conflict and women's well-being: Some observations. *Community, Work and Family*, *6*(3), 297–319.

O'Driscoll, M. P., Brough, P., & Kalliath, T. J. (2004). Work/family conflict, psychological well-being, satisfaction and social support: A longitudinal study in New Zealand. *Equal Opportunities International*, *23*(1/2), 36–56.

O'Driscoll, M. P., Ilgen, D. R., & Hildreth, K. (1992). Time devoted to job and off-job activities, interrole conflict, and affective experiences. *Journal of Applied Psychology*, *77*(3), 272–279.

Parasuraman, S., & Greenhaus, J. H. (2002). Toward reducing some critical gaps in work-family research. *Human Resource Management Review*, *12*(3), 299–312.

Parasuraman, S., Purohit, Y. S., Godshalk, V. M., & Beutell, N. J. (1996). Work and family variables, entrepreneurial career success and psychological well-being. *Journal of Vocational Behavior*, *48*(3), 275–300.

Peeters, M. C. W., Montgomery, A. J., Bakker, A. B., & Schaufeli, W. B. (2005). Balancing work and home: How job and home demands are related to burnout. *International Journal of Stress Management*,*12*(1), 43–61.

Poelmans, S., O'Driscoll, M., & Beham, B. (2005). An overview of international research on the work-family interface. In: S. A. Poelmans (Ed.), *Work and family: An international research perspective* (pp. 3–46). Mahwah, NJ: Lawrence Erlbaum Associates, Incorporated.

Posig, M., & Kickul, J. (2004). Work-role expectations and work-family conflict: Gender differences in emotional exhaustion. *Women in Management Review*, *19*(7), 373–386.

Rantanen, J., Pulkkinen, L., & Kinnunen, U. (2005). The big five personality dimensions, work-family conflict, and psychological distress: A longitudinal view. *Journal of Individual Differences*, *26*(3), 155–166.

Rowley, G., & Purcell, K. (2001). As cooks go, she went: Is labor churn inevitable?. *International Journal of Hospitality Management*, *20*(2), 163–185.

Stoeva, A. Z., Chiu, R. K., & Greenhaus, J. H. (2002). Negative affectivity, role stress, and work-family conflict. *Journal of Vocational Behavior*, *60*(1), 1–16.

Sumer, H. C., & Knight, P. A. (2001). How do people with different attachment styles balance work and family? A personality perspective on work-family linkage. *Journal of Applied Psychology*, *86*(4), 653–663.

Van Dyne, L., Jehn, K. A., & Cummings, A. (2002). Differential effects of strain on two forms of work performance: Individual employee sales and creativity. *Journal of Organizational Behavior*, *23*(1), 57–74.

Voydanoff, P. (2004). Implications of work and community demands and resources for work-to-family conflict and facilitation. *Journal of Occupational Health Psychology*, *9*(4), 275–285.

Voydanoff, P. (2005). The differential salience of family and community demands and resources for family-to-work conflict and facilitation. *Journal of Family and Economic Issues*, *26*(3), 395–417.

Watson, D., & Clark, L. A. (1984). Negative affectivity: The disposition to experience aversive emotional states. *Psychological Bulletin*, *96*(3), 465–490.

Watson, D., Clark, L. A., & Tellegen, A. (1988). Development and validation of brief measures of positive and negative affect: The PANAS scales. *Journal of Personality and Social Psychology*, 54(6), 1063–1070.

Wayne, J. H., Musisca, N., & Fleeson, W. (2004). Considering the role of personality in the work-family experience: Relationships of the big five to work-family conflict and facilitation. *Journal of Vocational Behavior, 64*(1), 108–130.

CHAPTER 13

The optimal hospitality leader: creating a thriving, self-motivating, leadership-followership organizational network

Dr. George Alexakis

Resort & Hospitality Management
Florida Gulf Coast University
Fort Myers, Florida

Introduction

Technological advances have caused the rapid decline in employment and purchasing power internationally. Global unemployment is now at its highest levels since the Great Depression (Rifkin, 2004). Although the Information Age has decreased the need for organizational workers, the hospitality industry remains labor intensive. The motto that "human resource is our most valuable resource" does not hold up to scrutiny in most organizations. There is typically a mountain of evidence refuting the claim, which can even elicit laughter among many hospitality employees.

Job satisfaction is inexplicably linked to a first-rate work environment. The human resources atmosphere is primarily a result of leadership. Motivation and empowerment are, in turn, directly linked to leadership. Along these lines, the chapter will discuss how hospitality leaders can create an environment that will cause self-induced (internal) motivation among all employees. The ultimate aim is to create circumstances in which managers and workers will self-motivate to progress in the direction of peak performance.

The chapter contains seven sections: (a) Leadership Described, (b) Leaders Utilizing Human Resources, (c) Mainstream Versus Multistream Leaders, (d) Motivation, (e) Creating a Motivating Environment, (f) Achieving an Empowering and Self-Motivating Organizational Environment, and (g) Conclusion. The chapter blends research and application with the ultimate intent of optimizing the hospitality organization's "most valuable resource:" its people.

Leadership described

There is vast disagreement over the term leadership. However, the leader makes a significant impact on an organization's success and longevity (Crother-Laurin, 2006). One leadership definition often used is, a process whereby an individual influences a group of individuals to achieve a common goal. Leadership may be defined as a commitment to the success of people surrounding the person that is thought to be leading. Another definition is accomplishing something through other people that would not have happen if the leader were not a factor. The word leadership was found by one researcher to be the predominant response when participants were asked what is their greatest obstacle hindering extraordinary products or services (Crother-Laurin). Most studies of the sort suggest that when it comes to resignations, employees quit their bosses not their companies. Thirty-five percent of the respondents answered yes in one survey to the question, "Was the attitude of your direct supervisor/manager the primary factor in your quitting a previous job?" Soft management skills or people skills are critical in battling high employee turnover. They also create a high-retention workforce or "retentionship" (Smith, 2002). The conservative rule of thumb among human resource experts puts the cost of replacing an employee in excess of that employee's yearly salary. Table A.1 lays out the typical reasons for the high cost of turnover (see Appendix A).

The literature is replete with leadership theories, the most contemporary typical being transformational leadership. It is commonly defined as developing an exchange and implicit transaction contract between leaders and followers that is supplemented with behaviors that lead to organizational transformation. There is usually a charismatic aspect to the transformational leader. This alluring element further spotlights the relationship between leaders and followers, rather than as a combination of leadership traits and behaviors. Many companies have gained from putting such leaders in place. While theories such as transformational leadership have their merits, they are not without their criticisms. For example, some studies have indicated that transformational leadership is based on the emotions of followers. Conger and Kannugo (1988) suggested that leadership is a process of attribution, which implies that people construct naive theories to explain relations between phenomena (Kelly & Michela, 1980). Conger and Kannugo concluded that people follow transformational leaders owing to the fact that they attribute to those leaders the ability to impose order, security, and direction in an otherwise chaotic and threatening world.

The inference is hard to ignore in light of the amplified power that the U.S. government and corporations have assumed since 9/11 under the pretext of safety and security concerns. Until very recently, the transformational leader phenomenon has represented a marked increase in Americans not questioning authority (Alexakis, Platt, & Tesone, 2006). The post-9/11 national mood translated into a similar atmosphere in corporate America, which has spelled a boon for coercive leaders. Kets de Vries (1989) explained transformational leadership in terms of transference that comes from the psychoanalytic field. In effect, there exists an unconscious redirection of feelings by a follower. The feelings are for an important person in the follower's past that are *transferred* or assigned to the leader. For instance, one could trust a charismatic leader who resembles a beloved parent in kindness, gregariousness, or enthusiasm; or be overly compliant to a leader who resembles a childhood friend. A transference reaction indicates that the followers are reacting to transformational leaders in terms of what they want to see. It is also often what followers see when they know little about the leader (Racker, 2001).

According to their studies, Popper and Lipshitz (1993) liken transformational leadership to a regressive expression of fantasies and yearnings to a past when people felt protected by strong authority figures. Leadership theories must be properly and repeatedly tested in the real world for them to have efficacy. Just because a particular buzzword is popular and "everyone is doing it" does not mean that it is correct or even useful. To consent to the existence of those fad leadership theories, one needs to complicate the theory by adding experimentally unsupported processes and ad hoc postulates (Conger & Kannugo, 1988). Hence, like hospitality services and products, leadership and motivation theories should be thoroughly examined to be certain they meet the industry's own exacting quality control standards.

There are two contrasting sets of assumptions that leaders make about human nature. Theory X is a pessimistic view of employees' performance propensities. Theory Y is an optimistic view of employees' performance propensities. Theory X thinking is not supported by the literature but still predominates managerial thinking (Alexakis *et al.*, 2006). Theory X managers and leaders are fast becoming a relic of the past. In any case, the fact of the matter is that leaders face dilemmas that require choices between competing sets of values and priorities. Leaders set a moral example that becomes the model for the group. Good leaders tend to align the values of their followers with those of the organization or movement. In a personal communication (Preziosi, 2007), one human resources educational specialist said that the four main qualities of highly effective leadership are: (a) vision, (b) empathy, (c) consistency, and (d) integrity. Effective leaders tend to

1. Be consistent, which usually contributes to stable performance, creates trust, and lowers employee turnover. Inconsistent leaders may cause employees to doubt higher-ups and be less inclined to give their best efforts.
2. Focus on the future. They see that the past is the best indicator of the future to gauge the direction of the organization if it does not undertake significant changes. They then visualize a future for which they are desirous.
3. Create change, once they evaluated the direction that the organization is likely to otherwise advance. They then look

for ways to effect change within their sphere of influence so that the organization is guided in an improved direction.

4. Create a culture based on shared values. They understand the fact that people are more likely to follow a program that they themselves have helped design. Likewise, every voice is heard or represented to get maximum buy-in among employees.

5. Establish an emotional link with followers. They do this by using their personal power, the power that can never be taken away from them.

6. Recognize that leaders are not above followers, are not better than followers, and should have an interactive relationship with followers.

7. Ultimately foster an emotional and social commitment to the organization that keeps people working and attached to the organization.

As maintained by business guru Stephen Covey, leadership is primarily a high-powered, right brain activity. It is not principally a science, but is more of an art; it is based on a philosophy. An individual has to ask the ultimate questions of life when dealing with personal leadership issues. Metaphorically speaking, leadership development is a journey of professional and personal development. In fact, to develop oneself as a leader is to develop oneself professionally and personally. Taking personal responsibility for one's actions is consistent among today's successful, ethical leaders. They make it their business to understand breadth, depth, and context before they act. They learn constantly and know that they must find out how to successfully teach others. They stay true to their own inimitable style. Finally, if they want those around them to change, they change themselves first.

Leaders utilizing human resources

In the broad context, humans today are required to use their labor to make enough money to live, which economists refer to as exchange. Few people would work at a job if they had no economic need. As such, they are resistant to working for others. It is perceived at some level, whether consciously or subconsciously, by most people as an implicit form of societally accepted exploitation. Employees make a decision to accept direction and responsibility, which industrial psychologists call balance. Regardless, the arrangement is one in which employee labor is more or less exploited by the organization.

Against such a backdrop, most people are resistant to work at a high performance level unless they find their jobs enjoyable. A recent national study revealed that "fewer than half (44%) of employees feel glad that they chose to work for their current employers …" (Harris, 2005, p. 1). Therefore, effectively leading others to provide superior quality and productivity in a hospitality entity is understandably a difficult job. Notwithstanding the foregoing, what effective industry leaders do is make work enjoyable, engaging, interesting, and otherwise intrinsically rewarding as an efficient means to further the organization's goals. Hartline and Ferrell (1996) discovered that one way to increase service quality is to improve employee job satisfaction, as the employee attitude impacts heavily on customer's perception of service quality. Peter Drucker once said, "The only things that evolve by themselves in an organization are disorder, friction, and malperformance." Organizations can be complicated. There are (a) multiple technologies, (b) myriad interconnected processes, and measureless assortments of responsibilities. Dealing with the intricacies associated with a tangible product, service, or idea can be a monumental task.

Despite the difficulties, leaders are to be responsible and accountable for everything at their level and below. To complicate their duties further, leaders are expected to be conscious of the organizational environment. Further, it is not enough for a leader to direct people and systems. Particularly in the hospitality industry, the leader should also be aware of subordinates' expert views. A leader's degree of empathy often plays an important role (Pescosolido, 2002); that is, the ability to feel another's emotional pain. A hotel industry study shows a striking association between profitability and how workers perceive their managers' behavioral integrity (Simons, 2002).

In most hospitality organizations, those in positions of power tacitly cooperate in self-seeking actions while these collective actions typically contribute to organizational failures. In such a complex system of behavioral anomalies, the question of how organizations survive and thrive is more puzzling than how they fail (Gordon & Lowe, 2002). Companies should be seen holistically as interrelated socioeconomic systems that need to adapt to particular markets (McColl-Kennedy & Anderson, 2002). Effective hospitality leaders will lean on the expertise of others, rather than engaging in autocratic decision-making.

When asked if there are enough resources in their organization, most people say no. Successful leaders continually inventory what resources they have and utilize them the best way possible. Through an optimum mix of available resources and an appropriate application of available systems and technologies, an effective leader implements operational, tactical, and corporate strategies that would enhance competitiveness, quality, turnaround, and flexibility. A progressive leader can meet an organization's goals and objectives by working through people. "Management is about coping with complexity," asserts Kotter (as cited in Steers, Porter, & Bigley, 1996, p. 620). The art of leadership involves sizing up the players and needs in each situation and constructing strategies suitable to the time and setting (Senge, 2006).

Today's leaders must realize that it is the human resources that can impinge on long-term profits and its success. This is particularly poignant in Canada and the United States, where the economies have markedly moved toward the service sector. Work-related outcomes are often tied to include job satisfaction, communication, and perceptions of the work environment. The hospitality industry's service and people orientations give it an edge over other sectors, because the profile of individuals attracted to the industry are by their very nature people-oriented.

Mainstream versus multistream leaders

The above discussion points to the inevitability of a transformation in thinking occurring about the effects of motivating others through leadership. Current theorists and practitioners are beginning to distinguish what are essentially the two types of leadership thinking in existence today: mainstream and multistream. Multistream leaders are more aware of the multiple tensions facing them (Dyck & Neubert, in press). Multistream leadership is of special relevance for individuals of the "Millennial" generation. The *Millennials* are people that were born between the years 1980 and 2000. The group represents almost 70 million people. The multistream approach "is being increasingly advocated by management professors and becoming more evident among vanguard practitioners" (Dyck & Neubert, in press, p. 1).

Beyond the typical concerns for an organization's financial viability and stakeholder interests, the multistream advances values, ecological concerns, ethical conduct, and social justice in a way never seen before. For instance, a look at the facts about how different people are ethically motivated is fast replacing those theories found in the latest leadership craze. Human resource development is seen as an (a) underutilized resource, (b) untapped source of profit, and (c) impending silver bullet. Tomorrow's leader will have the facts when assessing what does work and what does not work. How people are motivated remains one of the most talked about and least understood phenomena in leadership. The theories that support the reality of motivation have been tested and retested for many decades. Paradoxically, mainstream management and leadership literature has essentially ignored the research. People are not motivated by other people in any enduring way—people motivate themselves. Therefore, it is imperative and instructive for hospitality professionals to investigate the research that has been done on organizational leadership, motivation, and empowerment. The next section discusses the issue of self-motivation; specifically, how leaders can create environments in which others are likely to motivate themselves. It distinguishes between intrinsic and extrinsic motivation.

Motivation

For optimally efficient and effective hospitality leadership to occur, some basic understanding of intrinsic versus extrinsic rewards is central. Motivation is an internal feeling. It can be defined as a good attitude toward work (Merkle, Jackson, Zhang, & Dishman, 2002). Some would describe motivation as a reason for a particular act or set of actions. Punishment or a threat of punishment can work to get employees and managers to improve quality or productivity. Supervisors can cause performance to improve, so long as they are present. However, once the punishment or threat of punishment is not present, performance decreases, in many cases to below pre-punishment levels. The reason is that workers are then focused on avoiding the punishment or a threat instead of focusing on their work. The side effects can be detrimental to individual and organizational growth. Most of the serious management investigations that have been performed in the last half-century concur with the ineffectiveness of punishment and other Theory X approaches to motivation. However, the use of rewards is a generally accepted practice in the mainstream literature, regardless of the fact that rewards of all sorts undermine efforts to manage, lead, and teach workers.

Before discussing rewards, one has to make the distinction between job compensation and rewards—they are two different things. Compensation is defined as annual salary or hourly wages, bonuses, and perquisites that are not tied to performance. The definition excludes incentive schemes of any kind. For the following discussion, rewards are characterized as monetary incentives or other inducements that are linked in any way to a worker's performance. They include, but are not limited to (a) merit pay, (b) performance-based bonuses, (c) contests, (d) equity-based compensation schemes, (e) executive stock options, (f) incentive plans, and (g) verbal or other types of positive reinforcement.

As increasingly more companies base less of their employee pay on straight salary and look to other financial options, leaders are inundated with erroneous advice about the best approaches to take. Most of the conventional wisdom and public discussion about pay today is misleading, incorrect, or both. The result is that business leaders are adopting wrongheaded notions about how to pay people and why. Pfeffer's (1998, p. 110) research uncovered six myths about pay. The myths are what follow below

1. Labor rates are the same as labor costs.
2. Cutting labor rates will lower labor costs.
3. Labor costs represent a large portion of a company's total costs.
4. Keeping labor costs low creates a potent and sustainable competitive edge.
5. Individual incentive pay improves performance.
6. People work primarily for the money.

The author explained that, although pervasive, these myths are wrong. Leaders harm organizations by buying into and acting on these myths. Pfeffer warned that the myths result in an endless tinkering with pay, which accomplish little and are costly. Companies that have successfully transcended the myths about pay know pay cannot substitute for a working environment high on trust, fun, and meaningful work.

Mainstream inquiries into how business management leaders should motivate employees customarily promote the broad practices of incentives, recognition, and positive reinforcement. The premise that all these applications work is so grounded in contemporary "businessspeak" that the only discussions that seem to occur are axiomatic. Analysts discuss the usefulness of rewards and combinations of rewards that might produce intended results. The reality is that they (a) do not work for very long, (b) are not very useful in achieving the main goals of most organizations, and (c) have far too many significant and negative side effects for people and organizations (Kohn, 1993). They are ineffective for the same reason that indulgences are ineffective. It is because they are outside remedies for inside needs. Hospitality leaders should begin to understand that self-motivation is an internal affair.

There are several reasons that rewards such as incentives, recognition, positive reinforcement, bonuses, pay-for-performance plans (merit pay), and other bribes are ill-advised methods to motivate employees. What follows are five counterproductive characteristics of rewards

1. They tend to make employees focus on the minimum that is required to get the reward, thereby reducing work quality. For example, if someone needs to make a certain amount of sales to win two Superbowl tickets at their place of work, they will focus only on what they need to do to make the sale as opposed to do all the suitable things necessary to please the customer or do a good quality job. All too often, pleasing customers goes far beyond just making the sale. Customers become particularly irate once they sense the level of attention they are receiving has diminished as soon as their check clears.

2. They encourage people to act unethically. The employee in the above example is focused on generating sales to win tickets. The hypothetical company representative is thus more likely to be dishonest with the client to make the sale, which may hurt the client, company, or public (e.g., lying about the freshness of fish or the safety of spinach). The employee is more likely to bribe the client by giving away something "free" to make the sale. Beer representatives were notorious for giving away product to proprietors to acquire accounts. In some cases, they would "sponsor" parties or other personal social events for managers that had nothing to do with the organization itself. Beyond the moral implications, the customer is shortchanged, as the product that they are being offered may not be the best quality, but the one backed up with the biggest bribe. Further, the employee is more likely to persuade the client by giving something away that belongs to the company (e.g., a weekend stay at a hotel or an advantageous rate). The employee is more likely to cheat in a contest environment (e.g., arrange with certain customers for the product to be returned after the contest is over).

3. They are not moral; rather, they are controlling, coercive, and essentially bribes. For a leader to use rewards to get people to do what the leader wants them to do is tantamount to coercion. It discourages people from doing their job because they are paid to do it. Why should one get something to do the right thing? Recently, a hospitality leader hired someone who made it clear from the outset that the compensation was not enough. The leader said that no matter what he tried, the employee always had his hand out.

4. They inhibit individual insight. If employees are always being pointed to the direction of the proverbial carrot, they are not as likely to think about what direction they should be going in. By compelling compliance instead of creativity, the leader's job becomes more difficult because more time is spent telling employees how to do their jobs, instead of what to do. A chef, for example, is more likely to visit a manager frequently and ask many more questions about how to execute a banquet if there is a monetary reward at the end of the night for doing it the "right" way.

5. They stop working when the rewards stop. Like most extrinsic rewards, they are only effective while they are right in front of the rewardee. Rewards work at motivating until it is done. Besides being costly, it leads to unsatisfied feelings, and the above (Kohn, 1998).

Because so many people subscribe to the falsehood that financial incentives drive good performance, leaders often think that money can solve all their problems (Ewers, 2006). They often tie pay to performance when workers are not performing a certain way. If executives have not bought into the company's mission, they offer them stock options. What could be simpler than using financial incentives to improve performance? Too many managers overlook the fact that incentives can inspire bad behavior and often hurt performance as much as they help it. "When you tie money to incentives, people will not necessarily focus on what's best for the organization," says Sutton (as cited in Ewers, 2006). They will focus on what it takes to get the incentive, which encourages a path down a slippery ethical slope. The arrangement also encourages behavior that may not be best for the customer. For this reason, the practice of including a gratuity on a guest check is popular among many European foodservice establishments. Servers are less likely to oversell patrons simply to drive up the guest check and more likely to focus on enhancing the dining experience. The reward (i.e., tip) takes a backseat to the organizational goal (i.e., customer satisfaction). Another consequence is that employees will enjoy their work more and be less likely to experience burnout in due course. Employees do work for money—but they work harder for meaning in their lives. In reality, they work to have fun. Companies that ignore this fact are essentially bribing their employees and will pay the price in a lack of loyalty and commitment (Pfeffers, 1998).

Many people in the hospitality industry and the hospitality academy have witnessed first hand the destructive and divisive behavior that goes on after a merit pay system replaces cost of living increases. Managers and employees alike begin to work against one another instead of working as a team. They begin to jockey for position and ultimately start undermining each other for the scarce resources. The result of incentive plans, explains Scholtes (1990, p. 32), is as follows: "Everyone is pressuring the system for individual gain. No one is improving the system for collective gain. The system will inevitably crash." Corporate higher-ups are particularly susceptible to this type of competition (which is the converse of cooperation), as the incentive packages and bonus options are particularly appealing. Such deals can coax even the most ethical person to lose moral ground. Peter Drucker once said, "stock option plans reward the executive for doing the wrong thing. Instead of asking, "Are we making the right decision?" he asks, "How did we close today?" It is encouragement to loot the corporation." A study conducted in 2005 compared 435 companies that restated their earnings with those that did not. Researchers at the University of Minnesota found that the bigger the proportion of stock options in senior executives' payment packages, the more likely than other companies to have restated their finances (Ewers, 2006). The implication is that accounting fraud becomes more likely the more salary is connected to stock prices. Trying to make the stock go up is not a noble purpose. Although it is the foundation of shareholder capitalism, it does not make people get out of bed in the morning (Colven, 2006). The failure of ethics training programs provided by businesses to prevent their employees' unethical behaviors is not news. For example, Arthur Andersen developed a reputation for integrity and led the business community in ethics training, while at the same time Andersen auditors and consultants frequently behaved immorally, contributing to the collapse of Enron and WorldCom (Toffler, 2003). The findings in the study supported Trevino's (1986) viewpoint that ethical behavior is a function of a variety of personal and situational factors including moral development, norms, coercion, regulations, self-control, and ethics training. To prevent any or all unethical behaviors by implementing ethics training is an unrealistic goal (Williams & Dewett, 2005). The findings in the study imply that the fundamental purpose of ethics training should rely on how to arouse employees' ethical awareness. Personal insight is the preferable alternative to teaching employees what they can do or what they cannot do according to a policies and procedures manual.

As indicated by Gitlow and McNary (2006), extrinsic motivation comes from the desire for reward or fear of punishment. For instance, the feelings stimulated by receiving a bonus are caused by an extrinsic variable. They are initiated from someone else, not from the individual experiencing the feelings. Extrinsic motivation frequently restricts the release of energy from intrinsic motivation, because the individual feels judged or policed. Conversely, intrinsic rewards promote employee self-motivation and persistence.

Creating a motivating environment

In most cases, there are only two things that will significantly motivate someone—inspiration or desperation. The psychology of an individual typically determines whether they tend to be motivated more through feeling inspired (or impassioned) or through feeling desperate (or afraid). Insightful leadership understands that certain personalities are unlikely to be inspired by much. Effective leaders, at times, may even create circumstances that cause a particular employee to experience desperation. For example, a banquet manager may allow a new kitchen helper, who happens to be a complacent and passive individual, to struggle through a particular work problem instead of providing assistance.

Individuals can motivate themselves, but no one can motivate another person in any meaningful and sustainable way. Motivation is an internal force that compels. That is to say, self-motivation is the favored method and perhaps the only method of true motivation. Self-motivation is "a generalized non-specific tendency to persist in an activity in the absence of any kind of external reinforcement" (Saunders, Skinner, & Beresford, 2005, p. 371). A high performance employee team can be realized most economically by empowerment through creating an environment to encourage motivation within everyone. In such circumstances, the leader's role is only one of a facilitator in the motivation process. Through the process of empowerment, the leader has the power to harness and utilize the available intellectual capital. The language used is important to the discussion. All too often, leaders are given ways to "motivate employees." Instead the leader can be most effective when fostering, aiding, supporting, assisting, abetting, fostering, helping, backing, easing, promoting, furthering, cultivating, nurturing, sponsoring, and otherwise advancing the motivation level that is within a person.

Separating the work that needs to be done by each individual or group from the rewards (i.e., pay, benefits, perquisites, and other incentives) in their minds is paramount. Perceptive leaders know that it is hard to meet organizational objectives

277

through people when those same people are spending work time thinking about how they are going to pay their bills. A minimum threshold of remuneration needs to be in place for employees to feel that they are being paid fairly. This earnings level is essential for people to get their minds off thinking about their livelihood and basic needs. It is difficult to otherwise promote self-motivation in the workplace. Thus, Kohn's (1998) formula for how to do this distills most dependable theory, research, and practice into three short sentences

1. Pay people well.
2. Pay people fairly.
3. Having achieved 1 and 2, do everything possible to take money off people's minds.

Should a leader have difficulty in paying people well or fairly, there are many non-inducing compensation supplements that have been used for years to compensate employees for lack of income (see Appendix B). An increasing number of U.S. employers have also been offering non-traditional supplements in lieu of an appropriate salary that can get employees to the necessary minimum threshold. Colven (2006) related that leaders of several sought-after companies work to offer alternative benefits such as compressed work-weeks, four 10-hour days, Fridays off, subsidized lunches, etc. (see Appendix C). Such benefits and perquisites can assist decision makers considerably in creatively compensating employees for lack of living wage or salary. However, the added remuneration must be handed out symmetrically among all employees or it can lead to fighting, backbiting, cronyism, and the other undesirable effects of competition. Ultimately, a workplace that is more egalitarian and democratic is a workplace that is more cooperative. Such virtues add to performance levels that are positively reflected in quality and productivity of the goods and services offered to customers. Employees treasure the freedom to do their job as they think best, and great employers trust them. Being a great place to work pays (Colven, 2006).

Assuming that non-incentive-based compensation, benefits, and perquisites are collectively sufficient and fair, then how do hospitality leaders take money off the minds of their employees? The answer is both simple and complex: intrinsic motivation. The philosopher, Al Gini, opined, "Adults need meaningful work in the same way that children need interesting play, in order to fulfill themselves as persons." *Homo sapiens* and many other animals have an innate propensity to add meaning to their lives through work and play. The capacity to create and envision is central to humans and we must express ourselves through work or play that allows us to see the fruits of our labor and our creativity. If the nature of the work is properly appreciated and applied, it will stand in the same relation to the higher faculties as food is to the physical body, so said the philosopher and economist J. C. Kumarappa.

Critical to high performance and closely tied to capacity are worker's internal views of themselves and their jobs (Fournies, 1999). Factors such as self-esteem, work ethic, values, and quality orientation all play a major role in determining if workers can perform to standard. Other individual characteristics, such as fear of failure or punishment, and risk taking and avoidance can also influence performance levels. Fournies (1999) continued by arguing that trying to determine what needs level is motivating an employee places corporate coaches in the role of amateur psychologist. It is valuable for coaches to know, however, that "when an environment enables people to meet their need for esteem (competence, power, purpose, uniqueness) and growth (actualization through creative accomplishment), people become connected to that environment. Creating the right environment can build commitment" (Fournies, p. 421).

Intrinsic motivation comes from the sheer joy of doing an act, for example, the pleasure derived from a job well done. It releases human power that can be focused on the improvement and innovation of a system. Intrinsic motivation cannot be given to an individual; it comes entirely from within the person experiencing it (Gitlow & McNary, 2006). An intrinsic approach allows individuals to work, learn, and play with more flair and inventiveness, whereas the structured and compartmentalized way of doing things stifles people's creativity to problem-solve in today's hospitality world. The flaw with the linear model of cause and effect often found in the medical sciences and in much of society generally is that it excludes or minimizes the probability of dynamics. Intangibles require that a leader's decision calculus must sometimes result in a conclusion that the right investment may not linearly be best for the return on investment.

Gitlow and McNary (2006) found that a fertile environment could be created by managers for others to experience intrinsic motivation. Managers can promote joy in work by empowering employees to improve and innovate the work processes. One way toward this end is by managing to promote cooperation instead of competition. Conventional wisdom dictates that Americans believe in the value of competition because of four myths. They are as follows, accompanied by the authors' research conclusions that demonstrate the opposite

1. Competition is an unavoidable fact of life; it is part of human nature. Research shows that competition is a learned phenomenon. People are not born cooperative or competitive.
2. Competition motivates us to do our best. The evidence is overwhelmingly clear and consistent that competition rarely causes better performance. Superior performance not only does not require competition, it usually seems to require its absence.
3. Competition is the best, if not the only way, to have a good time in contests or at play. Play is the opposite of work and has no goal other than pure enjoyment. Many play activities have come to resemble work because of competition. The complete absence of play is an unhealthy thing for most people.
4. Competition builds character and increases self-confidence. A literature review concluded that cooperative learning situations, compared with competitive or individualistic situations, promote higher levels of esteem. The potential for loss is always present in competition; therefore, the more importance that is placed on winning in the society, the more destructive losing will be (Gitlow & McNary, 2006).

In a competitive environment, most people lose. The costs resulting from competition are unknown and unknowable, but they are huge. Competition makes sense if the aim of a system is to win; however, if the aim of a system is something other than to win, then cooperation makes sense (Gitlow & McNary, 2006).

There are many ways that employee collaboration, autonomy, and power sharing can positively aid an organization. The research supporting such structures has been around for years (Alexakis *et al.*, 2006). The paradox of autocratic organizations within nations of egalitarian principles is increasingly being exposed. Equally ironic is that the natural yearning towards social equality in the workplace can ultimately help institutions succeed financially. A more democratic workplace also has broader societal implications, as corporations are among the least examined institutions in the world. In light of the above discussion, the manager or leader must realize that subjugated people will impinge long-term profits and organizational success. Such awareness to the counter productivity of generally accepted leadership behavior is particularly imperative in the hospitality industry, where service is fundamental to success. The effectiveness of true democratic structures, the ramifications of demoralized employees, and the outcomes of power hoarding should be quantifiably measured and analyzed whenever feasible by hospitality leaders (Alexakis, Platt, & Tesone).

Achieving an empowering and self-motivating organizational environment

There is no dispute that employees want to trust their leaders. Nor is it also a secret that hospitality people tend to be more people-oriented than most other professions. The leader can play an important role in the mood and attitude of the employees who operate the organization. The outcome directly affects profit. As established previously, how employees feel does affect their level of customer service. More than ever, today's emerging hospitality Millennial generation is (a) sociable, (b) optimistic, (c) talented, (d) well educated, (e) collaborative, (f) open-minded, (g) influential, and (e) achievement-oriented (Raines, 2002). They want inclusiveness in the workplace. They are

used to being organized in teams—and to making certain no one is left behind. They expect to earn a living in a workplace that is fair to all, where diversity is the norm—and they'll use their collective power if they feel someone is treated unfairly (Raines, 2002). They look for leaders with honesty and integrity, because they want some great role models before they become leaders themselves.

Tomorrow's hospitality leaders will have to have an edge over others fighting for talent. Diversity, varied viewpoints, different styles, and dissenting opinions: all of these variances are necessary if a company is to renew itself and move ahead. Generational, cultural, regional, and personality differences are just some of the human variables that will need to be examined more closely. The astute hospitalier will be mindful of the various types of human diversity when hiring, training, and mentoring people. Equally important is that employment recruiters and selectors do a *cultural fit assessment* to determine the extent to which potential employee values match up and integrate with those of the hospitality firm. Apart from *values integration*, utilizing human diversity of all types can be the first significant step in creating an environment in which people will self-motivate and discover intrinsic rewards within the organization. After all, how can one create such an environment without understanding the target employee audience? This, of course, is if the Kohn (1998) premise is in place: people are being paid well and fairly.

For any generation at work, those that seek interaction with their leaders want to know that they are not being talked at, but talked to. One must contrast such an organization where the point of departure is asking what people need with an organization whose fundamental question is, in effect, "How can we get the employees to do what we tell them?" The former sort of workplace is about working with; the latter sort is about doing to. Rewards, seen from this perspective, are just one more way of doing things to people. They are basically "control through seduction" (Deci & Ryan, 1985). As one CEO has said, "No vision, no strategy can be achieved without able and empowered employees." Avoiding punishments and rewards (including positive reinforcement) is essential to indirectly meeting long-term organizational goals. Further, taking "value" out of evaluations can also go a long way towards a peak performance workplace. By simply describing an employee's work during the appraisal process and avoiding value-laden terms, employees can assign their own labels to their work performance. In the instance of a food server being evaluated by using words such as good, poor, outstanding, bad, the supervisor describes the work in an objective way without these terms. Here is a basic example of how appraisers can share their perspectives in an in depth way while giving employees the right to decide how they will feel about the information:

The number of compliments regarding your service level has steadily increased in the last year. Customers have recently taken to writing us letters praising your high level of affability. As far as working with others is concerned, some of the back-of-house staff has complained recently that you have been ornery and somewhat unreasonable with your food requests. One of the sous chefs said that you have taken to using profanity when things don't go your way. At the same time, by all accounts, you have proved that you work well with all of the front-of-house staff. They all admire your skill levels and respect your professionalism.

Notice that in the above evaluation piece, no value-laden terms were used. Instead of the supervisor sharing feelings about the performance level, the employee is left to decide how to feel about the perspective offered by the evaluation. This is the very essence of empowerment—deciding how to assess and label one's own performance. It encourages a self-evaluation of sorts. More so than the traditional evaluation process, it subtly dissuades defensive postures. After a few such evaluations, the employee begins a process of continual self-assessment that ultimately leads to self-insight and further empowerment, ownership, and self-motivation.

However valid the research is on internal motivation and despite the best efforts that have gone into fostering empowerment, there is little evidence that it exists in corporate America. According to organizational guru Chris Argyris (1998), empowerment is still mostly an illusion, because CEOs subtly undermine empowerment. Managers love empowerment in theory, but the command-and-control model is what they trust and know best. Argyris continues:

Internal commitment occurs when employees are committed to a particular project, person, or program for their own individual reasons or motivations. Internal commitment is very closely allied with empowerment. The problem with change programs designed to encourage empowerment is that they actually end up creating more external than internal commitment. One reason is that these programs are rife with inner contradictions and send out mixed messages like "do your own thing—the way we tell you." The result is that employees feel little responsibility for the change program, and people throughout the organization feel less empowered … [Leaders] must encourage employees' internal commitment; and to realize that morale and even empowerment are penultimate criteria in organizations. The ultimate goal is performance. (p. 99)

Georg Brandes once said, "The crowd will follow a leader who marches twenty steps in advance; but if he is a thousand steps in front of them, they do not see and do not follow him." The literature may seriously investigate the theories on leadership, motivation, and empowerment. It may use all the tools of science. However, it is always a struggle to challenge conventional wisdom. Although leaders can greatly benefit from Drs. Argyris and Kohn's prodigious research on motivation, prudence must be exercised in its implementation. Fear will often keep others from accepting it. Fear that they were wrong, in a culture where some leaders believe that "change the course," means admitting failure and admitting failure is tantamount to death. Fear has been presented as an acronym that stands for *False Evidence Appearing Real* or *False Expectations About Reality*. Even when there are clear and compelling reasons why people should change their leadership behaviors, they are fearful and resistant to change. However, if properly treated, the facts will prevail, clinch Argyris and Kohn's fame, and push the intrinsic movement away from an incendiary status to something that makes sense to everyone. Perhaps, then, there will be 12-step group for tragically optimistic positive-reinforcement fans.

Conclusion

Because of their high-frequency customer interaction, hospitality employees can be viewed as strategic weapons in the acquisition and retention of profitable loyal customers. However, the industry is challenged by human resource management issues. Often overworked and underpaid workers are devoid of effective continuous training programs, empowerment, and intrinsic rewards. The above-described motivation and empowerment practices can serve as scaffolds for hospitality leaders to construct progressive organizations and build the overall economic success of the industry. They would allow hospitality to be the trailblazer in organizational human dynamics. It is apt, since the hospitality industry is all about people, and people are the hospitality industry's most valuable resource.

References

Alexakis, G., Platt, A. R., & Tesone, D. V. (2006). Appropriating biological paradigms for the organizational setting to support democratic constructs in the workplace. *Journal of Applied Business and Economics*, 6(1), 17–28.

Argyris, C. (1998, May/June). Empowerment: The emperor's new clothes. *Harvard Business Review*, 76(3), 98–105.

Colven, G. (2006, January 11). The 100 best companies to work for 2006: By treating employees well, these firms are thriving. *Fortune*. Retrieved January 3, 2007, from http://money.cnn.com/magazines/fortune/fortune_archive/2006/01/23/8366990/index.htm

Conger, J. A., & Kannugo, R. N. (1988). *Charismatic leadership*. San Francisco, CA: Jossey-Bass.

Crother-Laurin, C. (2006, Fall). Effective teams: A symptom of healthy leadership. *The Journal for Quality and Participation*, 29(3), 4–8.

Deci, E. L., & Ryan, R. M. (1985). *Intrinsic motivation and self-determination in human behavior*. New York: Plenum.

Dyck, B., & Neubert, M. J. (2008). *Principles of management theory*. Boston, MA: Houghton Mifflin.

Ewers, J. (2006). Management myths: Maxims in need of a makeover. *U.S. News & World Report*. Retrieved March 3, 2006, from http://www.usnews.com/usnews/biztech/articles/060327/27eepfeffer.intro.htm

Fournies, F. F. (1999). *Coaching for improved work performance*. New York: McGraw-Hill.

Gitlow, H., & McNary, L. (2006). Creating win-win solutions for team conflicts. *The Journal for Quality and Participation*, 29(3), 20–26. Retrieved January 29, 2007, from ABI/INFORM Global database. (Document ID: 1154206691).

Gordon, J., & Lowe, B. (2002, March). Employee retention: Approaches for achieving performance objectives. *The Journal of American Academy of Business, Cambridge, 1*(2), 201–205.

Harris Interactive. (2005, May 6). Many U.S. employees have negative attitudes to their jobs, employers and top managers. *The Harris Poll*. Rochester, NY: Harris Interactive Inc. Retrieved January 5, 2007, from http://www.harrisinteractive.com/harris_poll/index.asp?PID=568

Hartline, M. D., & Ferrell, O. C. (1996). The management of customer-contact service employees: An empirical investigation. *Journal of Marketing, 60*(4), 52-70. Retrieved January 29, 2007, from ABI/INFORM Global database. (Document ID: 10281333).

Heneman III, H. G., & Judge, T. A. (2006). Voluntary turnover: Costs and benefits. *Staffing organizations* (5th ed.). New York: McGraw-Hill.

Kelly, H. H., & Michela, J. L. (1980). Attribution theory and research. *Annual Review of Psychology, 31*, 457–501.

Kets de Vries, M. F. R. (1989). Prisoners of leadership. *Human Relations, 4*(3), 261–280.

Kohn, A. (1993). Why incentive plans cannot work. *Harvard Business Review*, September–October54–63.

Kohn, A. (1998). Challenging behaviorist dogma: Myths about money and motivation. *Compensation and Benefits Review, 30*, 27–37.

McColl-Kennedy, J. R., & Anderson, R. D. (2002). Impact of leadership style and emotions on subordinate performance. *Leadership Quarterly, 13*(5), 545–559.

Merkle, L. A., Jackson, A. S., Zhang, J. J., & Dishman, R. K. (2002). Re-examining the construct validity of the self-motivation inventory. *International Sports Journal, 6*(2), 48–59. Retrieved January 24, 2007, from Research Library database. (Document ID: 139240951).

Pescosolido, A. T. (2002). Emergent leaders as managers of group emotion. *Leadership Quarterly, 13*(5), 583–599.

Pfeffer, J. (1998, May–June). Six dangerous myths about pay. *Harvard Business Review*, 108–119.

Popper, M., & Lipshitz, R. (1993). Putting leadership theory to work: A conceptual framework for theory-based leadership development. *Leadership and Organization Development Journal, 14*(7), 23–27.

Racker, H. (2001). *Transference and counter-transference.* Madison, CT: International Universities Press.

Rifkin, J. (2004). *The end of work: The decline of the global workforce and the dawn of the post market era.* New York: Penguin Group.

Saunders, M. N. K., Skinner, D., & Beresford, R. (2005). Mismatched perceptions and expectations: An exploration of stakeholders' views of key and technical skills in vocational education and training. *Journal of European Industrial Training, 29*(4/5), 369–382. Retrieved January 24, 2007, from ABI/INFORM Global database. (Document ID: 874917731).

Scholtes, P. R. (1990). An elaboration of Deming's teachings on performance appraisal. In G. N. McLean, S. R. Damme & R. A. Swanson (Eds.), *Performance appraisal: Perspectives on a quality management approach.* Alexandria, VA: American Society of Training and Development.

Senge, P. M. (2006). *The fifth discipline: The art and practice of the learning organization.* New York: Currency.

Simons, T. (2002). The high cost of lost trust. *Harvard Business Review, 80*(9), 18–19.

Smith, G. P. (2002). Top-ten reasons why people quit their jobs. *The CEO refresher.* Retrieved January 5, 2007, from http://www.refresher.com/archives13.html

Steers, R. M., Porter, L. W., & Bigley, G. A. (1996). *Motivation and leadership at work* (6th ed.). New York: McGraw-Hill.

Trevino, L. (1986). Ethical decision making in organizations: A person-situation interactionist model. *Academy of Management Review, 11*(3), 601–617.

Williams, S. D., & Dewett, T. (2005). Yes, you can teach business ethics: A review and research agenda. *Journal of Leadership and Organizational Studies, 12*(2), 109–120.

Appendix A

The costs of employee turnover

Table A.1 Voluntary Turnover: Costs and Benefits

Separation costs

A. Financial costs

HR staff time (e.g., exit interview, payroll, benefits)
Manager's time (e.g., retention attempts, exit interview)
Accrued paid time off (e.g., vacation, sick pay)
Temporary coverage (e.g., temporary employee; overtime for current employees)

B. Other costs

Production and customer service delays or quality decreases
Lost or unacquired clients
Leaves—goes to competitor or forms competitive business
Contagion—other employees decide to leave
Teamwork disruptions
Loss of workforce diversity

Replacement costs

Staffing costs for new hire (e.g., cost-per-hire calculations)
Hiring inducements (e.g., bonus, relocation, perks)
Hiring manager and work-unit employee time
Orientation program time and materials
HR staff induction costs (e.g., payroll, benefits enrollment)

Training costs

Formal training (trainee instruction time, materials, equipment)
On-the-job training (supervisor and employee time)
Mentoring (mentor's time)
Socialization (time of other employees, travel)
Productivity loss (loss of production until full proficient employee)

Other costs

Replacement employee not as experienced in job, even with training
Time to get up to speed with KSAO
These might require the time and expense to restructure work unit
Cost from not replacing employee immediately (i.e., time to recruit, select, hire)
Replacement more expensive in salary, because of growing expectations of emerging employees and because of the salary compression experienced by former employee

---

Note: Adapted from "Voluntary turnover: Costs and benefits," by H. G. Heneman III and T. A. Judge, 2006, *Staffing Organizations* (5th ed.). New York: McGraw-Hill.

Appendix B

Table B.1 Recognizable Employee Benefits and Perquisites to Compensate for Lack of Income

Relocation expenses
Paid vacations
Employee health insurance plan
Company car
Paid sick leave
Personal secretaries or assistants
Increase in job position title
Supplemental long-term disability insurance
Corner or window offices
Disability insurance
Executive dining rooms
Education reimbursement for job
Pension plan
Life insurance
Dental insurance
Supplemental life insurance
Supplemental medical insurance or reimbursement

Appendix C

Table C.1

Innovative employee benefits and perquisites to compensate for lack of income

Flexible hours or flex schedules
On-site child care center
Family days (for when children have a half day of school or hurricane or snow days)
Gym, recreational, and/or other health and wellness facilities
Discounted fitness club memberships
Paying, subsidizing, and buying power for wholesale club memberships
Movie, sporting event, community theater tickets
Employer mass buying power (to negotiate deals on consumer purchases)
Computer discounts (for employee home computer equipment)
Employee discounts (on employer goods or services)
Friends and family discounts (for employer products or services)
Cellular telephone
Laptop computer
Education and training (e.g., tuition reimbursement or management seminars)
Free personal seminars (e.g., investment planning or stress reduction)
Legal, financing, and investment counseling
Parking privileges or commuter dispensation (e.g., city transit pass)
Loan (and other forms of credit) with appealing rates
Paid time or comp time or payment for community or charitable activities
Fully paid luxury retreats
Bringing children and/or pets to work
Dependent care reimbursement
Free or subsidized on-site massages
Reimbursement for buying a hybrid vehicle
Sleep breaks at work
On-site concierge service for everyday errands (e.g., order and/or pick up photos, groceries, dry cleaning, flowers, etc.)
Vacation travel services
Free or subsidized car washes
On-site cafeteria with discounts on the healthier choices (even Burger King World Headquarters provides this, with healthy choices)
Ready-to-serve take-home meals
Continental breakfasts
Bring in lunch for everyone on fridays
Free or subsidized housecleaning services
Holiday-family parties
Telecommute or work-from-home days

If telecommuting, the following are additional items that can be provided

Home desktop computer
Computer printer
Fax machine
Printer cartridges
Pay for DSL (if telecommuting)
Cellular telephone
Desk supplies (e.g., pens, pencils, paperclips, paper, etc.)

CHAPTER 14

The path of least resistance? Choice and constraint in HRM strategy in the UK hotel sector

Nick Wilton

*Bristol Business School,
University of the West of England, UK*

Introduction

Guerrier and Deery (1998) suggest two central questions that are recurrent in HRM research in the hotel sector. Firstly, to what extent is the work of hospitality managers influenced by the industry context? Secondly, to what extent do hospitality managers engage in reaction or reflection? In this chapter, research-exploring patterns of HR practice and policy in the UK hotel sector will be used to address these questions. The chapter discusses the factors that appear to be influential in determining HRM strategy across the hotel sector and how different approaches to HRM translate into employee relations' practices in respect of employee involvement and participation, skills utilisation and employment flexibility. In particular, it discusses the contextual pressures on HRM in the sector, particularly those relating to labour and product markets, the extent to which HR managers in the sector are able to formulate a range of strategic approaches and how HRM strategy relates to wider competitive strategy.

HRM in the UK hotel sector

Traditionally weak social and legal regulation of employment, fragmented ownership, largely unpredictable product markets, an under-emphasis on training and an over-reliance on employees from the margins of the labour market have contributed to employment practices in the UK hotel sector being characterised as predominantly "bleak house" (Sisson, 1993) or "black hole" (Guest & Conway, 1999). The term "black hole" seems particularly applicable to the UK hotel sector as it refers to a system of employee management defined as having neither formal individual nor collective structures and practices. Guest and Conway (*ibid.*) suggest that "black hole" organisations are generally relatively small establishments[1] in labour intensive sectors and are characterised by low-pay, low levels of skills, training and employee involvement or participation and the high use of temporary labour resulting in both a lack of job security and high turnover[2]. Consequently, interest in

---

[1] The UK hotel sector is predominantly made up of small establishments with fewer than 10 employees.

[2] It would be mistaken to argue that the literature claims that the industry is completely homogenous in its employment patterns although most of what is written tends to paint a distinct picture of employee relations in the sector as predominantly "bleak house" and so that any establishments that diverge from this stereotype are the exceptions that prove the rule (Lucas, 1996). Similarly, Price (1994) argued that examples of poor practice were more prevalent than good practice (simply defined as adhering to practices encouraged or required by legal provision).

HRM practice in the UK hotel sector often relates to its reputation for exemplifying the "bad" or "ugly" extreme of employee relations (Guest & Hoque, 1994) and national surveys of employment practice have often shown this to be the case (Cully *et al.*, 1999; Lucas, 1995, 2002).

The UK hotel industry has also been described as being *"a sector dominated by the spirit of amateur management"* (Parsons & Cave, 1991, quoted in Guerrier & Deery, 1998, p. 151). Management is generally held to be *ad hoc*, reactionary, lacking in formality, and most acutely informed by the necessity for constant labour manipulation in response to unpredictable demand (Riley, 1993; Wood, 1992)[3]. Subsequently, Hales and Tamangani (1996) found that for hotel managers, *"the pressing needs of the immediate and recurrent often drive out longer-term consideration"* (p. 748) reflecting a hands-on, operational rather than a reflective, strategic approach (Guerrier & Lockwood, 1989; Purcell, 1993). This implies little conscious, strategic planning or cohesiveness of HR practices to the extent that Rowley, Purcell, Howe, Richardson, Shackleton, and Whiteley (2000) argue that the most fundamental skills deficit in the industry is that of strategic management itself.

It can be seen in the hotel sector, therefore, that the highly unpredictable nature of demand, a reactive, short-term approach to management and poor employee relations are closely related. Goodman, Earnshaw, Marchington, and Harrison (1998) ask whether the problems of high levels of absenteeism, labour turnover and general employee dissatisfaction within the industry are not so much an inevitable characteristic of the industry itself, but rather an outcome of the way in which management chooses to address its product and labour market context. By pursuing policies of employment casualisation and tight employee supervision and control with an emphasis on managerial prerogative employers are likely to alienate employees and create a workforce without trust in management, lacking commitment to the organisation and reinforce feelings of "them and us". This dynamic is likely to directly affect levels of service quality and overall organisational performance.

Shortcomings in HRM in the UK hotel sector are perhaps most evident in the utilisation of labour, a critical element of HR strategy (Lockwood & Jones, 2000). Larmour (1983) suggests

---

[3]This model of informal, *ad hoc* and reactive management with an emphasis on the short-term is not, however, limited only to the UK hotel sector. For example, Nankervis (1993) and Nankervis and Debrah (1995) paint a similar picture of the Australian hotel industry.

that the principal problem for hotel management is that of finding a suitable workforce, especially given the *"volatility of labour"* associated with high labour turnover and skills shortages (Rowley *et al.*, 2000, p. 53). However, in response to fluctuating demand, hotels managers will typically casualise a significant proportion of labour, which creates insecurity and low employee commitment and, in turn, precipitates further turnover and skills shortages. Hotel managers are therefore seen as being complicit in creating this vicious circle while often bemoaning the problems it creates for service provision. To compound this paradox, if we consider that most hotels conform to the dichotomous model of the flexible firm which has both core and periphery elements of labour (Atkinson, 1984)[4], unlike most organisations where periphery staff are relegated to non-essential activities, in hotel establishments peripheral staff are often no less involved in critical operations as core staff. Most notably, peripheral staff are often employed in "frontline" activities fundamental to the successful delivery of customer service and are, therefore, a key determinant of customer satisfaction (e.g. waiting staff, receptionists, porters and room attendants) (Guerrier & Lockwood, 1989; also, Deery & Jago, 2002). This proves problematic, therefore, when employers are unwilling or unable to offer conditions of employment that reflect the importance of these employees (Guerrier & Lockwood, 1989, p. 14) resulting in lower levels of employee commitment and service quality and perpetuating high labour turnover and skills shortages. Moreover, both pre- and post-entry training for many positions in the sector is typically held to be inadequate and, subsequently, employers are forced to hire inexperienced staff, often to key positions for which they are poorly prepared.

Strategic choice in the hotel sector

Much discussion of HR strategy in the hotel industry focuses on the extent that management is able to exert control over the industry context (mainly, the unpredictable nature of demand) and the extent to which managerial strategy is able to cope with the problems it presents (e.g. the need for high levels of labour flexibility). A central question is, therefore, to what extent are managerial decisions rational, proactive and strategic

---

[4]Where the workforce is comprised of a core of valued, skilled employees who enjoy security of employment are supplemented by semi-skilled and unskilled operatives working on temporary, casual or other non-standard contracts of employment and who enjoy less favourable terms and conditions.

or reactive and "forced" by the context in which decisions are made? This raises the question of the role of HR professionals in the hotel industry and whether it is essentially about "being there" to cope with the immediate operational problems or is there scope for strategic management choice.

Beer, Spector, Lawrence, Quinn Mills, and Walton (1984, p. 25) suggest that *"an organisation's HRM policies and practices must fit with its strategy in its competitive environment and with the immediate business conditions that it faces"* (p. 25), The interaction between business and HR strategy is, therefore, key to understanding patterns of HR practice. Porter (1985) suggests that two decisions need to be made by an organisation to arrive at a suitable type of competitive strategy. First, whether the basis of competition is to be cost or added value and, second, whether mass or niche markets are to be targeted. On the basis of these questions, four possible competitive strategies are apparent:

- Cost leadership: Selling standardised product to a mass market.
- Differentiation: Selling added-value product to a mass market.
- Cost focus: Selling a low cost product to a niche market.
- Differentiation focus: Selling an added value product to niche market.

Similarly, Gilbert and Strebel (1988) suggest that there are two constituents of competitive advantage for an organisation: lower delivered cost and higher perceived value. Gilbert and Strebel suggest that there is an "internal logic" to each business system that dictates the possible combinations of perceived value and delivered cost that must exist for the whole business system. It is the primacy of one or the other of these two constituents of competitive advantage which differentiates between organisations, depending on industry position and circumstances. Either strategic position can be adopted but they can be also used together to give and organisation a superior position by offering the highest perceived value for the lowest possible cost.

It is apparent that any of these strategies might apply to different hotels operating in different markets, however, the stereotypical picture of much of the UK hotel industry, in particular among smaller establishments serving the tourism sector, is that of cost leadership using Porter's typology. The "internal logic" of the hotel industry, especially smaller establishments, leads managers to adopt a competitive strategy predominantly based upon lowest delivered cost. Among certain types of hotels, however, it is clear that wider choice of strategy, and a greater focus on perceived value, is possible. For example, using Porter's model, a differentiation focus strategy would be most appropriate for boutique hotels or a differentiation strategy for hotels serving both a commercial and tourism market. This apparent diversity of appropriate competitive strategies in the hotel sector would be expected to result in similar diversity of HR strategy.

Bratton (2003, p. 49) defines human resource strategies as meaning *"the patterns of decisions regarding HR policies and practices used by management to design work and select, train and develop, appraise, motivate and control workers"*. Bamberger and Meshoulam (2000) suggest that these decisions centre around two main dimensions of HR strategy: "acquisition and development" and "locus of control". Acquisition and development is concerned with the extent to which HR strategy develops internal human capital as opposed to relying on external recruitment. Locus of control is concerned with the degree to which HR strategy focuses on monitoring employees' compliance with process-based standards as opposed to developing a psychological contract that nurtures social relationships, encourage mutual trust, and controls the focus on the outcomes themselves. HR strategy will depend on the emphasis put on each of these variables at different times, representing a distinction between commitment (or resource-based) and control (process-based) strategies (Hutchinson, Purcell, & Kinnie, 2000).

The majority of the UK hotel industry operates in a high volume, low cost product market and attempt to generate profits from increasing market share. Subsequently, the dominant "model" of HR strategy is one of process-based control, reflecting either bureaucratic and/or individual direct control, with a predominant focus on the external labour market. Such control would most likely be achieved by the use of Taylorised working practices such as job prescription, a high degree of specialisation, minimal training and a high degree of monitoring and direct supervision. Wage costs are minimised by the use of non-standard employment and subcontracting. Resource-based HR strategies which emphasise outcome-based control and a long-term commitment to labour, underpinning an added-value competitive strategy, are generally held to be very much the exception. Some research does, however, provide evidence of more complex patterns and a greater unevenness of HRM practices. Hoque (2000, p. 27) suggests that where there is *"scope for diversity in business strategies within any given industry, there is likewise scope for diversity in the approaches taken to HRM"* and that there is diversity in the UK hotel industry that is related to particular hotel characteristics such as hotel size and standard (Hoque, 1999, 2000). Hoque (2000) argues that rather than the hotel industry conforming to a "one size fits all" model, individual hotels tend to adopt approaches to employee management that "fit" business strategy according to "product market logic" (Evans & Lorange, 1989). The more successful the organisation is at achieving fit between product market, business strategy and HR strategy, the more successful it is likely to be in terms of achieving organisational outcomes. For example, he suggests that a high-standard hotel is best served by adopting a strategy of quality enhancement through fostering employee commitment (e.g. through employee involvement and consultation) and continuous improvement in service provision (including high levels of training).

On this basis of this discussion, it would be expected that a cross-sectional study of the hotel sector in the UK, covering a wide variety of hotel "types", would highlight both differences in competitive strategy and, subsequently, HR strategy. The following section discusses whether this was the case.

The research study

The research presented in this chapter sought to identify the patterns of incidence of particular employee relations practices and outcomes in the south west region of the UK[5]. Tourism-related industries provide significant employment and income for the South West and the region has an above average population of hotels. At the time of the research, the region represented 9% of total UK employment in the hotel sector (Office for National Statistics, 2002). Moreover, the regional hotel sector is diverse in its composition, ranging from the small, highly seasonal guest houses in the far South West (Cornwall & Devon) to large urban hotels serving both the tourism and business markets (e.g. in Bristol & Bath) and, as such, provided scope to explore a broad mix of both product and labour markets. In particular, the study sought to investigate the pervasiveness of the "black hole" model of employee relations, whether there was evidence of more "progressive" forms of HRM in certain sections of the industry and to explore the factors that might shape approaches to HRM, such as size and location of hotel establishment. On the basis of the assumption that management practice is largely dictated by

---

[5] For the purposes of the research, the South West refers to the counties of Cornwall, Devon, Somerset, Gloucestershire, Wiltshire and Bristol.

local labour and product market, mediated by size of establishment, then significant diversity of practice should have been revealed within this varied population of hotels.

Data were collected using a cross-sectional questionnaire survey of the HR policies and practices among 137 hotels and a number of follow-up interviews with managers with responsibility for HR issues in a sample of larger hotel establishments in the region[6]. The purpose of the questionnaire survey was to identify the patterns of incidence of particular employee relations practices and outcomes across the region. The qualitative interviews were then conducted to further explore employee relations management practice in the individual establishment, in particular the extent of formality in strategic HR planning. The interviews were used to probe the assumption that innovation in HR practice and either nascent or well-developed high-commitment HRM were most likely to be found in larger, higher quality hotels which would set them apart from the stereotypical managerial approaches characteristic of "black hole" firms. A key element was to investigate managerial rationale behind particular policies and the degree to which management felt constrained by their organisational context in HR decision-making.

The focus of the discussion here is on areas of HR practice that were felt most likely to indicate diversity in the formality of HR practice and differences in strategic approaches to HRM: employee communication, involvement and consultation, employment structures and labour flexibility and the incidence and attempts to address HR problems associated with the industry; skills shortages and high labour turnover.

Summary of research findings

Questionnaire survey • • •

Supporting the findings of previous surveys of HR practices in the UK hotel sector, the questionnaire survey suggested that informality of employee management was pervasive across hotels in South West England and there was only limited evidence of structured, proactive approaches to HRM among the sample. Certain assumptions regarding HRM in the hotel sector were found to hold true for the region. For example, the use of flexible labour, through both part-time and casual employment,

---

[6] The survey covered hotels with at least ten rooms. The smallest hotel in which an interview was conducted had 60 rooms and the largest had 289 rooms.

was widespread and the experience of skill shortages and high level of staff turnover was similarly endemic. Similarly, mechanisms used to consult or communicate with employees tended to be informal, "when necessary" meetings and unilateral forms of communications were predominant across the sample. However, some notable diversity was also identified within the sample and some interesting "contradictory" findings were made. For example, a small but significant number of respondents claimed to use formal means to communicate or consult with employees over a number of key issues including changes to working practices suggesting a more consultative approach to managerial decision-making than was expected[7].

However, analysis of the survey data suggested that some practices and issues in HR were not industry-wide conditions but appeared to be associated with particular organisational characteristics. Most importantly, size of establishment appears to be the most influential factor when considering the formality of, and approach taken to, employee relations and HRM. For example, larger hotels were more likely to have a specific manager with responsibility for personnel and employment matters[8], demonstrate greater concern for employment problems such as skills shortages and employee turnover and, while the use of numerical flexibility to manipulate labour supply was pervasive, were more likely to utilise part-time working as opposed to casual employment as the preferred mode of flexibility[9]. In addition, formality of communication and consultation increase with size of establishment (perhaps unsurprising given the likely complexity of employment structures and, therefore, communicational channels in medium to large hotels).

The survey suggested, therefore, that there exists a "crude" two-tier industry structure in the UK hotel sector. While much of the small hotel sector typified many of the "black hole" characteristics of the industry, some larger hotels appeared to apply greater formality to HRM. However, the extent of formality was also highly contingent on product and labour market context.

---

[7] As Hales and Klidas (1998) found, however, management is often quick to espouse the rhetoric of empowerment but rarely does this represent significant increase in employee 'voice' (especially at the organisational level) or, indeed, employee 'choice' over minor operational decisions.

[8] Suggested as being an indicator of formality in HR practice and policy (Kelliher & Johnson, 1997; Cully, Woodland, O'Reilly, & Dix, 1999).

[9] This perhaps represents a higher propensity or ability to support a permanent workforce in larger hotels that is able to supply a degree of flexibility through part-time employment rather than adopting a 'pruning' strategy more appropriate to smaller, leisure hotels.

The survey suggested that formal employee relations practices were more likely to be found in hotels located in urban centres serving the stable, commercial market rather than those hotels catering for the more unpredictable tourist trade. Hoque (1999), in a study of HR practice in large and medium hotels, divided establishments into three categories in terms of business strategy: those focusing on cost-minimisation or price competition, those focusing primarily on quality enhancement and those with an ambiguous approach to business strategy. Much of the survey sample appears to adopt a cost minimisation approach or, at best, an ambiguous strategy trying to balance the need for strict control over labour costs and the need for standards to be maintained. There was also evidence, however, to suggest that among larger hotels there may be evidence of hotels adopting competitive strategy of quality enhancement and with it a more formalised system of HRM.

Interviews with HR managers • • •

From the survey alone it was unclear whether this perceived formality in larger hotels was indicative of greater strategic thinking among management and how widespread strategic approaches to HRM were in the sector. Furthermore, it was debatable whether any greater formality was the result of management linking employee satisfaction to improved service quality and the pursuit of the former in order to achieve the latter or whether it was associated with the need for tighter control and supervision of a larger workforce. These questions formed the basis for the qualitative phase of the research. It was expected that the interviews conducted with HR/personnel managers in larger hotels would uncover a relatively consistent level of formality of HR practices. However, even in a small sample of largely "similar" establishments (hotels targeting the higher end of the hospitality market) considerable diversity in HR policy and practice was apparent. Relative diversity in overarching HR strategy was informed by a number of factors including the nature of ownership (whether independent or belonging to a UK or overseas chain), the approach of the wider organisation (if part of a chain), the management style of the general manager/personnel manager at the establishment and the location of the hotel and its associated labour market.

First, diversity was found in the area of employment structures and the utilisation of labour. Despite an almost universally high dependency on (either or both) part-time and casual labour in the hotels surveyed, the interview sample hotels displayed a range of approaches to the manipulation of staffing levels which tended to reflect a deliberate approach to HR planning and, in some cases, a particular competitive strategy. These included a seasonal establishment that managed to maintain a relatively large year-round workforce of full-time workers complemented by a large intake of casuals in the summer months, an approach informed by the owner's desire to retain key workers (despite the overhead costs associated with doing so out of season) and a scarcity of key skills in the local labour market at peak season. This was partially to support a business strategy of diversification (away from its main summer tourism market) to attract custom out of season (e.g. small business conferences, short breaks…). Alternatively, other hotels managed to address the problems of variable demand with little recourse to casual employment through other forms of flexibility such as cross-training and multi-skilling, reflecting an ambiguous business strategy, attempting to maintain tight control over costs while maintaining service quality.

The methods of communication used in the interview sample hotels also varied considerably from highly structured, bilateral consultative formats, to unstructured, informal, purely downward models. Several establishments went beyond managerial communication of strategic or operational information (using methods that ranged from regular (or irregular) general meetings through to an informal cascade through departmental managers). These hotels used staff forums or consultative committees as a deliberate attempt to engender employee commitment and to gauge employee satisfaction. Informal forms of communication, characterised by ideas of "open-door" policies or "as and when necessary", were again to be found in a variety of hotels, whether according to ownership or size. Again, the adoption of particular methods of employee communication and/or consultation tended to reflect both management style and HR strategy within an establishment, as discussed in the following section.

In relation to employee relations "problems", the majority of managers interviewed regarded labour turnover to be an issue at their establishment. However, managerial attitudes differed significantly in the extent to which they saw it as an avoidable problem and the extent to which they were willing or felt able to address it. One perspective considered high levels of turnover not to be of particular concern and an inevitable occurrence in the industry that was to be tolerated and, in some cases, contributed to maintaining low labour costs. Alternatively, other hotel managers regretted labour turnover which they felt impacted negatively on service quality and were actively attempting to address this problem, whether through supply-side approaches (e.g. through the refinement of selection processes and ensuring prospective staff were aware of the demands of the industry, especially regarding working hours) or measures to improve staff retention. A similar situation was apparent in the discussion of skills deficiencies. Skills shortages in the external labour market (at all occupational levels) were felt to be the most significant problem and all managers interviewed acknowledged the problems of recruiting adequately trained, experienced employees, regardless of location. Again, however, significant diversity was evident in the approaches taken to address the issue. Several hotels actively addressed the issues by attempting to improve recruitment procedures and to aid retention by offering better terms and conditions than their competitors. Other hotels appeared to accept inevitable shortfalls in supply of key skills and actively sought to de-skill certain tasks to minimise training and employment costs. Of course, external factors, for example the nature of the local labour market were largely to blame for the severity of the problem in a particular hotel, but the problem also appears to be inherent in the sector, relating to poor industry image and poor conditions of employment. This appeared to be an area of consensus in all hotels.

Management style in the interview sample

One means by which to classify approaches to employee management is to consider the management "style" that is reflected in the adoption of particular HR practices. Wilton (2006), using the same data as discussed here, outlines the approach evident in each of the interview sample hotels by referring to Purcell's (1987) model of management style based on degrees of individualism and collectivism[10]. Purcell suggests that a high degree of individualism (which emphasises individual employee development) is characterised by strong internal labour markets, comprehensive training schemes and extensive welfare provision. Such establishments are also characterised by payment systems that emphasise merit elements,

---

[10]While intended to map long-term management styles reflecting coherent strategic approaches, this model may also be a useful means of locating different managerial approaches within the hotel industry (Croney, 1988). Even though these approaches may not be deliberate in the sense of being planned and formulated as coherent business strategy, the model may still prove useful in mapping contingent management styles (Wilton, 2006).

the use of appraisals and assessment techniques and communication systems are likely to be extensive though a variety of media. In contrast, low individualism (which emphasises labour control) is characterised by tight fiscal controls (emphasising the commodity element of labour) and little priority to job security, with emphasis on the external labour market and employee discipline. Organisations that occupy the middle ground are characterised as paternalist and described as being those organisations that *"do not appear to place emphasis on employee development and career progression … nor are they dismissive of a sense of social responsibility towards their staff"* (Purcell, *ibid.*, p. 537). Hotels that formed the interview sample generally displayed a labour control or, at best, paternalist management style. Predictably, only a very limited number of hotels could be characterised as emphasising employee development by demonstrating a commitment to internal labour markets and attempts to forego a degree of numerical flexibility in favour of greater emphasis on employment stability.

The collectivism variable refers to the degree of "industrial democracy" found in an organisation and the means by which managers *"become to a greater or lesser extent accountable for their actions to employees, and where staff have some say in decision-making"* (Purcell, *ibid.*, p. 538). Wilton (2006) modified Purcell's original model to reflect the negligible presence of trade unions and organised collectivism in the sample establishments by using this axis to refer to the degrees of employee involvement in decision-making, ranging from absolute managerial prerogative (unilateralism) through employee cooperation to some degree of worker consultation. Most establishments where interviews were conducted could be argued to be essentially *unilateral* or *cooperative* (mainly through paternalist "open door" means of employee communication and involvement) in nature. The few hotels that were categorised as *consultative* were seen to demonstrate more inclusive employee participation mechanisms that rose above simply day-to-day concerns and which impacted upon immediate working conditions and, in some cases, represented strategic joint decision-making. Importantly, employee influence on managerial decision-making was portrayed as being relatively high in these hotels. Again, only one hotel in the sample (which was part of large international chain) appeared to reflect both elements of consultative collectivism and employee development; the hotel had both well-developed mechanisms for participative employee consultation and employment policies emphasising the importance of staff retention, skills and positive encouragement of functional flexibility.

Discussion

The research suggested, therefore, that generalisations about employee management in such a diverse industry are difficult to make and, given that managerial responses to the pressures and tensions of the industry are difficult to predict, a contingent approach is necessary to understand managerial practice, especially in relation to strategic HR planning. Elements of the industry context, for example the unpredictability of demand and the subsequent "need" for employment flexibility, appeared endemic to most hotels yet managerial responses to their environment were diverse. Therefore, while the industry itself provides the broader context, it is the immediate circumstance of the individual establishment that appeared to provide the greatest influence on employment practice. The research highlights both the diversity of employee relations policies and practices adopted by managers and organisations in the UK hotel sector but also the relative paucity of strategic approaches to HRM across the sector. Even where more considered approaches to employee management were evident, considerable diversity of responses to environmental pressures were also found. While the survey gives some indication that larger hotels are more likely to demonstrate greater formality of employee relations[11], the range of practices adopted, even within the selective interview sample, indicates that there is little uniformity even among similar establishments.

Lockwood and Jones (2000; citing Slack et al., 1995) suggest that there are four key factors that influence the operational complexity of a service or production process: volume of demand; variety of products and services offered; variation in demand; and the extent of customer contact. In the hotel industry, it is likely to be the combination of the first three factors (assuming that the level of customer contact is high across the sector) that are likely to exert most influence and be the prime determinants of competitive and HRM strategy. On the basis of this research, size of establishment appears to have significant implications in terms of the interaction between a particular hotel and its immediate context (i.e. labour and product market) partly because it is a significant indicator of other important characteristics (e.g. larger hotels are likely to be of a higher standard and belong to a larger organisation).

---

[11] There were incidences of smaller hotels adopting more progressive approaches to HRM (in the survey sample). Typically these were more upmarket establishments apparently adopting a differentiation focus approach to competitive strategy which informed a high commitment HRM strategy.

Larger hotels might deal with larger volumes of custom and offer a wider variety of services and products, yet it is the relative stability of demand in the commercial sector (which makes up the bulk of custom in many large hotels) that both requires and allows the adoption of a more coherent, formalised HRM strategy to contribute to organisational performance.

The (larger) hotels in the interview sample appear, therefore, to have a greater range of HR and competitive strategic options as demonstrated by the diversity of HRM practices and ethos that had been adopted. There were considerable differences, however, in the extent to which the HR managers interviewed appeared to recognise the range of alternatives available to them. While several managers were aware of the opportunity to adopt a long-term, commitment-based HR strategy, only a small number had adopted related practices, mainly in an *ad hoc* manner. Only one hotel (which was part of large international chain) had in place practices and policies that could be inferred to approximate to strategic, high-commitment HRM. Most managers appeared to be constrained by day-to-day concerns and tactical decision-making, whether at establishment or higher organisational level, which inhibited their ability to adopt a more cohesive strategy. The interviews suggest that even where there are alternatives available to management in the formation of competitive and HR strategy, management's failure to recognise them, or fail to see their benefit, is as much of a constraint as their environmental context.

Many factors affecting organisational performance in the hospitality industry lie outside the control of managers and it is unsurprising that few hotels in the study adopted a long-term HR strategy. Overall, the vast majority of establishments appear to conform to this largely stereotypical model of hotel management demonstrating little formality, establishments being characterised by a reliance on casualised labour and strict wage control. Using Hoque's (1999) distinction between different competitive strategies in the sector, the hotels in this study appear to compete on the basis of cost-minimisation or by adopting an ambiguous approach to business and HR strategy. Alternatively, a very small proportion of hotels, most commonly larger, higher-rated establishments belonging to a larger organisation, formed a distinctly different industry sub-sector. The internal logic for larger hotels serving the more benign commercial marketplace is, therefore, likely to be different to that of the smaller hotel sector coping with more unpredictable demand. As such, management of such hotels while still subject to particular idiosyncrasies of the sector was more likely to be formalised, less instrumental and more inclusive than that found in the rest of the sector. Employment was, therefore, likely to be experienced more positively with better terms and conditions on offer, opportunities for development and a greater emphasis on the stability of labour and skills flexibility.

The research presented in this chapter raises the question of whether a conscious (or unconscious) competitive strategy of cost minimisation simply represents managers taking the path of least resistance (and as such, rather than being a statement of incapacity in the face of external pressures is a legitimate response to these pressures), especially given that attempts to move away from such an approach would likely be viewed as high risk. Taking the perspective that the strategies of firms are best understood as sets of strategic choices (whether emergent or planned), a key issue is the *"degrees of freedom"* available to different firms in different sectors (Boxall & Purcell, 2003, p. 35). Thompson and McHugh (2002) suggest that the choice of HR strategy within a firm is governed by variations in organisational form (e.g. size), competitive pressures on management and the stability of labour markets, mediated by the interplay of employer–employee relations and worker resistance. Hyman (1987) argues that all management decision-making is merely tactical rather than strategic and this notion may be epitomised by hotel industry norms. Kochan, McKersie, and Cappelli (1984, p. 21, cited in Hyman, 1987, p. 29) suggests that *"strategic decisions can only occur when the parties have discretion over their decision, that is where environmental constraints do not severely curtail the parties' choice of alternatives"*. The research suggests that, in response to specific labour and product market pressures, for many hotels, both in the UK and elsewhere, the extent of choice in HRM strategy appears limited, given that a cost-minimisation business strategy appears almost irresistible. This might be used to infer, therefore, that some conceptions of strategic choice might exaggerate the ability of managers to make decisions and take action independent of the environmental contexts in which they do business (Colling, 1995) nowhere more so than in the hotel industry.

Many conceptualisations of strategic HRM are predicated upon a rational perspective of managerial decision-making where decisions are definable acts of planning, choice and action. Bratton (2003) suggests, however, that the assumption that a firm's business-level strategy and HR strategy have a logical, linear relationship is questionable given the evidence that strategy formulation is informal, politically charge and subject to complex contingency factors. As such the notion of consciously aligning business strategy and HR strategy applies only to the "classical" approach to strategy, where the manager is a reflective planner and strategist. Furthermore, the relationship between business and HR strategy is often said to be "reactive" in the sense that HR strategy is subservient to "product market logic" and wider corporate strategy. In the hotel industry, the process of strategic formulation would appear to be less clearly delineated. For example, HR "strategy" and practice in some hotels may well be determined primarily by local market conditions (e.g. the scarcity of particular skills leading to deskilling or the unpredictability of demand leading to the mass casualisation of employment) which, in turn determines, wider competitive strategy. Even in hotel establishments which are part of a larger chain (like most of those in which interviews were conducted) managers are likely to be trying to reconcile business strategy and environmental pressures and whatever HR strategy emerges is likely to be an amalgamation of policies and practices which are an *ad hoc* response to local market conditions and those imposed from senior management. This has more in common with Purcell's (2001) portrayal of HR strategy as *"emerging patterns of action"* that are likely to be formed intuitively, rather than a set of proactive edicts that are born from and complementary to competitive strategy.

Summary

What can be concluded from the research presented in this chapter is that a contingent approach is necessary to understand HRM practice and strategy within this highly diverse industrial sector as employer responses to the pressures and tensions of the industry are unpredictable. The complex relationship between product and labour market context, HR and wider competitive strategy in the industry appears to inform a broad range of responses from HR managers in the sector. Many hotels in the UK, including the majority of those covered by the survey, have high levels of operational complexity on the basis of serving highly variable product markets (as well as competing in difficult labour market conditions) that lends itself to a cost-minimisation "strategy" and a reactive, unitary management style. At best, they adopt an ambiguous strategy attempting to balance the need for strict control over labour costs and the maintenance of standards. Hotels that operate in the more stable commercial marketplace appear in a better position to adopt a proactive strategy of quality enhancement and associated HRM practices (whether or not as part of a coherent HRM strategy).

Adopting the matching model advocated by Beer *et al.* (1984), then arguably for many hotels a cost-minimisation business strategy, with attendant HR policies of high levels of numerical flexibility, deskilling and use of casual labour, is the ideal match for its competitive environment. In many hotels it appears that competing purely on the basis of price and, therefore, cost-minimisation through the manipulation of labour, sufficiently addresses for many of the fundamental strategic problem of via-bility in the marketplace. Given the volatility of demand in the sector this response appears rational. Where a strategy of qual-ity enhancement and high-commitment strategic HRM may be most useful is in those hotels where the "second-order" problem is to be tackled, that of sustained advantage; for those that wish to play in a higher level "tournament" (Boxall & Purcell, 2003, p. 33). Achieving viability is likely to be enough of an objective for many smaller hotels and the problems posed by trying to increase competitive advantage through strategic approaches are likely to be too costly to address. For managers in many hotels, the "degrees of freedom" in decision-making about both business and HRM strategy appear limited in response to spe-cific labour and product market pressures. However, referring to the "ideal types" of business strategy suggested by Porter and Gilbert and Strebel, it is apparent that among the inter-view sample hotels there is variation in competitive approaches dependent on their target market(s), their patterns of demand, hotel ownership and location. What is less apparent, however, is a conscious formation of a coherent HR strategy to underpin this competitive approach. In fact, in smaller hotels where an explicit competitive strategy of price competition and labour cost minimisation is the norm, there is perhaps greater "fit" between HR and competitive strategy.

Models of HR strategy tend to assume that an alignment of business strategy and HR strategy will improve organisational performance and competitiveness and that high-commitment-type HRM systems produce above-average results compared with control-type systems. A number of studies (Guest, 1997; Hutchinson *et al.*, 2000) have found that bundles of HRM practices are positively associated with superior organisa-tional performance. In the hotel sector, Worsfold (1999) sug-gests the adoption of HRM practices may result in significant improvements in organisational performance and service quality. However, Purcell (1999, p. 26) does report on the high-commitment HRM discourse that has led to "*extravagant claims on the universal applicability of the best practice model, implying one recipe for successful HR activity*". It might be the case, therefore, that in the hotel industry at least, an instrumental approach to labour control within an overall business strategy of cost minimisation is the logical strategic choice for some establishments and that apparently "poor" HR practice are reflective of management adopting a "strategy" by which to best achieve sustainability of their organisation.

Implicit in different competitive strategies is a particular set of employee responses to that strategy, or *"needed role behaviours"*. HR strategy is concerned, therefore, with the challenge of matching the HR philosophy, policies, practices and processes in a way that will stimulate and reinforce the different employee role behaviours appropriate for each competitive strategies (Schuler, 1989; Schuler & Jackson, 1987; Capelli & Singh, 1992). This might suggest that in an industry sector where customer interaction and service quality is paramount, an emphasis on labour control and cost-minimisation would not achieve the employee role behaviours required to produce competitive advantage. It can be inferred from the data collected in this study that, in many hotels, immediate operational concerns such as unpredictable demand and the manipulation of labour take precedence over concerns about service quality. In this scenario, management are likely to rely on the "goodwill" of employees to perform effectively without providing incentives for doing so (an approach which tends to favour paternalist styles of management). Combined, this goodwill and effective cost management are likely to ensure the survival of the hotel. For a large part of the sector, therefore, adoption of a strategy of control is arguably the path of least resistance for achieving viability in the marketplace and the adoption of a high-commitment HRM strategy would most likely be extremely difficult, highlighting that "best practice HRM" is not universally applicable (Purcell, 1999). Conversely, in hotels where consistently high service quality is essential, then best-practice HRM would appear to be of paramount importance to achieve sustained advantage. What seems apparent in this research is limited evidence of HR strategy formation and practical implementation of policies and practices to underpin a value-added competitive strategy in those hotels where it would be most beneficial to do so.

Even in organisations where an overall corporate strategy of quality enhancement and differentiation appears to have been adopted the extent to which this is translated into HR practice comes down to the ability and leadership of local managers to follow through these objectives in the context of specific environmental conditions (Purcell & Ahlstrand, 1994). Therefore, while most of the hotels in the interview sample operate in similar product and labour markets the ways in which management utilise and communicate with employees, and respond to HR "problems, was found to differ substantially. Although many of the hotels in the sample simply react in the most cost-effective manner (in the short-term), other hotels appear to have acknowledged the connection between staff retention, job satisfaction and service quality. The interviews with HR managers in the sector indicated that while much of the work of HR specialists and managers in the sector focuses on "tactical", day-to-day concerns, a long-term strategic perspective was possible and found in a small number of hotels. It is perhaps surprising that more did not adopt such an approach given the importance of service provision to both viability and sustained competitive advantage. Therefore, in the context of the survey data, even though larger hotels appear more likely to recognise this connection and display more formal or strategic approaches to HRM compared to the industry as a whole, this sub-sector still appears significantly divided in the extent to which managers appear able, willing or compelled to invest in associated practices.

References

Atkinson, J. (1984). Manpower strategies for flexible organisations. *Personnel Management*, *16*(8), 28–31.

Bamberger, P., & Meshoulam, L. (2000). *Human resource strategy*. California: Sage.

Beer, M., Spector, B., Lawrence, P., Quinn Mills, D., & Walton, R. (1984). *Managing human assets*. New York: Free Press.

Boxall, P., & Purcell, J. (2003). *Strategy and human resource management*. Basingstoke: Palgrave.

Bratton, J. (2003). Strategic human resource management. In: J. Bratton & J. Gold (Eds.), *Human resource management: Theory and practice* (3rd ed.). London: Palgrave.

Capelli, P., & Singh, H. (1992). Integrating strategic human resources and strategic management. In: D. Lewis, O. Mitchell & P. Sherer (Eds.), *Research frontiers in industrial relations and human resources*. International Industrial Relations Association, Madison, WI.

Colling, T. (1995). Experiencing turbulence: Competition, strategic choice and the management of human resources in British Airways. *Human Resource Management Journal*, *5*(5), 18–33.

Croney, P. (1988) *An Investigation into the Management of Labour in the Hotel Industry*, Unpublished MA thesis, University of Warwick

Cully, M., Woodland, S., O'Reilly, A., & Dix, G. (1999). *Britain at work. As depicted by the 1998 workplace employee relations survey*. London: Routledge.

Deery, M., & Jago, I. (2002). The core and the periphery: An examination of the flexible workforce model in the hotel industry. *International Journal of Hospitality Management, 21*, 339–351.

Evans, P., & Lorange, P. (1989). Two logics behind HRM. In: P. Evans, Y. Doz & A. Laurent (Eds.), *HRM in international firms*. Basingstoke: Macmillan.

Gilbert, X., & Strebel, P. (1988). Developing competitive advantage. In: J. Quinn, H. Mintzberg & R. James (Eds.), *The strategy process*. Englewood Cliffs, NJ: Prentice-Hall.

Goodman, J., Earnshaw, J., Marchington, M., & Harrison, R. (1998). Unfair dismissal cases, disciplinary procedures, recruitment methods and management styles. *Employee Relations, 20*(6), 536–550.

Guerrier, Y., & Deery, M. (1998). Research in hospitality human resource management and organisational behaviour. *International Journal of Hospitality Management, 17*, 145–160.

Guerrier, Y., & Lockwood, A. (1989). Core and peripheral employees in hotel operations. *Personnel Review, 18*(1), 9–15.

Guest, D. (1997). Human resource management and performance: A review and research agenda. *International Journal of Human Resource Management, 8*(3), 263–276.

Guest, D., & Hoque, K. (1994). The good, the bad and the ugly: Employee relations in new non-union workplaces. *Human Resource Management Journal, 5*(1), 1–14.

Guest, D., & Conway, N. (1999). Peering into the Black Hole: The downside of the new employee relations in the UK. *British Journal of Industrial Relations, 37*(3), 367–389.

Hales, C., & Klidas, A. (1998). Empowerment in five-star hotels: Voice or rhetoric? *International Journal of Contemporary Hospitality Management, 10*(3), 88–95.

Hales, C., & Tamangani, Z. (1996). An investigation of the relationship between organisational structure, managerial role expectations and manager's work activities. *Journal of Management Studies, 33*, 731–756.

Hoque, K. (1999). Human resource management and performance in the UK hotel industry. *British Journal of Industrial Relations, 37*(3), 419–443.

Hoque, K. (2000). *Human resource management in the hotel industry: Strategy, innovation and performance*. London: Routledge.

Hyman, R. (1987). Strategy or structure? Capital, labour and control. *Work, Employment and Society, 1*(1), 25–55.

Hutchinson, S., Purcell, J., & Kinnie, N. (2000). Evolving high commitment management and the experience of the RAC call centre. *Human Resource Management Journal, 10*(1), 63–78.

Kelliher, C., & Johnson, K. (1997). Personnel management in hotels: An update. *Progress in Tourism and Hospitality Research, 3*(4), 321–331.

Kochan, T., McKersie, R., & Cappelli, P. (1984). Strategic choice and industrial relations theory. *Industrial Relations, 23,* 16–39.

Larmour, R. (1983). Some problems faced by managers in the hotel and catering industry. *International Journal of Contemporary Hospitality Management, 2*(2), 89–92.

Lockwood, A., & Jones, P. (2000). Managing hospitality operations. In: C. Lashley & A. Morrison (Eds.), *In search of hospitality*. Oxford: Butterworth Heinemann.

Lucas, P. (2002). Fragments of HRM in hospitality? Evidence from the 1998 workplace employee relations survey. *International Journal of Contemporary Hospitality Management, 14*(5), 207–212.

Lucas, R. (1995). *Managing employee relations in the hotel and catering industry*. London: Cassell.

Lucas, R. (1996). Industrial relations in hotels & catering: Neglect and paradox? *British Journal of Industrial Relations, 34*(2), 267–286.

Nankervis, A. (1993). Enhancing productivity in the Australian hotel industry: The role of human resource management. *Research and Practice in Human Resource Management, 1*(1), 17–39.

Nankervis, A., & Debrah, Y. (1995). Human resource management in hotels: A comparative study. *Tourism Management, 16*(7), 507–513.

Office for National Statistics. (2002). *Labour force survey: March 2002*. London: Office for National Statistics.

Parsons, D. & Cave, P. (1991) *Developing Managers for Tourism*, National Economic Development Office, London

Porter, M. (1985). *Competitive advantage*. New York: Free Press.

Price, L. (1994). Poor personnel practice in the hotel and catering industry: Does it matter? *Human Resource Management Journal, 4*(4), 44–62.

Purcell, J. (1987). Mapping management styles in employee relations. *Journal of Management Studies, 24*(5), 533–548.

Purcell, J. (1993). Challenges of HRM for industrial relations research and practice. *International Journal of Human Resource Management, 4*(3), 511–528.

Purcell, J. (1999). Best practice and best fit: Chimera or cul-de-sac? *Human Resource Management Journal, 9*(3), 26–41.

Purcell, J. (2001). Personnel and human resource managers: Power, prestige and potential. *Human Resource Management Journal*, *11*(3), 3–4.

Purcell, J., & Ahlstrand, B. (1994). *Human resource management in the multi-divisional company*. Oxford: Oxford University Press.

Riley, M. (1993). Back to the future: Lessons from free market experience. *Employee Relations*, *15*(2), 8–15.

Rowley, G., Purcell, K., Howe, S., Richardson, M., Shackleton, R., & Whiteley, P. (2000). *Employers skill survey: Case study hospitality sector*. Nottingham: Department for Education and Employment.

Schuler, R. (1989). Strategic human resource management. *Human relations*, *42*(2), 157–184.

Schuler, R. S., & Jackson, S. E. (1987). Linking competitive strategies and human resource management practices. *Academy of Management Executive*, *1*(3), 207–219.

Sisson, K. (1993). In search of HRM. *British Journal of Industrial Relations*, *31*(2), 201–210.

Slack, N., Chambers, S., Harland, C., Harrison, A. and Johnston, R. (1995) *Operations Management*. Pitman Publishing, London

Thompson, P., & McHugh, D. (2002). *Work organisations*. Basingstoke: Palgrave.

Wilton, N. (2006). Strategic choice & organisational context in HRM in the hotel sector. *The Service Industries Journal*, *26*(8), 1–17.

Wood, R. (1992). *Working in hotels and catering*. London: Routledge.

Worsfold, P. (1999). HRM, performance, commitment and service quality in the hotel industry. *International Journal of Contemporary Hospitality Management*, *11*(7), 340–348.

Part Three

Developing human resources

CHAPTER 15

Employee orientation and mentoring programs

Bahaudin G. Mujtaba

H. Wayne Huizenga School of Business and Entrepreneurship
Nova Southeastern University
FL 33314, USA

Employee orientation and socializations programs are an important element of making sure employees are successful in achieving their goals and the goals of the organization. Human resource managers and staff are responsible for maximizing the productivity of their organization's human resources through effective employee orientation and mentoring programs. Through a comprehensive coverage of socialization and mentoring programs, this chapter provides a reflection of employee orientation and development practices that can be used by human resource staff members and departments.

Mentoring is an art as it requires experience, and it is a science since it can be formalized, structured, and taught. Now, more than ever in the global economy, it is critical to understand the skills of mentoring to effectively develop and influence others toward maximum individual and organizational productivity. We have all witnessed the changing needs of professional working adults and understand that some of the old methods of management are simply not adequate in today's world of global opportunities. The workforce has changed a great deal, and accordingly, so should how managers develop and work with their employees, colleagues, and suppliers throughout the value chain. With outsourcing, mergers and reorganizations becoming a constant in today's global business environment, managers, directors, and senior executives alike are being forced to learn new skills and acquire new knowledge so as to ensure effective communication for timely knowledge dispersion and competitiveness. Skill-sets have changed, and to be effective, *we* must change the way in which we manage, develop, and influence or lead others inside the organization and those outside of the organization throughout the value chain.

Employee socialization and indoctrination[1]

In global business environment of the 21st century, effective mentoring of personnel enhances internal business relationships, perceived career success, organizational commitment, overall job performance, and the reduction of turnover. When an organization invests monetarily into a person, it is best to establish a relationship with that person to ensure that he/she is receiving the best support possible. This is even more important for international assignments, diverse groups, and for those who deal with personnel in multinational corporations.

---

[1] For more comprehensive discussion of this material, see the author's book entitled "*Mentoring Diverse Professionals*," 2nd edition, 2007; Llumina Press.

Many businesses have paid the high price of losing key personnel due to the lack of an effective mentoring and socialization program regarding the culture of the organization and the countries involved. A major goal of mentoring is to support the new employee through good socialization and indoctrination practices. This chapter discusses best practices in mentoring new employees through effective socialization and indoctrination programs and provides an example of online peer review process which can be utilized in national and international environments.

The rapid "shift to a knowledge economy makes the knowledge, skills and competencies of employees the most significant drivers of company value," states Jennifer Schramm (2005). Schramm suggests that due to the rapid and growing pace of knowledge turnover, a greater investment in skills development is required in today's competitive global world. While employees must take personal responsibility for keeping up with new knowledge and skills, employers are required to take more of a formal role in order to retain and develop highly skilled employees for critical positions in the organization. Some employers have resorted to succession planning and development programs for their executive positions. However, a succession planning and development program must reach more employees if the process is to be successful in large culturally diverse global firms. Also, these large organizations must find effective ways for developing the talents of underrepresented groups as the workforce and customers are becoming culturally more diverse. It is important to note that one of the best and cost-effective means of ensuring the development and retention of qualified employees in a culturally diverse population is mentoring.

The term mentor applies to a person who helps another become familiarized with an organization's culture, people, and tasks in order to function effectively, and/or progressively move upward on the ladder of success, as defined by the internal culture. Depending on the assigned mentor and his/her influence in the organization, mentoring relationships can greatly enhance a person's growth and advancement opportunities. Mentoring can be formal and/or informal. Informal mentorship programs are natural connections that bond two or more individuals together based on some similarity, liking for each other, or common goals. On the other side, formal mentoring programs are developed purposefully by managers or the organization to partner a new employee with a veteran employee in the organization. Some common forms of mentorship include peer mentorship, supervisor/subordinate mentorship, and third party mentorship where the new employee is assigned an outside coach. Regardless of format or level of formality, mentoring programs tend to focus on familiarizing the new employee with the organization, career development opportunities, psychological well-being, while learning the "ropes" and politics of the culture, and role modeling. Of course, mentoring is not limited to employees, as it also applies to other individuals in the organization or community who want to learn new skills. For example, Michelle Roberts (2005) discussed how business school training in Arizona helps Afghan women establish and expand lucrative businesses. Roberts expanded on the story of how 14 Afghan women participated in a special program that assists them get the education to expand and/or build new businesses in Afghanistan. The 2-week training program at Thunderbird, the Garvin School of International Management, provides an overview of business school lessons covering marketing, strategizing, accounting, and the development of a business plan. The women have been paired with mentors who will continue to assist the mentees with their plans over the next several years. Since over 55% of the Afghan population are women and the fact that there are over 70,000 widows in Kabul alone, such training programs and mentoring assistance will equip Afghan women in starting small businesses to support themselves and their families.

According to Gordon Shea (1994), author of *"Mentoring: Helping Employees Reach Their Full Potential"* from the American Management Association's Publications, mentoring is "A developmental, caring, sharing, and helping relationship where one person invests time, know-how, and effort in enhancing another person's growth, knowledge, and skills, and responds to critical needs in the life of that person in ways that prepare the person for more responsibility, productivity and achievement." Shea (1994) stated that a mentor can be a person who has a beneficial or life-style altering effect on another individual as a result of personal one-on-one contact; one who offers knowledge, insight, perspective, or wisdom that is helpful to another person in a relationship which goes beyond duty or obligation.

A *mentor* is "a senior member of the profession or organization who provides support, coaching, feedback, acceptance, and friendship. A mentor creates opportunities for exposure, provides challenging and educational assignments, and serves as a role model and advisor" (Milkovich & Boudreau, 1994). Milkovich and Boudreau state that mentor relationships usually evolve informally, but firms can also encourage and formalize them. Successful formal mentoring programs are characterized by top management support, careful selection of mentors and mentees, an extensive orientation program, clearly stated responsibilities for the mentor and mentee, and established duration and frequency of contact between mentor and mentee.

Mentoring is usually one-on-one and very personal in nature. According to Shea (1994), mentoring is the value-added dimension in the continuum of development—teacher, tutor, coach, counselor, and then mentor. Effective mentoring requires listening, caring, and other forms of involvement between mentors and mentees. Mentoring provides a cumulative beneficial effect on mentees that counteracts many of the negative forces in society (Shea, 1994). Mentoring is being used to

- Achieve the interests of special groups and populations,
- Conserve and transfer special know-how,
- Encourage mentee contributions,
- Bring employees together in a new social environment,
- Help people reach their full potential,
- Enhance competitive position, and
- Develop a more civil society.

According to studies conducted by Cable and Parson (2001), as well as Cable and Judge (1996), it has been concluded that many job seekers select companies that share their personal values. Businesses also invest considerable monetary resources to hire people with the same attributable cultural values as the company. People seek normalcy which aspires to specific affective, cognitive, and behavioral patterns of people based on their level of cognitive dissonance. For example, as new employees enter a company, they seek to have commonality within their environment, which will reduce the level of self-efficacy or anxiety within the new organization. If new employees' perceive they have the same values with the company they are entering, the level of cognitive dissonance will be lower. The term used for this values congruency is the "Right Fit." Of course, people with the same nuances will benefit the organization because of similarities in values, beliefs, and work behaviors, which can lead to higher productivity and better teamwork. Hochwarter, Kiewitz, Gundlach, and Stoner (2004), cited Guion's (1998) definition of social efficacy in comparison to social skills of individuals as their study addresses the individual's ability to interact successfully with others to foster positive interpersonal relationships. However, their research was to determine the impact on task efficacy within the socialization process of the performance relationship within an organization. Their independent variables included career satisfaction to determine whether the relationships found for performance were comparable to other outcomes for social efficacy, based on task and interpersonal relationships. The results of their study on interpersonal relationships and task skill can be quantifiable and teachable within an organizational setting through vicarious learning, according to Bandura (1997) and Stajkovic and Luthans (1998), where task efficacy correlates with career satisfaction and performance measures of social efficacy. Their research studies found that high social efficacy is not enough to ensure desirable job performance or satisfaction levels for individuals in organizations. As such, task efficacy is needed because people need certain social skills (communication and coordination) to effectively work with other individuals. The socialization process within an organization is a very important function which establishes the foundation of affective job satisfaction and organizational commitment for the new employee. The employee must be able to adapt to his/her new work environment by assessing the organization's internal capabilities and to derive one's full capacity within this new environment. Successful socialization processes allow new employees to effectively understand their place within this environment. An effective socialization process creates value for the organization by escalating the process of a new hire to become proficient on the job more quickly, thus increasing overall effectiveness for the organization.

According to Griffeth and Hom (2001), new employees are confronted with six variables during their hire period

1. *Performance proficiency*. Knowledge and skills to perform the job.
2. *People*. The mentor partner and the type of relationship (formal or informal).
3. *Politics*. The power structure within the organization.
4. *Language*. The professional language unique to their profession.
5. *Organizational values/goals*. The vision and mission of the firm.
6. *History*. The traditions, customs, and stories of the firm.

According to Griffeth and Hom, employees who master these six variables achieve higher proficiency in overall job satisfaction and obtain the necessary socialization skills to become successful in their jobs. An effective socialization process provides the new hires with invaluable information in order for them to quickly adapt to their rightful place within the organization.

Cable and Parson (2001) espoused that organizational theory and behavioral patterns on socialization is the primary means for communicating organizational culture and ensuring stable values (Bauer, Morrison, & Callister, 1998). New hires seek conformity with their own personal value system and apply them to the new work environment. Griffeth and Hom (2001) categorized the socialization process for new employees into three stages

1. *Honeymoon period*. New hire—entry Level, 1–6 weeks.
2. *Reality shock period*. Individual/group/team development, 7–11 weeks.
3. *Resolution period*. Conflict resolution, 12–18 weeks.

Mentoring employees and colleagues

Businesses that exude value-added mentoring practices within the organization can realize actual growth in market share, capacity, infrastructure, and employee development. Effective mentoring practices provide employees with the needed skill sets to become fully competent on their jobs, based on another person's active involvement in the employees' growth and development. A mentor's involvement in an employee's development in the organization should be based on creating overall value for the organization, by facilitating value-added intangible outcomes. Value-added intangible outcomes result in long-term overall value for the organization through effective mentoring programs within an organization.

Grindel (2003, p. 517) stated that mentoring is the act of helping others learn while enhancing the employees' career development. The fundamental process of mentoring is to meet the desired goals by fulfilling the employees' performance roles and fulfillment of specific professional and personal attributes of the employee (Zachary, 2002). Others have discussed building an effective mentoring relationship and based on Zachary's (2002) model to propose the following assumptions

- Mentoring is an enriching process, which creates value-added experiences for both the employee and mentor.
- Mentoring is a process of collaboration and commitment.
- Mentoring is an art, which takes preparation and dedication on both parties.

Two of the most common mentoring and socialization practices used within the business environment of the 21st century are "self management training" and "realistic orientation programs for new employees" (ROPES). *Self Management Training* (SMT) is a mentoring and socialization practice in which the new employee engages his/her new environment with proactive and assertive aspirations to reduce uncertainty factors in the new business environment (Bauer *et al.*, 1998). Researchers of the SMT philosophy cite that new employees should alleviate stressors and conditions which cause anxiety and stress by socializing themselves to their new business environment through

- The creation of motivating situations for oneself within the work environment.
- Performing strategic (worldly view and self induced) tasks.
- Redesigning one's behavioral patterns and beliefs.

SMT includes self motivation and control on the part of the new employee. People who believe in themselves and focus on their abilities while staying the course for their own socialization process have a higher success and retention rate (Bauer *et al.*, 1998).

Realistic Orientation Program for New Employees, or "ROPES," was developed within the nursing profession to alleviate new employees' stress while creating technical competency for the new hires and to alleviate patient stress during medical procedures (Wanous, 1992). Wanous's ROPES program is used by both new employees and patients in hospitals who administer or undergo medical procedures and treatments. During the new hire period, employees are provided with ROPES instruction to accommodate the new employees' stressors on the job to allow the new hire to preview the processes and procedures which could impede their performance. The ROPES mentoring program is designed to provide new employees with

- Realistic information.
- Support and reassurance.
- Role models used to demonstrate technical and coping qualities.
- Collaboration of procedures to create effective learning.
- Rehearse opportunities for the required procedures.
- Enforcement of technical competency and self control.
- Opportunities to identify stressors and effectively manage them.

One of the best practices of ROPES is that it provides new employees with a support mechanism from other experienced employees. Also, experienced employees provide emotional support for the new employee and the patient during this process. One of the techniques utilized during the ROPES process for the new hire is that of adapting realistic or video-taped procedures, which allows the new employee to cope with what he/she must do in the medical procedure and learn the necessary skills for the job. During the ROPES procedures, groups and teams are utilized to enhance collaboration among the employees through discussions which can create better overall learning. The ROPES technique can be utilized in many professions to encourage effective new employee mentoring and socialization practices within the 21st century business environment through effective leadership and coaching skills. For example, the ROPES concepts, using effective coaching skills, can be used within the education, retail, service, and/or manufacturing industries.

Great mentors can use the skills of great coaches to lead associates to better performance before, during, and after the socialization process. As such, mentors should acquire the skills needed to coach employees for good performance, bad performance, and for no performance. Good mentors will always give support to associates, but when associates are not performing up to the standard for the job, it is necessary to provide effective coaching by asking leading questions to assist them in the thinking and solution generation process. When mentoring associates, coaches can help them solve problems they are having with the tasks they have been assigned. Every associate is likely to have difficulties with some task at one time or another. That is why the mentor's support is so vital. A good mentor will be able to spot an associate who is having trouble and coach him/her to a solution for the problem by asking good reflective questions. When supporting and leading associates, it is important to focus on the work results and not on the person.

Mentoring successes and pitfalls

The success of a mentoring and socialization process within an organization today is based on new employees' adaptation and success in what they can provide to the organization in value by applying their skills, abilities, and talents for the organization's benefits. Mentoring practices enhance employees' abilities to learn and adapt to their new environment faster while instilling and developing self confidence in them. According to Reisz (2002), about 77% of organizations that promote mentoring show increased employee performance and retention. Mentoring programs provide new employees opportunities to develop the necessary skills and abilities they will be expected to perform in the future.

Jayne's (2004) research concludes that executive development through mentoring is necessary today. People learn best from other people who have the experience and knowledge that can effectively be sought through a relationship. The contributors in this book can relate to this from both the corporate and education industry perspectives as they have mentors who guided them in dealing with new responsibilities, new cultures, and the stress of becoming a part of the "in-group" in the new environment. Such mentors transfer their knowledge to the mentee best when they know and engage the person. According to Reisz (2002), coaching and mentoring a future leader of an organization ensures that the potential leader is trained in a way that instills core competencies of the organization, which must be descended from one leader to the next, thus creating an overall vision for the potential prospective leader. The value-added leader encourages mentoring practices throughout the organization to create cross functionality. When a mentoring program is established, leaders must ascertain the degree of effectiveness in the organization by evaluating its success rate over a given time period. Once the mentoring program has been proven to be successful, internal benchmarks are created throughout the firm to ensure validity and reliability according to the organization's specific and measurable characteristics.

Mentoring practices within today's organization is a collaborative effort on the part of the mentor and the mentee. However, effective mentoring is a relationship built on trust, either professionally and/or personally, where the new employee confides personal information and characteristics to the mentor and the mentor guides the mentee toward effective growth and/or advancement opportunities.

According to Ragin, Cotton, and Miller (2000), formal mentoring relationships are developed by members in a third party (Murray, 1991) where the mentor and the new employee have not met prior to this process. As such, the formal mentoring relationship is formed based on convenience to quickly indoctrinate the new employee into the organization. In the informal mentoring relationship, both the mentor and mentored are motivated to enter the relationship by mutual identification and developmental needs. On the other side, formal mentoring relationships are developed based on specific organizational expectations to quicken the indoctrination time for new employees. According to Poldre (1994), formal mentoring programs can receive high notoriety; however, formal mentoring relationships are less likely to effectively socialize new employees with intrinsic rewards, based on relationships that are created for convenience rather than being personally invested in a person based on informal relationships. Kram's (1985) research on formal and informal mentoring relationships reflects differences in the time, length, and the structure of the mentoring relationship. Informal relationships are unstructured, which allows diversity of issues to be discussed and addressed for the mentored. The mentoring relationship is beneficial for both parties and the informality allows the relationship to flourish, grow as open discussions are created and they meet as often as they need, which according to Kram can last about 3–6 years. However, formal mentoring relationships are usually contracted to last between 6 months and 1 year, which denies the mentee the ability to collaborate, thus reducing the mentee's abilities to effectively socialize within the organization. Murray (1991) and Poldre (1994) concluded that the shorter duration time of the formal mentoring relationship may cause a reduction in the opportunity for the mentor to influence the new employees' organizational socialization process. The socialization phases for a new employee are crucial for the success of the new hire. Organizations that seek to quickly impose arbitrary, formalized socialization practices without the new employee in mind, and without regard to the person's values, skills, abilities, and experiences, are at risk of failing to provide the new employee with the correct intangible skills necessary to socialize him or her within the organization. Other risks and pitfalls of a mentoring process can include taking too much responsibility as a mentor or overextending one's time and resources, conflicting expectations from the mentor, lack of sufficient training and support for the mentors and mentees, "preaching" to the mentee, and not involving the mentee in the learning process.

Developing and mentoring minorities

Hispanics in United States represent the largest and youngest minority group today. As the number of Hispanics attaining higher education continues to grow, so will the number of Hispanics entering the professional job market. Successful Hispanic professionals are working to improve educational opportunities and break down barriers to entry into higher-paying jobs. Still, businesspeople of any race or background are unlikely to reach the top unless they build bridges and learn from associates from all walks of life. Domestic markets are increasingly multicultural, and global markets are critical to the future of more and more employers. So Hispanics are finding that the value of their backgrounds continues to appreciate in the increasingly diverse workforce in the United States and its surrounding partners. Nonetheless, the key lies in implementing career development and mentorship programs for high-potential Hispanic candidates as well as to create new ones where they do not exist. This section emphasizes the benefits of implementing mentorship programs in an organizational setting. In addition, several successful programs are discussed and recognized for their innovative and successful methods in Hispanic mentorship. By exposing Hispanic employees to the business world and nurturing their development, organizational mentorship programs will ensure that qualified and talented Hispanics are ready to take their place in the corporate world. Besides discussing how Hispanics are being recruited and retained in professional positions, this chapter offers material on the concept of Affirmative Action and success strategies for female managers.

Hispanics in the United States

With a population of 44 million, and an estimated purchasing power of more than $700 billion, the Hispanic community is now the largest minority group in the history of the United States. It is estimated that, by 2007, the domestic Hispanic population will top 50 million. Highly educated, ambitious Hispanics have made great strides in the fields of medicine, high technology, education, politics, and entertainment. But there is a glaring absence of Hispanics in the executive offices and boardrooms of corporate America. While Hispanics account for 10% of the workforce, they make up only 4.5% of decision-making executives. And because executive experience is necessary for selection to a company's board of directors, it follows that only 1.7% of these influential directors are Hispanics.

The disparity between Hispanic buying power and power-making corporate advances troubles those who study U.S. business trends that impact minorities—particularly the rapidly expanding Hispanic population. With a population of 44 million and growing faster than other groups, and a huge purchasing power, the Hispanic community now is the largest minority group in the history of the United States. It is estimated that, by 2007, the domestic Hispanic population will top 50 million (Hispanic Business, 2005).

Someone once commented that "It's been this sad, same story for 30 years. What we hear from corporations is that diversity is important, but not for critical positions. For many companies, this business of diversity has never been proven, never quantified." This cycle of inequality will continue as long as corporations continue to lack high-ranking, power-playing Hispanics to help pull other Hispanics up the chain of success. Often we see a company placing a Hispanic in an executive position that carries no decision-making power and no ties to the company's purse strings (Wallace, 2005).

Some have said that "Popular positions for Hispanics are director of diversity and human resources. Their only intent is to get the word out that they have hired someone of color for a top spot. That type of focus is counterproductive to diversity in the long run." In a study for Hispanic MBA Magazine, Donna Maria Blancero and Robert G. DelCampo revealed Hispanics are still mostly locked out of the corporate power structure, as they have been for decades. This makes retention of Hispanic employees at Fortune 1000 companies problematic.

These young Hispanics "hit" what DelCampo, a business management professor at the University of New Mexico in Albuquerque, calls the "adobe ceiling." "People, in general, are attracted to people just like themselves," DelCampo said. "In the corporate world, you need a hand up from someone who sees the talent in you. But there are no Hispanics in higher management to bring you up through the ranks. Knowing people is the key to moving up" (Blancero & DelCampo, 2002). The remaining sections provide examples of organizations that do a good job of attracting and retaining minorities through various mentoring programs.

McDonald's Corporation

McDonald's leaders believe that people are their most valuable resource as they compete with national and international fast-food giants throughout the world. They invest in their employees' growth and job satisfaction because it's the right thing to do and, perhaps, because their success as a business depends on their commitment to delivering outstanding value. The McDonald's system provides employment and growth opportunities to a vast number of minority groups in the United States and people around the globe. Their commitment to opportunity also includes support for their employee's education. For example, McDonald's Hong Kong offers employees free continuing education courses in business. McDonald's Argentina provides scholarships for employees to study in a degree-granting program that was developed in partnership with a national university. McDonald's UK offers approximately $1800 to each employee to invest in their education, training, or ongoing involvement in sports or the fine arts (VSA Partners, 2004). As can be seen, the McDonald's Corporation invests significant resources in training and retaining employees of diverse backgrounds. Every day, around the world, restaurant crewmembers receive structured on-the-job training and coaching in workplace skills and values. As a matter of fact, diversity initiatives was initiated at McDonald's back in the mid-1970s, under the guidance of former chief executive Fred Turner, who currently is senior chairman of McDonald's and a member of the board. It all started when Turner's daughters who were working at McDonald's shared some things with him about what was happening on their jobs. That led to the introduction of another initiative around diversity education in the late 1970s known as the "Changing Workforce Seminars." Supported by Turner and upper management, the seminars included education about the changing workforce overall, followed by career development seminars for women, African-Americans, and Hispanics (Smith, 2005).

While the seminars were one of the first diversity directives taken by McDonald's, the employees themselves had started informal networking activities on their own. Many of the employee networks were formed in the mid-1970s, and they include the Women's Leadership Network, Home Office Asian Network, McDonald's Black Employee Network, the Hispanic Steering Committee, and others. Those networks eventually evolved into the National McDonald's Diversity Advisory Council, which helped to start the Hispanic Business Vision initiative that focused on ensuring that the brand was more appealing and inviting to Hispanic consumers and employees, whether through bilingual signage, décor', new products, or even attitude (Smith, 2005). According to Courtney Smith, writer about McDonald's and their socially responsible actions, such efforts have given McDonald's a long-standing and distinguished record for diversity—as an employer, franchiser, and purchaser of good and services. They recognize not only a responsibility to provide opportunity, but also the advantages of having diverse backgrounds and perspectives in their system. Approximately 40% of McDonald's U.S. owner/operators are minorities and women. In 2004, they purchased more than $4 billion in food and paper products from U.S. minority and women suppliers. In their corporate headquarters and U.S. companies in 2004, approximately 26% of the managers, not including managers of company-owned restaurants, were minorities and 46% were women (VSA Partners, 2004).

McDonald's Corporation, Bank of America, Dell Computers, Disney World, and General Mills are among the Fortune 1000 companies, which have implemented successful strategies to improve the representation of Hispanics at their workforce. Their innovative programs as well as that of 10 other companies were included in a best practices study on employment by the Hispanic Association on Corporate Responsibility (HACR) (U.S. Wire, 2002). McDonald's strategic approach to hiring, retaining, and promoting Hispanics has resulted in greater representation at all levels of the company. The company supports Hispanic employees through its Hispanic Employee Networks, Hispanic Leadership Council, Hispanic Summits, and Hispanic Steering Committee. All of these groups, in one way or another, support Hispanic employees with career development, and provide the company with valuable information on Hispanic issues.

As a result of McDonald's efforts, today Hispanics represent 29.3% of its workforce and 18% of its restaurant managers. In addition, two of the three McDonald's USA presidents, and three of six McDonald's global presidents, are Hispanic. Ralph Alvarez and Henry Gonzalez are both U.S. Division Presidents, and Eduardo Sanchez is President of Latin America. The company, which is based in Oak Brook, Illinois, also boasts representation in its governance. Enrique Hernandez, Jr., chairman and chief executive officer of Inter-Con Security Systems, is a member of the board of directors.

"McDonald's senior leadership's commitment to Hispanic inclusion at all levels of its workforce as well as its governance has provided the company with the competitive edge to continue to excel as the number one restaurant chain in the world," said Anna Escobedo Cabral, president and chief executive officer of HACR.

Bank of America and BankAtlantic

At the second largest bank in the nation, Bank of America, corporate executives are increasing the representation of Hispanics in their workforce pipelines through a job training and scholarship program. The program has succeeded in bringing Hispanic talent as permanent employees and in encouraging low-income students to pursue a college degree. Bank of America is headquartered in Charlotte, North Carolina.

Bank of America's Youth Job Program teams up students with company executives and assigns them to a banking center where they receive job training. Upon completion of the program and graduation from high school, they receive a 4-year $10,000 scholarship. The program has served 315 students, of which 77 are currently still enrolled in 2005. Among the program graduates, 26% are Hispanics. Also 80% of graduates have continued on to higher education and 64% have been recruited to work for Bank of America.

Similar formal and informal mentoring strategies are being implemented by other banks, such as BankAtlantic in Fort Lauderdale, as mentioned by Anne Maree Norris on June 15, 2005 during a personal interview. Anne Maree is the Leadership Curriculum Manager at the BankAtlantic University (BAU) in South Florida. BankAtlantic managers attend a Fast Track Executive education program, where one of the modules provides coaching skills for them and Bahaudin Mujtaba often facilitates this session. Managers at BankAtlantic are formally coached and are expected to effectively coach their employees toward maximum productivity and goal achievement. Similarly, high achievers are mentored by various managers and leaders in the organization as part of their succession and development practices. The employees of this organization are one of the first in the industry that see themselves as a financial retailer, and as such, they are breaking industry rules by being open longer than traditional banks and serving consumers at the customer's convenience. Just like Nova Southeastern University, when they started offering weekend and evening classes at distant sites about 40 years ago to make learning convenient for non-traditional working adult students, BankAtlantic is breaking ground by being the first to make banking convenient for all their customers. Since BankAtlantic is a pioneer in making themselves available 7 days each week, and by being open until mid-night in some of its branches (or stores), their employees are committed to going the extra mile in order to make sure customers see and perceive them as "Florida's most convenient bank." In other words, their employee development programs, coaching sessions, and informal mentoring strategies seem to be working since their employees feel that they are a part of the team, and, thus, are committed to realizing their vision. BankAtlantic is an excellent example of a learning organization that is focused on attracting, developing, and retaining diverse individuals to take care of diverse customers. Such is the essence of effective leadership, mentoring, and coaching.

Dell Computers

Michael Dell started Dell Computers, and helped make this organization a giant success by selling computers directly to consumers. Michael Dell and Dell leaders believe in acting responsibly in the community; as such, they are committed to understanding and respecting the laws and cultures of the regions in which they do business. Diversity management is an integral aspect of their business strategy and it is an essential element of their corporate values. As such, Dell relies on the diversity of its personnel, suppliers, and customer communities to maximize innovation, growth, competitiveness, and customer satisfaction. They understand that expanding their association's network of suppliers, vendors, third parties, retail organizations, community members, and other industry leaders is critical to the success of their diversity program and initiative. Accordingly, as can be seen from their website on dell.com, Dell Supplier Diversity mission is "to deliver superior supplier performance through highly-qualified minority, women and small businesses that enhance the overall Dell Customer Experience, support continued economic growth in our diverse communities and increase global market share." Dell's Supplier Diversity provides equal access to potential business opportunities for small businesses; small disadvantaged businesses, woman-owned Small Businesses, Veteran-owned Small Business, Minority and Women Business Enterprises to participate as partners and suppliers of goods and services within their corporate supply chain. Dell leaders and employees realize that diversity helps to meet or exceed their customers' expectations and further helps them maintain a competitive advantage in today's global marketplace.

Walt Disney World

Walt Disney World corporation has implemented a wide-ranging International Labor Standards (ILS) program that includes policies, practices, and protocols designed to protect the interests of their workers and has, along with other firms such as the McDonald's Corporation, "joined together with a group of faith-based and socially responsible institutional investors to carry out a unique project that seeks to promote sustained compliance with labor standards mandated by their codes of conduct for manufacturers worldwide" (The Walt Disney Company, 2005). Disney leaders believe that "The growth and development of the Walt Disney Company is directly related to the growth and development of its human resources—our cast," as originally stated by the founder, Walt Disney.

Employees', their cast members', objective is to create a magical environment where people can shop, visit the park, and be guaranteed to receive a memorable experience. Walt

Disney valued his cast members and as such, the value of Disney's cast is evident by myriad employee benefits and "perks" which can include

1. Learning and development opportunities,
2. The Walt Disney Company Foundation Scholarship Program,
3. Educational reimbursement,
4. Educational matching gifts program,
5. Health, dental, life insurance and more,
6. Complimentary theme park passports,
7. Employee stock purchase program,
8. Disney TEAM discounts, including Disney products and merchandise,
9. Service awards, and
10. Childcare centers in Burbank and Orlando.

By valuing employees, Walt Disney created an organizational culture that is still focused on creating value for both customers and their employees. Through the numerous training programs available at the Disney Institute, Disney trains its management team to pursue the company's goals such as improving service quality, gaining a diverse workforce, building customer loyalty, and improving their brand's overall image. By paying close attention to its employee's hiring, training and development practices, Disney seeks to match employees to its corporate philosophy.

Furthermore, they seek diverse suppliers from around the world, and their suppliers are required to comply with its labor standards and codes of conduct. Because Disney has many international manufacturers, close attention is paid to the manner in which these companies govern themselves as to ensure that they comply with Disney's expectations. For instance, as per their contracts and policies, no supplier of Disney should use child labor as that would be in direct conflict with the company's standards and values.

At Disney World, all customers are highly valued since they are about family and fun. They value both their traditional and non-traditional customers. Some of their practices have been seen as somewhat controversial since they do not discriminate based on sexual orientation and same-sex marriages. As a matter of fact, in 2005, the 15th "Annual Gay and Lesbian Days" was scheduled for a celebration in their park. Of course, Disney neither endorses nor prevents attendance of any particular group in its parks. Disney has continued to maintain itself as a venue that welcomes all people regardless of their sex, religion, sexual orientation, ethnicity, or color even when their bottom line has been challenged. Similarly, they recruit, develop, and retain "cast members" of a diverse nature to support their philosophy of serving all individuals who attend their park.

Publix Super Markets

Publix Super Markets, Inc. is a Florida-based grocery chain which has over 130,000 employees and annual sales of about $20 billion in 2005. Publix serves over 1 million customers every day. Because of committed employees and organizational learning, Publix was the first supermarket chain to install electric-eye doors, Muzak, fluorescent lighting, and air conditioning in its stores. Publix was also one of the first companies to have water fountains, self-service shopping, shopping carts, and computerized scanning technology. Since 1997, Publix has been rated as one of the best companies to work for in America on several occasions.

A key differentiating factor in Publix's success formula can be attributed to the philosophy of its founder, Mr. George W. Jenkins who stated that " … some companies are founded on policy. This is wrong. Philosophy, the things you believe in, is more important. Philosophy does not change frequently … and is never compromised … we attempt to adapt a philosophy in such a way as to allow ordinary people to achieve the extraordinary … to reach higher … to look upon average with disdain." The philosophy of caring for people has been embedded in Publix's corporate culture throughout its stores. Publix associates understand that they are not just in the grocery business but also in the people business. Therefore, taking care of associates, customers, suppliers, and community members is important to Publix people and the communities which they serve.

George Jenkins once said that "Publix will be a little better place to work or not quite as good because of you." A philosophy of employee appreciation has been embedded in the culture of the organization; so when the upper echelon visits retail stores, especially during appreciation week, they make it a point to personally see and thank every associate. They understand that people need recognition and sincere thanks for their hard work and commitment to the company. Publix has received various rankings and awards for being a caring employer, an industry leader, and for being socially responsible in the community.

As a caring employer, Publix has received recognition from various groups and organizations, including

- One of BestJobsUSA.com's "Employers of Choice 500" (2001).
- One of the top companies in Fortune's list of "100 Best Companies to Work For" (2003).
- One of Central Florida Family magazine's top companies for working families (1999).
- One of Jacksonville Magazine's top 25 Family Friendly Companies (2002).
- One of the nation's Outstanding Employers of Older Workers, according to Experience Works (2002).
- Named by Child magazine as one of the Top 10 Child-Friendly Supermarkets (2003).
- One of the top 10 companies to work for in America in the book, "The 100 Best Companies to Work for in America" (Currency/Doubleday, 1993) and
- Won the 1996 United Way's Spirit of America award.

It is through various formal succession planning and development as well as informal mentoring programs that Publix is able to offer its employees an environment "where working is a pleasure" and its customers an environment "where shopping is a pleasure." Publix associates' success with customers originates from their belief that no sale is final or complete until the meal is eaten and fully enjoyed. Then, they have made a positive and lasting impression. Publix's guarantee, which every associate is aware of, reads that "we will never, knowingly disappoint you. If for any reason your purchase does not give you complete satisfaction, the full purchase price will be cheerfully refunded immediately upon request." Publix has made it a point to consciously recruit and retain diverse employees so they can effectively and efficiently satisfy the desires of their diverse employees. In its South Florida stores, Publix has dual signage for products as to better serve Hispanic and English speaking customers. Furthermore, Hispanic and Haitian employees have worked to provide products that are in demand by their diverse customers. Publix has become successful because their senior executives serve as mentors for all managers and managers serve as coaches to their diverse employees. Furthermore, their Diversity Development Program employees stay in contact with the communities in which they do business on a continuous basis as to determine their needs, desires, and best means of satisfying them. As such, they consciously recruit and retain diverse employees in each community to better satisfy the needs of all customers in the community in a proactive manner.

General Mills

For the number one cereal maker in the United States, General Mills, Hispanic representation in its workforce is an imperative to ensure the continued success of the company. Its successful recruitment strategy stems from the Chairman and CEO Steve Sanger's active and vocal support, the participation of Hispanic senior level employees and the Hispanic employee network to boost these efforts, clear accountability on each human resources function to ensure the development of the Hispanic employee pipeline to higher level positions, the measurement of results, co-mentoring programs, and the Hispanic revisit weekend program encourages potential new hires to join the General Mills family of employees.

General Mills is based in Minnesota, where Hispanics represent 3% of the population. Despite this, the company has successfully increased the representation of Hispanics in its professional levels from 2.5% in 1999 to 4% in 2005. In the year 2000, about 7% of recruits at the professional level were Hispanic.

Recommendations

According to the HACR's best practices study, a sound strategy for Hispanic inclusion in Corporate America's workforce should include the following

1. Company CEO and senior management's commitment to Hispanic inclusion.
2. An articulated and well communicated rationale linking Hispanic inclusion to the company's vision.
3. Accountability measures for managers in meeting Hispanic inclusion goals.
4. Use of a measurement system to determine gaps and monitor progress in Hispanic inclusion.
5. Career development programs for high-potential Hispanics candidates to address "pipeline" issues.
6. Support of mentoring and Hispanic employee networks to boost recruitment and career development efforts.
7. A communication plan that explains Hispanic inclusion goals at all levels of the company.
8. Strong partnerships with Hispanic community organizations to further employment efforts.

Mentoring steps and essentials

In designing and implementing a formal mentoring program, it is best to start with a template and/or a structured process. Using the immersion model of training, we can further dissect its Mentoring step into a seven-step process as suggested by Miller (2002) thereby creating an Employee Mentoring Model (see Figure 15.1). As such, the successful creation and implementation of a mentoring program would be inclusive of pre-planning, recruiting, training, matching, mentoring, evaluation, and ending.

The seven steps of the model, as described above and by Andrew Miller (2002), can include the following details

1. Pre-planning. This stage can involve setting up the steering committee, recruiting of the right individuals as staff members, and determining the basic criteria for the program.
2. Mentor and mentee recruitment selection. It includes determining who needs mentors, finding mentors, and marketing the program.
3. Preparation of mentees and mentors. This can include training, setting objectives, and creating agreements as per the needs of both mentors and mentees.
4. Matching mentees and mentors. Finding the right skilled or experienced individuals and matching each mentor with the right mentee as per the mentee's needs, desires, and personality.
5. Mentoring meetings. This can be done for the benefit of mentors and mentees as well as for interaction among them, or to assess the progress of this relationship for accountability, improvement, and reporting purposes.

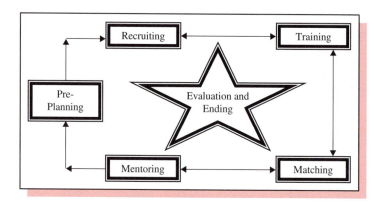

Figure 15.1
Mentoring Program Development Model.

6. Ending. It is best to formally bring a closure to a structured mentoring relationship through celebration and/or a formal event that provides recognition to the mentor, mentee and/ or to designated staff or project managers.
7. Evaluation and quality review. This final stage is simply for the purpose of continuous quality improvement where mentors' and mentees' input are integrated into the process for future mentoring programs.

Successful mentoring programs throughout various industries have certain commonalities that make them effective. According to some experts (Johnson, 2002), the main element of a strong mentoring program includes the fact that mentors

- Are selected based on specific qualifications, including soft and hard skills.
- Are provided sufficient training for their mentoring role.
- Continue to receive sufficient support throughout the mentoring process.
- Are appropriately paired with mentees based on the established criteria in the mentoring program.
- Establish strong relationships with mentees based on trust, honesty, and respect.
- Receive some form of recognition for their efforts in developing the mentee.

Johnson further explains that another element of a strong mentoring program is that "The mentoring program is evaluated and refined on an ongoing basis." Johnson mentions that it is very important for mentors to effectively work with mentees by adapting to the style and needs of the individual rather than always forcing the mentee to adapt to the mentor's style. As a matter of fact, Johnson mentions several tips for a strong mentor–mentee relationship which were provided by mentors in San Francisco through a survey (Johnson, 2002, p. 26), and some of these suggestions are

- Have regular contact, both formal and informal.
- Build trust through respect, open communication, and support.
- Make regular phone calls or contacts.
- Share your resources with the mentee.
- Encourage the mentee to be open and honest by providing him/her with such an environment.
- Socialize informally to strengthen the relationship.

- Be non-judgmental and never speak behind people's back.
- Listen and respond effectively to the mentee's questions and concerns.
- Be realistic and discuss the challenges mentee is likely to face.
- Be positive and offer support.
- Be accessible and be a coach.
- Show that the relationship is mutually beneficial if you are both successful. Explain how the relationship benefits you as a mentor.
- Work together since this is a joint relationship to create win-win for all parties.
- Be available, open, and honest. Be reliable, and follow through on activities and commitments.

As can be seen from the pattern of seeing the character traits of honesty and openness, it is fair to conclude that a high level of trust and respect are essential for successful mentor–mentee relationships. Portner (2002), in his book entitled *"Being Mentored: A Guide for Protégés,"* explains that "protégés get the most out of being mentored when they are able to take responsibility and be proactive in the mentoring process" (p. 20). Portner suggests that mentees do the following, as a start, to take responsibility for the relationship

- Take the initiative when it comes to having your needs as a protégé met.
- Avoid making assumptions about the mentor and his/her expectations.
- Solicit feedback from the mentor as a way to improve your knowledge, skills, and overall development.
- Listen well to receive feedback objectively.
- Construct ways to learn from seemingly untenable situations.
- Take responsibility for your personal well-being.
- Contribute to the learning of your colleagues in the organization. Teach what you learn to others, which is a good way of learning more.

As can be seen from the last element, both mentors and mentees can learn since mentoring is a learning process in itself. It is very possible that this relationship might lead to more learning for the mentor than the mentee. Nonetheless, both individuals must benefit from the relationship as it is a joint partnership. Furthermore, mentors and mentees must respect each other if they are to work together toward worthwhile ends.

Summary

As a manager, a mentor, a human resource professional, and/or a leader in the organization, one must continue to learn the best ways to create success for oneself and one's colleagues through effective employee orientation and mentoring programs. This can be done through both formal and informal mentoring programs. Of course, there are many ways to learn about leadership, management, mentoring, and coaching others.

When properly applied, formal mentoring in corporations can facilitate greater access to available growth prospects, applicable career development activities, educational opportunities, and more effective skills transfer between employees and among various departments. The implementation of a formal training and orientation program can become institutionalized and incrementally improved for effective socialization and inculcation of new employees into any organization. As demonstrated through faculty orientation and training process, formal mentoring not only facilitates learning rapidly in today's educational institutions, but it may also translate this development and learning into a sustainable competitive advantage. Companies can use the seven-step process, discussed in the chapter, to start and implement a mentoring program. The examples of major corporations provided further evidence that mentors can influence people for many years toward an organization's culture and objectives to enhance productivity and maximize bottom-line profits.

References

Bandura, A. (1997). *Self-efficacy: The exercise of control.* New York: Freeman.

Barnard, B. M. (2002). The benefits of mentoring. *SSM, 8*(4), 35–38.

Barnes, R. (2005). Hispanics absent in executive offices. *Hispanic Business.* Retrieved April 4, 2005, from http://www.hispanicbusiness.com

Bauer, T. N., Morrison, E. W., & Callister, R. R. (1998). Organizational socialization: A review and directions for future research. *Research in Personnel and Human Resource Management, 16*, 149–214.

Billett, S. (2003). Workplace mentors: Demands and benefits. *Journal of Workplace Learning, 15*(3), 105–113.

Blake-Beard, S. D. (2001). Taking a hard look at formal mentoring programs: A consideration of potential challenges facing women. *Journal of Management Development*, *20*(4), 331–345, 336–337, 339.

Blancero, D. M., & DelCampo, R. (2002). Hispanics in corporate America. Retrieved January 12, 2005, from: http://www.multiculturaladvantage.com/contentmgt/anmviewer.asp?a=668

Burgstahler, S., & Cronheim, D. (2001). Supporting peer–peer and mentor–protégé relationships on the internet. *Journal of Research on Technology in Education*, *34*(1), 59–74.

Cable, D., & Judge, T. A. (1996). Person-organization fit, job choice decisions, and organizational entry. *Organizational Behavior and Human Decision Processes*, *67*, 294–311.

Cable, D., & Judge, T. A. (1997). Interviewers' perceptions of person-organizational fit and organizational selection decisions. *Journal of Applied Psychology*, *82*, 562–577.

Cable, D. M., & Parsons, C. K. (2001). Socialization tactics and person-organization fit. *Personnel Psychology Durham*, *54*, 1.

Garvin, D. A. (1998). *Building a learning organization. Harvard business review on knowledge management* (pp. 47–80). Boston, MA: Harvard Business School.

Griffeth, R. W., & Hom, P. W. (1988). A comparison of different conceptualizations of perceived alternatives in turnover research. *Journal of Organizational Behavior*, *9*, 103–111.

Griffeth, R. W., & Hom, P. W. (2001). *Retaining valued employees*. California: Sage Publications.

Grindel, C. G. (2003). Mentoring managers. *Nephrology Nursing Journal*, *30*(5), 517.

Grundmann, F. P. (2003a). Corporate Best Practices 2002 Hispanic Workforce—Business case for Hispanic inclusion in corporate America. Retrieved March 10, 2005, from: http://www.hacr.org/research/scholarID.13/scholar_detail.asp

Grundmann, F. P. (2003b). Corporate Best Practices 2002 Hispanic Workforce—Retention: The role of mentoring. Retrieved March 10, 2005, from: http://www.hacr.org/research/scholarID.13/scholar_detail.asp

Grundmann, F. P. (2004). Hispanics or foreign national Latinos serving on FORTUNE 1,000 Boards. Retrieved March 10, 2005, from: http://www.hacr.org/research/scholarID.13/scholar_detail.asp

Hochwarter, W. A., Kiewitz, C., Gundlach, M. J., & Stoner, J. (2004). The impact of vocational and social efficacy on job performance and career satisfaction. *Journal of Leadership and Organization Studies*, *10*(3), 27.

Hom, P. W., & Griffeth, R. W. (1995). *Employee turnover*. Cincinnati, OH: South Western.

Jacques, R. (1996). *Manufacturing the employee: Management knowledge from the 19th to 21st centuries.* Thousand Oaks, CA: Sage.

Janssen, O., & Van Yperen, N. W. (2004). Employee's goal orientations, the quality of leader-member exchange, and the outcomes of job performance and job satisfaction. *Academy of Management Journal, 47*(3), 368–384.

Jayne, V. (2004). Executive development coaching pays. *New Zealand Management,* 47–52.

Johnson, H. (2004). The ins and outs of executive coaching. *Training, 21*(5), 39.

Johnson, K. F. (2002). *Being an effective mentor: How to help beginning teachers and succeed.* ISBN: 0-7619-4524-5. Corwin Press, Inc., A Sage Publications Company, USA.

Joiner, T. A., Bartram, T., & Garreffa, T. (2004). The effects of mentoring on perceived career success, commitment, and turnover intentions. *The Journal of American Academy of Business, 5*(1/2), 164–170.

Kram, K. E. (1985). *Mentoring at work: Developmental relationships in organizational life.* Illinois: Scott Foresman.

Kram, K. E. (1988). *Mentoring at work: Developmental relationships in organizational life.* Lanham, MD: University Press of America.

Kram, K. E., & Hall, D. T. (1989). Mentoring as an antidote to stress during corporate trauma. *Human Resource Management, 28*(4), 493–510.

Kram, K. E., & Isabella, L. A. (1985). Mentoring alternatives: The role of peer relationships in career development. *Academy of Management Journal, 28*(1), 110–132.

Milkovich, G. T., & Boudreau, J. W. (1994). *Human resource management* (7th ed., p. 459). Irwin, USA.

Miller, A. (2002). *Mentoring students and young people: A handbook of effective practice.* ISBN: 0 7494 3543 7. USA: Stylus Publishing, Inc.

Minter, R. L., & Thomas, E. G. (2000). Employee development through coaching, mentoring, and counseling: A multidimensional approach. *Review of Business, 21*(2), 43–47.

Mujtaba, B. G. (2007). *Mentoring diverse professionals* (2nd ed.). Llumina Press. ISBN: 1-59526-444-2. USA. Available at: http://www.llumina.com

Murphy, D., Campbell, C., & Garavan, T. N. (1999). The Pygmalion effect reconsidered: Its implications for education, training, and workplace learning. *Journal of European Industrial Training, 23*(4/5), 238–250.

Murray, M. (1991). *Beyond the myths and magic of mentoring: How to facilitate an effective mentoring program.* California: Jossey-Bass.

Muscatello, J. R. (2003). The potential use of knowledge management training: A review and directions for future research. *Business Process Management Journal, 9*(3), 382–394.

Olmeda, R. A. (2005). *Three Afghan teens try life in America*. Fort Lauderdale, FL: South Florida Sun-Sentinel. Retrieved on June 22, 2005, from: http://www.tallahassee.com/mld/tal-lahassee/news/nation/11936314.htm

Poldre, P. A. (1994). Mentoring programs: A question of design. *Interchange, 25*(2), 183–193.

Portner, H. (2002). *Being mentored: A guide for protégés*. ISBN: 0-7619-4552-0. Corwin Press, Inc., A Sage Publications Company, USA.

Raabe, B., & Beehr, T. A. (2003). Formal mentoring versus supervisor and coworker relationships: Differences in perceptions and impact. *Journal of Organizational Behavior, 24*(3), 271–273.

Ragins, B. R. (1989). Barriers to mentoring: The female manager's dilemma. *Human Relations, 42*, 1–22.

Ragins, B. R., Cotton, J. L., & Miller, J. S. (2000). Marginal mentoring: The effects of type of mentor, quality of relationship, and program design on work and career attitudes. *Academy of Management Journal, 43*(6), 1177–1194.

Reisz, S. (2002). *Mentoring: A cost-effective retention tool*. Ireland: Catalyst.

Roberts, M. (2005). Program helps women entrepreneurs. *The Herald*. Sunday January 23rd.

Schramm, J. (2005). Learning curves. *HR Magazine, 50*(2), 144.

Shah, A., Sterrett, C., Chesser, J., & Wilmore, J. (2001). Meeting the need for employee development in the 21st century. *SAM Advanced Management Journal, 66*(2), 22–28.

Shea, G. (1994). *Mentoring: Helping employees reach their full potential*. AMA Publications, USA.

Shea, G. F. (1997). *Mentoring*. Menlo Park, CA: Crisp.

Small Business. (2004). Small business: Finding and retaining qualified employees. Project completed by A. Amorio, C. Braun, A. Cheng, D. Gabon & A. Loehr in September 2005 in Managerial Communication and Ethics.

Smith, C. (2005). Delivering superior value through corporate social responsibility at McDonald's. Unpublished manuscript at NSU.

Smith, W. J., Howard, J. T., & Harrington, K. V. (2005). Essential formal mentor characteristics and functions in governmental and non-governmental organizations from the program administrator's and mentor's perspective. *Public Personnel Management, 34*(1), 31–58.

Stajkovic, A. D., & Luthans, F. (1998). Social cognitive theory and self-efficacy. *Organizational Dynamics*, *26*, 62–74.

VSA Partners. (2004). McDonald's worldwide. *McDonald's Corporation*, 1–83.

Wanous, J. P. (1992). *Organizational entry: Recruitment, selection, orientation, and socialization of newcomers* (2nd ed.). Massachusetts: Addison-Wesley.

Young, A. M., & Perrewe, P. L. (2000). What did you expect? An examination of career related support and social support among mentors and protégés. *Journal of Management*, *26*(4), 611–632.

Zachary, L. J. (2002). *The mentor's guide*. California: Jossey-Bass.

CHAPTER 16

Human capital development: a return on investment perspective

Robin B. DiPietro

Hospitality, Restaurant and Tourism Management
Department of Nutrition and Health Sciences
202G Ruth Leverton Hall
University of Nebraska-Lincoln
Lincoln, NE 68583

Objectives of chapter

The objectives of the chapter are as follows:

- To define the concept of human capital as it relates to the hospitality and tourism industries.
- To describe the concept of how people are a sustainable competitive advantage for an organization.
- To describe how the return on investment in human capital should be perceived by organizations as a way to measure the value of investment in people.
- To discuss the literature on human resource development, human capital, resource-based view of the organization, training and development, and how these constructs relate to a return on investment perspective.
- To review applications of human capital and return on investment in order to determine how to improve productivity and performance in firms.
- To apply a case study in order to ensure the transfer of knowledge and theory to practice.

Introduction

The chapter presents information concerning the benefits associated with investments in existing human capital within hospitality and tourism enterprises. It begins with an introduction that discusses the research framework. The author then discusses concepts and definitions concerning human resource development, human capital, resource-based view of the organization, training and development, and return on investment (ROI). Next, the service-profit chain will be reviewed as one of the strategic framework models that capture the essence of the role of human capital in the hospitality/service industry. Following that, a review of research is presented on the topic of human capital as it relates to the hospitality industry with a ROI perspective. Finally, applications of the concept of human capital and ROI will be discussed, as well as suggestions concerning directions for future research on the subject of human capital and ROI.

The chapter provides insights into the concept of human capital and the importance of the employee or "internal guest" within an organization. Researchers are in agreement that improving human capital management is a strong way to improve the financial performance of an organization (Hitt, Bierman, Shimizu, & Kochhar, 2001; Skaggs & Yound, 2004). There are many directions for future researchers to investigate areas that organizations may employ to improve the performance of human capital to ensure that external guests are satisfied in ways to encourage them to become lifetime guests of specific hospitality organizations. Research in the lodging industry has shown that it is four-to-seven times less expensive to retain a guest than to create a new one in competitive marketplaces, such as those that currently exist. The research in the lodging sector also shows that a 5% increase in customer retention can boost profits by 25% to 125% (McCarthy, 1997; Reichheld & Sasser, 1990).

Providing standardized levels of quality services will ensure that enterprises will experience growth in sales and guest satisfaction levels. Hospitality organizations rely on the competitive advantage of the service levels that they provide and the people that ultimately provide those services. Virtually everything else that is provided in a service business can be duplicated given time, with the exception of that exceptional service through the service providers within the organization. Ensuring that the money and time invested in human capital provides a ROI for hospitality organizations is critical for success in the global economy of the 21st century.

Human capital and return on investment

Service employees comprise the most important contribution for achieving a sustainable competitive advantage for specific hospitality enterprises. This is due to the industry's reliance on labor and services to provide quality experiences for guests. Human capital is the term used to describe a way of thinking about people who work for organizations. Human capital views people as assets that can be developed and are expected to appreciate over time. This is in contrast to the traditional way of thinking that regarded workers as expense lines on the profit and loss statement, which were thought to deplete an organization's financial standing.

In economic perspectives, capital is generally thought to be assets that serve as resources for a company. The term human capital is a component of capital and has many definitions, with most relating to the knowledge, skills and abilities that people bring to a specific job within an organization (Young, McManus, & Canale, 2005). Some describe human capital as a "commercially valuable skill" (Marcus, Ippolito, & Zhang, 1998, p. 490), while others describe human capital as "the attributes of a person or people that are productive in some economic context" in an organization (Econterms, 2004).

A more encompassing definition of human capital is the skills, knowledge, and expertise of employees in an organization, which includes the entire life experiences of each individual (Becker, 1964). Hospitality specific human capital has been expressed as the combination of a service-oriented employee, an empowered employee, and a committed employee that in combination creates a model for effective hospitality human capital (Young *et al.*, 2005).

Organizations in the hospitality industry have realized that all technological competitive advantages can be quickly duplicated by others. Technology is very imitable and should not be considered to be a sustainable competitive advantage (Tracey & Nathan, 2002). It is rare when an organization can create a unique competitive advantage that other organizations cannot copy in just a matter of time. Even the "secret sauce" that McDonald's created for the Big Mac was only patent protected for a limited amount of time. Therefore, in order to gain a sustainable competitive advantage, a company has to attract and hire the most qualified employees. This will result in a more long term, sustainable competitive advantage over time because no other company will be able to use their talents and to apply the various skills of the employees in the same combination to achieve the unique level of services provided by them. The concept of human capital recognizes that not all employees are created equal, and an organization's ability to recruit and hire the best, as well as create a culture of retention and service will give that enterprise an edge over other businesses.

In order to ensure that an organization receives a positive ROI for their efforts in recruiting and hiring the best, the hospitality managers also must be willing to train and develop their employees and supervisors in order to keep their skills cutting edge and more advanced than the competition. Following sections will provide some insights into the concept of human capital, how organizations should work toward developing their people to maintain that competitive advantage in providing positive service experiences, as well as various ways that organizations can ensure a positive ROI from their expenditures on the development of their human capital.

Research framework

Human resource development

Human resource development is defined as a process of developing and unleashing human expertise through organizational development and personnel training and development for the purpose of improving performance (Swanson, 2001). Human resource development is not the primary business of most organizations and it is often an afterthought for reactive enterprises. Human resources should be developed on the job as a way for organizations to gain a unique competitive advantage over the competition. Harbison (1973) believed that the wealth of an organization could be expressed in terms of the level of development and the effective utilization of human energies, skills, and knowledge for useful purposes. Those enterprises that focus energy toward developing the skills of their employees will gain an advantage that may not be readily duplicated by competing firms.

The human capital theory is related to the human resource development field. With the projected continued shortfall of talent available in organizations, developing people will become a significant area for resource enhancement within organizations (Fitz-enz, 2000). Because of this increased need for developing people, there is an increased need to evaluate human resource activities in economic terms. It will not be enough to ascertain the need for training and development, it will be critical to show a financial return on the investment made by organizations as a result of training and development initiatives. Financial analysis of human resource activities will require the analysis of the combined performance of the individual and the organization (Cascio, 1991). These factors will increase the need to determine the ROI for organizations from human resource development initiatives. It will not be enough to show a need for a training and development initiative; a ROI to the organization must also be shown.

In order to improve the effectiveness of organizations, the human resource departments will have to become more actively involved in the strategic planning process in organizations. It will be critical for organizations to ensure that all of the departments are aligned with the mission statement and vision of the company. Human resource practitioners will need to be involved in all facets of strategic planning in the organization to ensure that the focus of the organization can be achieved through the human capital in the organization. In order to achieve this, the human resource practitioner will need to be attuned to the state of the human capital in the organization and how it is helping or hurting the organization's long- and short-term chances of success. Without the involvement of the human resource department in the strategic planning process, a critical gap in the development and execution of the strategic plan will become evident.

Human capital

The concept of human capital became a topic of interest in the 1950s in the business and education literature. It was described by economist Theodore Schultz (1960) as human capacities that can be developed by education and in the family unit, which can be used productively (Traub, 2000). The concept came out of macro-economic theory and family studies, but was soon determined to play a big role in micro-economic theory relating to economic growth of organizations and individuals (Mincer, 1997). It was shown that there were impacts on the individuals' wages over time and on the overall organizational performance over time as human capital was developed throughout an organization. There were definitive returns to the individual and the organization through education and development of the human capital in the workforce (Becker, 1975).

The human capital theory comes out of the general systems thinking in that it regards organizations as systems, and the components of those organizations work together as subsystems to help ensure the success of the organization. This theory also stems from economic theory that states that businesses view people as assets rather than expenses. Nations prosper when organizations invest in the training and development of people (Fitz-enz, 2000; Rothwell & Sredl, 1992). The human capital theory also parallels the thinking of the resource-based view theory of the firm which views the organization as a group of resources and capabilities that are put together in order to achieve a purpose (Barney, 1991; Dess & Picken, 1999).

The human capital theory maintains that in order for organizations to prosper, they must hire superior people and also develop and train their current employees. People are the main competitive advantage that organizations have, and developing people in a way that will help the organization to achieve its goals can build a strong benefit for an organization (Fitz-enz, 2000; Luthans, 1998). The main tenet of this theory is that human resources are the active agents that produce and deliver the goods and services (Becker, 1975). Becker, who analyzed the human capital theory, found that investments in people improved the wages and employment of people, and also benefited the organization economically. This is especially true for hospitality organizations as they rely exclusively on people to deliver their services to the guest in a way that creates a memorable experience and can ensure a lasting and repeat guest (Pine & Gilmore, 1999). The primary "product" of a hospitality organization is the service experience that is provided through the people of the organization.

The assumptions guiding the human capital theory are as follows: (1) investments in training result in increased learning; (2) increased learning results in increased productivity; and, (3) increased productivity is reflected in increased wages and business earnings. The human capital theory is at its roots an economic theory for those who study human contributions to the economics of systems (Swanson, 2001).

The human capital assumptions described above should be included in the process of an operation of a business. Everything that happens in an organization is part of a process or system or series of processes. These processes take inputs, part of which are the human resources, and convert them to an output that is valued and desired by a guest. These outputs are products and services the organization sells. In a hospitality business, the primary product is the service that is provided to the customer. It is critical to determine which processes or people add value to the organization regarding the production of the product or service (Fitz-enz, 2000). The service-profit chain is one model that describes how the process of inputs and systems create a valued output for the guest (Heskett, Jones, Loveman, Sasser, & Schlesinger, 1994).

The service-profit chain works under the premise of a new paradigm shift in the service environment in the current economy. Front line workers or the actual service providers in organizations need to be the center of management concern. The investment in people development and technology that will aid in the delivery of the service should be the focus of management initiatives (Heskett *et al.*, 1994). Closely paying attention to recruiting and training practices and linking compensation to performance will help in the positive development of human capital in organizations. This is essential due to the role that employee satisfaction plays in customer loyalty and profitability. Heskett *et al.* (1994) have established a link from the internal customer or employee satisfaction to the external customer satisfaction and thus the overall profitability of the organization. This research puts the pressure on organizations to ensure that their human capital is being developed and are satisfied in their jobs in order to deliver on the service promises of the company.

The human capital theory supports the need for training and development in organizations in order to improve the skills and knowledge of individuals and thereby add value to the organization. In the move from an industrial to a knowledge-based economy, investments in people will need to be perceived as a positive investment by a company. A knowledge-based economy creates a need for organizations to have high functioning and intelligent people working for them. This will create the competitive edge that an organization needs. Despite the need for organizations to have highly trained people, that investment in people and their development will need to create a ROI for the organization. Human capital theory is developed around the premise that training and investment in people will improve the overall organizational performance. It is not only critical to train and develop people, but the follow up of measuring the ROI in human capital is essential to organizational success (Cascio, 1991; Fitz-enz, 2000; Phillips & Stone, 2002).

As human capital becomes more expensive to recruit, train and develop, increasing attention is being devoted to those factors that affect productivity. Empowerment, education, training, recognition programs, and technology will all play different roles in this paradigm shift, thereby affecting productivity in the future. The area with the greatest prospective impact on the overall productivity in an organization is training and development of the people or human capital in the organization (Cline, 1997).

Resource-based view

The resource-based view of the organization views the organization as a group of resources and capabilities that are put together in order to achieve a purpose (Barney, 1991; Dess & Picken, 1999). This theory takes the view that the people in the organization can create an advantage for an organization through the effective combination of talents and skills.

While past literature in business strategy has relegated the human resource function to the implementation stage of strategy rather than the development stage of strategy, current theoretical approaches argue that human resources and the organizational systems that develop the human resources in the company can generate a sustainable competitive advantage for an organization (Barney, 1995; Becker & Gerhart, 1996). Human resource departments help recruit, hire, train, and develop the human capital for the organization, but are not often involved in creating the strategy for the organization.

One classic strategy theory takes a strategic choice view, and suggests that companies select a "generic" strategy to compete in the environment in which they find themselves. Recent theorists have viewed organization strategy from a resource-based view, arguing that businesses develop sustained competitive advantage only by creating value that is rare and not easily imitated by the competition (Barney & Wright, 1997; de Chabert, 1998). The conventional sources of competitive advantage discussed in the strategic choice literature include factors such as technology, natural resources, productivity improvements, and low cost leadership. These factors have been shown to create value within an organization. Resource-based view theorists have argued that these traditional types of competitive advantages are becoming increasingly scarce, hard to develop and easy to imitate, particularly in comparison to well thought out employment and human resource systems (Murphy & Williams, 2004).

The resource-based view is predicated on the concept that in order to create a sustainable competitive advantage and produce value for the firm, individual policies produce the greatest results when they operate in a complex system that is not easily imitated (Barney, 1995). Resources are defined as the physical things a firm buys, leases, or produces for its own use, or the people hired on terms that make them effectively part of the firm (Penrose, 1959). In the 21st century, there are few if any competitive advantages that an organization can create that would have any lasting impact on an industry. Because of the scarcity and ability to imitate competitive advantages, a more lasting source of a sustainable competitive advantage are the people employed by an organization and the human capital that actually deliver the service in a hospitality or service organization.

Barney (1991) suggested that resources which can be used to create a sustainable competitive advantage must have:

- Value: external environmental usefulness;
- Rareness: unique resource;
- Inimitability: not easily copied; and,
- Lack of substitutability: cannot be replaced by other products/services or firms.

The ability of human beings to learn and thus constantly improve their services, to transfer their knowledge from one domain to another, and to combine other resources in more productive ways makes the human capital in an organization distinct from other types of resources that are available to an organization (Penrose, 1959). Human expertise is viewed as a separate resource class. It is viewed as a more intangible resource than the traditional profit generating resources, such as the manufacturing of goods.

Boxall (1998) uses the resource-based view of the firm, along with other human resource theories to outline the basic elements of a theory of "human resource advantage". In determining how firms build and defend competitive superiority through human resource strategy across the phases of the typical industry life cycle, Boxall (1998) suggests that human resources capable of yielding sustained advantage are those which meet the tests of rare value, relative immobility and superior appropriate ability. Firms which secure ongoing viability in their industry have the potential to build human resource advantage through superior human capital and organizational processes. These sources of superiority depend on the quality of the interest alignment between the firm and the employee, and employee development in the firm compared with industry rivals. It is for this reason that human resource strategies and the effective use of human capital in organizations are important sources of competitive advantage now and will continue to be so in the future. The current knowledge-based economy, along with the tough labor challenges in the hospitality industry during the end of the 20th century and continuing into the 21st century, has created a dramatic need for a paradigm shift in the area of human resources. The challenge for management will be creating value through people rather than using them as objects (Olsen & Zhao, 2002).

Training and development

Training and development is critical in improving the human capital of an organization, which then allows it to compete effectively in an industry. Training is typically viewed as giving someone a skill that they need to do their job effectively. For example, in the hospitality industry training deals primarily with the "hard skills" such as making a particular food item for a restaurant, serving a table effectively, or learning to check in a guest at a hotel. Development on the other hand tends to deal with the "soft skills" or improving a person's growth, whether in a job or in their personal life. Some examples of development programs may be time management or dealing with difficult people.

There is evidence in the hospitality industry of two trends with regards to training and development, there has been an increase in the amount of money spent on training and development in organizations, and there is evidence of much duplication of efforts in developing training programs (Cline, 1997; Sugrue, 2003). Many organizations develop their own internal training and development programs, but if the efforts were consolidated among the various segments of the hospitality industry, there could be some cost savings realized in creating more generic training programs that could have industry-wide applications (Cline, 1997).

Prior to the training of an employee is the necessity for organizations to do a better job of recruiting and hiring people. There is a deficit of qualified people in the hospitality industry looking for work, and an abundance of jobs. It is critical to attract the best people to an organization by creating an advantage that is unique to the enterprise. That may be to offer training and development at levels that are typically unheard of in the industry, or by creating a niche when it comes to the recruiting of talent. It is critical for organizations to determine what makes one company stand out from the rest when it comes to bringing great talent onboard.

It is becoming increasingly important for organizations to effectively train and develop the talented people that they hire once they are employed. It is important from a human capital perspective, and it is also important from the perspective of recruiting and retention of employees (Dess & Picken, 1999). With the current economic conditions in a time of vacant jobs and no one to fill them, it is becoming important to provide employees with a reason to choose a specific organization. Many employees are looking for an employer that is willing to help develop them and give them more skills to use at their current organization or in their future career. There is not the deep sense of long-term loyalty from employees anymore. If an employee is not happy with their pay and/or place of employment, they will leave. Today it is an employee's market, which gives talented people an advantage, as well as giving an advantage to those organizations that can provide a "value added" component for employees. Providing something extra in terms of incentives or benefits can get those talented employees interested in working with an organization (Dess & Picken, 1999).

Return on investment

Measuring the ROI in training and development programs intent on enhancing performance in an organization has always been a critical and yet elusive issue among practitioners (Phillips, 1997). ROI is determining the value of a human resource program through financial measurements that are acceptable to an organization. It is critical that organizations find a way to measure the investment into their human capital in the form of training and development with the returns that are experienced by the organization in the form of increased revenue and profitability. Despite the importance of measuring ROI, most companies do not have the systems in place to do so. This remains an illusive challenge that many human resource practitioners will have to address within their organizations.

Some of the barriers to effectively measuring ROI are: the additional costs and time that are required to correctly evaluate the programs; lack of skills and orientation for the human resource development staff; faulty needs assessment done with an organization; fear of failure and the unknown; lack of discipline and planning that is required to effectively evaluate the program; false assumptions made about the ROI process (Kraiger, McLinden, & Casper, 2004; Phillips, 1997). These barriers often dissuade organizations from even trying to perform an evaluation of an investment into human capital at all. Despite the difficulty and extra effort that is required to perform an effective evaluation of the ROI in human capital programs, it is important that organizations put the effort into this function in order to justify the expenses relative to the benefit that is achieved by the organization in the short and long run. Organizations need to determine how deep the evaluation of the training program needs to be, considering that many other programs implemented by organizations are not measured at all regarding ROI (Kraiger *et al.*, 2004).

Heskett *et al.* (1994) have found that there is a direct relationship between internal service quality that is provided to the employees of an organization by using positive workplace design, job design, employee selection and development programs, employee rewards and recognition, and the profitability of the company. This has been found to be the case because of the ROI in the above-mentioned tools and the employee satisfaction that occurs in the job because of them. When employees are satisfied, they tend to stay longer thus saving money on recruiting, hiring, and training costs. Their productivity increases because they are satisfied in their jobs and feel that they have the tools to effectively do their jobs. This converts to more satisfied customers who feel more loyal to the company. When employees are developed in a way that allows them to effectively do their jobs, they can then create experiences that the guest appreciates and sees as a unique feature of the organization. Customer satisfaction leads to customer loyalty which causes retention of them as customers, repeat business, and referral business to other people. This all leads to revenue growth and profitability that gives a positive ROI spent on the human capital in the organization (Heskett *et al.*, 1994).

Human resource practitioners have been traditionally convinced that their effort in training and developing human capital in the workforce of an organization adds value and is financially beneficial to that organization (Ramlall, 2003). Research over the past decade has linked investment in human capital with positive organizational outcomes in organizations (Huselid, 1995; Pfau & Cohen, 2003). A study done by Morrow, Jarrett, and Rupinski (1997) found that in a Fortune 500 company, training objectives that were aligned with corporate strategy produced a very high ROI on a company-wide basis. The study found that there was a 45% ROI in management training, and a 418% return for sales/technical training in the company.

The seven areas in which the human resource practitioner can add value to the organization that directly relate to a financial measurement and profitability are: strategic planning; acquisition of employees; training and development; organization change and development; performance management; reward system; organization theory and behavior (Ramlall, 2003).

Service-profit chain

The service-profit chain is a strategic framework model that suggests that the investments in employees, such as reward and recognition programs that are directly linked to individual performance results will lead to quality and productivity improvements that subsequently yield higher levels of service quality at lower costs. Such improvements will in turn influence customer satisfaction and loyalty, ultimately driving revenue growth and profitability (Heskett *et al.*, 1994).

There are direct benefits to organizations that think of their employees as human capital to be developed, rather than as expenses to be minimized. When the employees (or the internal customers) feel good about their jobs, they convey that in many ways to the external customer or the guest. The overall service delivered to the guest is improved and the value that the guest attributes to the service is higher. Heskett *et al.* (1994) discuss a "service-profit chain" that links together the way that employees are treated, how they feel about their jobs and the organization that they work with to the overall level of service that they give and the results that they deliver to their customers. The service-profit chain establishes a relationship between profitability of a company, customer loyalty, and employee satisfaction, employee loyalty, and overall productivity of the employee, and thus the organization that they work for.

The research shows that when organizations take the time to work with their employees and develop them to a point where they feel valued and treated with respect, this translates to overall good customer experiences. This creates customer satisfaction and a feeling of overall value about the organization (Heskett *et al.*, 1994). These positive feelings help a company to retain customers and over the life of that customer, this creates many additional dollars in revenue. Ritz-Carlton has estimated that a loyal customer is worth over $100,000 over his or her estimated 4-year relationship with the company (Bowen & Shoemaker, 1998). A good ROI in training and development will occur as a result of the overall positive treatment of the employee, which then translates down to the customer level.

Past research in hospitality and tourism

The hospitality industry has traditionally been plagued by extremely high rates of employment turnover, especially among hourly employees (Pizam & Thornburg, 2000). This high turnover creates a need in hospitality organizations to hire and train many people at any given time during the year. This fact creates a need throughout the hospitality industry to ensure that the investment in human capital is providing a return for the organization in financial terms or in improved human capital to serve the guests that frequent a hospitality organization. There have been some studies that have looked at the ROI specifically in hospitality organizations, which are discussed below.

One study was done to analyze the ROI through the framework of the service-profit chain. It looked at Southwest Airline, a company that is known for its proactive policies regarding employee satisfaction and loyalty (Heskett *et al.*, 1994). The data show that the policies that Southwest has for its employees, helps it to attain positive returns on investment in many areas. The profitability per revenue is higher than other organizations; on time arrivals were higher than other airlines; consumer complaints were lower than other airlines; passengers per employee were higher than other airlines; the number of employees assigned per aircraft was lower than other airlines. These hard measures show that in an organization like Southwest Airline, their positive leadership and proactive policies in developing a service-profit chain that ties positive employee satisfaction and loyalty actually translates to a positive ROI for the organization (Heskett *et al.*, 1994).

A recent study done by Young *et al.* (2005) showed that the intellectual capital of an organization is comprised of the human capital, structural capital, and customer capital of the firm. Structural capital is comprised of the technology and support systems in an organization. Customer capital is the contribution that customers make to the service and delivery systems, which comprises the overall value of customers. The human capital includes the values, culture, and philosophy that encompass the human capabilities that support the company objectives (Young *et al.*, 2005). The study found that in hospitality companies, human capital is comprised of service-oriented employees, empowered employees, and committed employees. They created a model of a hospitality human capital process that shows the relationship between these three types of employees and the strategic objectives of the firm that include treating employees well, providing extraordinary service, and providing shareholder value. In effect, the study proposed that even if human capital does not directly impact the financial performance of an organization, it works indirectly to help the organization accomplish its goals (Hitt *et al.*, 2001; Young *et al.*, 2005).

Another study done by Enz, Canina, and Walsh (2006) showed that investments in human capital in the hotel industry directly relate to higher overall performance by the organizations. The study was conducted with both full service and limited service hotels from 1998 to 2001. The study looked at performance data from 563 hotels of various sizes and classifications and found that hotels that invested more in their human capital through wages and development programs, while controlling for extraneous variables, realized higher operating income in future years. This shows a positive relationship between investment in human capital and the ROI in financial terms (Enz *et al.*, 2006).

The next section of the chapter looks at how human capital and ROI can and should continue to be applied to the hospitality and tourism industries and other service organizations.

Applications of human capital and return on investment

There are many ways that the information contained in this chapter can be used in a service based or hospitality or tourism organization. This information shows the need for development of human capital and the impact that developing human capital has on the hospitality or tourism organization of the 21st century. Many organizations do not have evaluation criteria in place for the investment that they make in human capital development programs. There are several levels of evaluation criteria that have been used in the evaluation of training and development, which include participant reaction and satisfaction with training, learning results, on-the-job application of training, and business impact of training. But few organizations implement evaluation programs measuring ROI (Phillips, 1997; Phillips & Stone, 2002). There are ways that this ROI can be calculated and then used for advancing knowledge in the organization, but often it is overlooked due to the time and cost issues involved, the lack of skills in the human resource department, faulty assumptions regarding the training, inaccurate objectives for training, and criteria that are difficult to isolate and measure (Phillips, 1997).

A study by Skaggs and Youndt (2004) found that in service organizations there is a relationship between the quality of human capital and the organizational performance. This study looked at the performance of 234 service organizations across 96 different industries and found that overall investments in human capital helped a firm to succeed. The study showed instances of higher levels of customer co-production or when the guest actually helps in the actual production process [i.e., self check in or check out at a hotel or partial preparation of a meal in a restaurant (i.e., salad bar)]. This actually helps to reduce the need for the organization to provide large investments in the development of human capital. On the other hand, higher levels of customer contact with the service provider however, required higher levels of investment in human capital. Organizations that have adaptable production and delivery systems where the customer can apply more variances to the product needed a higher level of human capital in order to ensure guest satisfaction (Skaggs & Youndt, 2004). This study in effect showed differences between the level of customer interaction and the ability to change the product or service. More intimate services require higher levels of training with lesser development investments in human capital required to provide more limited levels of service expected by guests within those operations.

Because of the inherent level of guest interaction with the processes provided in a hospitality industry organization, it will be important that more research be done regarding how to get the most returns out of human resource initiatives that are aimed at improving human capital. The fact that hospitality organizations cannot operate without human capital is another reason for the importance of the issue of human capital and the ROI achieved through development programs.

Directions for future research

Service organizations need to continue to look for ways to develop their human capital in order to create or maintain one of the only sustainable competitive advantages that they have. The people working in a service business or hospitality organization are one of the unique features of any enterprise. Delivering upon the service promise is one way that guests distinguish between one establishment and another. Future research needs to continue to be done in organizations by measuring the investment that they are putting into the human capital in their organizations, along with the return that they are getting either in a financial or non-financial way from those investments.

In the past decade, some studies have shown that improvements in human capital do impact organizations. These impacts have been shown to result in improved financial performance and higher employee productivity (Enz *et al.*, 2006; Huselid, 1995; Pfau & Cohen, 2003). The research has also shown dramatic returns on investment when training objectives are tied to organizational strategies (Morrow *et al.*, 1997). In order to advance the hospitality industry specifically and the service industry in general, more research will need to be done to tie the improvements in human resource initiatives regarding human capital (improving recruiting and selection programs, training and development programs, and ensuring that human resource programs are strategically based) with overall organizational performance.

Research needs to continue to be done in the hospitality industry around the world in order to determine where the gaps are in measuring human capital and their impact on the organization. There is a need for studies to be designed for various segments of the foodservice industry, events industry, tourism and travel organizations, timeshare industry, and further research in the lodging industry in order to provide answers that will guide paradigm shifts in the way that we think about human capital and their impact on the overall hospitality industry. A focus needs to be put on developing more research to guide the industry and create a best practices list for practitioners to be able to learn from.

Summary and conclusion

The hospitality industry carries with it a reputation of having low paying jobs and undesirable working conditions and hours (Cline, 1997; Pizam & Thornburg, 2000). Turnover is often thought of by managers as an inevitable part of working in the hospitality industry. This assumption is often based on the fact that organizations do not think of their employees as human capital or as internal guests who virtually make or break a service business due to their integral part in providing the unique service that in effect "is" the hospitality business.

Human capital is the term used to describe the attributes of people that are productive in an organization. As such, the best possible people need to be recruited and hired into an organization. It is critical that after the best are hired, they are trained and developed in order to adopt a true service mentality so that the service that they provide becomes the unique, sustainable competitive advantage for the organization.

Investing in human capital through investment in the growth and development of people in an organization will most likely bring a true ROI through the increased satisfaction of the employee and thus the guest. The recent studies examined have shown a financial ROI in creating stronger human capital, but further research needs to be done in order to derive best practices in the hospitality industry that others can grow and learn from. The best organizations currently invest in their human capital and it is paying dividends oftentimes beyond expectations. The rest of the hospitality industry should sit up and take note.

Case study/training exercise

Beachside hotel human capital dilemma

This is a case of two competing hotels, Sunrise Hotel and Beachside Hotel that are both located in a medium sized, tourism-based town in the Northeast U.S. The hotels are both competing for the same set of guests, as well as the same set of potential employees. They are both budget hotels, right next door to each other, with 60 guest rooms each and a view of the beach. The occupancy during peak season for the Sunrise Hotel is 98%, but during the winter months goes down to 65%. The Beachside Hotel has peak season occupancy of 90% and off peak occupancy of 50%.

Joe is the General Manager of Sunrise Hotel and has been in his current position for 5 years. He has been with Sunrise Hotel for a total of 10 years. He worked his way up at Sunrise Hotel from front desk agent to front desk supervisor, and finally to Assistant General Manager before he became the General Manager. He does a good job of screening potential employees for his front desk area of the hotel because he realizes the importance of that area of the hotel, especially in tourist areas. He also has incentives set up for excellent performance of the front desk agents and training and development programs designed to give everyone information that will help them do their job better. There is a sense of teamwork at Sunrise Hotel and that helps everyone want to do a good job. His guest satisfaction ratings for his hotel are overall excellent. On a rating scale of 1–10, his hotel averages a 9.

The average length of tenure of his employees is 4 years, and his current front desk supervisor was promoted from within, along with his Assistant General Manager. Because of the small size of the hotel, Joe is actually involved with all of the hiring decisions and helps to give training programs himself, along with his leadership team. The employee turnover at the Sunrise Hotel is 25% overall and that is primarily when hourly employees graduate high school or college and leave the Sunrise Hotel for a career somewhere else.

Brian is the General Manager of the Beachside Hotel and deals with a very different situation. Brian was brought in from another hotel in the same hotel group about 6 months ago. He was told by his boss that he needed to "fix" this hotel so that it would start having better customer satisfaction ratings and more return guests. Despite the fairly high occupancy noted during peak seasons, the off peak season occupancy is only 50%. Also noted by his boss, the occupancy should be as good as the Sunrise Hotel. Brian has been with his hotel group now for 2 years and he came out of the accounting and finance department in his old hotel. He has a great understanding of the numbers in the lodging industry, but has not been involved with the human resource aspects of the job.

The turnover of hourly employees at Beachside Hotel is 120% and that means that Brian is constantly running the hotel short handed and with new employees. The Beachside Hotel has been doing the hiring through a human resource practitioner in the hotel that was put in the position because she really could not handle serving guests at the front desk very well. Mary was promoted to human resources a year ago after she had one too many altercations with the guests at the front desk. The owner of the hotel wanted to make sure that she would not make any of the other guests angry, so he promoted her to a human resources practitioner. Since that time, she has been busy trying to keep up with hiring and she has had no time for training employees. Because she is so busy, paychecks often come out to employees late, there are no policies written down for employees to use as a guide for performance, customers are treated badly by new and poorly trained employees, and the departments of the hotel do not communicate very effectively and therefore everyone blames everyone else when things go wrong.

The average length of tenure of the front desk agents at the Beachside Hotel is 3 months and the customer satisfaction rating at the Beachside is a 6 out of a 10 possible rating. Most of the front desk agents that are hired come from other hotels in the area after they quit or are fired. Brian is not involved in the hiring for the hotel at all, and does not get involved with training and development. He spends most of his days looking at the financial reports for the hotel and analyzing average daily rate, occupancy rates, and REVPAR.

Brian knows that he has many problems to deal with and so he goes to the Sunrise Hotel to observe things over there for a while. He sees a happy crew and talks to Joe about how he is making that happen. Joe is happy to help, but wants Brian to go back and observe his employees first and come up with ways that he specifically can help guide Brian.

Class or small group discussion questions

1. What systems should Brian implement in order to start changing the human capital practices in the Beachside Hotel?
2. What could Brian learn from Joe in terms of the human capital aspects of running a hotel?
3. How could training and development programs be implemented in the Beachside Hotel in order to help with turnover and occupancy rates at the hotel?
4. How could a return on investment perspective help or hurt the Beachside Hotel in trying to compete with the Sunrise Hotel?
5. What other human resource initiatives could be undertaken by either the Sunrise Hotel or Beachside Hotel in order to help with the overall performance of their respective organizations?

Suggested solutions

This case study gives many examples of issues that could be improved upon in order to help with the human capital performance in the Beachside Hotel. The Sunrise Hotel offers many good practices that help to ensure a return on investment in their human capital practices. The low turnover, length of service of employees, and the positive ratings regarding guest satisfaction all point to the positive, human capital focused culture of Sunrise Hotel. The above questions give some discussion points that will help to focus students and practitioners on some of the positive actions that can be taken by Beachside Hotel to help improve performance and the tone of the company. Here are some partial solutions to the case study questions.

1. *In order to start changing the human capital practices at the Beachside Hotel, there needs to be a serious shift in the culture there. Since Brian did not have any human resources background, he does not get involved in hiring, training, and ensuring that these functions are used to build a stronger service culture. Mary, the HR practitioner, was put into place because she could not work with customers, yet she is now in charge of the internal customers in the organization, the employees. Brian needs to get involved in building a stronger culture by making sure that he works with Mary to make sure that she is focused on people and creating a positive atmosphere. Investments need to be made in training and development of the people currently employed at Beachside Hotel and also in the new people to build a committed workforce.*

2. *Brian should start out by learning more about the human capital in his own hotel first and getting himself immersed in the people of the company. The service profit chain starts internal to the organization and then looks to the external guest. Brian could then observe some of the human resource practices that are being used at the Sunrise Hotel and apply them to his own hotel. Joe gets involved in all of the hiring at the Sunrise Hotel as well as the training there. Brian should implement more of a focus in the top management of Beachside Hotel in order to emulate Joe's focus on developing a culture of service and in taking pride in the people that work for him.*

3. *Brian needs to focus on hiring the correct people for the various jobs at the Beachside Hotel and should then work with each person to determine what it would take to get them to be satisfied in their jobs. Training and development not only give people the skills that they need to be successful in their jobs, but also they help to develop people in other facets of their life, i.e., time management skills, money management skills, and even tuition reimbursement for college classes. These development classes help people feel a sense of connection with their jobs and would help them to be satisfied in their overall lives. The more satisfied employees are, the more that they tend to stay at a place of employment and the more they tend to satisfy the guest that they serve. Having the top management in a company get involved with the training and development of their people, helps them commit to their future growth and helps the employee feel that their employers believe in them.*

4. *Since Brian's job is to "fix" the Beachside Hotel, there will need to be an initial investment in order to get the human capital practices to a point where there are some significant improvements. These improvements will hopefully drive the service level up at the hotel and thus drive occupancy and repeat customers. There needs to be*

a return on investment focus for the hotel as they try to change the culture. It appears that currently, there is not a focus on investment in human capital at all and the cost is the low customer satisfaction scores, high turnover, and a lack of repeat guests. This hotel needs to encourage a focus on the human capital areas as well as focusing on the return on investment in this area. It needs to be noted that the return on investment may take a period of time to show a positive return, but hopefully the effort will be worth it.

5. *Some of the other human resource initiatives that could be undertaken by either or both properties are: regular and thorough performance reviews, 360 degree feedback programs, round table discussions with employees to focus on their needs, incentive programs to reward employees for positive performance toward the objectives of the organization, offer reward programs for guests in order to boost the level of repeat guests to the hotels, more open communication regarding progress toward the goals of the organizations in order to keep employees in the loop regarding performance, top management needs to focus on having a focus on the service profit chain regarding the internal guest satisfaction as well as the external guest satisfaction.*

References

Barney, J. B. (1991). Firm resources and sustained competitive advantage. *Journal of Management, 17*(1), 99–120.

Barney, J. B. (1995). Looking inside for a competitive advantage. *Academy of Management Executive, 9*(4), 49–61.

Barney, J. B., & Wright, P. M. (1997). On becoming a strategic partner: The role of human resources in gaining competitive advantage. Working Paper.

Becker, B., & Gerhart, B. (1996). The impact of human resources management on organizational performance: Progress and prospects. *Academy of Management Journal, 39,* 779–802.

Becker, G. S. (1964). *Human capital: A theoretical and empirical analysis, with special reference to education.* New York: Columbia University Press.

Becker, G. S. (1975). *Human capital: A theoretical and empirical analysis, with special reference to education* (2nd ed.). New York: National Bureau of Economic Research.

Bowen, J., & Shoemaker, S. (1998). Loyalty: A strategic commitment. *Cornell Hotel and Restaurant Administration Quarterly, 39,* 12–25.

Boxall, P. (1998). Achieving competitive advantage through human resource strategy; towards a theory of industry dynamics. *Human Resources Management Review, 8*(3), 265–288.

Cascio, W. F. (1991). *Costing human resources: The financial impact of behavior in organizations* (3rd ed.). Boston, MA: PWS-Kent Publishing Company.

Cline, R. S. (1997). The value of human capital. *Lodging Hospitality*, 53(10), 20–24.

de Chabert, J. (1998). A model for the development and implementation of core competencies in restaurant companies for superior financial performance. Unpublished doctoral dissertation, Virginia Polytechnic Institute and University.

Dess, G. G., & Picken, J. C. (1999). *Beyond productivity*. New York: AMACOM American Management Association.

Econterms. (2004). Definition of Human Capital. Retrieved August 25, 2006 from http://economics.about.com/cs/economicsglossary/g/human_capital.html

Enz, C. A., Canina, L., & Walsh, K. (2006). Intellectual capital: A key driver of hotel performance. *Cornell University Center for Hospitality Reports*, 6(10). Retrieved on September 2, 2006 from www.chr.cornell.edu

Fitz-enz, J. (2000). *The ROI of human capital*. New York: AMACOM American Management Association.

Harbison, F. H. (1973). *Human resources as the wealth of nations*. New York: Oxford University Press.

Heskett, J. L., Jones, T. O., Loveman, G. W., Sasser, Jr., W. E., & Schlesinger, L. A. (1994). Putting the service-profit chain to work. *Harvard Business Review*, 72(2), 164–175.

Hitt, M., Bierman, L., Shimizu, K., & Kochhar, R. (2001). Direct and moderating effects of human capital on strategy and performance in professional service firms: A resource-based perspective. *Academy of Management Journal*, 44(1), 13–28.

Huselid, M. A. (1995). The impact of human resource management practices on turnover, productivity, and corporate financial performance. *Academy of Management Journal*, 38, 635–672.

Kraiger, K., McLinden, D., & Casper, W. J. (2004). Collaborative planning for training impact. *Human Resource Management*, 43(4), 337–351.

Luthans, F. (1998). *Organizational behavior* (8th ed.). Boston, MA: Irwin McGraw-Hill.

Marcus, M., Ippolito, R., & Zhang, L. (1998). Shareholders and stakeholders: Human capital and industry equilibrium. *The Economic Journal*, 108(447), 490–509.

McCarthy, D. (1997). *The loyalty link*. New York: Wiley.

Mincer, J. (1997). The production of human capital and the life cycle of earnings: Variations on a theme. *Journal of Labor Economics*, 15(1), S26–S48.

Morrow, C. C., Jarrett, M. Q., & Rupinski, M. T. (1997). An investigation of the effect and economic utility of corporate-wide training. *Personnel Psychology, 50*(1), 91–120.

Murphy, K. S., & Williams, J. A. (2004). The impact of compensation on the turnover intentions of Outback Steakhouse managers. *Journal of Food Service Business Research, 7*(1), 63–81.

Olsen, M. D., & Zhao, J. (2002). *Forces driving change in the foodservice industry and competitive methods of multinational foodservice firms.* IH & RA White Paper.

Penrose, E. T. (1959). *The theory of the growth of the firm.* New York: Wiley.

Pfau, B. N., & Cohen, S. A. (2003). Aligning human capital practices and employee behavior with shareholder value. *Consulting Psychology Journal: Practice and Research, 55,* 169–178.

Phillips, J. J. (1997). *Return on investment in training and performance improvement programs.* Houston, TX: Gulf Publishing Company.

Phillips, J. J., & Stone, R. D. (2002). *How to measure training results: A practical guide to tracking the six key indicators.* New York: McGraw-Hill Publishing.

Pine, B. J., & Gilmore, J. H. (1999). *The experience Economy: Work is theatre & every business a stage.* Boston, MA: Harvard Business School Press.

Pizam, A., & Thornburg, S. W. (2000). Absenteeism and voluntary turnover in Central Florida hotels: A pilot study. *International Journal of Hospitality Management, 19,* 211–217.

Ramlall, S. J. (2003). Measuring human resource management's effectiveness in improving performance. *Human Resource Planning, 26*(1), 51–62.

Reichheld, F., & Sasser, E. (1990). Zero defections: Quality comes to services. *Harvard Business Review, 68,* 105–111.

Rothwell, W. J., & Sredl, H. J. (1992). *Professional human resource development roles & competencies* (2nd ed., Vol. 1). Amherst, MA: HRD Press.

Skaggs, B. C., & Youndt, M. (2004). Strategic positioning, human capital, and performance in service organizations: A customer interaction approach. *Strategic Management Journal, 25*(1), 85–96.

Sugrue, B. (2003). *State of the industry: ASTD's annual review of U.S. and international trends in workplace learning and performance.* Alexandria, VA: ASTD.

Swanson, R. A. (2001). *Assessing the financial benefits of human resource development.* Cambridge, MA: Perseus Publishing.

Tracey, J. B., & Nathan, A. E. (2002). The strategic and operational roles of human resources: An emerging model. *Cornell Hotel and Restaurant Administration Quarterly*, 43(4), 17–26.

Traub, J. (2000, January 16). What no school can do. *The New York Times*, pp. 52–61.

Young, C. A., McManua, A., & Canale, D. (2005). A value-driven process model of hospitality human capital. *Journal of Human Resources in Hospitality and Tourism*, 4(2), 1–25.

CHAPTER 17

Contributing to employee development through training and education

Debra Cannon

*Cecil B. Day School of Hospitality
Robinson College of Business,
Georgia State University,
Atlanta, GA, USA*

Introduction

Training and professional development are vital elements to hospitality organizations. Development of job skills and knowledge necessitate ongoing and consistent training processes. In addition, an organizational culture that supports continual quality improvement including exemplary guest service requires a commitment to ongoing effective employee training and development. Horst Schultze, former COO of the Ritz-Carlton Hotel Company and now President of West Paces Hotel Company, developer of some of the world's finest lodging properties, has described the role of training as "creating consensus between the employee and the customer" (Iverson, 2001). Without this consensus built on constant refinement of skills and knowledge, employees (the organization) cannot consistently meet and exceed customer (guest) expectations.

Although training is an essential component of any hospitality operation, it is not the "aspirin" of the industry. In other words, while training can positively impact many aspects of job performance, it is not a "cure all." Training should be considered when the goal is to make a difference in *knowledge, skills, and abilities (KSAs)*. Can training, therefore, correct job dissatisfaction? It depends on the *root-cause* (the primary reason or cause for a situation existing) of the dissatisfaction. If employees are less than satisfied because of uniforms in poor repair and lack of equipment to do their jobs properly, training will not be the appropriate choice. If employees are dissatisfied because managers show favoritism, do not treat employees with respect, and have less than effective communication skills, training for managers may be one of the necessary steps towards improvement.

In addition to targeting the appropriate behaviors through training, it is important for organizations to consider training as a *process*. It is not a one-time program or programs delivered sporadically in a piecemeal fashion. Training, ideally, should include a number of daily structured and unstructured learning opportunities. From the scheduled pre-shift line-up that affords a 5-minute reminder of several guest service standards to a supervisor coaching an employee in ways to improve and refine job performance, a number of opportunities exist daily for learning opportunities. Jim Sullivan, author and consultant to the hospitality industry, has noted that many managers mistakenly think of training as a project. Training does not have clear beginning and ending points as in a linear fashion. Instead, it is a cyclical pattern of collaboration that never ends (Sullivan, 2007).

The importance placed on training tends to fluctuate over periods of time. When business is down, often training is one of the first areas to be cut. Cutting training can have serious repercussions on any organization ultimately affecting the quality levels of service and products. Businesses in the United States spend, on average, about $826 annually to train each employee. This figure represents an increase of approximately $200 over the past 5 years. In comparison to other countries, the United States spends considerably less time on training (about 2% of the total work time) while Germany and Japan spend about five times more (Woods, 2006).

The training process

There are several key steps in the cyclical training process. The *training cycle* consists of eight steps beginning with developing and conducting a *needs assessment*. After the organization's priority needs are identified, *training objectives* can be established. The establishment of *training criteria* follows along with selection of trainees. Although many organizations forego the next step, *pre-testing* trainees, the benefits of a pre-test can be seen in the evaluation of a training program and being able to link results to the actual training activities. *Training methods* must be strategically chosen with the training objectives clearly in mind. The implementation of training follows. *Evaluation* is a step that is often overlooked and yet this step provides important *metrics* in determining the *return on investment* (ROI) of the training program. Each step in the training cycle will be described.

Conducting a needs assessment

Training programs should address identified needs that are relevant to the organization and, through a thorough analysis, have been determined to be linked to knowledge, skills, and/or abilities. A needs assessment is an important managerial tool that assists the organization in making sure that training activities will provide meaningful results to the organization.

There are a number of questions that are linked to the needs assessment process. These include

- What are the different ways of conducting needs assessments?
- How often should a needs assessment be conducted?
- How does a needs assessment target training needs? How is the link between data and training needs built?
- Who should conduct the needs assessment?

Organizations have the potential to collect data from a number of sources that can be utilized in the needs assessment process. For example, guest comments are typically collected from comment cards, letters, or surveys. In analyzing the comments from guests, there are two important elements to consider

1. What are the gaps between the experience described by the guest and the actual performance standards of the operation? For example, if the performance standard for a hotel is that guests will be checked-in within 3 minutes of their arrival at the front desk and the check-in time lapse was actually 8 minutes, the standard has not been met. The question then becomes is this a problem that can be addressed by training. If the root-cause of the delay is that front desk agents lack necessary computer skills, this problem can be targeted through training. If the problem is that the Property Management System (PMS) is antiquated and there are mechanical problems beyond the front desk agents' control, this most likely is not a training issue—at least for the front desk agents.

2. Guest perceptions are reality. The hospitality industry is run on perceptions and in conducting a needs assessment, the importance of perceptions has to be recognized. If several guests comment that service is slow or rude or not accurate, these opinions have to be addressed.

Other approaches in conducting a needs analysis include

- *Written surveys* of employees—These surveys would ask employees in what parts of their jobs do they struggle or what tasks do they find most difficult; where do the employees see gaps between the organization's standards and actual performance? In what areas would employees like to improve? What would make their jobs easier or more fulfilling?
- *Observation*—Gaps in performance can be identified through observation of employees conducting their work responsibilities.
- *Records/data*—Companies typically obtain a range of data such as safety records which show where accidents occur and how. An analysis of this information can determine if training is appropriate as an approach to accident prevention or reduction.
- *Employee performance reviews*—Individual training needs, as well as collective needs of employees, based on gaps in performance can be targeted through an analysis of employee performance reviews. This source of information

necessitates supervisors and managers conducting performance reviews so that there is an accurate and comprehensive portrayal of the employee's behavior.

- *Analysis of incoming employee skill/knowledge areas*—If organizations evaluate new employees, rather than assuming every individual starts with the same knowledge and skill levels, better initial orientation and training program can be designed.
- *Exit interview data*—Obtaining comments on training is highly recommended as part of the exit interview or survey. Employees leaving the organization should be asked if training was adequate, how it could have been improved and if there were certain areas of training—whether related to skills, knowledge, or abilities—that could have made a positive difference with their work.

A combination of several needs assessment approaches could be most effective in targeting training opportunities. In terms of how often a needs assessment should be conducted, it is more of an ongoing process than a one-time event repeated at certain intervals. For example, medically treated work-related accidents and illnesses, by law, must be documented. It is important that these records are reviewed on an ongoing and consistent basis so that preventative measures can be taken to avoid future accidents. Training employees in safe work behaviors would likely be one of several strategies to avoid future incidents. Likewise, exit interview data are collected on an ongoing basis. Ideally, these data should be grouped and reviewed every week or two to avoid the continuation of a problem that may be why employees are leaving the company. Employee surveys, however, would not typically be administered every week or month. A biannual or annual schedule would be more realistic with shorter follow-up surveys to monitor the progress of key priority problems or issues.

Many of the approaches in a needs assessment can be conducted by managers and employees. Others, such as the design of surveys, may necessitate outsourcing to consultants. A number of factors will determine if outsourcing is appropriate including the company's financial resources as well as the availability of internal expertise.

A vital question from the assessment information concerns the necessary action steps to address the gaps and problems discovered. When training is considered as a potential approach, several questions should be addressed

1. Is the problem or gap in work performance due to a lack of skills? Are the skills present and not being applied? If so,

why are the skills dormant? Is it because of role confusion in not understanding one's job tasks and how they should be performed? For example, does a host in a restaurant understand that part of the job responsibilities include a friendly greeting to arriving guests and explaining some of the daily specials on the menu? Or does the host provide a less than friendly greeting, presents the menu and then coldly leaves the table? Training is an appropriate step when there are these types of performance gaps.

2. Are the gaps in performance due to a training problem or to a *performance problem*? The distinction between training problems and performance problems is an important one. For example, in the situation with the host above, let's say that this individual has been trained. He was not only been told that a friendly greeting is important in his role as host but he has been reminded of this by his supervisor in frequent coaching interactions. One of the training techniques was role-playing where the employee demonstrated that he could provide a proper greeting and could explain the menu specials. His performance on the job is sporadic; sometimes, he meets the standards for the restaurant and often he does not. Providing training for this employee over and over will probably prove futile. The situation is not a training problem but a performance problem involving, at some point, a disciplinary approach along with proper documentation. The attempted training and coaching should also be documented. It shows the employer wanted the employee to succeed and tried through training to provide the necessary skill sets.

3. Is the problem or gap in work performance due to lack of knowledge? Similar to skills, employees must be provided with a foundation of knowledge to perform to their highest potential. As with skills, employees should be continually provided with the opportunity to increase their knowledge base with the most current and applicable information.

4. Are there attitudinal underpinnings of the identified performance gaps? Training cannot work miracles with attitudinal issues but it can positively impact them indirectly. An employee who has been trained in areas of interpersonal skills such as communication, conflict resolution, and teamwork may improve in demonstrating positive behaviors with co-workers and guests.

5. Are the gaps in performance reflective of work processes or systems? Deming, the "Father of Quality Management," emphasized that 80% of work errors are due to *systematic problems* (Walton, 1986). Training to impart information on better ways to organize work tasks and to layout work areas

can result in better employee performance in meeting organizational standards.

Once areas that are training-based are identified, priorities must next be established. Most companies do not have the resources in people, time, and money to handle all problems simultaneously. Key questions that may help in prioritizing the needs include

- Do the issues at hand deal with the organization's mission, goals, and objectives?
- Do the issues impact organizational performance?
- Do the issues impact the development of career paths?
- Do the issues involve the development of employees in career paths?
- Are the identified issues significantly impacting the organization negatively?
- Are there issues that need to be reviewed immediately? (Dolasinski, 2004)

Establishing training objectives and training criteria

As with a thorough and targeted needs assessment, establishing training objectives or goals is another essential component in the planning process. Training objectives should clearly answer the question of "Where do you want to end up?" (Cannon & Gustafson, 2002). Measurable objectives can greatly facilitate the evaluation of training.

An objective of "improving service" or "making guests happy" is problematic in numerous respects. What does improving mean? In what areas are improvements needed? Why specific things determine guest satisfaction or dissatisfaction? Training objectives should be: specific, measurable, achievable, relevant, and time-oriented. For example, a restaurant wanting to improve guest satisfaction may identify the following goal: Servers and hosts will know the description of every menu item, how the item is prepared (and alternative options of preparation if the guest requests), the ingredients in the dish (as well as what can be ingredients can be replaced.) This will be accomplished before the employee is put to work on their own (out of the orientation and initial training program), i.e. the information will be learned during the initial 5-day training program.

The goal is specific (100% of all items); measurable (written or verbal tests can be administered to see if the information is known); achievable (particularly with study guides and tastings provided during the learning period); relevant (with food allergies on the increase as well as other dietary and health concerns, this aspect of training is not only relevant but essential); and time-oriented (during the first week of training). This one objective would be appropriate for a training process that could be divided over 1–2 days with follow-up descriptions to take home for study. The focus is on knowledge although the delivery of this information would certainly involve presentation and even up-selling skills. A follow-up objective, once the information is learned, might be: Describe the items in a clear, concise and easy to understand manner emphasizing key adjectives that will help the guest appreciate the flavor and presentation of the particular menu item. Restaurants and other food service establishments often miss great marketing opportunities in the way menu items are described.

Training criteria is reflected in the training objectives and includes how the particular task should be performed and therefore measured. Training criteria should reflect the organization's standards. For example, a fine dining establishment may have a more formal standard in how employees interact and talk with guests as compared to a casual or quick service restaurant. This level of formality would be reflected in the training objective and in the assessment of the training.

Selecting the participating employees

Some training activities encompass all employees such as initial orientation programs and training for newly hired employees. Other training is selective such as preparing employees for upward movement in the organization. Supervisory or management development programs are of this nature. It should be remembered that training is considered a benefit provided by the organization—particularly in training programs that are selective. It is important for organizations to have delineated criteria for the selection of training participants to avoid potential legal problems such as *discrimination*.

A *trainee analysis* can be an effective management tool in optimizing training opportunities. This analysis includes developing a *trainee profile* so that important background information on the individuals can be reviewed in designing the activities. Questions to include in the trainee analysis include

- How experienced are the participants? What is their educational background? Their work experience?

- Will the information/skills to be covered vary in importance among the participants? If so, how and to what extent?
- What is the motivation for the participants to be involved in the training? Is it mandatory? Linked to upward advancement or a salary increase? Voluntary?
- What cultural differences exist in the group of participants? Language differences? Will translators be needed? Other supports?
- Are there any known disabilities among the participants that will require modifications in the planned training?
- What goals do the trainees personally have for the program?
- What learning styles exist among the participants? (Cannon & Gustafson, 2002)

Brief surveys or interviews can be used in answering the above questions. Pre-testing of participants can also be conducted to understand specific levels of knowledge and/or skills prior to training. Making the effort to pre-test participants can have additional benefits in determining if the changes in performance are linked to the training experience. For skills, the pre-test would require demonstration of the relevant behaviors. Knowledge can be pre-tested through written and/or verbal quizzes. In evaluating the effectiveness of the training process, the same quizzes or demonstration scenarios should be used in the post-test stage (after the training).

Establishing training methods

There are a multitude of different methods available to trainers. Nationwide, about 14% of training is delivered by computer with the clear majority (73%) delivered in a classroom setting (Woods, 2006). There are several important factors to consider before deciding on training methods

1. What are the objectives of the training activity?
2. What are the characteristics of the participating employees? What are their current ranges of skills and/or knowledge? Are there differences in language or other abilities that will have to be recognized in planning the training? How receptive will this group be to interactive training techniques? Are there any cultural factors that may reduce their willingness to actively participate? Are there any employees with disabilities and, if so, what type?
3. What are the restrictions regarding the training budget, the time employees can spend in training and the physical location for the training?

Because of the above factors, no one training method or technique is always the best. Typically, it is wise to include a variety of training methods. It is important for trainers to have background knowledge on *adult learning theories* and how in practicing *andragogy*, the teaching or training of adults, we learn differently than children (the teaching of children—peda-gogy). Adult learner theorist, Malcolm Knowles, stressed that adults need to know how the training activities will benefit them—in their jobs, careers, financially. The more immediate and direct these benefits are, the more likely the adult learner will be motivated to fully participate and optimize the learning opportunity. Adults also have the need to participate and be active learners. The quicker the time between learning new information and having the opportunity to apply or try it out, the better the training approach (Cannon & Gustafson, 2002).

It is also important that trainers understand the different learning styles and how training must be geared to visual learners, auditory learners, and kinesthetic learners. A fair assumption is that any group of employees will contain a representation of all learning styles. In designing a training program, that means that graphs, photos, illustrations will be important for the visual learners; talking through points and including discussions in the training will be important for auditory learners; and having a chance for hands-on activities will be necessary for kinesthetic learners.

Best training practices in hospitality

A sample of best training practices in the hospitality industry will reveal a multitude of different training approaches.

Olive Garden's DASH Training: The goal of DASH, which was rolled out to Olive Garden restaurants in September 2005 through November 2006, was to train employees on the company's new point of sale system. Hands-on training was conducted with 2328 restaurant managers and 3493 certified trainers ultimately including 40,000 team members. Quick-reference materials and Web-based training proved successful in reducing the project completion time by 33%.

MGM Grand Hotel—Las Vegas: Training was initiated in response to MGM's acquisition of the Mandalay Resort Group (MRG) in April 2005. MGM Grand University was launched as a support to this process. An e-management learning needs assessment was administered to get baselines on training priorities. A University Intranet was launched with descriptions of programs to facilitate employee registration. The result was 15,000 employees trained.

Starbucks—MyPartnerCareer.com: Training can also encompass career preparation as can be seen in Starbuck's new service for employees referred to as "partners" by the Seattle-based company. The web site www.MyPartnerCareer.com, was launched in May 2006. Through this web site, employees can create descriptions of themselves and their company aspirations which can be shared with others in the organization. Features also include a Career Resources section with department overviews, resume, and interview tools, and a "Top Opps" section spotlighting positions or functional areas in high demand. The site also offers a blog where employees can converse with experts on career growth, coffee facts, and leadership skills.

Continental Airlines: Continental hosted a recent Sky Team Ambassador training program at its Newark hob. The goal of the program was to align the frontline staff to better understand how the alliance works with their airline partners so that customers could be served better. As part of this program, Ambassador Forums were developed to allow hundreds of Sky Team employees to meet and interact in-person with representatives from the various member airlines. Attendees received informational material that could be used as reference material. The training covered everything from lounges and in-flight service to data points, such as destinations and hub locations (Wilson, 2007).

Brinker International, Inc.: Brinker, operator or franchisor of over 1500 casual dining restaurants including Chili's Grill & Bar, has created a "learning map" with the objective of helping restaurant managers understand the corporate mission and how to achieve the company's goals. Similar to board games, players draw activity cards that lead them into discussion about various strategies and behaviors. The concept is that if employees talk about a strategy, they connect with it and internalize it (Berta, 2006).

As can be seen from the above examples, employee training includes assorted techniques. Training is no longer limited to on-the-job training or classroom training. It includes web-based tools, intranets, blogs, in-person events, and even board games. The following are additional training techniques that are routinely used by hospitality organizations

- *Demonstration*—This is an essential training tool for skill-based positions. It is crucial that the demonstrated behavior is 100% reflective of company standards. Anything less will give the trainee the impression that lower standards are

383

acceptable. There is a method of utilizing demonstration in skill training that involves four steps that are sequential and should be followed in this order—*Tell, Show, Do, Review.*

1. Tell—The trainer tells the individual being trained what new skill will be presented and the importance of this skill. For example, "Today you are going to learn how to properly open a bottle of wine. Opening wine properly adds to the ambiance of the dining experience. It shows that you have the professional skills for a finer dining experience and also avoids ruining the wine by breaking off the cork or getting pieces of cork in the wine. There are also safety issues in opening a bottle of wine and you want to prevent accidents involving you and/or the guests." Questions should be welcomed and the trainer should urge the employee to be open with concerns and comments throughout the training process.

2. Show—The next step involves showing each step in completing the task. The training session on opening a bottle of wine would include how to prepare to open the bottle in getting the needed equipment (towel, proper corkscrew). The demonstration would include how to hold the bottle, where to place the corkscrew, how to turn it, and how to properly uncork the bottle. The training would also include what to do with the cork. The next training session would logically include how to pour the wine, when and how to refill, and where to place the wine bottle during the meal. The training is intentionally limited in scope. The trainer does not want to train on multiple tasks at one time.

3. Do—The employee now has the opportunity to perform the new task. This is done with the trainer watching every step. If there are any safety hazards as the employee performs the task, the trainer stops the employee immediately to avoid injury, describes what the hazard is, and how it can be avoided. With no safety hazards occurring, the trainer should allow the employee to continue through the entire task.

4. Review—After the employee finishes the task, the trainer reviews the performance. It is important for the trainer to always start with positive points in reviewing the employee's performance. Comments should be clear and constructive. Instead of just saying what was done incorrectly, suggestions should be offered on how to perform the task correctly. The trainer should always remain respectful of the employee and positive of the employee's attempts. After the review, the employee can return

to the "do" phase and repeat. Excessive repetition should be avoided because of fatigue and possible frustration. Sometimes going on to a new task and returning for repetitions later can prove fruitful. For knowledge-based training, the process is different in including the steps of: *Tell, Test, Review.*

- *Role plays*—This technique can help employees practice new skills in a safe environment and is most effective with small to medium size groups. The technique is particularly helpful with interpersonal skill training as well as supervisory and management training. There are following four stages in using role plays properly

  1. Provide background—In this stage, a reason is provided for the role play and any background information is provided about the situation that will be enacted. Time limits are also set at this stage.

  2. Conduct the role play—Volunteers are asked for and specific roles are assigned. In a group setting, individuals not in assigned roles can serve as observers. Clear instructions are provided for the roles. Observers are told what behaviors they should note.

  3. Debrief the participants—Participants give feedback about their reactions in their roles. Both positive and negative aspects of their performance should be noted. Observers can discuss their impressions with positive reactions noted first followed by negative.

  4. Close the session—This stage connects what has been learned and can be applied to real-life situations. Volunteers and observers are thanked for their participation (Cannon & Gustafson, 2002).

Typically trainers provide scripts for each role. With more advanced participants, the roles may be unscripted. This requires "thinking on the spot" by participants which may be more reflective of their actual behaviors. Unscripted roles are very unstructured, however, and the trainer must be prepared to provide specific feedback—both positive and negative.

Evaluation of training

The question of ROI for training processes has been deliberated by many industries including hospitality. Lashley (2002) emphasized that the attempts to link the costs of training to the gains often fail because a narrow range of financial measures is used when calculating the returns from a training investment. In his research of McDonald's restaurants, his findings supported training leading to improvements in service quality, employee satisfaction, and functional flexibility. He also found evidence of training's impact on employee turnover and productivity.

If an organization does not consistently evaluate the necessary metrics such as service levels, employee satisfaction, productivity, and turnover, the analysis of ROI becomes invalid. Likewise, if an organization does not accurately evaluate the costs incurred through training, an essential component of the analysis will be missing.

Evaluation of training can occur on several levels. The selection of evaluation approaches can enhance or deter the calculation of ROI. The levels of evaluation are

1. *Reaction*—This level of evaluation targets how employees felt about the training session(s). Did they enjoy them? Was the training interesting? Entertaining?
2. *Knowledge/skills gained*—This level evaluates how much information was acquired. A post-test, conducted after the training, in combination with the pre-test, could target before and after scores indicating almost exactly the amount of knowledge acquired through training. Similarly through demonstration, skills could be evaluated as new or refined skill sets. If organizations stopped at this level in the evaluation of training, what is not targeted is the extent to which the learning is transferred to new behaviors on the job.
3. *On-the-job behaviors*—This level of training evaluation is more helpful in determining ROI because evidence is sought regarding transfer of knowledge and skills from the training stage to being applied on the job. If knowledge and skills are not transferred to job performance, there will be limited, if any, ROI. The problem in stopping at this stage is that on-the-job behaviors are often difficult to quantify.
4. *Results*—This level looks for quantifiable business results in determining ROI for the specific training. For example, if training on pairing wine and food is provided to restaurant employees, the desired business results would be increased wine sales. While a manager could look for on-the-job behaviors (observing servers making wine recommendations based on items ordered; serving wine to more tables), the ultimate proof would be an increase in wine revenue.

Obtaining quantifiable data is often more difficult than the above example. For example, improvement in the "soft skills" such as interpersonal skills, communication, and service skills can be observed but putting an exact dollar figure on the improvements may be questionable. There are likely indicators of the impact of improvements in the soft skill areas. For example, is there a reduction in guest complaints? Has there been an increase in positive comments?

Although not applicable to every facet of a business, there are a number of quantifiable indicators that can be consistently measured and factored into the ROI for training. These include errors in work (order returned in a restaurant because prepared incorrectly; guest re-roomed in a hotel because a non-smoking room was requested and the guest was placed in a smoking room), employee turnover, accidents (employee and guest), breakage/waste—to name a few. For training targeted in these areas, are the results improving? If so, what is the dollar impact? There are industry averages of what one employee leaving costs an organization (typically estimated to be at minimum $2000 per employee and if a management-level or highly skilled employee, the cost of turnover may be $50,000 or more). Likewise, a company can calculate the cost of one employee work-related accident or the loss of one dissatisfied guest who does not return to do business with a hotel or restaurant.

Regarding the costs of training, the following are some of the costs that may be incurred by an organization

- Cost of the trainer—whether an internal employee or outsourced
- Cost of paying employees for the training sessions (typically necessary if the training is work-related)
- Training materials
- Loss of direct work productivity during the training

From orientation to life-long learning

As this chapter emphasized initially, training is a process. For organizations committed to the maximum development of their most important resource—humans—training is ongoing and consistently delivered. One of the first signs of an organization's commitment is the emphasis placed on the orientation of new employees. A well-planned orientation is a contribution to the new employee's success and retention. Statistics show that employee turnover is highest in the first 30 days of employment. The main reason for this high rate is the employee not getting off to the right start (Woods, 2006).

Orientations are categorized as "general property orientations" or "specific job orientations" These are not mutually exclusive and are typically offered together with the general property orientation preceding the specific job orientation. The general property orientation covers material that would be important for any new employee—regardless of their job positions. The history of the company, mission and goals, and the organizational structure are segments that would be typically included in the general property orientation. Company policies and procedures and the employee handbook are usually discussed. An introduction to the management team as well as a tour of the entire property are other helpful components. The specific job orientation would be conducted on the departmental level. This part of the orientation would cover the layout of the department, where employees sign-in and out, where they keep their personal belongings, how to alert the department if late or going to be absent and other operational aspects of the department (Woods, 2006).

Many organizations begin discussing the importance of training in the new employee orientation program. This is a very fitting beginning as an indicator of an organizational culture that supports the employee's development. The company's support can be present in many forms—from tuition reimbursement benefits to providing opportunities for employees to get professional certifications throughout their career.

Many certifications are offered through professional associations that help supplement training and education on the organizational level. The certifications can also span over a period of years spanning across one's career. For example, the Educational Institute of the American Hotel and Lodging Association has numerous certifications on the departmental level such as housekeeping, food and beverage, sales, engineering, and human resources. For the individual at a divisional or general manager level, the Certified Hotel Administrator (CHA) is an appropriate professional development goal (www.ei-ahla.com). The Club Managers Association of America (CMAA) offers numerous professional development options for club managers through their Business Management Institute series. CMAA also certifies club managers after pre-requisites are met of work experience and educational credits earned through the Certified Club Manager (CCM) designation. For the veteran manager who has established himself or herself as a leader in the club profession, has reached the CCM designation and has continued on to give to the industry and to his/her community, there is the Master Club Manager (MCM) designation (www.cmaa. org). Certifications are also offered by numerous other professional associations including Meeting Planners International, the National Restaurant Association, the American Culinary

Table 17.1 Examples of Professional Hospitality Certifications

Sponsoring Hospitality Association	Certification
American Culinary Foundation (ACF)	Certified Chef Educator; Certified Executive Chef; Certified Master Chef
Club Managers Association of America (CMAAA)	Certified Club Manager (CCM); Master Club Manager (MCM)
American Hotel & Lodging Association (AH&LA)	Certified Food & Beverage Executive (CFBE); Certified Hotel Administrator (CHA); Certified Hospitality Educator (CHE); Certified Hospitality Trainer (CHT); Certified Hospitality Supervisor (CHS)
Hospitality Sales and Marketing Association International	Certified Hospitality Marketing Executive (CHME)
Meeting Planners International (MPI)	Certified Meeting Manager (CMM)
Convention Industry Council (CIC)	Certified Meeting Professional (CMP)
International Special Events Society (ISES)	Certified Special Events Professional (CSEP)

Federation, Professional Convention Management Association, and the International Association of Assembly Managers. Almost any hospitality industry segment will have ties to a professional organization with a corresponding professional development program and certifications. Table 17.1 presents examples from several hospitality professional associations and the certifications offered by each.

References

Berta, D. (2006). Brinker maps out vision and strategy for employees, literally. *Nation's Restaurant News, 40*, 18.

Cannon, D. F., & Gustafson, C. M. (2002). *Training and development for the hospitality industry.* Lansing: Educational Institute of the American Hotel & Lodging Industry.

Dolasinski, M. J. (2004). *Training the trainer.* Upper Saddle River: Prentice Hall.

Iverson, K. M. (2001). *Managing human resources in the hospitality industry.* Upper Saddle River: Prentice Hall.

Lashley, C. (2002). The benefits of training for business per-formance. In N. D'Annunzio-Green, G.A. Maxwell & S. Watson (Eds.), *Human resource management* (pp. 104–117). London: Continuum.

Sullivan, J. (2007). How many times do I have to tell you? Employee training requires repetition to get real results. *Nations Restaurant News, 41,* 24.

Walton, M. (1986). *The Deming management method.* New York: Perigee.

Wilson, B. (2007). Sky team holds employee forums to review customer policies. *Aviation Daily, 42,* 6.

Woods, R. H. (2006). *Managing hospitality human resources.* Lansing: Educational Institute of the American Hotel & Lodging Industry.

Internet resources

www.acfchefs.org—American Culinary Federation

www.cmaa.org—Club Managers Association of America

www.conventionindustry.org—Convention Industry Council

www.ei-ahla.org—Educational Institute of the American Hotel & Lodging Association

www.hsmai.org—Hospitality Sales and Marketing Association International

www.ises.com—International Society of Event Specialists

www.mpiweb.org—Meeting Planners International

An HR practitioner's view: four actions that HR executives can take to get their services used

Robert C. Preziosi

H. Wayne Huizenga School of Business and Entrepreneurship, Nova Southeastern University, FL 33314, USA

Introduction

HR executives (execs) and their staff can increase the influence they have on organizations and on marketing their services. This view presents four actions that they can take to be a better business partner with their other departments. Human resources can make a great contribution if HR execs and HR staffs make a concerted effort to have their services used. HR needs to be seen as a department that is a consultative problem-solver and as the leader in all efforts that build upon this belief in appreciative inquiry.

It is commonly known that businesses need to focus on useful change if they are going to survive the future. The changes will be led by the human resource departments that have the foresight to incorporate drastic re-direction for organizations (Bendixen, Abratt, & Myres, 2001). The responses that HR execs must choose to take fall neatly into four actions. First, they must build different kinds of relationships. Second, they must be successful in their initiatives such that their reputation for success is known by all. Third, they must be recognized as responsive and having a sense of urgency. Finally, they must realize success for themselves and for their business partners throughout the organization.

Building of relationships

In building relationships, there are some categories of behavior that are necessary if HR execs are going to realize their desire to be a valued business partner. These areas include trust, long-term purpose, perfect attendance, provision of new services that are highly customized, and finally, sensibility and support.

Trust

First of all, while building trust, HR execs need to deliver what they say they deliver. If someone is promised a new job description by a certain date, that job description needs to be finished and in the hands of the person it was promised to.

Providing trust through use of information systems is a key way HR execs can enhance trust. To enhance productivity, they will seek out faster software that is easier to use for recruitment. Their efforts must include constant discoveries of ways to decrease the cost per unit outcome for each person they recruit. Another example could be built around a performance appraisal system. More likely than not, training is required. The training should be delivered in a timely fashion so that when the new performance appraisal system becomes operative, everyone is prepared to use it.

In some human resource departments, people only speak positively of others. This value of speaking positively of others is essential for the human resources department's function. It is necessary to use appreciative language. Also, the human resources department needs to find people who are problem solvers in their own departments and avoid placing blame.

Public and private support is also an important component to provide staff members. If coaching is needed, it should be done away from the action that leads to the need for coaching. Next, HR execs and HR departments should state a course of action, fully explaining changes before they are placed into effect. The bottom line in building trust is to deliver on your promises.

Long-term focus

Long-term focus is essential to build relationships for HR execs and HR departments. This means that HR needs to be futuristic in planning and thinking systems. This might certainly include succession planning and the design and delivery of leadership development. The HR department should visualize budgets more than once a year. It is important to look beyond the next 12 months. In order to do that, of course, HR must digest the corporate strategic plan. They must be fairly familiar with this strategic plan and know exactly what contributions will be expected from the department in delivering the key elements of the strategic plan.

One way to have a long-term focus is to do it by watching competitors and the actions they are taking. This can be within the same line of business, size of the organization, or in the same region of the state, country, or world. Knowledge of what they are doing helps human resources departments better understand what their strategy should be and potentially what they are overlooking. A final consideration suggests that HR strategy should be next to financial projection for the business. HR strategists must continue to speak for their piece of the pie and seek to expand HR activity so that financial projections are realized.

Leading the way is very important to long-term focus. This means that HR must create new internal programs that are cutting edge, or at least cutting edge to them. While on the subject of cutting edge, it is important to remember that creative people can make a great contribution in HR. It is important to hire staffs that are right brained, some that are left brained, and some that are equally comfortable with either set of activities.

Thinking long-term or strategically is a necessity; anyone who considers it a luxury will find it difficult to make HR contributions with a long-term focus. Because of this, HR departments should provide training in strategic thinking for themselves and other parts of the organization.

The last important element of leading the way is to remember that changing resource allocations when appropriate is essential. A budget is a guide. New business conditions or federal regulations that require reallocation of resources during a budget year should be addressed as quickly as possible. Businesses cannot be stuck in a rut due to poor monitoring of available resources.

Interdependence

HR execs need to show their HR staffs the connections that exist between HR jobs. Some focus on recruiting, while others focus on training or comp and benefits. It is crucial to show how these activities are related and how staff members move through the organization with arms locked walking forward. When showing connections among HR jobs, the best way to demonstrate this is to map out tasks and use process maps. When mapping past interdependencies, it becomes possible to show how many of the processes and procedures of HR interact with each other. It is also important, of course, to build interdependencies between HR and specific work units. You can assign a specific person to a specific unit or find another way to build interdependencies. The important thing is to build them because they create more energy. It is a broader understanding of HR business that can lead to better service for HR customers.

Aligning tasks with cost effective technology is also very important. Earlier, it was suggested that newer, more user-friendly software be used in recruiting. HR activities should use the most cost effective technology that is available within budget allocations. It is important for technologies to be able to interface for maximized efficiencies. This, of course, will lead to the establishment of a family of interconnecting procedures. This helps maintain a clear picture of the impact that HR has.

Also with regards to interdependence, it is important to keep in mind that success needs to cross grasp boundaries. As one unit or line of business is successful, the feeling of success must be diffused throughout the entire department or the organization. It is also important to accept the natural clustering of cross-functional teams. Rather than force lines of business or work units into some set of policies and procedures, it is beneficial to examine those already in existence and make every effort to work with what is there.

New services

The next focus point in building relationships is new services. A natural question is: what new services should be offered? And, of course, the first thing to do is identify with the executive management team what new services might be suggested by the combined strategies of the overall business and the HR department. This would involve identifying areas of need. This would also involve finding out existing strengths. Building on those strengths is a successful approach when identifying and providing new services. Another suggestion would be to try something weird. Weirdness tends to come natural. The point is to find something extraordinary that can be created by means of a new service to provide another success for the HR department.

Another great idea is to transport best practices from one organization to another. It is imperative to look inside the industry for something new that can be brought into an organization. Pay attention to the diversity of the HR department and the work force. This can often time lead to creation that does not happen when diversity is not present. Remember to always start with small projects and broadcast positive results.

For example, once I was delivering and introducing a supervisory skills training program for a very small group of supervisors. It was very successful, so my vice president decided to put it on the front page of the company newsletter. When I look back at that, I think, "Wow, that was a great way for a HR exec to sell the services of HR." Finally, sell the best practices. Let people know that the best practices are in their best interests. These can be transported into their own departments.

Customization

Customization is worth accomplishing if HR execs want their customers to respect what HR has to offer. Whatever the service, make it one of a kind—again, and again, and again. This makes it necessary to avoid the belief that one size fits all.

It is always necessary to balance customization with the need of consistent treatment of all employees. Remember to always make it a work in progress. Once it is out there, opportunities for improvement may present themselves. Those opportunities should be taken advantage of.

When creating more customization in HR services, get involvement. Establish a committee that includes HR folks and people throughout the organization. Ask for their opinion and discuss it until it becomes clear that it is building momentum. One thing to remember is customization activity requires simplifying as much as possible through integrated automation.

It is imperative to know the impact that customization efforts will have on the business. How does this impact operating procedures? How does it impact the bottom line, and does it impact employee moral? This will mean asking for feedback. Ask for feedback from throughout the organization. A short electronic questionnaire can provide lots of information. Also, remember to make or create a culture of acceptance. When creating a culture of acceptance, actions that are taken are accepted as more palatable throughout the organization.

Flexibility and support

The last focal point for building relationships has to do with flexibility and support. Always remember to frame feedback to make it useful. This means that focus groups, questionnaires, or other tools that are used should be thought through very clearly in terms of what information is needed. This means that it is important to stay true to the model that has been established, whether its' dealing with customization, new services, interdependence, long-term focus, or trust.

Maintain rationality as much as it is feasible. It is very easy to become victimized by emotional, irrational, and illogical perspectives. Stay, of course, on logical, rational, and objective pursuits. One thing that is pretty useful in identifying how to frame feedback based upon the model that is used is to mind map as much as possible. Mind map all the options. It makes it easier to make the appropriate choices. Also, another philosophy to follow is to know when to hold 'em and when to fold' em. What this means is that it is important to know when to stop being flexible. There is no formula or recipe. It is something that is just developed or felt internally.

Remember that support is a two-way street. Everyone can be an ally. Also, you can be an ally for everyone. Always show the numbers to strengthen support. Whatever kind of available data make sure some is available to present it. It strengthens arguments. Enlist everyone. Everyone can and should be involved in providing flexibility and support, but especially support.

Reputation

The first opportunity to develop or expand an excellent reputation begins with person-to-person communication. This includes the HR executive's communication with other senior executives, the staff of the HR department, and anyone else that the HR exec comes into contact with. The exec must be a role model for everyone to follow.

Develop high competency

It begins with the developing high competency in person-to-person communication. This means knowing your communication style. There are lots of MODELS available for development and utilization. HR execs should pick a model and use that to develop higher and higher competency in person-to-person communication. It may also be important from time to time to be flexible in style. Whenever you deal with a person whose style is different from yours, it may be easier to communicate with them by communicating in their style, and not to be so inflexible in using only your own style.

HR exec should also be familiar with cultural differences. Whether the culture differences are inside the organization or outside the organization, the issues are still the same. This includes culture differences in customs, words, and gestures. Because of differences, many times, we rush a communication to avoid the feeling of not being comfortable. Spending the time it takes to communicate with people so that your reputation is enhanced is a good solution to these uncomfortable situations. Build strength and confidence in staff and their person-to-person communication. Provide style training for them as well so they can improve their communication. This must be an ongoing requirement of the business of HR, and it must be timely. Whether people are expecting a communication at a certain time, or if they are just expecting you to respond, it is important to have a sense of urgency. They expect that you will see the importance of what they had to say and that you will respond quickly.

Referral networks

Another variable in reputation has to do with referral networks. These are people you exchange ideas with and who you consistently provide opportunities for. These are the people in your network. It begins with trust. It goes on to reciprocity. Remember to use these things sparingly, avoiding overuse and always appreciating the positive outcomes that come from them. Another aspect of the referral network includes building cross-functional networks. It is fine to have a mentor or a favorite person to have coffee with, but is also important to have someone from every function in your network. Remember to nourish members of the network by being available for them and doing the little things they find valuable.

Additionally, it is important to constantly assess the value of each member in your network. As I have found in the past, you may discover that there are people in your network who have no value and to whom you provide no value. Slowly separate yourself from them without harming the interpersonal aspect of the relationship. This means that you will add and subtract members of your network on an ongoing basis. This shows that your network is alive and well and functioning the way that you want it to function. You want it to function in giving and receiving.

Always maintain excellent relationships with staff members. The stresses and strains of HR work can cause us, from time to time, to strain relationships. Before everybody goes home, make sure that everyone is comfortable so that when they walk in the door the next morning, they are feeling positive and upbeat and not dragging in because of the "weight of the troubled relationship". Relate to all levels and functions throughout the organization. It is easy to be caught up in just learning to deal with the executive management team. People up and down the entire organization are contributing to the success of the organization, and all of them deserve attention from the HR exec.

Build diversity into the network. This includes many of the standard opportunities, such as gender, ethnic groups, etc. Build from different functions and levels in the organization. It is important to also keep in mind the aspect of generational diversity. This may be the most challenging issue for organizational diversity that we have seen in years. We are constantly reassessing the membership which was referred to us before.

It is important to carefully construct alliances. It is crucial that HR execs' inquiry in each department be seen as people who are supportive of the vision, mission, and values of the organization. It is true that sometimes we are known by the company that we keep. It is important to watch this carefully. Make sure that you include a personal friend in your network. In this case, personal means someone who you may see socially after work or go to a sporting event with, something of that nature. Just be aware of the proper socialization protocol within the organization.

I always felt the real reason for creating a network was so that I could identify ways to help people. Networks existed to find ways to give opportunity to people. It is important to emphasis giving, as I call it, but it is very important to receive. People in your network who never give and always take can be energy draining. Watch out! Remember to avoid the "I owe you one" syndrome. This kind of score keeping is disruptive. If you try to keep some kind of an even slate, you will get lost in score keeping and forget the true value of the network.

Use opinion leaders

When it comes to person-to-person communication, there may be nothing as energizing as using opinionators or people whom others greatly value the opinion of. Opinionated leaders are those folks who have a lot of people listening to what they have to say, regardless of the issue. These are the people who are responsible for the best storytelling about the organization. Consequently, they are always heard.

Always know where you stand with the opinion leaders. While certainly it is important to have them on your side, if you are not, you need to know that. Identify who your supporters are. Make sure they are people of integrity. Spend time with opinion leaders and supporters, and run your ideas by them. This could be value-adding time, as opposed to a half hour social conversation. They are a good barometer of what might and might not fly. Everyday, some political capital is used in dealing with opinion leaders. Never use all of your political capital at once. You do not want to be caught without any.

It is important to always speak for yourself. People must know that you are your own mouth piece. Do something for opinion leaders as often as you can. Let them know that you value them. Also, inform them that they bring value to who you are and what you do. Go further up into the organization chart, if necessary, when finding opinion leaders. Opinion leaders are not just those at your level. They can be everywhere. I remember once having a great relationship with a member of the board. This person was two or three levels above me, but I saw the need to seek out his opinion. I upgraded because it was necessary. Finally, observe the impact of the actions of opinion leaders and the impact that they have throughout the organization. Note the impact they have on things that are specifically related to HR.

Sense of urgency

The next thing that you will find important in building reputation is having a sense of urgency. This means that we should always be shifting gears for higher speed. HR must have a reputation for getting things done quickly. This could require the HR exec to change the framework of delegation in the HR department. If necessary, so be it. Once again, it is important to mention technology. Use technology that is efficient and effective. Avoid using technology just because it is there and available, especially if it is not efficient.

Remember to prioritize quickly so that you can act quickly. It is important to make decisions carefully. This means acquiring as much information as possible. It can also mean having a decision matrix. Include all of the HR procedures and processes that you can. It can lead to faster and higher impact actions from the HR department. One thing to watch out for is over-commitment. Take on only what you can get done back in a reasonable amount of time. It is ok to say "no" once in a while.

Responsiveness

The requirements for HR execs to be more agile have been growing in recent years. Technology has helped cause that. The need to respond quickly and accurately is now a strategic business requirement for many organizations. The major components of this responsiveness include total information, brand awareness, benefits of quick responses, demonstrating success, training people on new services, building a reputation, and positioning yourself within your department.

Total information

The most important blend through which to filter information flows are the blends of other people. The HR exec needs to view needs from the other person's perspective, rather than as a senior exec, a line employee, or even someone within a chart.

It is essential to determine a framework for information needs. In many ways, it is like establishing a decision matrix. The framework must include what HR needs to know, who needs to know it, the time that they need to know it, and in what format that it should be provided. It is also important within the framework to determine who is going to be the provider of the information. Attention to detail is very important in developing that information for the framework.

One thing that I have learned is that some data information seems to be more valid and reliable than others. Thus, it is always important to know your data sources. A previous history with the data source is terrific. You know exactly what you can expect. When a new data source is being developed, it is necessary to test the data to insure that it is providing what you need. This is true for both internal and external information and data sources. It is also important to determine whether the data collection is from a friendly source or an unfriendly source. A friendly source is one that has your interest at heart. An unfriendly source is one that has its own agenda or is seeking to destroy the concept of win-win in the information processes of HR.

Data collection processes need to be monitored. This is true whether you are using an employee survey, focus group, work samples, organizational archives, or some other form of data collection process. The process needs to be one that the HR exec feels is of high integrity. Monitoring may lead to modification. Modification is fine, when necessary. It is a good idea to change and improve the situation even if you have to swallow your pride. Make certain all the criteria that you established for successful data collection are used. These would include exactly what you think you would include, things such as timelines, formatting, and ease of use. Perhaps the most important aspect is the timeline. Make certain that there is an established deadline for receiving the data and/or information.

When you are working with in house or external sources, it is very important that fact always be distinguished from opinion because the rational drives the leaders in HR. It is very important that we know whether we are dealing with a fundamental truth, or whether we are dealing with someone that has particular feelings towards the given situation.

Brand awareness

When considering brand awareness, it is important to consider the answers to the following questions, including: (1) What is your department best known for?, (2) What is it that your department does better than anything else?, and (3) Are you fortunate enough to have an HR department that does everything so well that each and every HR activity or program is well liked and received by everyone? The best way to obtain this brand awareness is to consistently assess your existing brand strategy. This means identifying various programs that may require greater awareness throughout the organization or in specific functions and upper levels throughout the organization.

Staying on top of brand awareness means that you must talk constantly to your users in order to know what they are thinking. Just talking to the executives is a trap. This does not mean that the HR execs must talk to all people at all levels from all functions, yet this would be a great idea if it were feasible. HR folks need to be talking constantly to the people who are using HR services.

Some of these conversations may lead to the use of new branding strategies. Changing brand strategy is a part of the world of marketing. The willingness to make changes makes it easy for an HR exec to clear up a misconception that people might have for the HR departments. These may be uncovered from time to time. These misconceptions may be minor in nature or they may require major surgery. The willingness to make the change is the key to short- and long-term success. When these changes are made, it is wonderful to take advantage of other people's success in applying it to your own situation. Importing someone else's best practices for branding HR is a highly beneficial action.

Benefits of services

Responsiveness is a dual pronged issue. Although it is necessary that everyone knows what the benefits of services are, it is also important that everyone feels that the services offered are based upon the strategy that impacts the business. In order to accomplish this, every HR staff person needs to be a part time generalist, becoming very familiar with every aspect of HR activities. It is true that many questions should be referred to a specialist, such as the comps and benefits manager or the training supervisor. It is also true that people need to be able to answer the easy or simple questions in order to demonstrate their breadth of knowledge of what is going on in HR. It is important to know what people like and dislike. This information can help us assess what we are doing and it can also help us to determine where we need to do a better job of branding in selling our services. It can lead to different statements about the features or benefits of a particular HR service, activity, or program.

Ease and access are very important variables when it comes to benefits for services. Access may be live or hard copy. It can also be completely need driven. The bottom line is that people will be able to get it quickly in an understandable format. Another aspect of this is that while selling services and making access easy, it is important to know that whatever positioning you may be using for HR services is beneficial across generation, gender, etc.

The HR exec and the HR department should be seen as partners, not as controllers. HR should be doing whatever is feasible to help people to be successful. There will be times when this means taking a position because of a principle or law. HR policies, practices, activities, and programs should be seen as means for enhancing business success. Knowing the benefits with the largest impact is an important source of information. This allows HR to make connections based upon highly valued results. This impact should be based on some quantitative information.

Whenever some aspect of delivering services is working, it may be time to call upon your network for help. It may be time to pull people together and have a face-to-face meeting about a certain issue or aspect that is not going well. Seize the opportunities to consider what can be done differently. The execution of that plan is critical to perceived success.

Demonstrate success

How do you know when you are successful? What criteria for success have you established? Always have a set of criteria in place that allows you to determine how successful you are. This is a very, very important aspect of responsiveness. You need to respond when people wonder how HR is doing. An important aspect in this, of course, is knowing how your users define success. You may even want to include some of their definitions of success among your criteria. What you really want to do is meld together the success strategy of the HR exec and HR department and the success strategy of people that you are providing services to.

This may sound like there is need to keep score—which there is. A scorecard of departmental standing should be developed. Then send it to the appropriate people. It may or may not be something for the whole world to see, but it certainly will be able to sell different folks inside the organization on how and what HR is doing.

A fundamental managing principle in considering success is a focus on incremental success. Whenever a big bang or development appears, it is a great opportunity to sound the trumpets. Regular, incremental success goes a long way and shows people the favorable trend. HR execs and departments will always be selling successes. This means that we will always be winning over our detractors. The requirement of being optimistic is so important yet being realistic is critical as well.

Train people on new services

When introducing a new service, make sure that all your people know everything. It may be something new coming from your comp and benefits unit, your recruiting unit, or your training unit, but make sure that everybody is familiar with the change. A good side of that is, of course, that the people you serve know as much as they possibly can. If there is any doubt, provide training.

This is a good time to think through legal issues that should be considered before, during, and after the training. Legal issues are ever present and will not go away. The need to quickly run things through legally is a healthy approach when considering how these services are going to introduced and operationalized.

The important issue is training users. The answer to this question should be based upon a small trial to see if people will need the training or not. If training is required, make sure that all the HR folks that are doing training get together and work from the same page, presenting little or no variation in presentation. The new service is a new service and this is what it looks like, sounds like, and how it works. Make sure you measure the impact of the training. An on-going aspect of this may include providing refreshers. A colleague and I once worked together every year; he was the comp and benefits executive and I was the training executive. Everybody, every year, went through updated training because it was a task done yearly and we thought that people needed to be refreshed. It is the same as needing to refresh yourself every year when you work on your income taxes.

Build a reputation

Remember that reputation begins with orientation. It is true that your recruiters have an impact on the opinion of new employees. An employee has other data collections that also affect reputation, yet orientation is a key. It normally includes more than one person and it offers an introduction to the organization, so the orientation should be a great one. You can only do this if you know what your reputation is built upon. This, of course, gets back to the whole branding effort.

Reputation is everyone's responsibility. If an HR exec tries to build a reputation alone, a lower level of success will be obtained. Everyone needs to be focused on reputation. It is important that everybody needs to repair damage to a reputation when it is identified. The repair effort, however, should always include the HR exec. You do want everyone to build the reputation, but a repair opportunity really should be led by the HR exec. This could also include a well positioned and accomplished mentor for the HR exec. Mentors are a wonderful help around issues of reputation. We must take the time to chat with them so that we can get help in repairing the damage.

This probably sounds like you need to care deeply about your reputation. You do. It is not possible to care too much about your reputation. It does not just include your reputation at work either. In your neighborhood and around town when people know where you work and what you do can form an opinion about you and your organization. The issue here is that reputation is not just an inside the office issue. Thus, it is important to walk the talk. It also is important to know when to hold them and know when to fold them. Actually, you always just hold on to your reputation and you never fold.

Position yourself in the department

It is important to position yourself as a business partner. One of the actions that is, such an important part of this business partnership is that you show your return on investment to other executives. HR spends a lot of money. Every single penny must be spent wisely, creating positive impacts. Showing executives how well HR uses its financial resources by showing the positive ROI to staff and line executives is quite conducive to promoting yourself as a business partner to them.

You may not like to blow your own horn, but often times it is necessary to let people know how HR is contributing. This will avoid people taking HR for granted. It will also avoid people thinking that HR is a necessary evil. When you tell others how HR is a contributor, you consistently will find it easier to get support for what you are trying to accomplish. All of the things you should be trying to do, of course, should always be on the cutting edge, given the resources that you have to spend on HR activities, processes, and programs.

Influencing skills are important resources. Influencing is a little bit art, but mostly skill. Have you read about or attended a training program on influencing skills? I have found such training to be very, very valuable. And when the training is over, of course, it is important to use the skills. Shying away from good influencing behavior just is not an option.

Everyone has heard how important it is to spend time with opinion leaders. It also is important to spend time with well-positioned people. Top leaders are sometimes well positioned and some times they are not. Well-positioned people have the respect and the ear of key executives in the organization. Spend time with well-positioned people and discuss business issues with them. If they want it to be a social conversation, let them drive the conversation for a couple of minutes, but re-emphasize the business that you wish to discuss with them and state your case. This will help you maintain your seat at the table. If you are more expert at this than others, you will have a greater chance of success.

Realize success

It is true that success comes to those who work for it. HR execs and HR departments that get their services used consider this use successful. Create a reproach that you want to use and execute it. Be certain to include the following elements in your plan and in the execution of that plan for the realization of success. The elements include the management of expectations, the reporting of measures, quality, details, the competency of staff, the sale value, the enhancement and measurement of performance, and lastly, the feedback process.

Manage expectations

Managing expectations begins with knowing what the short-term goals are for the organization and the HR department. This requires HR folks to listen carefully to the dilemmas expressed by business units. Also, the HR exec needs to be aware of any dilemmas that may exist in HR itself. When uncovering dilemmas, it is important to ask a few questions, but to spend more time listening.

Equally as important as managing expectations is the need to discuss the current strength of each business unit and the strength of HR itself. In the spirit of appreciation, it is essential to know who has what strength because that information will help HR to succeed in one of the most important tasks, succession planning.

It is important to be precise on how you can approach the resolutions of dilemmas and the development of the current strength. It is important to be clear about what you have the capacity to deliver as a HR department and on what things you will need outside expertise for. Also, be precise on when you can deliver. People appreciate knowing timelines.

Thus, knowing your own capacities is essential. In this case, capacity is a strength and a weakness. This will present over promising. A final important issue is to get agreement on the roles that folks other than HR have. Whenever collaboration is required and when problems need to be solved in any dilemma, an essential approach is to get an agreement on everybody's role, particularly the roles of the business unit that are being helped.

Report measures

The line of measurement plan for all customers is essential. The simpler, the better. I was reading an article recently that stated that the only information sought out by others is a simple statement about how the company or department is doing. A report to appropriate executives is always a wise move. Discuss with your boss which executives need which measures of information. The provision of interim reports may be important. A wonderful approach for reporting information is to put it all on a website and make it available for people whom you have identified as needing the measurement information. Making reports on-line makes more sense and is a better use of HR time than sending reports out individually, even when using e-mail. When appropriate reports are available for people to download, you can avoid assembly line reporting.

Models for measuring ROI are good measurement tools for HR. It is possible to find excellent examples in the literature. If preferred, you can develop your own as well. Double check your models and make sure that you establish criteria for varying levels of success. Everyone in your department should be completely informed about the entire system of reports. This makes them aware of the level of success and allows them to be of service when someone calls or e-mails them looking for information.

Reports that you write should be impactful, not technical. They should be able to be read quickly and should leave the reader without questions. A worthwhile target is to have each report be no more than one page. This will help the HR department to not over-report. Finally, be certain that your models, your information, and your reports all relate to business results.

Quality

Much of what we know and do about quality has been thoroughly addressed. This section may be more of a review than anything else. To ensure quality, actions include: (1) hiring HR staff who believe in quality, (2) consistently and constantly auditing quality, (3) willingness to make changes if the audit suggests that necessity, (4) setting standards for quality in all HR activity and programming, (5) avoiding making quality an end in itself, (6) asking customers for quality feedback, and (7) willingness to borrow and reframe best practices from other successful HR groups.

Details

There is a constant need to determine what level of detail is required throughout the efforts in order to realize success. It is easy to say that reminding everyone that it is all in the details would be enough, but of course, this is not true. It is important to specify a level of detail. Once that level of detail has been established, no one in HR should settle for anything else than full details. This has been determined through discussion and agreement on what level of detail is required for the management of success throughout HR.

Staff competence

HR execs must make every effort to hire competent staff and build their expertise over time. This may be the most important consideration in the realization of success. There are always some appropriate actions for HR execs to take and make sure that others in HR take appropriate actions.

First of all, for staff competence to be realized, the staff must be cross-trained. This is highly motivational for the human resource department because it allows the HR exec to moderate the peaks and valleys of job loads. A successful HR department can be even more successful if the time and energy spent in cross training is time and energy that grows people into new areas of development particularly that resembles a promotion or perception of a promotion to the employees.

Other actions include the provision of training updates, including in house and out house for all HR staff. Avoid favoring training for one HR sub-function over another. Articles to read that address new HR policies and practices should be given to all of the HR folks. A discussion of those materials should follow the assigned reading. Finally, formal HR education should be encouraged and incentives should be offered for the staff to become accredited by the Society for Human Resource Management (SHRM).

Another interesting option could be to assign staff to spend one day per year in a line business unit working as a line employee. This keeps them up to date with the tasks that they are hiring for. There also is certain to be conversations about the good things that HR does and new things that employees would like HR to do. Rotating staff among all business units on a constant basis will have a tremendously positive impact.

It is essential to conduct an HR competency study every year. A competency study published by SHRM is the place to start. It is always important to know how well HR is doing in developing its competency over time. When opportunities for improving competency arise, it is important to (1) make funds available to send staff to professional conferences, (2) make sure they receive special training in coaching, consulting skills, and team building, and (3) be a mentor to them or help them to find a mentor. All the actions taken to enhance staff competence should show value, and this means that staff will take actions that impact productivity, quality, customer service, and cost reduction.

Enhance user performance

Since HR exists to be of service to many others, it is important to remember that HR does not exist for its own purposes. HR exists to help line business units be successful in what they want to accomplish. Enhancing user performance begins with the confirmation of user application of new HR policies and procedures. When a new policy, procedure, or program is introduced, it is critical to clarify the appropriate actions that must be taken if and when those actions become necessary. The people that we are trying to help often times are overwhelmed with things to do, which then causes them to ignore certain areas that may need attention.

Staff should always feel like they are partners with line units. It is critical to avoid the "we versus they" mentality. Partnering with line units should include offering consulting help to line units and should also involve coaching a person or people in line units as the need appears.

Another way to enhance user performance is to conduct general and specific training needs on HR issues, especially those programs with a high priority designation. Of course, it is critical to require that the people who are supposed to be present are going to be there. Avoid letting people miss training that they need to attend. Aligned with that is the need to maintain a knowledge management system of stories from business units. Stories will always come up when training is provided. They should be captured and be used for learning processes continuously in the organization.

It is important to avoid over-segmenting user groups. This means avoiding smoke stack organizational structures, as it clouds many things in the organization and sends the perception of a lack of fairness. When meeting with users regularly, it is important to meet across functions. Finally, consider providing score sheets for all user groups on user performance. This will take some development time and energy, but is a useful way to draw attention to what you feel line units need to be addressing.

Feedback process

Feedback should be multi-directional. When it is multi-directional, it provides opportunity for feedback to be seen through multiple channels. This is essential to the work of HR. As was mentioned earlier, it will be helpful to conduct focus groups for HR departments. Focus groups were mentioned, but referenced in the context of conducting focus groups to find out what line units need. In this case, we are talking about conducting focus groups of HR by an appropriate consultant. The HR exec should be a part of other department focus groups as it is appropriate.

As much as possible, encourage face-to-face feedback rather than electronic feedback. Though useful, electronic feedback is often times not 100% what it needs to be because you do not have the opportunity to see people's facial expressions and other body language. Whether you choose face-to-face or electronic feedback provision, be certain to listen to all stakeholders. Everyone needs a voice.

When providing feedback, it is more important to provide positive feedback than negative feedback. This does not mean to avoid negative feedback when it is required. What it does mean is that a work place will be more energized with a greater ratio of positive to negative feedback, as opposed to a one-to-one ratio of positive to negative feedback. Getting immediate feedback in critical situations is also very important. Avoid being judgmental, but listen objectively, focusing on information and consequences.

Conclusion

The intention of this article was to provide a set of ideas that you could call principle, tenets, or practices of HR and actions that can be taken by the department to get their service utilized. Do keep in mind, though, that what's been presented here is a total action plan. The idea is that HR execs do them all with the remainder of HR assisting.

It is easy to write about what should be done in isolation, but in reality, they are all in some kind of a stew feeding off of each other. They are constantly in motion. It is essential to keep all efforts coordinated. HR needs to come across as responsive, organized, focused on success, and concerned about reputation. Nothing, of course, is more important than HR efforts to build relationships for, with, and through everyone in the organization. Everyone should be targeted to form new relationships.

Finally, HR execs should use every conversation to tell a story about the impact of human resources. This needs to be done in a subtle way. You must avoid giving the impression that you are always pounding on your chest. Selling services must be your top priority, and that is best communicated by telling stories about HR impact. An earlier version of this chapter appeared in Employment Relations Today, Wiley Interscience, Summer, 2006, Volume 33, Number 2, pages 43–56.

Reference

Bendixon, M., Abratt, R., and Myres, H (2001). *Knowledge products: Their conceptualization and properties*. Bestuursdinamika, 10(3), 1–17.

Part Four

Critical human resource issues

CHAPTER 19

Employee management and innovation

Michael Ottenbacher

School of Hospitality & Tourism Management
San Diego State University
San Diego, CA 92182, USA

Introduction

Given increasing global competition and even more rapid changes in technology and in consumer needs and expectations, hospitality firms' ability to innovate is regarded more and more as a key factor in ensuring success. Hospitality firms can no longer rely on their existing service portfolio, as customers increasingly demand and expect—and competitors will do their best to provide—new and improved services. To succeed in such a turbulent environment, hospitality businesses must systematically develop innovations and become more customer focused (Cooper & Edgett, 1999). In this context, innovation can be seen as a fundamental marketing activity and an important resource for the survival and growth of service firms. Accordingly, customer focus requires managers to understand customer needs and behavior and to manage service encounters between employees and customers in ways that create satisfaction (Lovelock & Wirtz, 2004).

Innovation should be viewed as an opportunity to succeed in a competitive world, because it is through innovations that businesses strengthen their competitiveness and effectively create value for consumers (Drucker, 1985). In addition to creating value, hospitality firms should also differentiate their services from those of their competitors and find new ways to attract customers and improve service quality by offering innovative products and services. Because service firms such as hospitality businesses often have the same hardware, differentiating their services is quite challenging. However, they can distinguish their services and create value with their software, their employees. From this perspective, employees with customer contact can be seen as a competitive advantage for the firm. Harrison and Enz (2005) argued that the individuals who make up a hospitality business should be regarded as the organization's most valuable assets.

The most influential factor in service work is the direct contact between front-line employees and the customer. Interaction between the customer and the customer service worker can be seen as "the moment of truth" for the firm (Carlzon, 1987, p. 3). This is the moment when the consumer forms important impressions about the firm, which influence his or her future decisions. One unpleasant service encounter between an employee and the customer can negate the overall excellent performance of all the other employees. Consumers tend to concentrate on the weakest incident when evaluating the whole hospitality service experience; therefore, hospitality services are only as good as their weakest element. While a small, independent hotel might only have several hundred of these moments of truth every day, a large chain such as Marriot or Hilton might have several million moments of truth a day. Employees with customer contact can therefore be seen as a competitive advantage or disadvantage for the firm. Consequently, it is important for management to ensure that all customer service workers always act toward customers in the appropriate way.

Although the importance of employees has been noted in service innovation studies (de Brentani, 2001), our knowledge about their role and the issue of how to best manage human resources with regard to the outcome of service innovations is still relatively scarce. Furthermore, at the start of the 21st century, human resource literature still appears to have failed to study front-line employees. Human resources management (HRM) practices developed primarily from manufacturing are not always applicable to the more complicated social reality and greater variability of service industries (Korczynski, 2002). Accordingly, the task and challenge is to derive knowledge and conduct research that can add to our understanding of the specific nature of HRM in service work and service innovation. This chapter, therefore, addresses the gaps in the literature by examining the impact of employee management practices on hospitality innovation success.

First, the term *innovation* will be explained, followed by a discussion of why employee management is important in the service sector. A review of HRM practices in the hospitality industry will illustrate why employee management practices are also critical for this segment. Next, the relationship between employees, management, and hospitality innovation will be presented, including four key aspects of employee management practices that are critical in regard to hospitality innovation.

Innovation

Schumpeter (1934), who was one of the first to develop a theory about innovation, defined five areas in which companies can introduce innovation: (a) generation of new or improved products, (b) introduction of new production processes, (c) development of new sales markets, (d) development of new supply markets, and (e) reorganization or restructuring of the company. Another very useful definition was provided by Burgelmann and Maidique (1996), who reasoned that innovations are "the outcome of the innovation process, which can be defined as the combined activities leading to new, marketable products and services and/or new production and delivery systems" (p. 2). Successful innovations are, in general, the result of both effectively designed structures and professionally implemented processes.

Previous research into service innovation shows that success does not depend on the result of managing one or two activities very well. Instead, it is the result of a more comprehensive approach that manages a large number of aspects competently and in a balanced manner (Johne & Storey, 1998). Basically, the proficiency of the market-oriented development process and the focus on the synergy between the requirements of the new service and the resources of the firm influence the success of a new service. In addition, the attractiveness of the marketplace and the ability to launch innovations that respond to the demands of the market help determine the financial success of the firm. Product advantage has been identified as the number one success factor in product development. In services, however, while the service product is important, it is not considered to be the key success factor. The perceived quality of the interaction with the customer is of greater relevance for new services (de Brentani, 1991). The expertise and enthusiasm of front-line staff is a particularly crucial aspect, as it has a direct effect on customers' perception of service quality. Although previous studies have identified the important role that employees play in service innovation success (Atuahene-Gima, 1996; de Brentani, 2001), the HRM practices that facilitate the development of market-oriented innovations are poorly understood.

Importance of employee management in the service industry

Service employees are enormously critical to the success of the organization they represent, because they directly impact on customers' satisfaction (Zeithaml & Bitner, 2000). Because having a customer focus produces better service quality, service firms should be customer-oriented (Hartline, Maxham, & McKee, 2000). Furthermore, employees are responsible for personifying and implementing a customer-oriented strategy, because customers often judge a service firm largely on the service received from employees (Parasuraman, Zeithaml, & Berry, 1985). Therefore, it is important that managers understand how they can encourage employees to carry out a customer-oriented strategy.

The attitudes and behaviors of service employees can significantly influence customers' perceptions of the service. Therefore, service organizations must find ways to effectively manage their service employees' attitudes and behaviors so that they can deliver high-quality services (Chebat & Kollias, 2000). The human element in services means that service quality depends heavily on human resource strategies (Zeithaml & Bitner, 2000), which are management's tools for effectively managing its employees. However, it is often challenging for management to control employees in service firms (Schneider & Bowen, 1995). The argument is, therefore, that employees will be customer focused only if management can gain employee commitment to a service culture, rather than obedience (Canning, 1999). Groenroos (2000) has characterized a service culture as a culture in which everybody appreciates good service, and in which good service is given to the internal and external customers.

Employee management in the hotel industry

Because of the importance of gaining a competitive advantage, employee management is an important element of organizational planning within the hospitality industry. Employee management considerations, such as the ability to attract qualified staff, are one of the top concerns of hospitality managers (Enz, 2001). Unfortunately, many hospitality organizations at both the small and corporate levels neglect to recognize the tactical importance of human capital considerations (Harrison & Enz, 2005). In many hospitality firms, the critical customer-contact jobs are performed by the newest, least trained employees, who are often hired on a part-time basis only. Furthermore, they are often unskilled and have low salaries. However, they can have a major influence on profits and on customer experiences of service quality.

The impact of HRM within the labor-intensive hotel sector has been highly under-researched (Hoque, 2000). Hoque described the hotel industry management style as autocratic, ad hoc, low empowerment, and lacking long-term strategic vision. Goldsmith, Nickson, Sloan, and Wood (1997) also had a pessimistic opinion about the professional and innovative adoption of HRM practices in the hotel industry. Their view was supported by the research of Kelliher and Johnson (1987), who found that personnel management practices were highly simplistic and reactive rather than strategic and systematic.

Price (1994) studied 241 hotel operations in the UK and concluded that HRM practices in the hotel sector are not all ideal or professional. One of the key findings was that there is a strong correlation between the size of an establishment and the quality

419

of its HRM practices. This finding leads to the conclusion that although the majority of large hotel organizations or chains seem to have adopted professional HRM practices, this development has not reached smaller operations (Goldsmith *et al.*, 1997).

Baum (1995) had a more positive view. He argued that hotel operations should view and use HRM strategies as a competitive advantage. Indeed, Anastassova and Purcell (1995) found that hotels had moved away from an autocratic management style, and results of a study by Gilbert and Guerrier (1997) indicated that hotels empowered their employees. Similarly, Harrington and Akehurst (1996) found that a very high percentage (82%) of hotels within their sample invested resources to train employees in quality-related endeavors. The results of a study by Enz and Siguaw (2000) suggest a positive view of employee management in the U.S. hospitality industry, in that successful hotel operations have learned how to deploy human resources to build and sustain a competitive advantage in their services. The development and implementation of excellent human resources systems create value for customers and profitability for hotel organizations (Enz & Siguaw, 2000). Hoque's (2000) research revealed a high reported usage of HRM practices, particularly in relation to recruitment and selection techniques, empowerment, and training of employees. Hoque's results suggested that the HRM theory and practice of hotels may not be as divergent as previously believed, and that the better performing hotels were those that adopted a quality approach in their HRM practices.

Yet, the role of employee management practices in the success of service innovation has largely been neglected, despite the general acceptance that service employees play a critical role in customer satisfaction formation and perceptions of service quality (Storey & Easingwood, 1998). So, how can hospitality firms effectively manage their employees so that they are an asset to the organization rather than a negative influence on innovation success? Given the crucial importance of employees in the service industry, it is the aim of this chapter to discuss how employee management practices contribute to the success of hospitality innovations.

Employee management factors that are related to innovation success

The following sections outline findings from a wide-ranging literature search, as well as from empirical studies of successful innovation management in the hospitality industry conducted by the author and his colleagues (Ottenbacher & Gnoth, 2005; Ottenbacher & Gray, 2004). These findings suggest that the four HRM practices that are most important for success in hospitality innovation are (a) a strategic approach to HRM, (b) training of employees, (c) behavior-based evaluation, and (d) empowerment of staff.

Strategic human resource management (SHRM)

The organizational strategy literature has moved toward the resource-based theory of competitive advantage, emphasizing the internal resources of an organization and viewing human resources as a source of value (Bae & Lawler, 2000). Competitive advantage through employees is becoming more important, because other sources of competitive advantage are easier to access and therefore easier to copy (Pfeffer, 1994). However, the link between SHRM and innovation is poorly understood, partly because of a lack of consensus on how to define SHRM (Martell & Carroll, 1995). This lack of a consistent definition of SHRM is due to insufficient development of appropriate theoretical constructs (Guest, 1997). The key difference between traditional conceptions of HRM and SHRM is the extent to which HRM is integrated with the strategic decision-making processes that direct organizational efforts to cope with the environment (Bennett, Ketchen, & Schultz, 1998). A suitable definition of SHRM may therefore be "the pattern of planned human resource deployments and activities intended to enable an organization to achieve its goals" (Wright & McMahan, 1992, p. 298).

Organizational researchers have stressed the merit of SHRM, which is the practice of developing appropriate human resources policies that are in line with organizational strategy (Lado & Wilson, 1994). SHRM should also have a market orientation (Huselid, Jackson, & Schuler, 1997), because it is important for firms to adapt the HRM practices to any challenging needs of the market (Bowen, Schneider, & Kim, 2000). In addition, the resource-based view suggests that management should view its employees as an asset rather than as a cost factor (Bennett *et al.*, 1998; Bowen *et al.*, 2000; Huselid *et al.*, 1997; Lado & Wilson, 1994; Pfeffer, 1994). The premise underlying SHRM is that firms adopting a particular strategy require human resources practices that differ from those required by firms adopting alternative strategies (Jackson & Schuler, 1995; Lado & Wilson, 1994; Wright & McMahan, 1992). In order for an organization to benefit from having a SHRM vision, management has to (a) choose a strategy that enhances the unique characteristics of a firm's human talent, and (b) establish human resources policies that increase the value of these human assets (Bennett *et al.*, 1998).

Empirical research suggests that SHRM practices as a whole affect a firm's performance (Bae & Lawler, 2000; Harris & Ogbonna, 2001; Huselid *et al.*, 1997). For example, Huselid *et al.*'s study of 293 U.S. firms drawn from a wide range of industries found significant relationships between SHRM effectiveness and employee productivity, cash flow, and market value. This finding suggests that organizations that want to improve their performance should focus their attention on harnessing their human resources (Harris & Ogbonna, 2001). Hospitality innovations that are supported by an SHRM approach achieve higher financial results (Ottenbacher & Gnoth, 2005). Thus HRM practices of successful projects are strategic, unique, and integrated, and therefore difficult for competitors to duplicate. As a consequence, the firm has the ability to attract excellent staff.

Training

Training entails improving employees' knowledge, skills, attitudes, or social behavior, or any combination of these (Cascio, 1989). Training of employees is critical in order to enhance front-line expertise (de Brentani & Cooper, 1992; Storey & Easingwood, 1998) and in launch preparation (Cooper, Easingwood, Edgett, Kleinschmidt, & Storey, 1994; Edgett, 1994). If a service firm wants to have a competitive advantage through its human resources, it must invest in the necessary training programs to ensure that the workforce has the appropriate skills and abilities, not only to meet short-term requirements, but also to anticipate changing job requirements over time (Kochan & Dyer, 1993). Service employees need not only technical skills and knowledge training, but also training in interactive skills (Schneider & Bowen, 1995), so that they can provide courteous, caring, responsive, and emphatic service for innovation projects. Bowen *et al.* (2000) argued that training for new services should cover issues of emotional labor (Hochschild, 1983). Thus, investment in training and the development of employees is a crucial element in HRM, because service firms have first to develop and generate the competencies that are necessary to produce the desired output for the new service, which will in turn be valued by customers.

The adaptability of service employees in service encounters is a key factor affecting performance. Adaptability, however, requires systematically structured training for service employees, so that they can manage different role demands (Chebat & Kollias, 2000). Employee development is an investment; by providing flexible and adaptive employees, it enables the firm to survive and grow (Beer, Spector, Lawrence, Mills, & Walton, 1985). In organizations whose employees viewed the HRM practices under which they worked in more positive terms, customers reported that they received superior service quality (Schneider & Bowen, 1992).

A strong commitment to training in the hospitality industry has been associated with several benefits, such as improved self-esteem of employees, reduced turnover, higher customer satisfaction, and stronger commitment to the organization (Roehl & Swerdlow, 1999). Enz and Siguaw (2000) argued that in the hotel sector, employee training has become an increasingly critical factor in increasing service quality, reducing labor costs, and increasing productivity. Ottenbacher and Gnoth (2005) showed that firms with successful hospitality innovation projects consider training to be a high priority. Furthermore, these firms provide interpersonal as well as general skills training, in a systematically structured manner. Overall, however, hospitality organizations do not spend particularly high amounts of money on training.

Behavior-based evaluation

Hartline *et al.* (2000) argued that behavior-based evaluation of front-line employees is a factor that management can control in order to support a customer-oriented strategy. Behavior-based evaluation focuses on front-line employees' customer-oriented behavior (e.g., friendliness) rather than specific work-related outcomes (e.g., quotas). Behavior-based evaluation is particularly suited to employees with customer contact, and it encourages employee performance that is consistent with customer expectation of service quality (Zeithaml, Berry, & Parasuraman, 1988). This type of staff performance evaluation is designed to reduce role conflict and ambiguity and to encourage employees to focus on improving customer service experiences rather than outcomes such as quotas (Chebat & Kollias, 2000). Employees who have positive and encouraging managers are also likely to have better interactions with customers, who in turn are likely to experience superior service quality (Schneider & Bowen, 1995). Learning theory corroborates the conclusion that behavioral employee evaluations are an excellent tool for supporting desirable employee behaviors (Hartline *et al.*, 2000).

Furthermore, research has shown that behavior-based evaluation also increases employee competencies (Cravens, Ingram, LaForge, & Young, 1993), job satisfaction (Oliver & Anderson, 1994), and adaptability (Scott & Bruce, 1994). A study into the U.S. hotel sector also indicated that behavior-based evaluation is positively related to employees' organizational commitment (Hartline *et al.*, 2000). In contrast, staff evaluations based on financial outcomes can be harmful to the long-term success of the firm, particularly if a focus on short-term profits diverts attention from improving customer satisfaction (Anderson & Oliver, 1987). Successful hospitality innovation projects evaluate front-line employee performance in terms of ability to provide courteous service, resolve customer complaints and problems, and meet customer needs. Successful projects also evaluate the employees' degree of commitment to customers and to the organization (Ottenbacher & Gnoth, 2005).

Empowerment

Empowerment refers to the power and autonomy that employees are given to exercise control over job-related situations and decisions (Conger & Kanungo, 1988). The empowerment of service industry staff is almost unavoidable (Chebat & Kollias, 2000), because employees need flexibility to adapt their behaviors to the demands of each service encounter (Argyris, 1998). The more heterogeneous services become, the more employees need to adapt their behaviors to specific needs (Chebat & Kollias, 2000). Bowen and Lawler (1992) suggested that empowerment is recommended when service delivery involves managing a relationship, as opposed to simply performing a transaction. Reasons for establishing a relationship with customers are (a) to increase loyalty, (b) to get ideas about improving the service delivery system, and (c) to obtain ideas for new services.

Empowered employees are likely to have more confidence, which enhances their creativity and problem-solving skills (Kelley, Longfellow, & Malehorn, 1996). Further advantages include faster responses to customer needs and problems, and enthusiastic and warm customer interactions (Bowen & Lawler, 1992; Lovelock & Wirtz, 2004). However, despite broad support, empowerment has practical limits, and the effects of empowerment require further empirical proof (Argyris, 1998; Chebat & Kollias, 2000). Hospitality managers who give employees power and autonomy to exercise control over job-related situations and decisions may contribute to enhanced staff–customer relations. Successful innovation projects allow employees to use their discretion to solve problems; furthermore, the hospitality management trusts employees, transfers many responsibilities to them, and encourages and provides opportunities for personal initiatives (Ottenbacher & Gnoth, 2005).

Research into the German hospitality industry did not suggest that selective staffing is related to performance (Ottenbacher & Gnoth, 2005, Ottenbacher & Gray, 2005). The nonimpact of selective staffing is surprising, because preliminary interviews indicated that this factor was a key predictor of hospitality innovation success. Indeed, the literature argues that staff selection is the most potent management device for ensuring that organizations have willing staff who are able to deliver quality service and stay motivated to perform in a customer-oriented way (Zeithaml & Bitner, 2000). Inadequate hiring and selection procedures may also lead to the hiring of employees with skill deficiencies and result in service quality problems (Zeithaml *et al.*, 1988). One explanation for the non-impact of selective staffing is that staff shortages might make it harder for managers to be as selective as they would like to be. For example, at the start of the new century, the German hospitality sector was unable to fill 80,000 job openings. The limited role of selective staffing should therefore be interpreted with caution. Hospitality managers should be careful about the consequences of not being selective in their staffing efforts.

Conclusions

This chapter has focused on the important role played by service employees in hospitality innovation, and it has outlined how hospitality managers can encourage employees to implement a customer-oriented innovation strategy. A customer-oriented strategy not only produces better service quality but also improves the chance of success for hospitality innovations. In order to encourage employees to implement a customer-oriented innovation strategy, hospitality firms should implement appropriate HRM strategies and incorporate them into the firm's strategic business planning and innovation activities. Managers should also evaluate front-line employees' performance in relation to customer-oriented behaviors—such as their ability to provide courteous service and meet customer needs— rather than specific work-related outcomes such as quotas or sales. Employee training programs should be given a high priority, and firms are advised to provide interpersonal and general skills training to improve the introduction and delivery of new services. Empowerment is often preached but not always practiced. Managers should transfer responsibility, provide opportunities for personal initiative, allow employees to use their discretion and judgment in solving problems, and trust employees to deliver quality services. Careful hiring and selection of staff may help to ensure higher quality service and greater customer satisfaction.

In summary, hospitality innovation success is not the result of managing one or two activities very well, but of managing a large number of aspects competently and in a balanced manner. The results of studies in the hospitality industry emphasize the importance of employee management as a critical aspect of hospitality innovation management. It pays for hospitality businesses to invest in the internal human resource capabilities and to view employees as an asset rather than a cost factor.

References

Anastassova, L., & Purcell, K. (1995). Human resource management in the Bulgarian hotel industry: From command to empowerment. *International Journal of Hospitality Management, 14*(2), 171–185.

Anderson, E., & Oliver, R. L. (1987). Perspectives on behavior-based versus outcome-based salesforce control systems. *Journal of Marketing, 51*, 76–88.

Argyris, C. (1998, May/June). Empowerment: The emperor's new clothes. *Harvard Business Review*, 98–105.

Atuahene-Gima, K. (1996). Differential potency of factors affecting innovation performance in manufacturing and services firms in Australia. *Journal of Product Innovation Management, 13*, 35–52.

Bae, J., & Lawler, J. J. (2000). Organizational and HRM strategies in Korea: Impact on firm performance in an emerging economy. *Academy of Management Journal, 43*(3), 502–517.

Baum, T. (1995). *Managing human resources in the European tourism and hospitality industry: A strategic approach*. London: Chapman and Hall.

Beer, M., Spector, B., Lawrence, P., Mills, D., & Walton, R. (1985). *Human resource management: A general manager's perspective*. New York: Free Press.

Bennett, N., Ketchen, D. J., & Schultz, E. B. (1998). An examination of factors associated with the integration of human resource management and strategic decision making. *Human Resource Management, 37*(1), 3–16.

Bowen, D. E., & Lawler, E., III. (1992). The empowerment of service workers: What, why, how, and when. *Sloan Management Review, 33,* 31–39.

Bowen, D. E., Schneider, B., & Kim, S. S. (2000). Shaping service cultures through strategic human resource management. In T. A. Swartz & D. Jacobucci (Eds.), *Handbook for services marketing and management* (pp. 439–454). Thousand Oaks, CA: Sage Publications.

Burgelmann, R. A., & Maidique, M. A. (1996). *Strategic management of technology and innovation.* Chicago, IL: Irwin.

Canning, V. (1999). *Being successful in customer care.* Dublin, Ireland: Blackhall.

Carlzon, J. (1987). *The moment of truth.* Cambridge, MA: Ballinger.

Cascio, W.F. (1989). *Managing human resources: Productivity, quality of work life, profits.* New York: McGraw-Hill.

Chebat, J.C., & Kollias, P. (2000). The impact of empowerment on customer contact employees' roles in service organizations. *Journal of Service Research, 3*(1), 66–81.

Conger, J. A., & Kanungo, R. N. (1988). The empowerment process: Integrating theory and practice. *Academy of Management Review, 3,* 471–482.

Cooper, R. G., Easingwood, C. J., Edgett, S., Kleinschmidt, E. J., & Storey, C. (1994). What distinguishes the top performing new products in financial services? *Journal of Product Innovation Management, 11,* 281–299.

Cooper, R. G., & Edgett, S. J. (1999). *Product development for the service sector.* Cambridge, MA: Perseus Books.

Cravens, D. W., Ingram, T. N., LaForge, R. W., & Young, C. E. (1993). Behavior-based and outcome-based salesforce control systems. *Journal of Marketing, 57,* 47–59.

de Brentani, U. (1991). Success factors in developing new business services. *European Journal of Marketing, 25*(2), 33–59.

de Brentani, U. (2001). Innovative versus incremental new business services: Different keys for achieving success. *Journal of Product Innovation Management, 18,* 169–187.

de Brentani, U., & Cooper, R. G. (1992). Developing successful new financial services for businesses. *Industrial Marketing Management, 21,* 231–241.

Drucker, P. F. (1985). *Innovation and entrepreneurship: Practice and principles.* London: Heinemann.

Edgett, S. (1994). The traits of successful new service development. *Journal of Services Marketing, 8*(3), 40–49.

Enz, C. A. (2001). What keeps you up at night? *Cornell Hotel and Restaurant Administration Quarterly, 42*(2), 2–9.

Enz, C. A., & Siguaw, J. A. (2000). Best practices in human resources, *Cornell Hotel and Restaurant Administration Quarterly, 41*(1), 48–61.

Gilbert, D., & Guerrier, Y. (1997). UK hospitality managers past and present. *Service Industries Journal, 17*(1), 115–132.

Goldsmith, A. L., Nickson, D. P., Sloan, D. H., & Wood, R. C. (1997). *Human resource management for hospitality services.* Oxford, UK: International Thomson Business Press.

Groenroos, C. (2000). *Service management and marketing: A customer relationship management approach* (2nd ed.). Chichester, UK: Wiley.

Guest, D. E. (1997). Human resource management and performance: A review and research agenda. *International Journal of Human Resource Management, 8*, 263–276.

Harrington, D., & Akehurst, G. (1996). Service quality and business performance in the UK hotel industry. *International Journal of Hospitality Management, 15*(3), 283–298.

Harris, L. C., & Ogbonna, E. (2001). Strategic human resource management, market orientation, and organizational performance. *Journal of Business Research, 51*, 157–166.

Harrison, J. S., & Enz, C. A. (2005). *Hospitality strategic management: Concepts and cases.* Hoboken, NJ: Wiley.

Hartline, M. D., Maxham J. G., & McKee, D. O. (2000). Corridors of influence in the dissemination of customer-oriented strategy to customer contact employees. *Journal of Marketing, 64*, 35–50.

Hochschild, A. R. (1983). *The managed heart: Commercialization of human feelings.* Berkeley, CA: University of California Press.

Hoque, K. (2000). *Human resource management in the hotel industry: Strategy, innovation and performance.* London: Routledge.

Huselid, M. A., Jackson, S. E., & Schuler, R. J. (1997). Technical and strategic HRM effectiveness as determinants of firm performance. *Academy of Management Journal, 40*(1), 171–188.

Jackson, S. E., & Schuler, R. S. (1995). Understanding human resource management in the context of organizations and their environments. In M.R. Rosenzweig & L.W. Porters (Eds.), *Annual review of psychology* (Vol. 46, pp. 237–264). Palo Alto, CA: Annual Reviews.

Johne, A., & Storey, C. (1998). New service development: A review of literature and annotated bibliography. *European Journal of Marketing, 32*, 184–251.

Kelley, S. W., Longfellow, T., & Malehorn, J. (1996). Organizational determinants of service employees' exercise of routine, creative and deviant discretion. *Journal of Retailing, 72*(2), 135–157.

Kelliher, C., & Johnson, K. (1987). Personnel management in hotels: Some empirical observations. *International Journal of Hospitality Management, 6*(2), 103–108.

Kochan, T. A., & Dyer, L. (1993). Managing transformational change: The role of human resource professionals. *International Journal of Human Resources Management, 4*, 569–590.

Korczynski, M. (2002). *Human resource management in service work.* New York: Palgrave.

Lado, A. A., & Wilson, M. C. (1994). Human resource systems and sustained competitive advantage: A competency-based perspective. *Academy of Management Review, 19*(4), 699–727.

Lovelock, C. H., & Wirtz, J. (2004). *Services marketing: People, technology, strategy* (5th ed.). Upper Saddle River, NJ: Pearson Education.

Martell, K., & Carroll, S. J. (1995). How strategic is HRM? *Human Resource Management, 34*(2), 253–267.

Oliver, R. L., & Anderson E. (1994). An empirical test of the consequences of behavior- and outcome-based sales control systems. *Journal of Marketing, 58*, 53–67.

Ottenbacher, M., & Gnoth, J. (2005). How to develop successful hospitality innovation. *Cornell Hotel and Restaurant Administration Quarterly, 46*(2), 205–222.

Ottenbacher, M., & Gray, B. (2004). The new service development process: The initial stages for hotel innovations. *FIU Hospitality Review, 22*(2), 59–70.

Parasuraman, A., Zeithaml, V. A., & Berry, L. L. (1985). A conceptual model of service quality and its implications for future research. *Journal of Marketing, 49*, 41–50.

Pfeffer, J. (1994). *Competitive advantage through people: Unleashing the power of the work force.* Boston, MA: Harvard Business School Press.

Price, L. (1994). Poor personnel practice in the hotel and catering industry: Does it matter? *Human Resource Management Journal, 4*(4), 44–62.

Roehl, W. S., & Swerdlow, S. (1999). Training and its impact on organizational commitment among lodging employees. *Journal of Hospitality and Tourism Research, 23*(2), 176–194.

Schneider, B., & Bowen, D. E. (1992). Personnel/human resources management in the service sector. *Research in Personnel and Human Resource Management, 10*, 1–30.

Schneider, B., & Bowen, D. (1995). *Winning the service game.* Boston, MA: Harvard Business School Press.

Schumpeter, J. A. (1934). *The theory of economic development.* New York: Oxford University Press.

Scott, S. G., & Bruce, R. A. (1994). Determinants of innovative behavior: A path model of individual innovation in the workplace. *Academy of Management Journal, 37*, 580–607.

Storey, C., & Easingwood, C. J. (1998). The augmented service offering: A conceptualization and study of its impact on new service success. *Journal of Product Innovation Management, 15*, 335–351.

Wright, P. M., & McMahan, G. C. (1992). Theoretical perspective of strategic human resource management. *Journal of Management, 18*(2), 295–320.

Zeithaml, V. A., Berry, L. L., & Pasuraman, A. (1988). Communication and control processes in the delivery of service quality. *Journal of Marketing, 52*, 35–48.

Zeithaml, V. A., & Bitner, M. J. (2000). *Service marketing: Integrating customer focus across the firm.* Boston, MA: McGraw–Hill Companies.

Development of a sustainable tourism hospitality human resources management module: a template for teaching sustainability across the curriculum[1]

Dana V. Tesone[2]

Rosen College of Hospitality Management, University of Central Florida, Orlando, FL 32819, USA

[1]This chapter is a reprinted version of: Tesone, D.V. (2004). Development of a sustainable tourism hospitality human resources management module: A template for teaching sustainability across the curriculum. *International Journal of Hospitality Management, 23*(3), 207–237. (Permission for this reprinted version has been granted by the editor.)
[2]The author is an Associate Professor of Hospitality Management in the Rosen College of Hospitality Management at the University of Central Florida, Orlando, FL, USA.

Introduction

It would seem that two methods of concept delivery prevail within hospitality and tourism management programs at institutions of higher learning. The first method is to provide specific courses designed to cover topics that fall within an appropriate concept and the second would be to deliver those topics "across the curriculum" (infusion into the content of various courses).

Most hospitality and tourism educators would agree that concepts associated with sustainable tourism practices are crucial components that should be included in programs intended to develop the knowledge and skills of future industry leaders. One group called BEST—Business & Entrepreneurial Sustainable Tourism, is comprised of academics and industry practitioners representing various sectors of the tourism industry, worldwide. The leaders of this group are guided by a strong belief that sustainable tourism principles should be practiced in all aspects of tourism operations on a daily basis. The leaders and volunteers of BEST gathered on several occasions over a number of years in "think tank" formats to develop frameworks for programs of study aimed at the teaching of sustainable tourism "across the curriculum" of coursework offered in Tourism programs at institutions of higher learning.

The following module on sustainable tourism practices in hospitality/tourism human resources (HR) management is the outcome of the first think tank that was conducted in Bongani, South Africa. The author developed this first module in conjunction with the leaders of BEST, who provided formative and summative reviews. It is intended for infusion into hospitality/tourism HR courses and to serve as a template for future modules of sustainable tourism practices, as applied to other courses.

Preface

This module is intended as a supplement to be used in existing courses and training programs in hospitality and tourism human resource management (HRM). The purpose of this supplement is to generate an awareness of sustainable tourism principles and practices that may be applied to the management of hospitality HR. It is the assumption of this module that participants will be in the process of attaining knowledge and skills in the general aspects of HRM under the tutelage of a learned instructor using a generic textbook or training manual. With this in mind, the module is constructed in a manner that focuses solely on those activities that would pertain to a HR practitioner positioned within a Sustainable-based Tourism Organization (STO). Careful steps have been taken to avoid potential overlap with general principles associated with hospitality HRM throughout the construction of this module.

Instructors who would like to infuse sustainable practices into a HRM course or training program may use the module in a variety of ways. One approach would be to allocate a small portion of class time (approximately 15 minutes) for the coverage of each of the nine micro-modules that are consistent with the topic of instruction. The nine independent micro-module topics are formatted to be congruent with the layout of most HRM textbooks. Another option would be to use the entire module as a case study to provide learners with exposure to the unique HR challenges associated with the establishment and maintenance of a sustainable hospitality/tourism organization.

Regardless of the manner of use adopted by an instructor, the micro-modules are designed to require no more than 15 minutes of class time and may be delivered in any sequence deemed appropriate by the instructor. The first micro-module addresses organizational and structural HR issues, with the next section focusing on STO recruitment and selection strategies. The third and fourth micro-modules respectively provide employee orientation and training information that is specifically relevant to STOs. Performance standards, performance appraisals, and compensation strategies for STOs are the topics of the next three micro-modules (5, 6, 7). Micro-module 8 describes retention strategies for STOs, with the final micro-module (9) addressing employee exit procedures.

Each micro-module concludes with open-ended questions for discussion and a glossary of terms that are specific to the practice of HRM within sustainable hospitality organizations. The entire package is less than 40 pages in length and is written in a crisp and easy-to-understand style that is suitable for most learning audiences.

Micro-module 1: organizational structure and context

Objective

At the end of this micro-module, readers will be able to:

- Appreciate that sustainable principles should be a part of corporate goals and an organization and the organizational structure should be appropriate to local culture.

Introduction

It is common knowledge that the practice of HRM is prevalent in most organizations ranging from small-to-medium-to-large scale corporations. The current-day HR manager has direct influence on the strategic direction and thinking of both private and public sector organizations.

Tourism is the broad umbrella that drives related indicators within local and national economies. Hospitality organizations are driven by public (governmental) and private (institutional) sector tourism policies and practices. The proliferation of telecommunication technologies along with the development of multinational hospitality organizations has generated an awareness of tourism policies on a global level. Sustainable tourism is a long-term collaborative systems approach to establishing and maintaining harmonious relationships among hospitality/travel-related organizations and the social, cultural, and environmental aspects associated with tourist destinations.

While the process of sustainable tourism involves the establishment and maintenance of harmonious relationships, the goal (desired outcome) is the creation of continued viability and development of tourism-related entities. Hence, proponents of sustainable tourism engage in a process of creating a mutually beneficial balance between the macro-environment (social, cultural, and environmental aspects) and the microenvironment (internal workings of a specific organization). The objective (goal) of this process is the institutionalization of the tourism industry as a contributor to the socio-cultural welfare and development of each and every destination. In essence this goal seeks what might be called a "triple-win" outcome. Successful sustainable tourism initiatives result in positive outcomes for consumers (guests, travelers, and customers), organizations (commercial enterprises), as well as society (indigenous people and cultures). But how does the practice of hospitality HRM fit into this picture?

Career paths

As part of the commitment to the social environment of the community, HR practitioners in sustainable tourism-based organizations (STO) must determine the career goals and desires of host country citizens. While certain individuals will exist who do not possess progressive career aspirations, there will be others who will view the organization as a means to pursue professional development activities. For this reason, job design processes should provide a clear snapshot of knowledge, skills, abilities, and attitudes for every position within the organization through job descriptions and job specifications.

The job descriptions and job specifications provide foundational information to track logical paths of career progression among the many disciplines found within the operations and administrative areas of a medium-to-large hospitality enterprise. Once these paths are discovered, HR practitioners may engage in career counseling activities aimed at communicating activities to attain the necessary job requirements for internal promotions. HR practitioners may choose to take this one step further through formal succession planning programs coupled with training development activities.

Many cases of global expansion within hospitality organizations include the placement of expatriate managers from home nations into positions at host country locations. STO strategies might be aimed at the temporary placement of such individuals until citizens of the host nation are adequately prepared to assume senior management positions. An advantage to this strategy would be the assimilation into the mainstream culture of the host nation by establishing a representation of senior management positions that are held by qualified host nationals.

Proportion of local staff members

It makes good business sense for HR practitioners to scan the external environment of the host nation to determine the statistical representation of various groups of individuals by ethnicity, age, sex, race, national origin, and in some cases religion. Once the demographics for the locale are discovered, the HR manager would enact strategies aimed at a statistical representation within the organization that is somewhat similar to those evident within the region.

Some reactive hospitality organizations might claim to have sufficient numbers of represented groups within their companies. Upon further inspection, however, it could be determined that the representation exists exclusively for lower level position holders. This would not be the case for an STO, as the HR practitioners in such an organization would possess objectives for appropriate levels of group representation among all levels of the organization. In this case, career path objectives would become one strategy used to balance the representation of various classes of individuals in middle and senior level positions. Other strategies would exist within the established plans for recruitment and selection of staff members.

Figure 20.1
Organization Stakeholder Groups

Policy and governance from an external context

Who are the stakeholders or "constituents" served by HRM practitioners? In actuality, HR practitioners have the same responsibilities in the area of stakeholder service as any other corporate manager. The stakeholder group consists of shareholders (stockholders in publicly traded firms), employees, customers, and the community. The trick here is "balance". In a healthy organization, the needs of each stakeholder group will be satisfied more-or-less equally. On the other hand, dysfunctional companies will serve the needs of one stakeholder group (the shareholders, for instance) at the expense of another group (such as the employees). When this happens, the senior HR manager is at odds with the value system of the organization (or at least the CEO) and will attempt to stabilize the imbalance in the interests of both groups. In organizations that are committed to the practice of sustainable tourism, the role of the HR practitioner as a shareholder group stabilizer is particularly crucial. Figure 20.1 provides a description of the stakeholders as the people who the HR practitioner and every other manager in the sustainable tourism-oriented organization should serve in balanced proportion.

Shared ownership

In cases of organizational expansion strategies is common for corporate entities to engage in partnerships that result in multiple ownership of an operation. Usually this strategy is based on cost of capital and shared risk-taking in unproven markets. For instance, a start-up project may include limited partners such as real estate developers, construction firms, and multinational investment bankers. A proven STO ownership strategy is to include organizations and individual investors that exist within the targeted host country, if the legal environment permits such collaboration. In some cases it is permissible for certain government agencies of the host nation or republic to possess an ownership interest in a hospitality enterprise.

Similar to the case stated in favor of group representation among an organization's employees, shared ownership interests held by host country nationals helps the parent corporation assimilate into foreign national cultures. Additionally, successful enterprises contribute to the local economies through returns on investment to host national private and public entities.

Employee ownership strategies take the form of profit sharing and stock acquisition in some nations. This is not appropriate in all nations, however, in those countries with economies that lean toward individual accumulation of assets, employer ownership strategies may serve to motivate individuals to achieve organizational success factors such as growth and profit.

In some cases it may be appropriate to focus on "psychological" employee ownership through programs such as participative decision-making and team building activities. While these would not be well received in all social environments, certain "collective-thinking" cultures would expect this type of psychological ownership to exist within the organization.

Organizational structure and management

HR practitioners within STOs recognize the fact that organizational cultures should become micro-mirrors of the culture within the local and national societies. A number of factors external to the organization should be considered prior to establishing internal structures and management practices. Typical considerations from the "external environment" include social/political, economic, competitive, technological, and cultural factors.

HR managers working in sustainable tourism-based organizations will construct job analysis processes based on the social and cultural factors that exist in the surrounding environment. The findings of job analysis activities are used to determine the managerial structure of the hospitality organization. That structure will drive the spans of authority that exist for each manager. For instance, in cultures that value "authority" relationships, organizations will tend to possess a tall management hierarchy with multiple layers of management and narrow spans of management authority. Other nations may design the organization to be structured in a flat pyramid style with wide spans of management authority to facilitate decision-making activities on the part of most employees. Nations that value "individualism" may find this organizational structure to be appropriate.

We know that the key driver for any organization is its mission. The mission describes the purpose for the organization's existence, which includes the values and philosophies for that enterprise. The mission is the broadest objective that drives the firm. Missions that include the values of perpetuation and evolution drive sustainable organizations. An STO is a "mission driven" organization, which means that the mission is the key driver for all of the management objectives for the enterprise. Hence, "sustainable objectives" or targets for performance direct an STO.

The global-to-local mindset

One way to describe the mindset of STO HR practitioners would be to say, "They think globally and act locally." This describes the mental approach that is taken to establish balance between the macrocosm and the microcosm. For instance, a group of host country enterprises could be said to each represent a subsystem of a larger system called the multinational corporation. That corporation could be considered to be a subsystem of a larger system called the hotel industry and that industry would be a subsystem of global tourism. When HR managers frame their thinking in this manner, they see each entity as a node within a much larger pattern. Sustainable tourism views these patterns as an evolving ecosystem.

Multinational firms engaged in sustainable tourism will empower HR practitioners at the property level to balance performance factors with the socio-cultural needs of each respective host country. This practice is driven by a philosophy that healthy local operations contribute to performance on a global level.

People and community management

A hospitality organization is only as good as its people and the management of those people should take place in close cooperation with local community activities. The HR manager must take steps to align closely with the needs of the local community through social assimilation to ensure that the practices within the organization are consistent with the values of that society. The HR practitioner should become a participant with those agencies in the community that promote initiatives such as social welfare, education, and community service. There is a twofold benefit to this practice. First the HR manager acts in the capacity of "ambassador" to the community. Second, the HR manager uses what is learned through these activities to enhance the level of community awareness among the managers of the organization.

Questions for discussion:

1. Do you think hospitality organizations should become STOs? Why, or why not?
2. When you think about the stakeholder group called "the Community," would this group be considered to be more or less important for an STO? Why?
3. If you had a choice of becoming an HR practitioner for a regular hospitality organization or one includes sustainable tourism practices, which would you choose? Why?

Glossary of terms

Community	Outside stakeholders who are not within other stakeholder groups.
Stakeholder group	Groups of constituents for an organization.
Sustainable tourism	A long-term collaborative systems approach to establishing and maintaining harmonious relationships among hospitality/ travel-related organizations and the social, cultural, and environmental aspects associated with tourist destinations.

Micro-module 2: STO recruitment and selection strategies

Objective

At the end of this micro-module, readers will be able to:

- Realize that a local focus and equitable approach should be used in recruitment, and sensitity to local cultures and local community needs is important.

Introduction

The key factor that differentiates HRM from personnel administration is the strategic nature of acquiring, developing, and maintaining human capital. Since the break from personnel administration, HR managers have been included in the over-all strategic direction if a firm, which places the HR manager within the senior management of the organization. The strategies for recruiting and selecting employees for a sustainable tourism-based hospitality organization must balance the human capital needs for the business with a long-term approach of community citizenship with the host nation.

The key driver for recruitment and selection strategies from the external environment is the labor market for all hospitality organizations. The labor market consists of individuals who possess knowledge, skills, abilities, and attitudes that are consistent with the tasks, duties, and responsibilities required of employment positions. These, as well as the volume of individuals needed in each job classification are determined through the process of job analysis, which is the key activity within the process called job design. The job design process yields a number of positions in each job classification that must be filled through recruitment and selection activities.

The HR manager for an STO that is operating in a secluded area within a developing nation would be faced with even more daunting recruitment and selection challenges. A reactive organization would be tempted to place needed skilled positions with expatriates from more developed nations to solve this dilemma. However, this strategy would be in contrast with a mission that is based on sustainable tourism principles. The HR manager for an STO would devise strategies to develop the skills-base within the local population to provide career opportunities to members of the host nation. An outside share-holder could argue that this strategy would be cost prohibitive. However, the skilled HR practitioner would counter this argument by demonstrating that the exorbitant costs associated with expatriate placement could be better invested into the development within the local community. From a cost/benefit analysis perspective, the HR manager could easily show how the same investment in the community could yield a greater return on investment, relative to the short-term benefit of the huge level of expenses associated with expatriate placement.

Local focus at all levels of the organization

STOs may be said to "Think globally and act locally." This saying is particularly true of recruitment and selection activities for an organization that operates in a host nation. Factors such as language, culture, and management must reflect the local norms for acceptability. Multilingual employees may be preferred in hospitality organizations that cater to guests from eclectic national origins. The hospitality organization should attempt to assimilate the internal workings of the company with the cultural values of the host nation. In some cases the "local flavor" will become part of the marketing and promotional strategies to attract guests to resorts located in host nations. HR practitioners must ensure that procedures for attracting and hiring applicants are consistent with the local laws and customs.

Equity issues and disadvantaged groups

While many developed nations legislate equality in hiring practices, some developing nations may not have these protections for workers. However, the STO would perceive an ethical responsibility to build equality safeguards into all of its policies concerning workers. One particular advantage to doing business in some developing nations is the opportunity to provide economic stability to disadvantaged groups within the society. Hospitality operations are often labor intensive, which means that large numbers of employment opportunities exist within the local vicinity of such a business. While the community may appreciate the decline in unemployment levels that may result when large numbers of people are hired, the STO would take this responsibility further by providing progressive career development opportunities for workers.

Implications of seasonal/migratory labor

While certain industries engage in employment practices that may be construed to exploit the labor available to them, this is not an option for hospitality STOs. Since the STO is a good community citizen, it would be inappropriate to engage in practices that take advantage of the host country workers. The same would be true for migratory workers from other nations.

The nature of the hospitality industry calls for certain percentages of the total workforce to include part-time workers. The definition of part-time workers varies across cultures. But a traditional definition of less than one full-time equivalent could be applied on a global basis. Another employment option is to hire "on-call" or casual workers to perform functions on a project basis. Regardless of the mix of workers involved in an STO, the key consideration is to treat all employees with the respect and dignity that would be expected by the leaders of the community for its citizens.

Cultural sensitivity

On a positive note, certain developing nations possess populations that naturally exude a spirit of hospitality, which provides a natural transition into service-oriented positions. On the other hand, the people of some developing nations confuse the concept of service with the notion of "servitude." STOs in these nations are faced with the challenge of providing attitudinal training to those individuals who are selected for service-oriented positions. Such training initiatives, as well as all interactions concerning the recruitment and selection processes require excellent skills in the area of interpersonal relations and communication.

Mission and policies

The key-differentiating feature of an STO is a mission statement that articulates a commitment to sustainability principles. If the mission drives the organization, the activities associated with recruitment and selection must also support sustainability. The result of this thinking will be manifested in practices associated with skill analysis that will focus on recruitment and selection functions aimed at long-term sustainability for the organization.

Questions for discussion

1. In an STO, which function is more complex, the recruiting or selection process? Maybe you think they are equally intricate? Which is more important? Why?
2. Think about a scenario in which you have a choice of using expatriate managers versus those from a given host country. What would be the cost/benefit of each choice?
3. If you were a HR manager, would you prefer to work for a reactive hospitality organization or an STO? Why?

Micro-module 3: STO orientation programs for new employees

Objectives

At the end of this chapter, readers will be able to:

- Comprehend local environmental and cultural issues in relation to orientation.

- Apply training that is ongoing; supporting progression including to managerial levels for locally recruited staff; sensitive to local culture; and incorporating understanding the application of sustainable tourism practices.

Employee orientations

New employee orientations fall within the category of knowledge training. For this reason the sessions are conducted in a classroom setting with a training facilitator, who is often the training manager herself. This process is an exchange of the custody of the new employees from the domain of the employment manager over to the training manager. Most organizations benefit from two types of new employee orientation. The first may be referred to as a general orientation session(s), with the second phase referred to as the department orientation session(s). In many cases the department manager will act as the facilitator for department orientation programs.

The primary objective of orientation programs is to assimilate new employees into the organization. This means that the new employee should be made to feel comfortable with the new position by learning a little about the organization and the people who work there. The reason for assimilating new employees into the organization is to familiarize them with a strange and new work environment. Think about the first day you spent in a new job or at a new school. The experience is almost hostile because you are entering an unknown environment that is full of people who are strangers to you. The first immediate psychological response for most people in this situation is to refrain from returning to the uncomfortable environment. If they are persistent, however, the environment becomes comfortable to them in a short period of time. The purpose of the new employee orientation is to ease this transition into the organizational environment, by sharing information that explains the "what's, why's, and where's" in an effort to make the new workers comfortable in their new positions with the organization.

New employee engagement

STO Training Managers are adept at transitioning new staff members into the organization through orientation techniques that fully engage the participants as members of a new microcommunity. The psychology of newly acquired employees is based on the understanding that people bring a host of mental and emotional backgrounds with them into the organization. HR managers view individual employees as "holistic beings," which impacts the methods used for interpersonal communications. The goal of all managers is to fully engage an individual into the workplace by using communication methods that are consistent with each person's psyche to ensure that each person will understand his or her role as a member of the organization. At the same time, each person is reassured that organizational membership does not require loss of personal identity.

Focus and background on sustainable tourism principles and practices

One of the affective learning outcomes for orientation programs is to instill a sense of personal pride on the part of an individual for becoming a member of the organization. Sustainable tourism-based organizations are naturally aligned with this inclination since they are acutely aware of their role as corporate citizens of the host community. It would be an appropriate strategy to base a thematic approach to each orientation session on the sustainable tourism objectives for that organization. This is a conceptual approach in which the Training Manager paints a "big picture" of sustainable tourism and articulates how each principle and practice within the organization fits into that landscape.

Local environmental and cultural awareness integration

An elegant induction program will continuously infuse comparisons of the organization's culture with that of the local environment to emphasize the similarities that make the two systems seem as one. This has a twofold benefit. First, it enhances and reinforces cultural awareness on the part of each participant. Second, it reassures each individual that the leadership of that organization respects the psychological validity of personal cultural values. The goal of this orientation process is to fully embrace group similarities and respect individual identities.

Creating a strong sense of community attachment

Training managers who represent STOs will take extra care to ensure that orientation sessions are consistent with the values of the host community. This is done through language, gestures, meeting formats, attire, and proxemics (space/distance/formality issues). The goal of an STO orientation should be the appearance that the values of the organization reflect those of the host community. The overriding theme of this orientation approach should be to reinforce the concept that the organization is a composite of the community and exists as a contributing citizen of that environment.

Local specific corporate culture

Most operations within host countries are part of larger corporate entities, with some being multinational in scope. One strategy employed by sustainable tourism-based organizations is the creation of "hybrid" corporate cultures at the operations level within specific host countries. In addition to creating a relationship of positive corporate citizenship at the community level, this strategy facilitates a local identity that is consistent with the values of most host country nationals. Again, the articulation of the relationship from local community to a global scale requires a conceptual approach on the part of the Training Manager. Inductees should be assimilated into a local corporate identity in terms of values, attitudes, and beliefs and then be shown the ripple effect of that identity on regional, national, and ultimately global levels within the corporation.

Questions for discussion

1. One task of the training department in an organization is to conduct orientation programs. Is this particularly important for an STO? Why?
2. It is no secret that there is a labor crisis in the hospitality industry as well as certain other service sectors. Could orientation training play a role in lessening the crisis? How? Could the practice enhance community relations? How?

Glossary of terms

Assimilate   Adapt to an environment and its people.

Micro-module 4: STO training and development strategies

Objectives

At the end of this chapter, readers will be able to:

- Comprehend local environmental and cultural issues in relation to orientation.

- Apply training that is ongoing; supporting progression including to managerial levels for locally recruited staff; sensitive to local culture; and incorporating understanding the application of sustainable tourism practices.

Local training focus throughout the organization

The key to providing training programs within an STO is to ensure that all processes are consistent with the social norms of the host nation. For instance, corporate training documents may be developed in the local language of the home company and should be converted to the most popularly used languages of the host nation. Facilitators should possess fluency levels of the languages spoken among the majority of trainees. Also, training program design and delivery should meet with the educational customs of the local culture. Seating arrangements and other layout formats for training rooms should resemble educational settings that are familiar to host nationals. Other factors of cultural relevance that should be incorporated into training design would be levels of formality, group dynamics, and types of role-play scenarios.

The organization should provide an articulation of progressive training and education policies and opportunities that are made available to various levels of employees. These policies should be made available through employee handbooks, bulletin board postings, and meeting announcements. The company should convey an interest in the personal and professional development of its employees. When possible, alliances should be made with appropriate education and social agencies from the local community. Training programs should seek to expand beyond knowledge and skills for the workplace through the offering of "life-enhancement" training options.

Incorporation of local values and culture

Since training initiatives are crucial for STOs, one strategy is to employ "tandem" training managers (one from the host nation working with one from the home nation of the corporation). At first glance this appears to be a duplication of salaries. However, this temporary placement strategy could yield the equivalent of 5-years of assimilated cultures in a period of one-to-two years. With this strategy, the primary directive for the home country trainer would be a process of emersion into the culture of the host country, while the opposite would be the directive of the host nation representative. Within a short period of time a "hybrid" training culture would emerge within the STO resulting in seamless assimilation of all trainees into the new culture, which represents a blending of home and host nation values, attitudes and beliefs. This is a very powerful strategic technique that forms a solid bond between the STO and the host nation community.

Development programs for promotional opportunities

Sustainable tourism-based organizations will make every effort to prioritize the development training of local employees who are seeking management positions. In keeping with the "human capital" aspect of the employment relationship, proactive organizations take steps to identify talented workers for potential career advancement with the organization. The identification process occurs through performance appraisals. Performance appraisals are just one aspect of performance management systems, which combine strategic planning initiatives with performance evaluation criteria. One aspect of this process is to identify individuals within the workplace who possess the desire and potential to pursue career advancement with the organization.

Development programs may be conducted within in the organization (in-house) or through external training activities. Most organizations provide for a combination of internal and external training development programs. There are other aspects to development training in addition to management development programs. In keeping with the "human capital" approach to worker development; any set of competencies that enhances the worker as a holistic being may be considered to be a form of development. Some organizations refer to these types of programs as human development programs. For instance, certain quick service restaurants that hire very young workers will assist those workers in earning college degrees. While, those college degrees may not be in the field of restaurant management, these programs are offered as employee retention strategies, with the organization benefiting from the human development aspects attributed to the workers, as they progress through their academic training. STOs that provide for human development training are viewed as contributors to the host community, while benefiting from the employment of "self-actualizing" individuals, even though they may not be ultimately pursuing careers in our industry. These types of programs at the local level encourage a process of life-long learning for all members of the organization.

Implications of training for sustainability

While all training processes should be consistent with the local cultural value systems, training content would not be restricted to the local norms. Instead, the local cultural customs training could be used as a benchmark of comparison to the cultural aspects associated with other cultures to provide a holistic sense of cultural diversity training for all members of the staff. This awareness presents opportunities to incorporate principles and practices in sustainable tourism as part of the training process. For instance, skills training in the areas of service and guest relations would be provided from the perspective of global awareness. At the same time, management development programs should include programs aimed at the development of skills in the areas of conflict resolution, leadership, and crisis management.

All training should be customized to suit the cultural values of the local community. However, this does not suggest that training programs should be designed in a subjective manner. All training must be standardized to ensure that all employees achieve the same learning outcomes. A significant portion of the training budget should be allocated to management development programs aimed at training for careers rather than specific jobs.

Questions for discussion

1. Is it possible to run an STO without a serious commitment to training programs? Why?
2. Why is it important for STOs to provide training for careers as opposed to training just for specific jobs?
3. Most operations managers think that training is a waste of money. How might you convince them otherwise using a sustainable tourism-based organization argument?

Micro-module 5: sustainability through performance standards

Objectives

At the end of this chapter, readers will be able to:

- Perceive the importance of participation in developing ethical, adaptable, and negotiated performance standards that are appropriate to local context and sustainable principles.

- Know the importance of providing employee support during employment and post-employment through such policies as opportunities for job growth, good quality of personal life (including family), and skills training to aid with future employment.

Professional management

Professional managers within STOs know that their job is to clearly articulate objective standards for performance up front and to reinforce those standards every day. Performance standards should reflect values of the local community, as well as those that are consistent with sustainability. Since sustainability exists within the core values of an STO, these organizations tend to operate "mission driven" corporations, in which the mission drives all of the important decision-making processes and items that are not related to that mission are considered to be minor issues. The mission values are communicated throughout the organization via the "mission statement", which is a brief written description of the purpose for that organization. It is the responsibility of senior managers to establish and communicate the mission for the corporation. The managers audit the mission on an annual basis to verify its accuracy, given factors from the external environment, which exists outside the organization. The mission should clearly articulate the posture of an organization as possessing the core values of sustainability that ultimately become evident in daily management practices.

Training for careers rather than jobs

While job training will certainly be an important factor in most cultures, the goal of the STO HR practitioner is to train for careers. A career is a lifetime progression of jobs that are more challenging, yet professionally fulfilling. All career development programs should be consistent with the norms for professional life subscribed to within a host nation. For instance, some countries respect positions of authority, so management careers may be acceptable in such an area. In collectivist cultures, most individuals may prefer team-oriented contributory positions. The intended and achieved positions throughout a person's professional life constitute a "career path" for that person. HR practitioners may find it appropriate to develop the career paths of those employed within the STO. In such cases, the practitioner would arrange for development training and succession planning for each interested worker.

Adaptable performance standards to local context and sustainability

One practice that is common among centralized organizations is to establish and enforce consistent standards for performance for all hospitality locations. This may not be suitable for sustainability within a given locale. STOs seek to blend within the local and national environments. Hence, adaptability is the way to do business when it comes to performance expectations and evaluations.

Evaluation of human resource opportunities

HR practitioners scan the environments for resources as part of the planning process for doing business in multinational locations. In the case of HR, managers are seeking knowledge, skills, and abilities that are consistent with the needs of a hospitality organization. STO managers look at this issue from two perspectives. First, they seek those talents that are valued by the organization. The second practice includes providing opportunities for individuals within the community that would not exist in the absence of the hospitality organization. This two-way approach is intended to balance the needs of the organization with those of the local community.

Culturally relevant motivational and evaluation techniques

When applied to the workplace, human motivation is defined as the willingness to perform in a professional capacity. Motivation is influenced by factors such as personality, experience, and culture. It is important for HR practitioners to understand the psychology of individuals and groups of workers. Since the social environment influences motivation, it is necessary for the HR practitioner to understand the cultural norms within the host nation and local communities. Each culture seems to demonstrate behavioral patterns based on value systems concerning issues such as, authority figures, formality of interactions, collectivism, individualism, and others. HR practitioners within STOs strive to create organizational cultures that resemble the community environment through the creation of culturally sensitive policies.

Discussion questions

1. Do you think a manager who acts unprofessionally while working in one nation will act differently when transferred to another nation? Why or why not?

2. Are the people in a given community aware of the management practices within the hospitality organizations that do business in that community? Could this have an affect on the reputation of the tourism industry among members of that community?

Micro-module 6: STO performance appraisals

Objectives

At the end of this module, readers will be able to:

- Perceive the importance of participation in developing ethical, adaptable, and negotiated performance standards that are appropriate to local context and sustainable principles.
- Appreciate that participation in developing ethical, adaptable, negotiated appraisal standards that are appropriate to local context and sustainable principles are of significant importance.

Introduction

This micro-module presents a systems approach to performance standards and appraisals. When STOs determine performance appraisal criteria at the same time as the development of standards and procedures, the result is a holistic performance management system. A performance management system provides planning, identification, and encouragement through the communication of standards, as well as the process for the evaluation of actual performance. The performance management approach is the practice of proactive managers to ensure objective standards and performance evaluation criteria. Reactive organizations often succumb to the negative outcomes of low morale, high employee turnover, and decreased productivity associated with subjective management practices. Supervisory subjectivity is the antithesis of the professional management standards subscribed to by sustainable tourism-based organizations.

The purpose of performance measurement is to provide feedback to employees about their performance and to take actions to facilitate improvement, as well as provide recognition of successful performance levels by giving rewards. Actually, this is not a stand-alone process, as some managers would have us believe. Instead, it is a multidisciplinary approach to people management that requires daily observation and communication through coaching, mentoring, and disciplinary warnings on the part of the supervisor. The effectiveness of these practices is related to the levels of awareness on the part of the supervisor concerning the service perspective, leadership practice, worker motivation, and work life development.

Performance appraisals

STO HR practitioners recognize the need for sensitivity to the cultural norms that exist within the host nation and local community. For instance, in some cultures, it may be the expectation for performance standards to be established by the senior managers of the organization and mandated to the staff at-large. In other settings, individual employees may possess the expectation of having input to the process of setting organizational standards. To ensure sustainability, it is a generic practice to negotiate certain standards for performance at the host nation organizational level. This is not to say that guidelines established by the home corporate office will be negated, but to some extent it may be appropriate to modify those standards at the local operating level. For instance, in some Polynesian cultures tattooing is a common practice among individuals of all generations. The corporate home office for the hospitality organization may subscribe to a grooming policy prohibiting tattoos that are visible while wearing a uniform. At the property level in a Polynesian nation, it may be appropriate to disregard this policy in the interest of demonstrating an authentic local appearance by members of the staff.

Savvy HR practitioners will engage the services of an individual or group of people of high-level social acceptability from the host nation to assist with establishing a set of performance standards that are culturally relative. In most cases, the hospitality enterprise possesses an interest in preserving local cultural customs as part of the "guest experience." Hence, a hybrid set of culturally acceptable practices serves the business interests of the enterprise, while providing for cultural sustainability—a double "win" for the organization and the host community.

In many cases employees expect to gain performance feedback directly from the immediate manager. However, this is not true in all cultures. In certain societies it is extremely important for individuals to "save face," or maintain levels of dignity in social settings. In such instances business negotiations follow protocols that preclude person-to-person interactions to avoid potential embarrassment on the part of a given individual. Negotiators in these countries use third party intermediaries to present messages in an effort to save face for all individuals involved in the business deal. The issue of saving face may be true for performance appraisals, as well. HR practitioners in certain host nations may elect to provide third party individuals to share performance feedback on behalf of a given manager, in order to save face for both parties.

Staff ownership of the appraisal process

In certain cultures, the concept of "psychological ownership" is achieved through participative decision-making activities, such as Management by Objectives. However, participative schemes are not welcomed by the standards of all societies. Absent the practice of participative management, acceptance levels of the appraisal system by the majority of the workers within the organization could create a sense of psychological ownership. Workers seem to be motivated to attain peak performance levels in a work environment that fosters a sense of ownership on the part of the employees.

Staff problems and grievances

As can be expected of any system, employees will occasionally perceive problems with the performance appraisal process. Sometimes these problems are communicated as perceived unfair treatment, which constitutes workplace grievances. Reactive managers sometimes work from the assumption that all grievances are without merit or frivolous in nature. This is a mistake, since proactive managers know that perception is reality in the mind of the perceiver. Hence, individuals with complaints or grievances must be heard. A performance appraisal process should have a mechanism for the lodging of grievances via a "due process" policy. STOs are likely to have such a mechanism that provides for third party hearings, multiple level reviews, and rapid notification of determinations to employees regarding such matters.

In nations that hold "saving face" as an important value, formal grievance systems may be considered to be contrary to the social norms for behavior. In such cases, the grievance procedure could be replaced with alternative communication processes, such as third party mediation.

Questions for discussion

1. Some hospitality organizations provide centralized formal appraisal processes that are applied to all operating

properties to ensure consistency throughout the corporation. Would this be an appropriate strategy for an STO? Why?

2. Should an STO HR practitioner always implement partici- pative decision-making processes within the organization? Why?

Micro-module 7: STO compensation and motivation

Objective

At the end of this module, readers will be able to:

- Integrate an ethos associated with sustainable tourism into the workplace with critical elements that include such prin- ciples as equitable and transparent pay, non-cash benefits, and empowerment.

Introduction

As we know from our HR training, the organization spends a good deal of financial resources to recruit, select, train, and develop its employees. Some organizations throw these invest- ments down the drain by failing to realize that simple man- agement activities are required to maintain a staff of satisfied employees. When employees become dissatisfied, they find jobs in other organizations. They sometimes realize later that they had better work lives with the former employer, but by that time it is too late to return to the former place of employ- ment. The particularly sad fact is that the best employees will be the first to leave. In such a case, the organization has spent large dollars in staffing and training activities only to realize later on that they are retaining mediocre workers at best.

When this happens, the shareholders put pressure on the organization to limit its allocation of recruiting and training budgets, since it becomes evident that the managers are wast- ing money on selecting and developing the skills of employees who simply go to work for the competition. How many times have general managers been heard to say, "Why should we spend money on employees to prepare them to go work some- where else?" This is dangerous thinking that serves as an incen- tive for talented HR practitioners to seek positions with more proactive organizations. This spiral continues as the HR per- sonnel are replaced with cut-rate semi-trained practitioners. In such a case the company controller proudly notifies the share- holders that expenses in the HR office have been cut in half and that the training budget has been eliminated altogether.

The scenario is not possible within a sustainable tourism-based organization, since an STO remains focused on the "big picture" by balancing shareholder interests with those of the community constituents. STOs attract highly trained proactive HR practitioners, who possess knowledge and skills in the area of employee retention strategies. Further, these practitioners recognize that practices associated with effective employee exit procedures serve as both learning systems for the organization and positive relations vehicles with the community at large.

Fair compensation

In typical organizations, compensation practices are primarily driven by labor market variables and competitive practices. There are three basic strategies within this realm of doing business—to become the wage leader, wage "meeter", or wage laggard. Compensation policies within STOs, however, require more creative thinking on the part of HR managers to include an overriding mission of enhancing the standard of living for hospitality workers. The opposing force to this type of thinking falls within the realm of organizational labor costs and the solution lies within the domain of productivity. As workers in hospitality organizations develop the capacity of producing higher levels of outcomes (products and services) by using fewer resources (costs) the result is the ability to "do more with less." Over time the organization will require fewer numbers of individuals in certain positions to accomplish outcomes that meet established quality and quantity standards. When this happens, it is feasible to appropriately compensate more productive workers, which enhances the standard of living for those individuals. These types of organizations encourage "value-added" managers who continually seek to enhance productivity levels of the workforce.

While productivity improvements would be good for the financial standing of the organization, this strategy could be viewed as being in contrast with local economic interests of a host country. Certain developing nations would expect STOs to provide full employment levels through job opportunities for unemployed individuals. This appears to be in contrast with enhanced productivity strategies, as it could be argued that higher levels of efficiency and effectiveness would cause the elimination of positions within an organization. This scenario produces two strategic opportunities for the STO.

One option would be to enact a strategy aimed at providing employment opportunities to as many individuals as can be supported by the hospitality organization. Since the result of this strategy would be inflated labor costs, the organization would seek to support those expenses through increased pricing or reductions in material resource expenditures. The justification for such a strategy would be the appeasement of local and national employment interests.

Another option could include productivity enhancement strategies coupled with retention policies, such as a commitment to refrain from employee layoffs. In this case, the goal would be to train workers who are displaced by productivity improvements for higher levels of work. Improved systems usually yield new demand for higher level positions. For instance, an STO could find a way to reduce the number of individuals required to provide room attendant services. The individuals who are displaced by this system could be trained to provide butler services to guests, which would be a higher level of work that provides enhanced "value" from the guest perspective. Improved guest value perceptions drive justifications for pricing increases. In this case, the organization is able to retain high employment levels with enhanced productivity and higher average daily rates. This type of thinking generates "spirals" of productivity enhance that benefits workers and guests, as well as the organization and the economic needs of the local community.

Fair financial benefits

The reason employers offer benefits to employees is to compete with other organizations in the industry and geographic location in terms of creating employee loyalty to the organization. The importance of benefits seems to vary with age groups. For instance younger workers seem to place less emphasis on retirement benefits than older workers. Workers with families place higher emphasis on family benefits, as opposed to individual benefits, and so on. Also, benefit packages vary dramatically among different global locations based on the perceived role of employers as providers of certain individual and social needs. The main intent of employee benefits is to reward individuals for membership within a specific organization.

The importance of benefits also varies among individuals within various cultures. For instance, social structures that emphasize individual independence may weigh the value of benefits differently than those espousing social collectivism. The perception of "fairness" of benefit distribution will also vary across cultures. For example, some societies value equal pay and benefits despite length of service or performance levels, while others support seniority and merit differential systems. In some locations it may be permissible to alter remuneration based on family needs, such as numbers of dependents, while such a consideration could be considered to be preposterous and even illegal in other nations.

Job status and prestige

From a motivational perspective, it is important to note that compensation means different things to different people. The obvious meaning of pay systems is the economic ability to obtain the necessities and perhaps a few luxuries in life. Beyond that, there is a psychosocial aspect of compensation that equates to social status, a means of keeping score with the "Joneses", or feelings of psychological self-worth. For those individuals who value personal achievement, growth may be a motivational factor associated with compensation levels. When the scholars tell us "money is not a motivator," what they are really saying is that the meaning of money motivates people beyond the money in and of itself.

Certain positions within hospitality organizations possess natural levels of social status and prestige. Most of these are management and professional positions, with compensation levels that exceed those of lower level positions for the most part. For instance, hotel General Managers are often noted as pillars within a local community and often find they are involved with upper strata social circles. In some developing nations certain non-supervisory line positions possess levels of social prestige, usually based on the earning potential of the jobholder or the prominence of the clientele directly served by that jobholder.

Participation in decision-making and shareholding activities

It is true that participative decision-making practices enhance employee "buy-in" to organizational standards and procedures. One exception would be in host nations that have the expectation of high power/distance and low tolerance for the ambiguity that goes hand-in-hand with decision-making activities. The trick is for HR practitioners to be aware of the social values of individuals from the local community. Alternative strategies through motivational compensation practices may be employed in those areas were participative processes are not desired by most employees.

In some nations it is permissible for employees to participate as organizational shareholders through benefits such as employee stock option plans, profit sharing and gain share programs. These forms of compensation can motivate workers to enhance productivity if they clearly understand the relationship of their job duties to the financial outcomes of the organization. In localities that do not condone this form of employee benefit, alternatives performance based incentives such as commissions and bonuses may serve as motivational tools for performance enhancement.

Discounting and living conditions

Astute managers will conduct orientation sessions that demonstrate the overall value of compensation for a jobholder. Using visuals, such as pie charts, the workers are made to realize that direct wages represent just a small portion of overall earnings, when factors such as medical benefits, other insurance, and perquisites are added together. In remote locations, it is a common practice to provide staff housing units for employees. Also, meal benefits are commonly provided at nominal or no cost to the workers. These types of benefits significantly reduce living expenses and may be used to attract and retain lower wage earning workers. It is important to provide safe and comfortable living communities when providing staff housing. Amenities, such as laundry facilities, low cost restaurants, and entertainment facilities enhance the quality of life in these communities.

Work environment/conditions

One advantage to working in hospitality organizations is that the environment is usually pristine and luxurious. STOs should take care to ensure the "back of the house" reflects the guest areas in terms of sanitation, safety, and ambience. Some STO's permit employees to use recreational and entertainment facilities as a benefit of employment. For some workers these are truly appreciated as they are permitted to use amenity areas that most individual pocketbooks could not afford. These types of benefits are sometimes bundled with wellness programs, which demonstrate that the organization cares for the welfare of its employees.

Other factors associated with compensation practices

Family values are also a very high concern in certain host communities. HR practitioners in STO's should consider the impact of employee job duties on family life in these localities. This consideration may lead to a variety of creative employment scenarios such as job share, flextime, and day care programs.

A large number of employees within a hospitality organization provide guest services that warrant service charges or gratuities. In some cases legal regulatory agencies possess jurisdiction over this form of compensation; but most nations leave the regulation of gratuities to the discretion of the hospitality enterprise. As is the case with every other HR practice, care should be taken to ensure that gratuities and service charges are distributed in a culturally defined fair and consistent manner. A variety of systems such as tip pooling, distribution based on hours worked, and station rotation policies may be used to provide equal distribution of gratuities.

Cost of living issues are always a concern when constructing compensation strategies. The infrastructure associated with hospitality enterprises in some developing nations could cause shifts in local economies by inflating the overall cost of living, limiting housing supply, increasing demand for leisure industries, and other impacts. It is likely that certain economic impacts will be positive, while others may be detrimental to the local population. Compensation managers must consider the big economic picture when forecasting the compensation needs of workers over time.

Discussion questions

1. Consider an example of a large resort hotel in a developed nation metropolitan area versus one located in a remote area of a developing nation. What compensation strategies would be required of the latter that would not be issues in the first example?
2. All compensation strategies must be considered with a degree to sensitivity to the host community. How does this potentially impact the motivation of workers from the host nation?

Micro-module 8: STO employee retention

Objective

At the end of this module, readers will be able to:

● Integrate an ethos associated with sustainable tourism into the workplace with critical elements that include such principles as equitable and transparent pay, non-cash benefits, and empowerment.

Introduction

While recruitment and selection activities are aimed at attracting individuals to vacant positions within a hospitality organization, retention strategies focus on keeping talented workers as company employees. A number of HR sub-strategies feed into retention outcomes. Compensation practices, for instance, are designed to reward employees for organizational membership and performance. Other strategies include employee relations, recognition programs, and career development. HR practitioners in STOs should pay close attention to the symptoms that indicate the overall "health" of the workplace in terms of worker impressions concerning "quality of work life."

A number of techniques are used to measure the "organizational climate," which consists of the general perceptions of employees concerning the work environment. One indicator of organizational climate is employee morale. HR practitioners should continually interact with work groups on an informal daily basis to observe levels of employee morale. A more formal method of identifying worker satisfaction levels is to administer "attitude surveys" with the majority of the staff and to analyze the findings in terms of workplace strengths and weaknesses. Most sustainable organizations conduct formal surveys at least once per year to identify areas of employee morale that require management interventions. However, it should be noted that some cultures find the activity of questionnaire distribution to be offensive, which could result in poor levels of response, as well as a lack of reliability concerning survey findings.

Another indicator of worker satisfaction is employee "turnover rates." By dividing the total number of voluntary and involuntary employee separations by the total employee population, HR practitioners can calculate turnover rates. While the total rate of turnover may indicate a trend of workplace problems, more succinct analysis is required to pinpoint management intervention areas. HR practitioners will identify turnover statistics by position and department to localize specific problem areas within the organization. Perhaps the most succinct tool for identifying workplace problem areas is through the practice of "exit interviews," which are conducted with those individuals who are leaving their positions. A HR practitioner will meet with an exiting employee prior to the final date of work to engage in a candid and confidential conversation concerning the perceptions of that worker concerning her or his position, department and the overall organization. Of course, this practice should be modified or even eliminated within certain cultures. But in the event the practice is conducive to the local environment, the information would be collated and analyzed to identify trends that may adversely affect employee retention within the organization.

As is the case with all multinational sustainability initiatives, it is possible that the issue of employee turnover may not have merit in certain cultures. For instance, in a nation that values and subscribes to "lifetime" employment, rates of employee departure are very low. In these cases, employee turnover cannot be considered as a measure of the organization's well being.

Complaint and grievance procedures

In certain cases, HR managers will be surprised to learn that the reason individuals are leaving their positions is due to the perception that they did not have an internal vehicle to voice opinions and concerns about their work activities. For instance, an individual may have encountered problems with other workers that could have been easily solved had the supervisor been aware of the situation. This is an example of a worker "complaint" about the work environment. HR practitioners in STOs proactively establish employee "Complaint Procedures" for these types of scenarios.

One form of complaint that focuses on the perception of "unfair treatment" in the workplace is called a "grievance." An employee may lodge a grievance in the event that he or she feels she is being treated differently than others within the job classification. Again, the HR department should articulate an established "Grievance Procedure" for these types of complaints.

STOs take steps to provide complaint and grievance procedures on different levels from informal to formal activities. On an informal level, all supervisors and managers in the organization are encouraged or required to practice "open door" policies. This is a mechanism in which individuals with grievances or general complaints may feel free to discuss their situation with the immediate supervisor at the time of occurrence.

On a more formal level, employee handbooks should list the steps in voicing complaints and grievances to third parties within the organization. Usually employees will be encouraged to pursue this process only after an attempt has been made to resolve an issue at the departmental level. However, in some cases, such as harassment it may be appropriate to seek the counsel of a third party immediately. In these cases the third party consists of designated HR practitioners who are trained in the practice of employee counseling.

While at first face it may seem that complaint and grievance procedures provide focus on negative aspects of work, they are valuable tools for managers to diagnose perceived injustices in the workplace. It is the duty of HR practitioners to safeguard retention efforts by continually learning about individual perceptions of the work environment—both good and bad.

Consistent with all of our discussions, local cultural compatibility is the key concern with all STO practices. In the case of grievances, formal processes may not be effective. For instance, in collectivist societies informal grievances through third parties are more effective than those commonly used in the USA or Europe, as discussed in a previous module.

Quality of life issues

It has been said that hospitality workers live to work, while those in other industries work to live. It is true that the nature of the industry does create a sub-culture lifestyle due to hours of operation and the social nature of the business. However, HR practitioners must realize that each individual possesses a life outside the organization. STO managers are trained to be sensitive to the personal needs of workers in areas such as, family responsibilities, health and welfare, rest and relaxation, human development, as well as social and economic status. Collectively, these issues and more comprise a topic called "quality of life." From a workplace perspective, job positions should provide for the pursuit of life-quality through things such as, paid vacations, paid holidays, health and welfare benefits, reasonable scheduling practices, and human development initiatives. From a holistic perspective, work comprises a large portion of an individual's lifestyle (approximately 2000 hours per person per year for a fulltime worker). This is why HR practitioners in STOs seek to know the "whole person" by identifying their life situations, needs, wants, and ambitions. They seek to strike that balance between providing quality of life within the workplace and having the workplace contribute to external quality of life issues.

Quality of supervision

Perhaps the most important person in the work life of an individual is the direct supervisor. The professional demeanor of that supervisor is the difference between stimulating work and drudgery within a position. It has been said that people do not quit jobs; they just quit other people. This refers directly to the way individuals are treated by their immediate supervisor. For this reason, the hospitality organization possesses an ethical duty to provide "professional management" within the workplace.

Professional managers are those who are thoroughly trained to perform in the capacity of leadership. These managers must possess the technical, relational, and conceptual skills associated with leading other people. In STOs, management training should also include applied psychology, interpersonal communication skills, as well as teambuilding and leadership skills. STOs ensure that an individual is thoroughly trained to act as a professional manager before placing that person in a supervisory position. This is in contrast to the haphazard promotion of individuals who have demonstrated good technical skills to simply fill a supervisory vacancy. In the case of the latter, the hospitality organization is contributing to its own increase in employee turnover.

Company policies

The executive management team must support all activities within the organization. The way this is done is through corporate missions that feed into objectives and strategies for direction of the hospitality enterprise. At the operating level, these strategies are converted into policies, standards, and procedures to guide every worker within the hospitality organization.

In STOs the general policies of the organization take into account the strategies for sustainability. These strategies are then converted into HR policies similar to those mentioned above. Mission driven sustainable hospitality organizations will ensure that all HR policies feed into the ultimate objective of social and cultural assimilation. In practice, this involves professional people management within a holistic paradigm that balances the needs of the organization and the individuals who interact with the enterprise.

Questions for discussion

1. What are the benefits of professional management within an STO?
2. How should a HR practitioner from the USA modify retention practices for an STO doing business in Japan?

Glossary of terms

Health	General state of well being that is free from dysfunction.
Quality of work life	Perception of positive existence in a work environment.
Organizational climate	Perception of workers concerning the general state of the organization.
Quality of life	Perception of a positive lifestyle.

Micro-module 9: STO employee exit process

Objective

At the end of this module, readers will be able to:

- Recognize the impacts on individuals, families, and vulnerable local communities of separation in less privileged societies.

Introduction

HR practitioners spend most of their time and energy attracting and retaining quality workers. However, they must also practice professional procedures for employee exit from the hospitality organization in order to preserve sustainability as good community citizens. While the goal of every good HR practitioner is to minimize employee turnover, it is not desirable to bring that statistic to a level of zero. The reason for this is that individuals from the outside environment re-energize those who have been with the corporation for a while. For instance, if all senior managers within a hospitality operation were promoted from within the organization and stay in place for many years, the scope of thinking among that group would begin to become closed, since all members are from the same internal environment. If new members are added to that group once in awhile, ideas from outside the organization are introduced. New ways of looking at issues revitalizes the thinking process within groups of decision-makers. The same dynamic is true at every level of the organization. So, reasonable levels of employee turnover are actually rejuvenating for the STO. Since employee turnover is a fact of organizational life, the HR practitioner must become adept at providing professional exit procedures for those seeking new opportunities with other organizations.

Voluntary exit

Individuals who chose to leave the organization on their own free will are considered to be "voluntary separations." In most cultures it is appropriate for these people to give reasonable notice of the intent to leave their positions within the organization. This gives the managers of the organization time to replace the vacated position. One of the finalization procedures for these individuals is a formal meeting with a HR representative to discuss the reasons for leaving the organization, as well as to find out the perceptions of that person regarding the experiences of being employed with the organization. This is really a fact-finding process, in which the HR practitioner follows a pattern of open-ended questioning used to ascertain the thoughts and feelings of the exiting individual.

A secondary purpose of the exit interview meeting is to generate positive final impressions on the part of the exiting employee concerning the organization. This is important because the departing individual will become a spokesperson as an alumnus of the organization. One goal of sustainability is positive public relations within the industry and the general community at large. Hence, the goal of the HR practitioner is for people to exit the organization with positive impressions to be shared with other individuals outside the organization.

Immediately upon the completion of the exit interview, the HR practitioner will record all observations to include actual quotes from the interviewee as well as intuitive impressions from the interaction. This information could be entered into a database for an analysis of trends that indicate the positive and negative perceptions of separating employees about their experiences with the organization. HR practitioners will use the information reinforce those positive impressions (strengths) and correct negative perceptions (weaknesses), in an effort to improve the workplace environment.

As mentioned in a previous module exit interview procedures are only effective in those nations that find the practice to be appropriate for workers and organizations. Some cultures find this practice to be embarrassing and offensive. In such cases the exit interview process should be modified or abandoned by the STO. The key to all STO functions is compatibility with the value system of the host nation.

Involuntary exit

There will hopefully be few cases in which individuals will be asked to leave their positions with the hospitality organization.

These cases result from either chronic poor performance or incidents of misconduct on the part of that employee. While such a scenario is unpleasant for the exiting worker, HR practitioners realize that these cases support the overall welfare of the organization and those people who do perform in accordance with expectations.

HR practitioners in STOs realize the severity of such an action in the mind of the person being separated. That person is being released from a micro social environment, which is like being banished from a society. Also, that person is losing a source of financial income, which equates into an economic survival issue. The goal of the HR practitioner in such cases is to mitigate the sense of loss and to maintain that person's sense of dignity. It is important for practitioners to remember that the person being released is not a "bad person." He or she was simply unable to comply with the standards for employment.

In some nations, involuntary exit from an organization is not an option. Certain societies subscribe to "lifetime" employment values where losing a job would be considered to be an unbearable disgrace to an individual. Cases of performance problems in some of these cultures require managers to move individuals into positions that are consistent with the worker's abilities. Some social value systems support the movement of a worker into a position with no responsibilities at all. While this scenario will cause the worker to "lose face," it is still preferred to the level of disgrace associated with involuntary separation from the company.

The exit interview in these situations should include an opportunity for the separated employee to share his or her impressions concerning organizational prior to the incident that caused separation, as well as to voice their impressions of the situation leading to termination. Prior to this point, there should have been an opportunity for the employee to provide testimony in his or her defense. This is referred to as "due process," which should be provided to employees as part of a "covenant of good faith and fair dealing" on the part of the organization. The purpose of giving one more opportunity to voice a defense on the part of departing employee is simply for that person to be heard once again by a HR practitioner. If the due process was handled correctly, the employee should understand the issues resulting in the separation. Why do practitioners invest this time and energy into an involuntary separating employee? The objective here is for that person to leave the organization with a sense that he or she was listened to and that the organization was fair in dealing with the situation. Where appropriate, the HR practitioner may offer to assist with outplacement services in such cases.

Grievance procedures

Sustainable organizations should uphold a policy of providing procedures to hear employee complaints and grievances. One of the questions that should be asked of employees with negative perceptions of their experience with the organization is whether they pursued these procedures prior to deciding to leave the organization. Sometimes the employee will experience a less than favorable decision regarding a grievance. The STO should ensure that such matters result in a clear and convincing description as to why a grievance was not upheld. This determination should be a matter of record that could be reinforced at the exit interview. In cases where a person did not use the procedure, it should be clarified that the procedure was communicated clearly and that the organization wishes that the person had used the vehicle for articulating the nature of their discontent.

As discussed in a previous module, grievance procedure format and formality levels will vary across cultures. STO HR managers should be prepared to modify or even abandon such practices in localities that do not support such policies.

Summary

Some managers may contend that exit procedures are a waste of time and money. Managers in STOs realize the importance of positive community relations. It should be remembered that all employees are members of that community and will share their perceptions of employment experiences with other citizens. For these reasons, the hospitality organization must be viewed as being fair, uniform, and consistent in all dealings with its employees. It would be unrealistic to expect that all individuals will leave the organization with positive opinions. However, if the organization does business in a fair and impartial professional manner, the majority of personal opinions will be positive in nature. These opinions collectively impact the status of the organization as a member of the community. Positive community relations contribute to organizational sustainability.

References

Clarke, J. (2002). A synthesis of activity towards the implementation of sustainable tourism: Ecotourism in a different context. *International Journal of Sustainable Development, 5*(3), 232–239.

Hobson, K., & Essex, S. (2001). Sustainable tourism: A view from accommodation businesses. *The Service Industries Journal, London, 21*(4), 133–146.

Risko, V. J. (2002). Preparing teachers for reflective practice: Intentions, contradictions, and possibilities. *Language Arts, Urbana, 80*(2), 134–145.

Tesone, D. V. (2003). Human resource management for the hospitality industry: How the practitioners do it. Boston, MA: Pearson-Prentice Hall.

Strategic human resources management issues in hospitality and tourism organizations

Fevzi Okumus

Rosen College of Hospitality Management
The University of Central Florida
Orlando, FL 32819, USA

Introduction

This edited textbook has an ambitious agenda as it covers an extensive list of HRM concepts and topics in the hospitality and tourism (H&T) industry. Having read all previous chapters in this text, one may think that writing this final chapter would be a relatively easy task since summarizing emerging issues from this text would be sufficient for this final chapter. On the other hand, one may also expect that this final chapter should go beyond what has already been said in the text and provide further insights and directions for practice and future research. This chapter aims to achieve the latter. In particular, it aims to (1) identify and discuss critical HR issues, (2) explain importance of following a strategic human resources management (SHRM) approach, (3) discuss how HR departments can become strategic partners and players in the strategy process, (4) how they can help H&T organizations create and maintain a competitive advantage, and finally (5) how they can positively influence overall performance in H&T organizations.

This chapter was prepared through several overlapping phases. First, the relevant literature was reviewed both in the generic HRM field and also in the H&T field. Next, a series of discussions were undertaken with HR managers and senior executives from H&T organizations. Similar discussions were also held with HR academics and researchers from hospitality colleges. Next, based on the literature review and interview findings, a list of HR issues was compiled. After analyzing these critical HR issues, it emerged that the ability to manage people strategically is the main critical HR issue in H&T organizations. Under this area, four strategic HR issues were identified and discussed. The chapter first briefly discusses current HRM issues. Next, the emergence and importance of the SHRM perspective is explained. Following this, four strategic HR issues are discussed. Finally, the chapter ends by stating several key conclusions and provides recommendations for practice and future research.

Current human resources management issues

The management theory has evolved through several distinctive stages including the classical, the behavioral, and the contemporary management perspectives (Schermerhorn, 2008). Due to space limitation, the evolution of the management field will not be explained here. However, interested readers may find detailed explanations on this in numerous generic management texts.

In parallel to the evolution of the management thought, the HR field has also evolved in several distinctive stages. These include the personnel management, the human resources management, and the SHRM eras (Harrell-Cook, 2002; Tesone, 2005). As stated by Harrell-Cook (2002) the personnel management perspective was dominant until the 1960s that viewed labor as a production cost and suggested that organizations should find the most economical ways to do a job. Work was divided into different parts, and given step-by-step guidelines so that even unskilled workers could perform it. The personnel function was responsible for recruitment, job analysis, performance reviews, wages, benefits, training, record keeping, and labor relations (Harrell-Cook, 2002).

The HRM perspective emerged in the 1960s after realizing that employees could create added value for organizations not only in reducing cost but also in improving quality of products and developing new ideas (Harrell-Cook, 2002). To be able to achieve this, organizations started paying more attention to training, motivation, and development of employees and managers. In other words, rather than viewing employees as a cost center, this perspective suggested that employees need to be treated as one of the key resources since that could create added value to organizations.

Starting from the 1990s, intensive competition, technological developments, and demographic changes made business environments more complex and turbulent than ever. As a result, traditional sources of competitive advantage such as cost leadership or differentiation in markets (Porter, 1980) were not sufficient to be competitive (Pfeffer, 1994). Organizations needed to find alternative ways to create and maintain their competitive advantage. Human resources then become an important factor in creating and maintaining competitive advantage (Bartlett & Ghoshal, 2002). As a result, organizations and scholars started paying more attention to managing HR strategically (Bartlett & Ghoshal, 2002; Wright, Dunford and snell, 2001; Brockbank, 1999; Harrell-Cook, 2002; Galang, 2002).

Certainly these three perspectives which are briefly explained above have had implications on managing people in organizations. Each of the above perspectives has put forward propositions aiming to help organizations in managing their employees. In reality, there is perhaps a hierarchical and integrative relationship among these views. We should therefore see their development as a chronological evolution of the HRM field. Scholars and practitioners have advocated new perspectives in order to eliminate the limitations of previous perspectives and offer better solutions to practitioners so that they could overcome their challenges and problems and achieve superior performance. Although the SHRM perspective has received more attention lately, some of the key issues which were identified by the personnel management and the HRM perspectives are still important and continue to receive a considerable attention both in practice and in the HR literature.

In order to identify critical HR issues in today's H&T organizations, a comprehensive literature review was undertaken both in the generic HRM field[1] and in the H&T field[2]. This review identified a number of critical HR issues which are listed in Table 21.1. The list in Table 21.1 should not be considered inclusive of all critical HR issues. Different issues may be identified by others and certain HR issues listed in this table may be named differently or combined with other issues.

One can easily recognize that a very high majority of the issues listed in Table 21.1 are included in most HRM textbooks. This current edited text also has chapters on some of these issues listed in this table. It can be claimed that critical HR issues listed upper side of Table 21.1 received more attention during the personnel management era whereas those issues listed at the middle of Table 21.1 received more attention during the HRM era. Finally, those issues listed at the bottom of Table 21.1 appear to have received more attention during the last two decades. For example, Carrig (1997) identifies 14 HR activities/issues most of which are also listed in Table 21.1. Rather than grouping them under the personnel management, the HRM, and the SHRM perspectives, Carrig groups those HR issues under transactional, traditional, and transformational HR perspectives and stated that they are continuum of HR activities.

Brockbank (1999) proposes that there are two types of HRM perspectives which are operational and strategic. Operational HR activities are routine, day-to-day delivery of HR practices.

---

[1] Some of these sources include Anderson (1997); Bartlett and Ghoshal (2002); Becker, Huselid and Ulrich (1997); Wright et al., (2001); Hatch and Dyer (2004); Barney and Wright (1998); Baruch (1998); Becker and Ulrich (1997, 2006); Brocbank (1999); Carrig (1997); Effron, Gandsossy, and Goldsmith (2003); Ferris, Hochwarter, Buckley, Harrell-Cook, and Frink (1999); Pfau and Kay (2002); Lepak, Bartol, and Erhardt (2005); Losey, Ulrich, and Meisinger (2005); Oakland and Oakland (2001); Pfeffer (1997); Rucci (1997); Ulrich (1997); Ulrich, Losey, and Lake (1997); and Wright (1998).

[2] Some of these sources include Baum Fulford and Enz (1997); Nickson (1998); Worsfold (1999); Hoque (1999b); Cho, Woods, Jang, and Erdem (2006); D'Annunzio-Green, Maxwell, and Watson (2000); Enz (2001); Enz and Siguaw (2000); Guerrier and Deery (1998); Hoque (1999a); Kusluvan (2003); Lu and Chiang (2003); Lucas and Deery (2004); Nickson (1999); Tesone (2004); Tracey (2004); Tracey and Nathan (2002); Wood (1997); Woods (1999); and Zhang and Wu (2004).

Table 21.1 Critical Human Resources Management Issues

Issues Received Attention during the Personnel Management Era
• Record keeping
• Legal issues
• Selection and recruitment
• Compensation and benefits
• Labor productivity
• Performance management
• Retention and turnover
• Training and development

Issues Received Attention during the Human Resources Management Era
• Motivation and empowerment
• Communication
• Safety of employees and managers
• Stress management and burnout of employees and managers
• Diversity management
• Female employees and managers
• HR issues in mergers and acquisitions
• Impact of crises and disasters on HRM
• HRM in international/global organizations
• Emotional labor
• Managing conflict

Issues Received Attention in the Strategic Human Resources Era
• Outsourcing HRM function
• Managing change
• Managing innovation
• Impact of information technology on HRM practices
• Human capital and Talent Management
• Leadership development
• Developing high performing teams
• Knowledge management
• *HRM as a strategic partner and player in the strategy process*
• *HRM and competitive advantage*
• *Designing comprehensive HRM systems*
• *HRM and performance*

The strategic level of HRM activities are complex and involve long-term, comprehensive, planned, integrated, and value-added activities. Brockbank further notes that strategic HR can contribute to competitive advantage of a firm either reactively or proactively. In its former mode, HR aligns the company's HR practices with the company's business strategy and facilitates organizational change. In its proactive mode, HR participates in strategy development, creates a culture of creativity and innovation across the firm, and links internal processes and structures with ongoing changes in the external environment. Following Brockbank's groupings, those critical issues listed upper side of Table 21.1 can be categorized as more operational HRM practices whereas those activities listed at the lower part of the table are considered more strategic HRM activities.

Barney and Wright (1998) use the terms of 'little HR' and 'big HR'. Little HR activities are daily practices, whereas big HR activities are often related to HR actions and practices which play a key role in the strategic direction of an organization. Those critical issues listed upper side of Table 21.1 can be seen more as little HR activities whereas those activities listed at the lower part of the table can be seen as more big HR activities.

The focus in the HR field has moved from problem driven actions to proactive strategic HR actions (Barney & Wright, 1998; Becker & Huselid, 2006; Brockbank, 1999; Ferris, Hochwarter, Buckley, Harrell-Cook, & Frink, 1999). Those issues listed in Table 21.1 are all important and as stated by Carrig (1997) they are continuum of HRM practices. However, ability to manage HR strategically is the most important HR issue in all organizations (Bartlett & Ghoshal, 2002; Becker & Huselid, 2006; Brockbank, 1999; Pfeffer, 1994). The following sections will discuss why managing HR strategically is important and which issues are particularly crucial in this process.

Managing human resources strategically

Senior executives and formal reports of corporations often claim that employees and managers are their most important assets. However, many decisions and actions put into practice demonstrate a relatively low priority on HR activities in organizations (Barney & Wright, 1998; Oakland & Oakland, 2001). When there is an attempt to cut cost, HR activities particularly training programs, wages, and headcounts are the first to take into consideration (Barney & Wright, 1998). There are perhaps several H&T companies such as Southwest Airlines, Four Season Hotels, and Ritz Carlton that have usually followed and implemented exemplary HRM practices. However, overall the H&T companies have a reputation of following poor HRM practices (Lucas, 1996; Price, 1994; Tracey & Nathan, 2002; Wood, 1997).

According to the strategic management theory, an organization's success can be measured by looking at how far it has achieved its intended goals and objectives. Certainly, there are numerous factors that affect this outcome but without its employees' skills, knowledge, and abilities, an organization can achieve very little (Harrell-Cook, 2002; Schuler, 1992). According to Brockbank (1999), managing HR strategically is the only way to achieve competitive advantage in this complex and dynamic business environment. However, Brockbank (1999) further claims that very few companies have been able to follow proactive strategic HRM practices. It emerges that in order to manage human resources strategically; there are four very closely related requirements for H&T organizations. These are listed below and each of them is discussed in the following pages.

1. HRM should become a strategic partner and a player
2. The HRM function should contribute to creating competitive advantage
3. All HRM activities should be closely coordinated and evaluated as a system
4. The HRM function should demonstrate impact of their activities on performance

These above four factors are particularly chosen believing that they are the most important strategic HR issues in H&T organizations and through taking these issues into consideration and making them happen, H&T organizations can overcome their HR problems and challenges and manage their people strategically.

The HRM function should become a strategic partner and a player

Traditional HR departments in many organizations have no vision, are often out of touch with employees, their work is inefficient, and their impact on the bottom line is not often measurable (Stewart, 1996). Supporting this, Wilkerson (1997) found that 60% of expenses of HR departments were related to hiring, training, and performance management and only 10% of their expenses were associated with strategic planning and strategic direction of companies.

In an empirical research study Maxwell (1994) found that HR practices did not play a key role in strategic planning in hospitality organizations in the UK. Tracey and Nathan (2002), note that HR has a negative image in many hospitality organizations and is seen only as an administrative-support unit. These authors further claim that HR "gets much lip service but no respect" and it plays "a subservient and reactionary role in the business-planning process" (Tracey & Nathan, 2002, p. 18). They further note that

"many business leaders fail to fully consider HR influences when making long-term plans. While most executives acknowledge the importance of HR for implementing strategy plans—"making it happen"—we have seen few who formally incorporate HR concerns when developing a strategic direction." HR is primarily viewed as an "enabling" function, responsible for implementing "the plan," and thus largely ignored during the initial planning stages" (p. 17).

If the HR function is to play a key role in aligning an organization's HR capabilities with the strategic orientation of the firm, the HR function has to become a strategic partner and a player in the process of strategy development and implementation (Harrell-Cook, 2002). However, this requires that the HR function needs to be fully integrated into the formulation and implementation of strategies (Harrell-Cook, 2002; Leonard, 2002; Tracey, 2004). Having a significant role in the strategic management process of an organization does not mean that the HR function simply provides information for senior executives and helps the company implement decisions. Having such a strategic role requires that HR managers have the ability and authority to influence the formulation of strategies and also as a strategic player, they participate in the implementation of these strategies and measure their intended outcomes (Brockbank, 1999; Harrell-Cook, 2002). This requires that HR executives directly report to the CEO and they have a seat in senior level boardroom meetings.

Woods (1999) claims that the HR function in H&T organizations is at a crossroad and there are two possible futures. The first option is that HR will evolve and become a strategic partner. For example, in some H&T organizations such as Southwest Airlines, Four Season Hotels and Resorts, and Marriott International, HR already has a strategic role in terms of participating in the strategy formulation and implementation process. The second option is that HR will disappear and be replaced by a combination of outsourcing and technology. There are examples that many organizations have downsized HR. Woods (1999) notes that if H&T companies will follow the second option, there will be 'constant employee shortages, legal problems, diminishing revenues and returns and eventual bankruptcy' (p. 455). Therefore, the only way to go forward for H&T organizations is to make sure that the HR function has a strategic role in the strategic management process of these companies so that a sustainable competitive advantage can be achieved through people.

The turnaround strategy of Continental Airlines can be given as a good example of how HR function can move beyond its traditional roles and become a strategic partner and a player (Carrig, 1997). After many years of operating at a loss,

Continental Airlines was almost bankrupt in 1994. There was a hostile work environment due to years of conflict between employees and management. The company ranked last in most ratings. After having 10 CEOs in 10 years, a new leadership team of Gordon M. Bethune (CEO) and Greg Brenneman (COO) took over the company in 1994. They devised a turnaround strategy and one of the key components of this strategy was their HR strategy which was called 'Working Together' (Carrig, 1997, p. 278). This new HR strategy created a working environment of dignity and respect with the ultimate goal of all employees feeling valued and enjoying coming to work. In particular, they introduced profit sharing and new performance measures to create and maintain reliable performance. They hired successful executives from other companies, revised their employees' manual, shared information with employees through open, honest, and direct communication, and made their executives work very closely with frontline employees. They used outsourcing and technology when necessary and made their HR function as a strategic partner in turning around the company. As a result, the company achieved superior performance results not only in financial aspects but also in satisfaction of internal and external customers (Carrig, 1997).

Achieving competitive advantage through people

It can be helpful to refer to different views on how organizations can create and maintain competitive advantage. For example, Porter's (1980) five forces industry structure analysis framework and his generic business strategies (cost leadership, differentiation, and focus) are often used to analyze companies' competitive advantage. It is assumed that by looking at competition and competitive strategies in an industry, the threat of new entrance and substitutes, and the bargaining power of buyers and suppliers, companies can identify their competitive advantage and may choose to follow one of the generic business strategies: cost leadership, differentiation, or focus. Through these deliberate and planned activities companies can achieve competitive advantage.

The research-based view is proposed as an alternative view to analyze competitive advantage of firms (Barney, 1991). Unlike Porter's positioning view, the resource-based view suggests that competitive advantage comes from a firm's unique resources. However, in order for a resource to be competitive advantage, it must be *valuable, rare, inimitable, non-substitutable,* and the firm should be organized in a way that it can effectively and efficiently exploit the resource (Barney & Wright, 1998; Galang, 2002). Following Porter (1980), it was assumed that competitive advantage could be achieved by creating barriers to entry, achieving economies of scale, protecting patents, accessing capital, and regulating competition. However, due to globalization and rapid economic, technological, and socio-cultural changes, it has been recognized that companies need to be innovative, adaptable, quick, and efficient when using and developing their resources and abilities (Pfeffer, 1994). According to Itami (1987) these are invisible abilities and resources. Knowledge, experience, and dedication of employees and mangers are often accepted important factors in creating and developing unique resources and competencies (Becker & Huselid, 1999; Svelby, 1997; Wright et al., 2001). Bartlett and Ghoshal (2002) state that

'In the competitive-strategy model in which many of today's leaders were trained, sophisticated strategic planning systems were supposed to help senior managers decide which businesses to grow and which to harvest. Unfortunately, all the planning and investment were unable to stop competition from imitating or leapfrogging their carefully developed product-market positions … people are the key strategic resource, and strategy must be built on human-resource foundation. As more and more companies come to that conclusion, competition for scarce human resources heats up' (pp. 34–35).

In short, employees are now seen as an important source of competitive advantage (Bartlett & Ghoshal, 2002; Ulrich and Brokcbank 2007; Barney & Wright, 1998; Hatch and Dyer, (2004); Pfeffer, 1994, 1995; Wright, McMahan & McWilliams (1994). According to Harrell-Cook (2002), HR can create value through reducing costs and differentiating products/services so that not only higher prices can be charged but also customer satisfaction and loyalty can be achieved. By following the resource-based view, if HR activities are to be valuable, they should contribute to the company's performance, if they are to be rare, only very few firms should possess such good HR activities. If HR activities are to be inimitable, competitors should not be able to easily copy HRM practices of a firm. Then HRM can be considered as a source of competitive advantage. However, the organization has to be organized and managed so well so that all these HR and competencies support each other and they are utilized together (Barney & Wright, 1998).

For example, after looking at five successful firms such as Southwest Airlines, Wal-Mart, Tyson Foods, Circiut City, and Plenum Publishing Inc., Pfeffer (1994, 1995) noted that the source of competitive advantage for these companies changed over time. Pfeffer concluded that competitive advantage of these firms did not only came from technology, patents, or strategic position, but also came from their exemplary HR activities. For example, Southwest Airlines' competitive advantage greatly comes from its very well trained, productive, and dedicated workforce and managers. Over the years, this company has managed to operate fewer employees per aircraft, fly more passengers per employee, and has more available seat miles per employee. They have won the Triple Crown award because of the fewest lost bags and fewest passenger complaints (Pfeffer 1994; Barney & Wright, 1998; Quick, 1992).

The inimitability of the value created by the HR activities closely links with history and social culture of the firm (Barney & Wright, 1998). The HR system of the firm evolves over many years and is shaped by the organization's unique culture, history, and founders. For example, an organization may deploy the same or similar policies and practices of their competitors but it may not be able to easily duplicate the history and culture in which those practices are embedded (Harrell-Cook, 2002). The strong and unique organizational culture has made Southwest Airlines the most successful airline in history. Continental Airlines, United Airlines, and Delta have attempted to compete with Southwest Airlines by providing low cost service to a number of destinations. However, they have not been able to deliver superior performance. Herb Kelleher, the co-founder of Southwest Airlines stated that even if their competitors achieve same level of cost structure and quality service, they cannot create the spirit of Southwest employees' attitude towards service (Barney & Wright, 1998; Quick, 1992). In other words, as noted by Barney and Wright (1998), how Southwest Airlines has developed and managed their people has been a source of sustained competitive advantage for this company since they have created a culture where employees have been loyal and dedicated to their company, their HR practices have been rare, and have been virtually impossible to imitate these practices as well as their organizational culture.

Four Seasons Hotels and Resorts is another company which is famous with its multiple exemplary HR practices. The HR practices of this company have been based on a guiding principle—The Golden Rule—"Treating others as we would wish to be treated" (Nagabhushan & Ganesan, 2004, p. 9). In 2006, for the eighth consecutive year Four Seasons was named as one of the best 100 companies to work for in America (Four Seasons Hotels and Resorts, 2007). Marriott International is another company which has been also named one of the best 100 companies to work for in America. As explained by Prashanth and Gupta (2004) Marriott International employs multiple exemplary HR management practices because they believe that their employees' attitude toward their customers create value and competitive advantage. J. W Marriott (2001) states

'That guest's room may be our product, but our associate's caring attitude is our value. We can't measure it with statistics, and we can't manufacture it. We can deliver that value only if we can attract, retain and inspire the best people—with what we call "The Spirit to Serve" (p. 17).

To sum up, competitive advantage comes from firm-specific unique skills rather than general skills, high performing teams more than individuals, and HRM systems rather than single HR practices (Barney & Wright, 1998; Pfeffer, 1994). In order to create and maintain a competitive advantage, H&T organizations should be able to create firm-specific skills, high performing teams, and human capital. As stated by Bartlett and Ghoshal (2002) companies compete for talents and vision rather than products and markets, therefore investing in finding and developing talents and creating a vision should be seen as essential requirements. The HR function particularly plays a key role in finding and developing talents through developing comprehensive HR systems so that sustainable competitive advantage can be achieved through people. The following section will discuss creating cohesive HR systems.

Strategic human resource management systems

The SHRM perspective emphasizes that organizations need to develop HR management systems as solutions to business problems rather than developing single HR practices in isolation (Becker & Huselid, 2006). For example, when explaining how successful companies achieved competitive advantage through their people, Pfeffer (1994, 1995) proposed 13 closely related HR practices. These include employment security, selectivity in recruitment, high wages, incentive pay, employee ownership, information sharing, participation and empowerment, self managed teams, training and skill development, cross utilization and training, symbolic egalitarianism, wage compression, and promotion within. However, he suggests that these practices need to be considered as a package of interrelated practices rather than single independent practices. It is because it may be easy to copy one practice but not easy to imitate closely coordinated numerous HR practices (Pfeffer, 1995).

Individual HR practices may not be rare, inimitable, and non-substitutable (Galang, 2002). However, a package of HR practices which are often embedded in organizational culture and structure can be rare and hard to imitate. In other words, HR practices are most effective when they are implemented together successfully in a coherent system (Harrell-Cook, 2002). This means that rather than seeing HR practices in isolation, they should be viewed together as a system. If organizations are to achieve competitive advantage from HR practices they have to practice the best selection, training, and reward systems (Barney & Wright, 1998). The reason for this is that individual HR practices may not create sustainable competitive advantage.

Certainly, this does not mean that individual HR practices are unimportant. The challenge for organizations is to develop a highly interdependent HR system that can create a synergistic effect and also makes it difficult for competitors to imitate (Barney & Wright, 1998). The package of interrelated HR practices which are aligned with the organization's goals and strategies can be referred to as a high performance works system (Galang, 2002). Rather than focusing on each HR practice, H&T organizations need to look at them as a system and try to create coordination and synergy among multiple HR practices. According to Barney and Wright (1998) very few companies spend much time and resources on coordinating each of the various HR sub functions and have been able to achieve synergy among their HR practices. Galang (2002) also states that designing and maintaining a cohesive HR system is particularly challenging.

Fitz-Enz (1997) states that an HR leader needs to have the eight best human asset management practices which include

1. A constant focus on adding *value* in everything
2. *Commitment* to a long-term strategy
3. Proactive approach to create a *culture* where managers are aware of how culture and systems are linked together for consistency and efficiency
4. A genuine concern for multiple ways of *communication* with all stakeholders
5. *Partnering* with people within and outside the organization
6. Aiming a high level of *cooperation* and involvement
7. The willingness and ability to take *risk and innovate* work practices
8. Having *competitive passion* to search for improvement

Enz and Siguaw (2000) suggest that successful hospitality companies need to bundle multiple good HR practices together.

However, on the other hand, Tracey and Nathan (2002) argue that HR departments in many hospitality organizations fail to execute even the most basic HR functions effectively. "Many firms' policies and practices are archaic, inflexible and do not directly benefit those who are most keenly affected by HR actions" (p. 17). As a result, HR departments are often seen as cost centers and they cannot prove that their activities positively influence the company's performance. The following pages will discuss measuring impact of HR practices on performance.

Measuring impact of HR practices on performance

Employing numerous good HRM practices together increases skills and motivation of employees. This then leads to higher productivity and enhanced worker efficiency (Pfeffer, 1994). In return, this influences positively customer satisfaction, sales volume, profit ratios, and reduced cost (Harrell-Cook, 2002; Pfeffer, 1995). Measuring how specific HR practices and initiatives influence on organization's performance can be good indication of how far an organization is successful in employing its HR practices. In addition, closely measured practices will be valued by employees and managers. Therefore, 'The need to demonstrate the impact of HR on a firm's performance is a current and future priority' (Warech & Tracey, 2004, p. 377).

We often hear that effective HR management is one of the most important factors in creating a competitive advantage (Bartlett & Ghoshal, 2002; Gronfeldt & Strother, 2006; Pfeffer 1995; Tracey & Nathan, 2002). However, according to a research study carried out by the American Management Association (Condodina, 1997), a very high percentage of executives and managers (86%) outside HR function perceive HR as a non-revenue producing overhead department and it does not contribute to companies' overall performance. In this research only 16% of the participants believed that HR delivered value to their organizations.

Measuring the impact of HR practices on performance is not an easy task. It is rather a complicated process. Academics in the generic HR field have tried to investigate whether there is a link between HR strategies and systems and a firm's performance. Previous studies found a strong relationship between HR strategies and a firm's financial performance (Becker & Huselid, 1998; Huselid, 1995; Paauwe & Richardson, 1996). For example, Huselid (1995) carried out a cross sectional study in 968 publicly held US firms and found that these firms could gain about $27,000 in sales per employee and about $18,000 in firm market value per employee from one standard deviation increase in their high performance work system. Becker and Huselid (1998) also carried out research in 740 firms and found that firms investing in HR practices had greater market value per employee.

A number of examples can be given about how implementing our numerous HR practices can impact on a firm's performance. For example, Harrell-Cook (2002) explains how NUMMI and Nordstrom developed and implemented exemplary HR practices which lead to superior results in both firms' performance. NUMMI, a joint venture between Toyota and General Motors (GM) reopened a closed GM facility in 1982. They hired (85%) GM workers who were laid off when the plant had been closed earlier. Toyota introduced new HRM practices: Training in problem solving, teamwork, elimination of work rules, changes in wage structure, and emphasis on communication. From being one of GM's poorest performers, NUMMI became one of the best performing plants in the US within 2 years, ranking highest in both productivity and quality. Similar to NUMMI, designing and implementing exemplary HR practices helped Nordstrom to achieve superior performance (Harrell-Cook, 2002).

Cho, Woods, Jang, and Erdem (2006) investigated the impact of HRM practices on organizational performance in the lodging and restaurant industries. They found that some HRM practices had significant effects on the turnover rate of non-managerial employees. Companies that involve more employees in quality of life, quality circle, and labor–management participation programs are more likely to experience lower turnover rate of non-managerial employees. Their study investigated the relationship between the use of 12 HRM practices and organizational performance measured by turnover rates for managerial and non-managerial employees, labor productivity, and return on investments. The results of management participation program, incentive plans, and pre-employment tests are more likely to experience lower turnover rates for non-managerial employees.

During our discussions with senior executives and HR managers, they often stated that reduced labor turnover, facing no or minimum legal cases related to HR, increased customer satisfaction, and increased number of loyal customers should be seen indicators of how good HR practices impact on performance. Supporting these claims, particularly related to customer satisfaction, previous studies found that customers leave companies for different reasons. However, it is claimed that more than half of customers leave companies because of a negative attitude toward customer and poor treatment by a company employee (Jones & Sasser, 1995; Reicheld, 1996).

The Gallup employee engagement study grouped employees into three categories: engaged employees, neutral, and disengaged employees (Gallup, 2007). This study found that about 29% of employees are engaged and they are committed to work. About 56% of employees in organizations are neutral who show up and do what is expected but do little more than expected. Finally, about 15% of employees are disengaged and these employees destroy customer relationships. The lower productivity and negative behavior of these disengaged workers cost the US economy annually about $328 billion (Gallup, 2007). This implies that organizations first need to design and implement good HR strategies and practices to increase the percentage of engaged employees and reduce the percentage of neutral and disengaged employees.

Poor HR practices can have detrimental affect on strategy development and implementation efforts in H&T organizations. For example Okumus (2004) illustrated how poor HR practices at a leading hotel group almost failed the deployment of a yield management strategy in that company. In order to implement this strategy, the company spent over $6 million and offered specific training workshops for hotel managers, front office managers, and reservation staff. However, due to poor HR practices, the company had a very high percentage of labor turnover. Most of those managers and staff who attended revenue management workshops left the company which clearly meant that there were not qualified people in many hotel units to use the sophisticated revenue management software. In addition, due to previous cost cutting attempts by the head office, many employees and even managers were not committed to the company and they were often suspicious of all projects and strategies coming from the head office. Changing and improving HR practices in this company was almost beyond the power of those managers and executives who developed and implemented this yield management strategy. In other words, poor HR practices were a company wide issue in this hotel group and they were hurting the company not only in daily operations but also in strategy development and implementation efforts. In short, as stated by Okumus (2003, 2004) good HR practices are essential to create an organizational culture and structure in organizations where employees and managers are engaged and committed to the company.

To sum up, employing multiple exemplary HR practices can lead to increased performance in different areas in H&T

organizations. Becker and Huselid (2006) conclude their seminal article by following statements

"The empirical literature demonstrating that HR could influence meaningful financial outcomes was once a novel and exciting results for managers. But that time has passed. To a substantial degree, managers now "get it" and do not have to be persuaded that the quality with which they manage the workforce has strategic impact. What they need now is help in understanding how to generate and sustain potential results" (p. 921).

Most readers would agree with these statements and further question why HR departments are not becoming strategic partners in H&T organizations and why they do not play a key role in creating sustainable competitive advantage through people. The following section will briefly discuss these issues.

Impediments to moving towards SHRM

A number of reasons can be given to explain why H&T organizations may not undertake necessary steps to move towards SHRM. According to Harrell-Cook (2002) one of the main reasons why HR is not aligned with the organization's overall strategy is that firms do not often have formal strategic plans and goals. Although large H&T organizations may have long-term strategies and formal strategic plans, a very high majority of H&T organizations worldwide are small and medium sized organizations and the only strategic goal of them is often to make money and survive. Another reason is that the HR function has earned a negative image in many H&T organizations (Tracey & Nathan, 2002). As stated earlier, HR management practices are not very much valued in H&T organizations (Kelliher & Johnson, 1987, 1997; Price, 1994). HR practices are often seen as the soft side of business believing that HR is an administrative-support area and it does not generate any revenue. For example, Tracey and Siguaw (2002) state that "HR plays a subservient and reactionary role in the business-planning process ... human resources gets much lip service but no respect" (p. 18).

A further challenge in this process is that senior executives and managers may still have the traditional view of labor as an input and cost center which can be easily found (Harrell-Cook, 2002). For example, to transform HR into a strategic partner, the CEO and other senior executives should fully understand and support SHRM perspective, clearly understand what type of competencies that employees and managers should have to implement the business strategy, and how the HR system will develop those competencies (Becker & Huselid, 1999). Beer (1997) claims "CEOs want a more strategic HR function but often do not understand what this entails" (p. 93). Bartlett and Ghoshal (2002) further claim that managing change in an organization is inevitably challenging but changing the mind-set of senior executives is even harder. They state that 'Very few top executives have been able to transform themselves from being analytically driven strategy directors to people-oriented strategy framers' (p. 35).

In addition, many managers and executives may perceive that moving to SHRM may take a long time and require substantial resources and changes in their organizations (Harrell-Cook, 2002). Especially when firms face internal and external crises and challenges, they may focus on solving immediate challenges and problems rather than trying to employ SHRM. Company wide politics and conflicts may prevent the transition to SHRM. If HR managers have more power in the strategic management process, executives from other functional areas may not be happy with sharing their power and resources (Harrell-Cook, 2002).

Finally, characteristics and competencies of HR managers may be a major factor preventing a move to SHRM in H&T organizations (Beer, 1997). Galang (2002) and Johnson (1997) claim that to manage HR strategically, HR managers and executives should possess certain skills and competencies. They further note that it is often difficult to find the right people with such skills and competencies. Carrig (1997) notes that "if human resource departments must transform themselves into value creators, most of the employees who currently work in HR do not fit the new model" (p. 287). It is because HR departments often have no vision, HR people cannot often see the big picture, HR is inefficient in terms of processing and disseminating information and HR is out of touch (Stewart, 1996; Woods, 1999). Bartlett and Ghoshal (2002) note that many old-school HR executives often realize that neither their training nor their experience have prepared them to take a leading role in the strategy process. In support of the above statements, Johnson (1997) explains what a CEO looks for in a new HR leader

I don't want a typical HR type. I don't think I even want someone from HR. I want this person to be the brightest, smartest, bravest, most strategic and highest potential individual on this management team. That's probably not going to be someone from HR (p. 130).

HR managers and executives in many organizations are often good at doing their day-to-day activities but they have a lack of vision and they do not understand much about business and cost issues (Carrig, 1997; Leonard, 2002). They need to understand issues related to cost and profit and illustrate the positive impact of HR practices on the bottom line (Galang, 2002). They should have a clear understanding about the business, the industry, competitors, company's strategy, direction, and competitive needs. They should be able to move away from traditional HR functions and develop partnerships with other functional areas to offer solutions to company wide problems and illustrate their impact on the company's performance (Harrell-Cook, 2002). Leonard (2002) states that CEOs now spend more time with their HR executives. Therefore, HR executives should be more passionate about their jobs and work on their powers of persuasion to raise the profile of their departments in their companies.

Yeung, Brockbank, and Ulrich (1997), and Galang (2002) suggest that HR managers and executives should (1) have knowledge about business particularly, customers, market, competitors, technology, and cost issues, (2) develop HR mastery which refers to the ability to design and implement HR practices, (3) develop change management skills, (4) have personal credibility so that employees and managers in other functional areas would respect and trust them, and (5) have good interpersonal skills. To sum up, as stated by Carrig (1997), Ulrich (1997), and Galang (2002) HR managers and executives should know how to deal with multiple roles.

There has been a trend that HR departments now employ fewer employees and managers. This is because many HR roles and responsibilities have been transferred to line managers (Brannen, 1996; Galang, 2002; Tracey & Nathan, 2002). This implies that in addition to developing HR managers and executives, line managers in many different functional areas need to be trained and developed about SHRM issues on an ongoing basis. This further implies that it is essential to establish good working relationships and communication channels between HR and line managers.

Conclusions and recommendations

This chapter aimed to discuss critical HR issues, the importance of following a SHRM approach and its relationship to a competitive advantage, and overall performance in H&T firms. Several conclusions can be drawn from the above discussions. First, the HR field has evolved form the personnel management era to HRM and then to the SHRM era. It is no longer perceived that the HR function is only responsible for just record keeping, hiring, training, and compensation (Ferris *et al.*, 1999; Lepak *et al.*, 2005). It is now expected that the HR function has to have a strategic role in H&T companies.

The second conclusion is that there are numerous critical HR issues that H&T organizations face. However, being able to manage people strategically is the most important critical HR issue in today's H&T organizations. This requires that the HR function has to become a strategic partner and help H&T organizations create and maintain a competitive advantage through people. In order to achieve this H&T organizations have to develop and employ numerous exemplary HR practices and align all these practices among themselves as well as with the company's overall strategy.

Another conclusion is that, the HR function has to prove that employing numerous HR practices and managing HR strategically influence companies' overall performance positively. Being able to prove and demonstrate their efforts on performance can give the HR function a stronger position within H&T organizations. However, one should also underline the fact that designing all exemplary HR practices may not guarantee success for H&T organizations. Other functional strategies as well as external factors should also be considered when measuring success and performance. What is clear that good HR practices have played a key role in the success of many H&T companies such as Southwest Airlines, Marriott Hotels International, and Four Seasons Hotels and Resorts. It is apparent that no hospitality organization has been successful without following good HR strategies.

The final conclusion is that although it is expected that managing HR strategically is beneficial to H&T organizations, there are multiple impediments and barriers preventing organizations from moving towards adapting the SHRM perspective. Overcoming such impediments and making the HR function a strategic partner may not be an easy task to achieve in a short period of time. One essential factor in this process will always be finding and developing executives as well as HR managers who would view HRM practices more from the strategic management perspective. Certainly, this requires breaking the traditional old HR paradigms and changing organizational culture and structure of H&T organizations where the HR function is seen as a strategic partner rather than as a cost center. Following suggestions of Becker and Huselid (2006), Brockbank (1999), Pfeffer (1997), Ricci (1997), and Woods (1999) a radical shift has to occur in the minds of many senior executives as well as HR managers. In addition, these managers and executives have to be equipped with new skills and competencies. In this process, both senior executives as well as HR managers should understand the value of people in the firm and their role in creating a competitive advantage. In addition, they need to understand and demonstrate how HR practices influence performance of a firm. To be able to do this, HR managers and executives need to be equipped with new skills and abilities so that they not only understand business issues, competitors, financial issues, managing change, and conflict management, but also demonstrate good communication and interactive skills. Strong support from senior management team members, particularly from the CEO, is necessary in this process.

Before finishing this chapter, it is perhaps essential to question how HRM courses should be taught in H&T programs at universities. Most HRM textbooks focus on traditional HR activities such as job analysis, HR planning, recruitment, training, compensation, and motivation. As stated by Chadwick (2005), HR courses are not often taught from the SHRM perspective. Teaching HRM courses more from the SHRM perspective requires that content and delivery style of HR courses have to be changed. Several important questions can be proposed for instructors to consider when they develop and deliver HRM courses from the SHRM perceptive. It is hoped that while trying to answer such questions, students can understand and practice principles of the SHRM perspective. Several closely interrelated questions (Chadwick, 2005) include

- If an organization designs and implements good HR practices, will any of their competitors notice their good HR practices?
- Why do customers choose a specific company rather than its competitors?
- What particular activities contribute to financial performance of an organization?
- What products/services does an organization really sell, and how can they be differentiated?
- How can a firm leverage its strategic capabilities and can HR practices play a role in this process?
- How can HR practices create value to a firm so that this firm can differentiate itself from its competitors?

Finally, despite all the research and publications, the SHRM literature in the generic management field is still in its infancy (Harrell-Cook, 2002). If this is the case in the generic HR management field, one can question how far the HR literature progressed in the H&T field. Previous studies already noted that despite much effort and numerous research studies in the field, the HR literature is still limited in the H&T field (Guerrier & Deery, 1998 Lucas & Deery, 2004). Given this, based on the discussions throughout this chapter, it can be suggested that more empirical research is needed for H&T organizations to investigate

1. whether HR departments have become strategic partners and players in strategic management of H&T organizations,
2. to what extent do HR practices help H&T organizations create and maintain competitive advantage,
3. to what extent H&T organizations employ exemplary HR practices simultaneously and whether they are aligned with their overall strategy and strategic direction,
4. whether there is a positive relationship between specific HR practices and the performance of H&T organizations, and finally,
5. what kind of challenges and impediments there are (have been) to moving towards SHRM practices in H&T organizations.

References

Anderson, R. (1997). The future of human resources: Forging ahead of falling behind. In D. Ulrich, M. Losey & G. Lake (Eds.), *Tomorrow's HR management—48 thought leaders call for change* (pp. 146–154). New York: Wiley.

Barney, J., & Wright, P. (1998). On becoming a strategic partner: The role of human resources in gaining competitive advantage. *Human Resources Management, 37*(1), 31–46.

Barney, J. B. (1991). Firms resources and sustained competitive advantage. *Journal of Management, 17*, 99–120.

Bartlett, C., & Ghoshal, S. (2002). Building competitive advantage through people. *MIT Sloan Management Review, 43*(2), 34–41.

Baruch, Y. (1998). Walking the tightrope: Strategic issues for human resources. *Long Range Planning, 31*(3), 467–475.

Baum, T., & Nickson, D. (1998). Teaching human resource management in hospitality and tourism: A critique. *International Journal of Contemporary Hospitality Management, 10*(2), 75–79.

Becker, B. and Huselid, M. (1998). "High Performance Work Systems and Firm Performance: A Synthesis of Research and Managerial Implications", *Research in Personnel and Human Resource Management, 16* (1), pp. 53–101.

Becker, B., Huselid, H., & Ulrich, D. (1997). *The HR scorecard.* Boston, MA: Harvard Business School Press.

Becker, B., & Huselid, M. (1999). Strategic human resources management in five leading firms. *Human Resources Management*, *38*, 287–301.

Becker, B., & Huselid, M. (2006). Strategic human resources management: Where do we go from here? *Journal of Management*, *32*(6), 898–925.

Beer, M. (1997). The transformation of the human resource function: Resolving the tension between a traditional administrative and a new strategic role. In D. Ulrich, M. Losey & G. Lake (Eds.), *Tomorrow's HR management—48 thought leaders call for change* (pp. 84–95). New York: Wiley.

Brockbank, W. (1999). If HR were strategically proactive: Present and future directions in HR's contribution to competitive advantage. *Human Resource Management*, *38*, 337–352.

Carrig, K. (1997). Reshaping human resources for the next century—lessons from a high flying airline. *Human Resources Management*, *36*, 277–289.

Chadwick, C. (2005). The vital role of strategy in strategic human resource management education. *Human Resource Management Review*, *15*(3), 200–213.

Cho, S., Woods, R., Jang, S., & Erdem, M. (2006). Measuring the impact of human resource management practices on hospitality firms' performances. *International Journal of Hospitality Management*, *25*(2), 262–277.

Condodina, J. (1997). Echoes from the line: HR lacks strategic initiative. *HR Focus*, *74*(7), 21.

D'Annunzio-Green, N., Maxwell, G., & Watson, S. (2000). Human resource issues in international hospitality, travel and tourism: A snapshot. *International Journal of Contemporary Hospitality Management*, *12*(3), 215–216.

Effron, M., Gandsossy, R., & Goldsmith, M. (Eds.). (2003). *Human resources in the 21st century.* New York: Wiley.

Enz, C. (2001). What keeps you up at night? Key issues of concern for lodging managers. *The Cornell Hotel and Restaurant Administration Quarterly*, *42*(2), 38–45.

Enz, C., & Siguaw, J. (2000). Best practices in human resources. *The Cornell Hotel and Restaurant Administration Quarterly*, *41*, 48–61.

Ferris, G., Hochwarter, W., Buckley, R., Harrell-Cook, G., & Frink, D. (1999). Human resources management: Some new directions. *Journal of Management*, *25*(3), 385–415.

Fitz-Enz, J. (1997). The truth about best practices: What they are and how to apply them. In D. Ulrich, M. Losey & G. Lake (Eds.), *Tomorrow's HR management* (pp. 217–226). New York: Wiley.

Four Seasons Hotels and Resorts. (2007). A career with four seasons. Accessed at http://www.fourseasons.com/employment/a_four_seasons_career/#division_5 on May 11 2007.

Fulford, M., & Enz, C. (1995). Human resources as a strategic partner in multiunit-restaurants. *The Cornell Hotel and Restaurant Administration Quarterly, 36*(3), 24–29.

Galang, M. C. (2002). The human resource department: Its role in firm competitiveness. In G. R. Ferris, M. Ronald Buckley & D.B. Fedor (Eds.), *Human resources management* (4th ed., pp. 583–607). New Jersey: Prentice Hall.

Gallup. (2007). Engaged employees inspire company innovation. *Gallup Management Journal.* Accessed on 15th April, 2007, from http://gmj.gallup.com/content/24880/Gallup-Study-Engaged-Employees-Inspire-Company.aspx

Gronfeldt, S., & Strother, J. (2006). *Service leadership: The quest for competitive advantage.* Thousand Oaks, CA: Sage.

Guerrier, Y., & Deery, M. (1998). Research in hospitality human resource management and organizational behavior. *International Journal of Hospitality Management, 17*(2), 145–160.

Harrell-Cook, G. (2002). Human resources management and competitive advantage: A strategic perspective. In G. R. Ferris, M. Ronald Buckley & D.B. Fedor (Eds.), *Human resources management* (4th ed., pp. 30–42). New Jersey: Prentice Hall.

Hatch, N., & Dyer, J. (2004). Human capital and learning as a source of sustainable competitive advantage. *Strategic Management Journal, 25*(12), 1155–1178.

Hoque, K. (1999a). New approaches to HRM in the UK hotel industry. *Human Resources Management Journal, 9*(2), 64–76.

Hoque, K. (1999b). Human resource management and performance in the UK hotel industry. *British Journal of Industrial Relations, 37*(3), 419–443.

Huselid, M. (1995), "The Impact of Human Resource Management Practices on Turnover, Productivity, and Corporate Financial Performance", *Academy of Management Journal,* 38 (3): 635–72.

Itami, H. (1987), *Mobilizing Invisible Assets,* Cambridge, MA: Harvard University Press.

Johnson, H. (1997). Don't send me one of those typical human resource people. In D. Ulrich, M. Losey & G. Lake (Eds.), *Tomorrow's HR management* (pp. 130–136). New York: Wiley.

Jones, T., & Sasser, W. (1995). Why satisfied customers depart. *Harvard Business Review, 73*(6), 88–91.

Kelliher, C. and Johnson, K. (1987), "Personnel management in hotels — some empirical observations", *International Journal of Hospitality Management,* 6 (2), pp. 103–108.

Kusluvan, S. (Ed.). (2003). *Managing employee attitudes and behaviors in the tourism and hospitality industry.* New York: Nova.

Leonard, B. (2002). What do CEOs want from HR? In G. R. Ferris, M. Ronald Buckley & D.B. Fedor (Eds.), *Human resources management* (4th ed., pp. 4–8). New Jersey: Prentice Hall.

Lepak, D., Bartol, K., & Erhardt, N. (2005). A contingency framework for the delivery of HR practices. *Human Resource Management Review, 15*(2), 139–159.

Losey, M., Ulrich, D., & Meisinger, S. (Eds.). (2005). *The future of human resource management: 64 thought leaders explore the critical HR issues of today and tomorrow.* New York: Wiley.

Lu, Z., & Chiang, D. (2003). Strategic issues faced by Ontario hotels. *International Journal of Contemporary Hospitality Management, 15*(6), 343–345.

Lucas, R. (1996). Industrial relations in hotels and catering: Neglect and paradox. *British Journal of Industrial Relations, 34*(2), 267–286.

Lucas, R., & Deery, M. (2004). Significant developments and emerging issues in human resource management. *International Journal of Hospitality Management, 23*(5), 459–472.

Marriott, J. (2001). Our competitive strength: Human capital. *Executive Speeches, 15*(5), 18–21.

Maxwell, G. (1994) 'Human Resources Management and Quality in the UK Hospitality Industry – Where is the Strategy' *Total Quality Management,* 5 (3) pp. 45–52.

Nagabhushan, M., & Ganesan, S. (2004). *Case study on Four Seasons Hotels and Resorts.* Bangalore, India: ICFAI Business School. (Distributed by the European Case Clearing House.)

Nickson, D. (1999). Human resource management in hotel accommodation. In C. Verginis & R. Wood (Eds.), *Accommodation management: perspectives for the international hotel industry* (pp. 201–215). London: International Thompson Business Press.

Oakland, S., & Oakland, J. (2001). Current people management activities in world class organizations. *Total Quality Management Journal, 12*(6), 773–788.

Okumus, F. (2003). A framework to implement strategies in organizations. *Management Decision, 41*(9), 871–883.

Okumus, F. (2004). Implementation of yield management practices in service organizations: Empirical findings from a major hotel group. *The Service Industries Journal, 24*(6), 1–25.

Paauwe, J., & Richardson, R. (1996). Introduction. *International Journal of Human Resource Management, 8*(3), 257–262.

Pfau, B., & Kay, T. (2002). *The human capital edge.* New York: McGraw-Hill.

Pfeffer, J. (1994). *Competitive advantage through people.* Boston, MA: Harvard Business School Press.

Pfeffer, J. (1995). Producing sustainable competitive advantage through the effective management of people. *Academy of Management Executive, 9,* 55–72.

Pfeffer, J. (1997). Does human resources have future. In D. Ulrich, M. Losey & G. Lake (Eds.), *Tomorrow's HR management—48 thought leaders call for change* (pp. 190–196). New York: Wiley.

Porter, M. (1980), *Competitive Strategy: Techniques for Analyzing Industries & Competitors,* New York: The Free Press.

Prashanth, K., & Gupta, V. (2004). *Case study on human resource management: Best practices at Marriott International.* Hyderabad, India: ICFAI Center for Management Research. (This case study is distributed by the European Case Clearing House.)

Price, L. (1994). Poor personnel practice in the hotel and catering industry: Does it matter? *Human Resource Management Journal, 4*(4), 44–62.

Quick, J. (1992). "Crafting an Organizational Culture: Herb's Hand at Southwest", *Organizational Dynamics,* 21 (1), 45–56.

Reicheld, F. (1996). Learning from customer defections. *Harvard Business Review, 74*(2), 56–69.

Ricci, A. (1997). Should human resources survive? A profession at the crossroads. In D. Ulrich, M. Losey & G. Lake (Eds.), *Tomorrow's HR management—48 thought leaders call for change* (pp. 197–204). New York: Wiley.

Schermerhorn, J. (2008), *Management,* Danvers, MA: John Wiley& Sons, Inc.

Schuler, R. (1992). Strategic Human Resource Management: Linking People with the Needs of the Business', *Organizational Dynamics,* 21(1), pp. 18–32.

Stewart, T. (1996). Talking on the last bureaucracy. *Fortune, 133*(1), 105–108.

Svelby, K.E. (1997), *The New Organizational Wealth: Managing and Measuring Knowledge-Based Assets,* San Francisco, CA: Berrett-Koehler Publishers.

Tesone, D. (2004). Development of a sustainable tourism hospitality human resources management module: A template for teaching sustainability across the curriculum. *International Journal of Hospitality Management, 23*(3), 207–237.

Tesone, D. V. (2005). *Human resource management for the hospitality industry: A practitioner's perspective.* Upper Saddle River, NJ: Prentice Hall.

Tesone, D. (2005), *Human Resources Management in the Hospitality Industry: A Practitioners Perspective*, New Jersey: Pearson, Prentice Hall.

Tracey, B., & Nathan, A. (2002). The strategic role and operational roles of human resources. *Cornell Hotel and Restaurant Administration Quarterly*, *43*, 17–26.

Tracey, R. (2004). Human resources roundtable 2003. *Cornell Hotel and Restaurant Administration Quarterly*, *45*(4), 373–375.

Ulrich, D. (1997). HR of the future: Conclusions and observations. *Human Resource Management*, *36*, 175–179.

Ulrich, D., & Brockbank, W. (2007). *The HR value proposition*. Boston, MA: Harvard Business School Publishing.

Ulrich, D., Losey, M., & Lake, G. (Eds.). (1997). *Tomorrow's HR management*. New York: Wiley.

Warech, M., & Tracey, B. (2004). Evaluating the impact of human resources: Identifying what matters. *The Cornell Hotel and Restaurant Administration Quarterly*, *45*(4), 376–387.

Wilkerson, J. (1997). The future is virtual HR. *HR Focus*, *74*(3), 15.

Wood, R. (1997). *Working in hotels and catering* (2nd ed.). London: International Thompson Publishing.

Woods, R. (1999). Predicting is difficult, especially about the future: Human resources in the new millennium. *International Journal of Hospitality Management*, *18*(4), 443–456.

Worsfold, P. (1999). HRM, performance, commitment and service quality in the hotel industry. *International Journal of Contemporary Hospitality Management*, *11*(7), 340–348.

Wright, P. (1998). Introduction: Strategic human resource management research in the 21st century. *Human Resource Management Review*, *8*(3), 187–191.

Wright, P., Dunford, B., & Snell, S. (2001). Human resources and the resource based view of the firm. *Journal of Management*, *27*(6), 701–721.

Wright, P., McMahan, G., & McWilliams, A. (1994), "Human Resources and Sustained Competitive Advantage: A Resource-based Perspective," *International Journal of Human Resource Management*, 5 (3): 299–324.

Yeung, A., Brockbank, W., & Ulrich, D. (1994). Lower cost, higher value: Human resource functions in transformation. *Human Resource Planning*, *17*(1), 1–16.

Zhang, H., & Wu, E. (2004). Human resource issues facing the hotel and travel industry in China. *International Journal of Contemporary Hospitality Management*, *16*(7), 424–428.

Index